ORDERED LIBERTY

ORDERED LIBERTY

Rights, Responsibilities, and Virtues

James E. Fleming
and
Linda C. McClain

Harvard University Press
Cambridge, Massachusetts, and London, England   2013

Library of Congress Cataloging-in-Publication Data

Fleming, James E.
Ordered liberty : rights, responsibilities, and virtues / James E. Fleming and Linda C. McClain.
p. cm.
Includes bibliographical references and index.
ISBN 978-0-674-05910-8
1. Civil rights—United States.
2. Constitutional law—United States.
3. Civics.
4. Civil society—United States.
5. Cultural pluralism—United States.
6. Liberalism—United States.   I. McClain, Linda C.   II. Title.
KF4749.F55   2013
320.01'1—dc23   2012014823

For Our Family

"That ill deserves the name of confinement which hedges us in only from bogs and precipices. . . . The end of law is not to abolish or restrain, but to preserve and enlarge freedom: . . . where there is no law, there is no freedom."

—JOHN LOCKE, Second Treatise of Government

Contents

ORDERED LIBERTY

Rights, Responsibilities, and Virtues

In recent years, communitarian, civic republican, and progressive thinkers and politicians have argued that our constitutional system takes individual rights too seriously, to the neglect of responsibilities, virtues, and the common good. "No rights without responsibilities," a slogan of Third Way thought, encapsulates this perceived imbalance.[1] Similarly, President Barack Obama in his inaugural address called for a "new era of responsibility."[2] Liberal theories of rights, critics argue, exalt rights over responsibilities, licensing irresponsible conduct and spawning frivolous assertions of rights at the expense of encouraging personal responsibility and responsibility to community. These theories, critics say, require neutrality among competing conceptions of the good life, undermining civil society as "seedbeds of virtue" and precluding government from promoting good lives. Worse yet, liberal theories justify rights of autonomy on the ground of "empty" toleration of wrong conduct instead of respect for the personal capacity for responsibility or recognition of the substantive moral goods or virtues promoted by protecting such rights. Finally, liberal theories take rights too absolutely, to the subordination of responsibilities, virtues, and the common good, and in doing so debilitate the political processes and impoverish judgment. Ronald Dworkin's famous book, *Taking Rights Seriously,* with his idea of rights as "trumps,"[3] is the *bête noire* of proponents of such charges of irresponsibility, neutrality, wrongness, and absoluteness. Liberalism, critics claim, promotes "liberty as license" rather than securing "ordered liberty."

This book answers these charges against liberal theories of rights. We propose an account of rights that (1) takes responsibilities as well as rights seriously, permitting government to encourage responsibility in the exercise of rights but not to compel what it holds is the responsible decision; (2) supports what we, following Michael Sandel, call a "formative project"[4] of civil society and government promoting responsibility, inculcating civic virtue, fostering citizens' capacities for democratic and personal self-government, and securing ordered liberty and equal citizenship for all; (3) justifies rights of autonomy on the basis not of "empty" toleration, but of toleration as respect, together with the capacity for responsibility and the substantive moral goods furthered by securing such rights; and (4) protects basic liberties (such as freedom of association and rights of autonomy) stringently but not absolutely, through reasoned judgment concerning ordered liberty without precluding government from encouraging responsibility or inculcating civic virtues. We develop an account of responsibility that takes rights seriously, avoids submerging the individual into the community, and appreciates the value of diversity in our morally pluralistic constitutional democracy. We defend our understanding of the relationships among rights, responsibilities, and virtues by applying it to several matters of current controversy: reproductive freedom, the proper roles and regulation of civil society and the family, education of children, clashes between First Amendment freedoms (of association and religion) and antidiscrimination law, and rights to intimate association and same-sex marriage.

The battle over same-sex marriage illustrates the value of our defense of rights in relationship to responsibilities and virtues. The irresponsibility critique of same-sex marriage charges that redefining marriage severs the rights of marriage from responsible sexuality, procreation, and parenthood. Marriage becomes "just another lifestyle choice." To the contrary, we argue, same-sex couples seeking to marry want the rights, responsibilities, and goods of marriage. In *Varnum v. Brien,* recognizing same-sex marriage, the Iowa Supreme Court rejected the argument that same-sex couples could not achieve the goods of marriage because they could not procreate naturally. It held that such couples were similarly situated to opposite-sex couples with regard to government's purposes in regulating marriage because they were "in committed and loving relationships, many raising families," and "official recognition of their status provides an institutional basis for defining their fundamental relational rights and responsibilities."[5]

Our analysis of the rights-responsibilities dichotomy will emphasize that a leading source of the problems in this area is the failure to distinguish and relate two different conceptions of responsibility: *responsibility as autonomy* or self-government and *responsibility as accountability* to community. We examine the tensions between pursuing accountability and protecting autonomy. An additional source of problems is that most liberals, worried about preserving individual freedom, have feared to tread where communitarians, civic republicans, and progressives rush in: the terrain of responsibility and civic virtue. We aim to fill this void. If Dworkin's *Taking Rights Seriously* is the canonical exposition and defense of liberal rights and why they matter, our book aims to provide a guiding framework for pursuing ordered liberty—"to secure conditions favorable to the pursuit of happiness"[6]—through taking responsibilities and civic virtues as well as rights seriously.

To be sure, some liberal political theorists, most prominently William Galston and Stephen Macedo, have taken steps to fill this void, persuasively arguing that liberalism has a proper concern with civic virtues.[7] We tackle the jurisprudential task of reckoning with leading critiques of constitutional rights and developing the most defensible ordering of rights, responsibilities, and virtues in the American constitutional order. Moreover, while many civic liberals focus on fostering the capacities and preconditions for democratic self-government, we defend the crucial role of constitutional rights in securing the capacities and preconditions for not only democratic self-government (what we call "deliberative democracy") but also personal self-government ("deliberative autonomy"). By doing so, we provide a jurisprudential anchor for a constitutional liberalism that is analogous to John Rawls's political liberalism.[8] It is a synthesis of liberalism, civic republicanism, and feminism.

Dworkin has labored mightily and productively on the terrain of rights and responsibility. In *Life's Dominion* and *Is Democracy Possible Here?* along with *Justice for Hedgehogs,* he uses the language of responsibility to justify a right to decide for oneself issues of ethical value in one's own life.[9] This move is part of his ambitious "hedgehog" argument for "value holism"—the integration of the domains of ethics, personal morality, political morality, and law. We argue that his notion of each person's "special responsibility" for his or her own life exemplifies the relationship between rights and responsibility. But we resist his move to what Rawls called a "comprehensive liberalism" as distinguished from a "political liberalism,"[10] and we believe our constitutional liberalism is more appropriate in a morally pluralistic polity such as our own.

As in *Securing Constitutional Democracy,*[11] we aspire to secure the preconditions for democratic and personal self-government: first, the basic liberties that are preconditions for *deliberative democracy* to enable citizens to apply their capacity for a conception of justice to deliberating about and judging the justice of basic institutions and social policies as well as the common good, and second, the basic liberties that are pre-conditions for *deliberative autonomy* to enable citizens to apply their capacity for a conception of the good to deliberating about and deciding how to live their own lives. As in *The Place of Families*,[12] we apply a framework for fostering capacity, equality, and responsibility in circumstances of moral pluralism. We advance a formative project for securing and respecting the capacities for both deliberative autonomy and deliberative democracy, addressing the division of labor between government and the institutions of civil society in such a project. "Perfectionism" is the term sometimes given to the idea that government should actively help citizens to live good and valuable lives.[13] Some criticize political liberalism for ruling out perfectionism. Our constitutional liberalism posits the responsibility of government and civil society to help persons develop their moral capacities for self-government and, in that sense, live good lives. To that extent, it is a mild form of perfectionism.

Rights and Irresponsibility: Encouraging Responsibility

In Chapters 2 and 3, we take up the irresponsibility critique: that liberal theories of rights license irresponsible conduct instead of promoting ordered liberty. We defend a liberal conception of the relationship between rights and responsibility against familiar communitarian, civic republican, and progressive criticisms.

Rights and Irresponsibility

A marked discontent with rights and "rights talk" is a staple in a broad range of contemporary discourses, as are calls for a turn to responsibility and "responsibility talk."[14] Rights are juxtaposed against responsibility as if the two were inversely or even perversely related to one another. Indeed, rights are said to license irresponsibility. Academics, politicians, and the popular media claim that Americans increasingly invoke rights talk and shrink from responsibility talk, resulting in an explosion of frivolous assertions of rights and a breakdown of responsible conduct. The problem is framed as "too many rights" and "too few responsibilities."[15] Proposed solutions appeal to "rights *and* responsibilities."

Chapter 2 examines a cluster of questions about the relationship between rights and irresponsibility. What is it about rights that triggers the irresponsibility critique? Do legal rights include a right to be irresponsible and, if so, why defend them? Does the structure of legal rights discourage or preclude individual, community, or societal reflection on right conduct and efforts to foster responsible behavior? Have liberal justifications of legal rights invited discontent by neglecting the relationship between such rights and responsibility? How much of what is at issue in charges of irresponsibility is really about rights, as distinguished from legally prohibited behavior?

We distinguish two strands of the irresponsibility critique: "immunity" and "wrongness." The immunity critique recognizes that a legal right creates a realm within which one is free from coercion and not legally responsible or accountable to others for social costs or harms resulting from one's actions. The problematic implications of this immunity are that rights are trumps, overriding the common good, and that they insulate a right-holder from the moral scrutiny or disapproval of others. The wrongness critique observes that having a legal right to do something does not mean that it is the right thing to do. Regrettably, critics claim, rights talk suggests that the existence of a right implies the nonexistence of responsibilities constraining its exercise. This suggests that having a legal right to do something is a sufficient reason to do it or, worse, that legal rights equal moral rightness. We grant that legal rights do not equate with moral rightness, but we deny that they send a message about moral rightness, moral insulation, or the absence of responsibility. In support, we point to the employment of moral suasion and the language of responsibility in contemporary debates about several constitutional rights.

We also challenge the dichotomous treatment of rights and responsibility by showing that presuppositions about moral capacities and moral responsibility undergird liberal justifications of constitutional rights like those we advance. We put forward a formative project for securing the preconditions for the development and exercise of such moral capacities and moral responsibility. Doing so promotes ordered liberty. The possibility of irresponsible conduct is a cost of recognizing and protecting rights, a cost that is generally preferable to shifting the locus of moral responsibility from individuals to the community or the government.

Taking Responsibilities as well as Rights Seriously

No constitutional right draws the irresponsibility critique more frequently than that of a woman to decide whether to terminate her pregnancy.

Critics challenge the *immunity* the right provides: a pregnant woman should not be insulated from public persuasion against abortion. Abortion also illustrates the *wrongness* prong of the irresponsibility critique: the right to choose abortion is a right to do wrong, permitting women to commit an immoral, irresponsible act. Moreover, it "licenses" irresponsibility by others, such as women's male partners and a society indifferent to human life.

In Chapter 3, we assess the irresponsibility critique in the context of this constitutional right. We use communitarian Mary Ann Glendon (the author of *Rights Talk: The Impoverishment of Political Discourse*) and liberal Ronald Dworkin (the author of *Taking Rights Seriously*) as foils. We observe that Dworkin himself has turned, in more recent work, to responsibility to justify rights. Communitarian critics of rights like Glendon and liberal champions of rights like Dworkin, we explain, emphasize two different, although related, meanings of responsibility: *responsibility as accountability* to community versus *responsibility as autonomy* or self-government, respectively. In the present context, responsibility as accountability connotes being answerable to others for the manner and consequences of exercising one's rights, whereas responsibility as autonomy connotes self-governance, that is, entrusting the right-holder to exercise moral responsibility in making decisions guided by conscience and deliberation. The irresponsibility critique highlights the tension between pursuing responsibility as accountability (emphasized by communitarians) and protecting responsibility as autonomy (stressed by liberals). We illustrate that tension by contrasting the critique of abortion rights articulated by Glendon with the defense of such rights elaborated by Dworkin. We focus on the Supreme Court's decisions in *Planned Parenthood v. Casey* (reaffirming the right of a woman to decide whether to terminate a pregnancy) and *Gonzales v. Carhart* (upholding the "Partial-Birth Abortion Ban Act").[16]

We criticize Glendon's account of responsibility as accountability—which would permit the government to compel what it holds to be the responsible decision by prohibiting abortion—because it would eviscerate responsibility as autonomy. Like Dworkin, we argue that people live up to the freedom that a right to procreative autonomy protects by exercising their ethical responsibility of reflection in deciding matters of serious moral concern. The government may encourage responsibility in making decisions such as whether to terminate a pregnancy but may not coerce what it thinks is the responsible decision.

We also assess the *incapability* version of the irresponsibility critique of abortion rights. This argument maintains that any woman who terminates a pregnancy cannot be *responsible* for her decision in the sense of acting knowingly and freely: she must have done so either because she lacked proper information about what an abortion is or what help is available, or because she was pressured or coerced by others. Inevitably, she will suffer regret. The seeds of this argument were sown in *Casey*'s portrait of abortion as posing psychological peril for women, but *Carhart* and a flurry of state restrictions take this argument further in new and disturbing directions.

Opponents of legal abortion are not the only critics of rights—and of the right of privacy in particular—for neglecting issues of responsibility. Progressive and feminist theorists who support legal abortion, such as Robin West, argue that constitutional rights have social, moral, and political costs. As against Dworkin's call for "taking rights seriously," she calls for "taking responsibilities seriously" by grounding rights to reproductive freedom in the capacity of women to decide responsibly. A rights approach, by "insulating" the abortion decision from public scrutiny, "obfuscates the moral quality of most abortion decisions." [17] Furthermore, she advances what we call the *negative liberties* critique of rights: framing the right to abortion as a negative right to be free from governmental interference legitimates the government's failure to provide the preconditions for reproductive justice, or positive rights, to women facing the decision whether to terminate a pregnancy. Such positive rights stem from the public responsibility to meet pregnant women's needs and to address, more broadly, the social and economic conditions leading to unwanted pregnancy and the absence of social supports for parenthood.[18]

To preview our constitutional liberalism's project for taking responsibilities as well as rights seriously: as against the irresponsibility critique, it takes responsibility (as autonomy) seriously by permitting government to encourage reflective, responsible exercise of rights; as against the incapability critique, it grounds the right to decide whether to terminate a pregnancy in women's capacity to decide responsibly; and as against the negative liberties critique, it lends no support to public irresponsibility, for it conceives the Constitution not merely as a charter of negative liberties protecting people from government, but also as a charter of positive benefits imposing affirmative obligations upon government to secure the preconditions for reproductive justice. Thus, constitutional liberalism aspires to secure the preconditions for ordered liberty, not liberty without responsibilities.

Rights and Neutrality: Inculcating Virtues

In Chapters 4 to 6, we consider the neutrality critique: that liberal theories of rights require neutrality among competing conceptions of the good life, undermining civil society as "seedbeds of virtue" and precluding government from promoting good lives and inculcating civic virtues and public values. Against this critique, we defend a formative project of civil society and government promoting responsibility, inculcating civic virtues, fostering citizens' capacities for democratic and personal self-government, and securing ordered liberty and equal citizenship for all.

Civil Society's Role in Cultivating the "Seedbeds of Virtue"

In Chapter 4, we consider the cultivation of responsibility and virtue through civil society (a realm between the individual and the state that includes the family and religious, civic, and other voluntary associations). The erosion or disappearance of civil society is a common diagnosis of what underlies civic and moral decline in America, and many (whom we designate as "civil society–revivalists") propose reviving civil society as a cure.[19] Civil society–revivalists have analyzed the erosion of civil society and the "seedbeds of virtue" as a consequence of an excess of liberal virtues, such as tolerance taken too far. On this view, the American experiment of liberal democracy presupposes certain traits of character that make "ordered liberty" possible, but liberalism cannot create or sustain those virtues.[20] Instead, it fosters "liberty as license." We reject this view.

We pose some questions for civil society–revivalists. Does civil society cultivate seedbeds of virtue—our foundational sources of "competence, character, and citizenship"[21]—to foster democratic self-government? Or is its more vital purpose to serve as a buffer against the government? Should government attempt to secure "congruence" between democratic values and the values of voluntary associations,[22] or would such an effort offend commitments to pluralism and diversity? Is the decline of civil society due to a flawed liberal conception of the person as an "unencumbered," sovereign self? Do civil society–revivalists ask the right questions or offer the best solutions when they focus on the family and its supposedly weakened capacity to serve as a seedbed of civic virtue? Have gains in equality and liberty contributed to the decline of civil society and civic virtue? Finally, would a revitalized civil society support democratic self-government or supplant it?

We grapple with these questions and outline a conception of the roles and regulation of civil society in our morally pluralistic constitutional democracy. Working within the framework of Rawls's political liberalism, and guided by key feminist commitments, we argue that the associations of civil society play the critical roles of underwriting a stable constitutional democracy and fostering persons' capacities for democratic self-government. Associative ties also help persons to realize the important good (in Rawls's terminology, the "primary good") of self-respect.[23] This function of associations relates particularly to aiding persons' development of their capacities for personal self-government. Even as associations play these roles, the principles of justice shape the domain of associational life. Political liberalism distinguishes between the domain of the political and the domain of civil society, yet it posits a relationship of mutual support. We explore the "liberal expectancy" of congruence between these two domains,[24] but illuminate how our constitutional order protects discontinuities between them.

We argue that civil society is as important for securing the capacities for deliberative autonomy as for promoting the capacities for deliberative democracy. We examine the tensions between protecting civil society as a realm of personal self-government—and a buffer against the government—and expecting that it will function as a school for responsible democratic self-government. Our constitutional liberalism, by fostering these capacities for self-government, pursues ordered liberty, not liberty without virtues.

Government's Role in Promoting Civic Virtues

In Chapter 5, we turn from civil society's role in cultivating "seedbeds of virtue" to government's role in a formative project of promoting civic virtues, focusing on the shared authority of parents and government in fostering capacities for democratic and personal self-government. Discontent with liberal toleration often goes hand in hand with attraction to perfectionist conceptions of the responsibility of government to undertake a formative project of shaping or steering citizens pursuant to a vision of human virtue, goods, or excellence.

The recent Supreme Court has conceived the U.S. Constitution merely as a charter of *negative liberties,* protecting people from government but not imposing affirmative obligations upon government to pursue positive benefits. By contrast, we conceive the Constitution also to be a charter of *positive benefits:* an instrument for pursuing good things like the ends proclaimed in the Preamble, for which We the People ordained and established the Constitution.[25] The Constitution does not merely protect us from government. It constitutes us as a people and as citizens. Despite Madison's famous strategy in *The Federalist* No. 51— "supplying . . . the defect of better motives" by relying upon checks and balances and making "[a]mbition . . . counteract ambition"[26]—the realization of the Constitution's ends and indeed the maintenance of the constitutional order requires a formative project of cultivating civic virtues in responsible citizens. Such a formative project, with such positive benefits, is necessary to secure ordered liberty.

The Constitution supports government's role in fostering persons' capacities for democratic and personal self-government. (As discussed in Chapter 4, families and other institutions of civil society are also significant sites in which this development should occur.) These terms capture two significant dimensions of self-government protected in the American constitutional order.[27] Our schematic draws on political liberalism, which (as elaborated by Rawls) posits that free and equal citizens have two moral powers: the capacity for a conception of justice and the capacity for a conception of the good.[28] Our constitutional liberalism conceives the first moral power as pertaining to democratic self-government: preparing people for participation in democratic life. It conceives the second moral power as relating to personal self-government: enabling people to decide how to live their own lives. Cultivating capacities for both moral powers has a vital place in a formative project for constitutional liberalism.

Education of children is one of government's most significant formative responsibilities. Education is vital for preparing children for both personal and democratic self-government. Its dual purpose is to foster "succe[ss] in life" along with responsible citizenship (paraphrasing *Brown v. Board of Education*[29]). We focus on the role of civic education in such a formative project.

There is tension between preparing children to live in a diverse, morally pluralistic society, in which toleration is a virtue, and respecting the rights of parents to instruct their children in a particular way of life that rejects such "modern" virtues as toleration.[30] Indeed, "teaching tolerance" is a flashpoint for parents who object that such instruction conflicts with their prerogatives to teach their children values. We illustrate these controversies by examining several cases in which religious parents and students objected to school curricula or programs aimed at teaching tolerance. In resolving these controversies, it is important to remember that our constitutional order does not allocate absolute authority over children either to parents or to the state. Accordingly, many education theorists speak of schools as serving a complementary or "compensatory" role in teaching civic knowledge, skills, and virtues that children may not learn elsewhere.[31] Indeed, to the extent that schools may be uniquely situated to carry out certain forms of civic learning, retaining this shared authority is important. We look at homeschooling as a test case for how our constitutional liberalism would reconcile the dual authority of parents and schools to educate children.

Conflicts between Liberty and Equality

As we show in Chapters 4 and 5, there is a basic tension in the U.S. constitutional order between two important ideas about the relationship between civil society and government: families, religious institutions, and other voluntary associations of civil society are foundational sources or "seedbeds" of virtues and values that undergird constitutional democracy; and yet these same institutions are independent locations of power and authority that guard against governmental orthodoxy by generating their own distinctive virtues and values. The first idea envisions a comfortable *congruence* between norms fostered by nongovernmental associations and those inculcated by government. The values and virtues cultivated in each domain, in other words, are in agreement.

What happens, however, when values and virtues generated by nongovernmental institutions *conflict* with political values and virtues? The second idea about the relationship between civil society and government recognizes this potential for conflict. Government's formative project of cultivating good citizenship may clash with the formative tasks of religious institutions and other voluntary associations, just as it may clash with those of families. To adapt the parlance of civil society, what if certain associations sow bad seeds or are weedbeds of vice instead of seedbeds of virtue?[32] The possibility of this conflict invites the question of how much pluralism a healthy constitutional democracy can sustain in a system in which multiple sites of sovereignty (or authority)[33] coexist alongside the ideal of unity amidst diversity. What limits must government respect when it regulates or encourages behavior to advance political virtues or values?

In Chapter 6, we analyze such conflicts and show how constitutional liberalism justifies the use of antidiscrimination law to secure the status of equal citizenship for everyone. In doing so, we tell two stories about clashes of rights: a story about clashes between freedom of association and equal protection, and the mutual adjustment of conflicting basic liberties to secure the family of basic liberties as a whole; and a second story about congruence and conflict between protecting freedom of religion and association, on the one hand, and protecting against discrimination on the basis of race, sex, and sexual orientation, on the other. We use these two stories to illustrate two tools that government may use in a formative project of securing the status of equal citizenship for all: outright prohibition of discrimination or exclusion upon certain bases such as race, sex, or sexual orientation; and conditioning benefits or subsidies upon a group's not discriminating on such bases.

To advance the first story, we focus on *Roberts v. United States Jaycees*[34] (forbidding the Jaycees to exclude women) and *Boy Scouts of America v. Dale*[35] (permitting the Boy Scouts to exclude homosexuals). We also use these cases to illustrate the tool of outright prohibition of discrimination on certain bases such as race, sex, or sexual orientation. To tell the second story, we focus on *Bob Jones University v. United States*[36] (upholding the Internal Revenue Service's revocation of a fundamentalist Christian university's tax exempt status because of its racially discriminatory policies) and *Christian Legal Society v. Martinez*[37] (upholding a public university's enforcement of antidiscrimination norms by not subsidizing a student religious organization's freedom to exclude homosexuals). Our analysis of these cases also illustrates the tool of conditioning benefits or subsidies upon a group's not discriminating on certain bases.

Both stories—and all four cases—illustrate the struggles between the formative projects of civil society and government and between competing visions of diversity and pluralism. We conclude by examining a new generation of conflicts of rights: arguments for religious exemptions when states extend civil marriage to same-sex couples. Our constitutional liberalism provides a framework for resolving clashes of rights so as to promote ordered liberty and equal citizenship for all, not the absolutism of one liberty to the exclusion of other constitutional commitments.

Rights, Wrongness, and Disagreement: Justifying Rights in Circumstances of Moral Pluralism

Some discontent with rights relates to the justifications that liberals offer for them. In Chapters 7 and 8, we turn to the wrongness critique: that liberal theories ground rights of autonomy in empty toleration of wrong conduct instead of the substantive moral goods or virtues promoted by protecting such rights. We take up two diametrically opposed repub-

lican challenges—perfectionism and minimalism—to liberal justifications of constitutional rights of the sort we propound. Both perfectionist
and minimalist arguments raise questions about the best way to justify
rights in circumstances of moral pluralism, in which disagreements
about the good life may be intractable. In addressing these arguments,
we further develop our formative project for securing ordered liberty in
our constitutional democracy.

Autonomy versus Moral Goods

In Chapter 7, we take up Michael Sandel's perfectionist charges that liberal justifications of constitutional rights are too thin: they represent a
"minimalist liberalism" and an impoverished vision of freedom and justice that exalts choice without regard for the moral good of what is chosen.
Sandel argues that justifications for rights should rest upon the substantive moral worth of the choices and conduct protected by rights.[38] Therefore, in interpreting constitutional rights like privacy, courts should move
beyond liberal toleration and autonomy arguments about protecting individual choices to perfectionist moral arguments about fostering substantive human goods or virtues. For example, in *Lawrence v. Texas,* the
Supreme Court should have justified protecting homosexuals' right to privacy not on the basis of homosexuals' freedom to make personal choices,
but on the ground of the goods or virtues fostered by homosexuals' intimate associations, such as commitment, nurture, and intimacy.[39] In his
recent work, drawing on Aristotle's conception of justice, Sandel conceives rights and freedom in terms of cultivating virtues and forming good
citizens, not merely respecting autonomy. He argues that the question
raised in *Goodridge v. Department of Public Health*—whether to recognize same-sex marriage—cannot be resolved by arguments appealing to
"liberal nonjudgmental grounds," but "is fundamentally a debate about
whether gay and lesbian unions are worthy of the honor and recognition
that, in our society, state-sanctioned marriage confers."[40]

We grant Sandel's point that issues of moral goods and worth are central to these controversies. However, we reject his antithesis between
autonomy arguments and arguments from substantive moral goods and
virtues. We examine the opinions in *Lawrence* and *Goodridge,* differentiating what Sandel sees as the liberal strains from the perfectionist
strains. The liberal elements bespeak concern for choice as such, while
the perfectionist elements voice concern for substantive moral goods and
virtues such as commitment, intimacy, and security. We show that each
opinion is infused with arguments sounding not only in autonomy but

also in substantive moral goods and virtues. Thus, both opinions weave together liberal and perfectionist strands. We offer a similar analysis of the California Supreme Court opinion in *In re Marriage Cases*.[41] Finally, we illustrate how arguments about rights work together with arguments about virtue or worth by analyzing the New York legislature's enactment of the Marriage Equality Act. We show that our constitutional liberalism, despite Sandel's criticisms, can justify constitutional rights on the basis of both respecting autonomy and cultivating virtues. Both are essential to ordered liberty.

Minimalism versus Perfectionism

Unlike Sandel, who has put forward a perfectionist critique of liberal theories like ours for being minimalist, Cass R. Sunstein has developed a minimalist critique of such theories for being perfectionist.[42] In Chapter 8, we focus on minimalism versus perfectionism in the justification of constitutional rights. Sunstein charges that liberal theories of rights of the type we advance are too thick: they sponsor "maximalist," "perfectionist" constitutional interpretation by the judiciary that intrudes too deeply on the political processes, ignores the risks of backlash, and exaggerates the institutional capacities of courts to the detriment of democratic capacities.[43] He develops a "minimalist" republican constitutional theory, with narrow and shallow justifications for constitutional rights. He contends that courts should eschew both autonomy arguments about choices (such as those liberals like us make) and moral arguments about goods (such as those perfectionists like Sandel make) in favor of seeking "incompletely theorized agreements" on particular outcomes and "leaving things undecided" in order to allow democratic deliberation to proceed. Thus, in *Lawrence,* the Court should have avoided deciding whether homosexuals, like heterosexuals, have a right to privacy or autonomy and instead struck down the law banning same-sex sodomy (but not opposite-sex sodomy) on the ground of desuetude: "Without a strong justification, the state cannot bring the criminal law to bear on consensual sexual behavior if enforcement of the relevant law can no longer claim to have significant moral support in the enforcing state or the nation as a whole."[44]

We rebut Sunstein's criticisms of liberal perfectionist justifications for the right to privacy or autonomy. We present a tale of two courts addressing the controversial issue of same-sex marriage, comparing the minimalist *Baker v. State* (civil unions short of marriage are sufficient to accord common benefits) and the perfectionist *Goodridge* (nothing short of marriage will accord liberty and equality).[45] Furthermore, we show the journey from Sunstein's *The Partial Constitution*[46] to his minimal Constitution to be an odyssey of "the incredible shrinking constitutional theory" with a perilous withering away of rights driven by worries about moral disagreement and the limited capacities of courts as compared with legislatures. We argue that our constitutional liberalism, notwithstanding Sunstein's criticisms, is not too intrusive on the political process, is not undercut by fears about backlash, and does not presuppose the exaggerated capacities of philosopher judges living on Olympus. We substantiate these arguments in Chapter 9. Over and against minimalism, we defend the mild perfectionist approach to justifying constitutional rights that we developed in Chapter 7: respecting autonomy along with cultivating virtues and moral goods.

Rights and Absoluteness: Protecting Rights Stringently but Not Absolutely

Finally, in Chapter 9, we address the absoluteness critique: that liberal theories of "taking rights seriously" treat fundamental rights as "trumps" or absolute exemptions from governmental pursuit of goods. We assess this critique in the context of the Supreme Court's protection of basic liberties under the Due Process Clause. We show that the absoluteness critique is misplaced as against the cases and our constitutional liberalism, which protect such basic liberties stringently but not absolutely.

The Myth of Strict Scrutiny for Fundamental Rights: The Rational Continuum of Ordered Liberty

The Equal Protection and Due Process Clauses are said to protect fundamental rights that trigger "strict scrutiny." In a famous statement, Professor Gerald Gunther wrote that under the Equal Protection Clause, strict scrutiny is "strict in theory and fatal in fact"; he also stated that under that clause, rational basis scrutiny is deferential in theory and nonexistent in fact.[47] Gunther thus dramatically phrased the Supreme Court's hankerings for absoluteness and for frameworks that automatically decide cases without requiring judgment: laws are either automatically unconstitutional (on the first tier) or automatically constitutional (on the second tier). Such hankerings are subject to Glendon's criticisms about rights talk's "illusion of absoluteness" and "impoverishment" of judgment.[48] She contends that absolutist rights talk has led Americans carelessly to deploy "the rhetoric of rights" as though rights trump everything else and to develop a constitutional jurisprudence of rights isolated from "common sense," reasonable, and necessary limitations on rights in a system of "ordered liberty." She suggests that liberal theories take rights too absolutely, to the exclusion of encouraging responsibility and inculcating civic virtue.

In Chapter 9, we explore the analogous hankerings for absoluteness and avoidance of judgment under the Due Process Clause in cases protecting rights of liberty or autonomy. These cases are at the center of our concern throughout this book. Dissenting in *Lawrence,* Justice Scalia stated that, under the Due Process Clause, if an asserted liberty is a "fundamental right," it triggers "strict scrutiny" that almost automatically invalidates any statute restricting that liberty. If an asserted liberty is not a fundamental right, it is merely a "liberty interest" that triggers rational basis scrutiny that is so deferential that the Court all but automatically upholds the statute in question.[49]

Lawrence deviated from this regime, striking down the statute forbidding same-sex sexual conduct by using an intermediate standard—what we call "rational basis scrutiny with bite." Consequently, Scalia chastised the Court for not following the rigid two-tier framework that all but automatically decides rights questions one way or the other.[50] In equal protection cases, Scalia has cried foul because strict scrutiny for affirmative action plans has not been "fatal in fact," but has required judgment.[51] In due process cases, he has cried foul because rational basis scrutiny for laws forbidding same-sex sexual conduct has not been nonexistent in fact. In both domains, and in the application of both tiers, he has called for absolute, automatic decisions that do not require judgment. Such a constitutional jurisprudence manifests both the illusion of absoluteness and the impoverishment of judgment.

We expose the myth of strict scrutiny for fundamental rights under the Due Process Clause. We show that the only case under that clause ever to recognize a fundamental right implicating strict scrutiny—requiring that the statute further a compelling governmental interest and be necessary to doing so—was *Roe v. Wade.*[52] And we point out that those aspects of *Roe* were overruled in *Casey,* which substituted an "undue burden" test for strict scrutiny and pointedly avoided calling the right of a woman to decide whether to terminate a pregnancy a "fundamental right."[53] Going through due process cases protecting liberty and autonomy—from *Meyer v. Nebraska* (1923)[54] through *Casey* (1992) and *Lawrence* (2003), we show that due process jurisprudence is not absolutist nor does it reflect an impoverishment of judgment.

To the contrary, the cases protecting basic liberties under the Due Process Clause reflect what *Casey* and Justice Harlan called "reasoned judgment" concerning our "rational continuum" of "ordered liberty."[55] Indeed, the cases themselves dispel any illusion of absoluteness concerning rights of privacy or autonomy and manifest judgment of the very sort that Glendon calls for and that Scalia would banish. The constitutional liberalism developed in this book does not seek to protect rights absolutely or to avoid judgment in interpreting rights. Instead, it justifies reasoned judgment, protecting important rights but not precluding government from encouraging responsibility or inculcating civic virtues.

Epilogue

We conclude with an epilogue on pursuing ordered liberty through taking rights, responsibilities, and virtues seriously.

CHAPTER TWO

Rights and Irresponsibility

I t is a common refrain: Americans focus excessively on rights, to the detriment of responsibilities. Reflection on the relationship between rights and responsibilities goes deeper than diagnosis of current moral, legal, and social problems. It extends to analysis of the very design of our constitutional system. For example, during the 1991 bicentennial of the ratification of the Bill of Rights, *Harper's* asked a group of scholars and political figures to "carry on the founders' conversation." They pondered whether a "Bill of Duties" should complement the Bill of Rights, taking as their point of departure the claim that although "the vocabulary of rights is nearly exhausted ... the vocabulary of responsibilities has yet to emerge."[1] Most of the respondents declined to endorse a bill of enforceable duties, but some called for bringing a new communitarian perspective balancing rights and responsibilities to bear on the moral, legal, and social issues of our time.[2]

Proponents of "rights *and* responsibilities" trace the responsibility deficit not only to the silence of our governing documents about responsibility but also to the structure and rhetoric of American "rights talk" and the "morally incomplete" language of rights. One alleged consequence of the imbalance between rights and responsibilities is the erosion of personal responsibility and the institutions of civil society, such as families and religious, civic, and other voluntary associations. These "seedbeds of virtue" are necessary to inculcate the traits of character on which the preservation of ordered liberty depends but which rights talk neglects. The new communitarians seek "[t]o rebuild America's moral foundations [and] to bring our regard for individuals and their rights into a better relationship with our sense of personal and collective responsibility."[3]

Political leaders, both Democrats and Republicans, have sympathized with this new communitarianism and its focus on responsibility. As a candidate, Bill Clinton ran on a Democratic Party platform charging the Republican Party with a twelve-year "nightmare" of "irresponsibility and neglect." As President, he called for a "new ethic of personal and family and community responsibility," through which Americans would "demand more responsibility from all" and "take more responsibility" for themselves.[4] The Republican Party countered with its own call to "restore the American dream" and "restore a proper balance between government and personal responsibility."[5] The Third Way politics pioneered by Clinton, the Democratic Leadership Council, and the Progressive Policy Institute proposes a "new social compact based on individual rights and responsibilities."[6]

As a candidate, Barack Obama wrote of how Americans' "individualism has always been bound by a set of communal values, the glue upon which every healthy society depends," and by obligations to family and nation. These appeals to community, along with Obama's declaration that we are "not from red states, not from blue states, but from the United States," led sociologist Amitai Etzioni, founder of the "responsive communitarian" movement, and prominent journalists to label Obama a communitarian.[7] In his inaugural address, President Obama called for a "new era of responsibility—a recognition on the part of every American that we have duties to ourselves, our nation and the world"—and contended that such duties give meaning to "our liberty."[8] Obama, like his Democratic and Republican predecessors, also voices communitarian and Third Way themes that there are many social problems that government alone cannot solve and supports governmental partnerships with community- and faith-based groups.

The refrain of "too many rights, too few responsibilities" and the appeal to "rights *and* responsibilities" in themselves do not explain how rights undermine responsibility.[9] To assess the irresponsibility critique, we must get a clearer picture of what sorts of responsibilities the communitarians believe are in need of restoration (e.g., moral, social, or legal) and to whom such responsibilities are owed (e.g., to self, family, community, country, or the world). This chapter examines a cluster of questions about the relationship between rights and responsibility. What is it about rights that triggers the irresponsibility critique? Do legal rights include a right to be irresponsible and, if so, why defend them? Does the structure of legal rights discourage or preclude individual, community, or societal reflection on right conduct and efforts to foster responsible behavior? Have liberal justifications of legal rights invited discontent by neglecting the relationship between rights and responsibility? How much of what is at issue in charges of irresponsibility is really about rights, as distinguished from legally prohibited behavior?

Because the irresponsibility critique encompasses a complex cluster of charges about rights, we need to focus on specific proponents to sharpen our analysis and to do the critique justice. We shall focus on two comprehensive, articulate, and influential formulations: those of Harvard Law School Professor Mary Ann Glendon, especially in her book *Rights Talk: The Impoverishment of Political Discourse,* and those expressed in "The Responsive Communitarian Platform: Rights and Responsibilities," whose primary authors are communitarian sociologist Amitai Etzioni, civic liberal political theorist William Galston, and Glendon (and whose signatories include prominent communitarians, civic republicans, and progressives). We acknowledge that these new communitarians have many precursors and contemporaries. They represent the best foils here because of their application of the irresponsibility critique to constitutional rights.

First, we explicate the irresponsibility critique of rights and the calls for responsibility. Second, we argue that a significant component of the irresponsibility critique is a social critique: that a flight from individual responsibility coupled with an increased demand for rights have led to a dearth of civic virtue and a growth of social pathology. We question the connection posited between legal rights and those phenomena. Finally, we put forward a jurisprudential analysis of the irresponsibility critique. We distinguish two strands of the critique: legal rights permit right-holders to act with legal *immunity,* and legal rights allow people to act without regard to moral *rightness.* We grant that legal rights do not equate with moral rightness, but we reject the claims that legal rights send a message about moral rightness, moral insulation, or the absence of responsibility. In support, we point to the employment of moral suasion and the language of responsibility in contemporary debates about a number of constitutional rights.

We also challenge the dichotomous treatment of rights and responsibility by showing that presuppositions about moral capacities and moral responsibility undergird liberal justifications of constitutional rights like those we advance. Liberals believe that the possibility of irresponsible conduct is a cost of recognizing and protecting rights, a cost that is generally preferable to shifting the locus of moral responsibility from individuals to the community or the government. Yet, liberals need not hold that the costs of rights never justify restricting or regulating individual freedom. Thus, the irresponsibility critique misunderstands the notion of "rights as trumps" as being more "absolutist" than it actually is. We return to these matters in Chapters 6 and 9. Our constitutional liberalism pursues ordered liberty, not absolute rights without responsibilities.

We argue that the freedom that rights provide makes possible the exercise of responsibility and that leading liberal justifications for rights are not silent about this relationship between rights and responsibility. As a schematic device, we argue that communitarian and liberal talk about responsibility emphasize two different, although related, meanings of responsibility: *responsibility as accountability* to community versus *responsibility as autonomy* or self-government, respectively. As we use the terms, "responsibility as accountability" connotes being answerable to others for the manner and consequences of the exercise of one's rights, whereas "responsibility as autonomy" connotes self-governance, that is, entrusting the right-holder to exercise moral responsibility in making decisions guided by conscience and deliberation. If liberal rights talk seems silent about responsibility, as the communitarians claim, it may be due in part to these very different conceptions of responsibility. The irresponsibility critique highlights the tension between pursuing the goal of responsibility as accountability (emphasized by communitarians) and protecting the principle of responsibility as autonomy (stressed by liberals). In Chapter 3, we illustrate that tension with the example of the right to procreative autonomy.

In Search of "Rights and Responsibilities"

In *Rights Talk,* Glendon argues that rights talk impoverishes political discourse and civic life because it drives out or obscures the language of responsibility. Diagnosing a lack of fit between, on the one hand, a rights talk that is silent about a rights-bearer's correlative responsibilities and, on the other, a deep American belief that persons should be personally responsible for their actions, Glendon argues that the law's silence about responsibility may even appear to send a message that it condones irresponsibility.[10]

What is wrong with rights talk? Glendon submits:

> Our rights talk, in its absoluteness, promotes unrealistic expectations, heightens social conflict, and inhibits dialogue that might lead toward consensus, accommodation, or at least the discovery of common ground. In its

silence concerning responsibilities, it seems to condone acceptance of the benefits of living in a democratic social welfare state, without accepting the corresponding personal and civic obligations. In its relentless individualism, it fosters a climate that is inhospitable to society's losers, and that systematically disadvantages caretakers and dependents, young and old. In its neglect of civil society, it undermines the principal seedbeds of civic and personal virtue. In its insularity, it shuts out potentially important aids to the process of self-correcting learning. All of these traits promote mere assertion over reason-giving.[11]

Glendon illustrates these lamentable features of American rights talk with examples from constitutional, family, and tort law.

Glendon casts her critique of the inattention to responsibilities in American rights talk in the form of a comparative legal anthropology of "libertarian" versus "dignitarian" conceptions of the person and of rights.[12] She argues that the United States, influenced by the Anglo-American tradition, reflects the first. Her primary illustration is Justice Brandeis's proclamation that the "most comprehensive of rights and the right most valued by civilized men" is the "right to be let alone."[13] This lone "rights-bearer," she claims, is "imagined as an independent, highly autonomous, self-determining being." In "the American rights tradition," the "highest priority" is "on individual freedom from governmental constraints. Rights tend to be formulated *without explicit mention of their limits* or of their relation to *responsibilities* or *to other rights*."[14]

By contrast, the conception of the person in "dignitarian systems," influenced by the Romano-Germanic tradition, makes explicit that "each person is constituted in important ways by and through his relations with others." Glendon contrasts Brandeis's formulation with the German Constitutional Court's declaration that "The image of man in the Basic Law is not that of an isolated, sovereign individual." In many other post–World War II constitutions, as well as in the United Nations Universal Declaration of Human Rights (UDHR) and in Catholic social teaching, she argues, rights are grounded in a normative framework of human dignity and "specific rights are typically formulated so as to make clear that they are related to one another, that certain groups as well as individuals have rights, and that political entities, as well as citizens, have responsibilities."[15]

Gauging the scope of Glendon's critique is difficult. At its narrowest, it is a meditation on the comparative silence in American governing documents, such as the Bill of Rights, concerning responsibilities. This silence contrasts strikingly with European constitutions and rights proclamations such as the French Declaration of Rights and Duties and with Article 29 of the UDHR, which states that "[e]veryone has duties to the community" and that everyone's rights and freedoms are subject to limitations "for the purposes of securing due recognition and respect for the rights and freedoms of others and of meeting the just requirements of morality, public order and the general welfare in a democratic society."[16] As an exercise in comparative legal anthropology, Glendon's critique is a reflection on how differences in such founding texts shape different conceptions of the person. (As we respond to various critiques of rights and liberal conceptions of the person, we will encounter again Glendon's "lone rights-bearer" (Chapter 3) and meet such near-kin as the supposed radically autonomous, "sovereign" self characteristic of "expressive individualism" (Chapter 4) and the "unencumbered self" able to stand apart from all relationships (Chapter 7).)

At its broadest, Glendon's critique is a social critique of American society and American attitudes about freedom untempered by a sense of personal responsibility and civic duties. Her leading example is a survey of teenagers reporting their perception that what makes America special is that they are free to do whatever they want, without limit. As a jurisprudential analysis, her critique attacks the characterization of rights as trumps and absolutist formulations of rights that are silent about responsibility and that appear to preclude deliberation about the common good. Our public documents and our rights talk encourage a careless and exaggerated way of speaking and thinking about rights, as if liberty meant license. Yet she points out that the interpretations of rights by judges, lawyers, contracting parties, and others reveals that rights are not without limits.[17]

Why is our rights talk silent about responsibilities? Does the silence matter? On the one hand, Glendon locates the undeniable differences between the American Bill of Rights and the French Declaration of Rights and Duties in the different intellectual pedigrees of the American and French Revolutions (Lockean individual rights and self-interest versus classical and Rousseauean civic virtue and duty). On the other hand, she downplays the American and European textual differences by arguing that the American Founders did not need to adopt a bill of legal duties because they relied on the institutions of civil society to restrain and temper individual self-interest and the exercise of rights. Invoking speeches by the Founders, Glendon and other proponents of an unwritten "constitution of responsibility" stress the role of morality and religion as the ultimate supports for maintaining a republican form of government, for respecting rights, and for making "our experiment in ordered liberty" possible. Relying particularly on Alexis de Tocqueville's nineteenth-century observations of Americans, Glendon argues that the "seedbeds of civic virtue"—such as families, associations, and the constraints of morality and religion—once played a vital role in educating Americans about rights and responsibilities.[18]

In Glendon's view, the silence of our governing documents concerning responsibility would not matter so much if these institutions were still germinating virtuous citizens with the requisite character traits for "ordered liberty." However, that traditional, richly textured social fabric is wearing thin, and Americans increasingly view law as the primary, if not only, source of teaching about morality. She traces the rise of rights talk to a significant shift in constitutional law in the 1950s and 1960s to a focus on individual rights and an eschewal of ordinary politics in favor of judicial vindication of rights. This "rights revolution" brought with it an equally significant social phenomenon, a change in "habits of thought and speech."[19] The result is a rights-laden discourse that makes public dialogue and deliberation about responsibilities and the common good difficult and fosters attitudes that the Founders would have criticized as "liberty as license."

Clearly, Glendon's tale contains an important then/now contrast. She contends: "[T]he liberal principles enshrined in the United States' founding documents were political principles that were never meant to serve as moral guides for all of social and private life." Moreover, their silence about responsibility reflected an expectation that the institutions of civil society and individual states would address "the responsibilities that are correlative with rights." But when legal images of personhood "migrate into other contexts" of social and private life, and when these institutions atrophy, so that the law becomes the primary carrier of values, these images can become "mischievous." In today's more "legalistic and heterogeneous society," citizens "tend to regard the Supreme Court's pronouncements not merely as legal rulings but also as moral teachings grounded in the country's most sacred civic document." This reinforces the "excessive individualism in American law."[20]

Glendon maintains nonetheless that the social fabric is not threadbare and that rights talk obscures a still-intact civil society, with its "communities of memory and mutual aid." She marshals "evidence" that America has "indigenous languages of relationship and responsibility" available to refine rights talk.[21] (In Chapter 4, we assess Glendon's arguments concerning the institutions of civil society as "seedbeds of civic virtue.")

As with her critique of rights talk, judging the scope of Glendon's proposed corrective is difficult. On the one hand, she claims that her goal is a refined rhetoric of rights that would keep "competing rights and responsibilities in view." She urges that we address such matters as: whether a particular issue is best conceptualized as involving a right; the relation a given right should have to other rights and interests; the responsibilities that should be correlative with a given right; the social costs of rights; and the effects a right may have on the durable protection of freedom and human dignity.[22]

On the other hand, matters such as how to link rights with responsibilities and how to factor in social costs of rights appear to raise questions about the content of and limitations on rights. Glendon appears to consider, as refining rights rhetoric, not only greater judicial attention to the publicity effects of judicial opinions but also greater judicial willingness—even when a fundamental right is asserted—to countenance "moral fabric" arguments and to consider whether they justify the use of the criminal law to express and maintain a "widely shared moral view" (e.g., through sodomy laws).[23] Moreover, although she rejects importing European declarations codifying limitations on rights and correlative duties to communities, she finds them instructive and proposes that the former West Germany's restrictive abortion law would better serve American women than the right of privacy has (an argument we assess in Chapter 3).[24] All this suggests a substantive critique of the content of rights.

Assessing the Irresponsibility Critique as a Social Critique

Situating the irresponsibility critique in the context of a number of contemporary critiques of American society suggests that certain components of it are a social critique aimed less at legal rights as such than at American society and "rights culture." Those components include the claims that: Americans want rights without the responsibilities of citizenship; the legacy of the 1960s includes not only the civil rights movement but also a challenge to authority that led to the crumbling of moral authority and tradition and an explosion of self-indulgent and socially harmful behaviors; and Americans today debase the value of genuine legal rights by making frivolous claims to rights while fleeing personal responsibility and shifting blame to others. The new communitarians tie all these social phenomena together with the thread of a decline of responsibility. We do not assess fully their accounts of the problems of American society. Rather, we question whether legal rights, liberalism, and an "excess" of liberal virtues are to blame for these social phenomena.

The Quest for a Responsible Citizenry

The irresponsibility critique of rights explores the indispensable relationship between freedom and responsibility. The American experiment in ordered liberty, the communitarians argue, depends on such traits of character as self-control, self-restraint, and respect for the rights of others, as well as a willingness to assume responsibility for oneself, one's family, and the health of America's institutions.[25] Freedom, in other words, depends on both responsibility as autonomy and as accountability.

The communitarians argue that, to a disturbing degree, Americans manifest "a strong sense of entitlement—that is, a demand that the community provide more services and strongly uphold rights—coupled with a rather weak sense of obligation to the local and national community."[26] To the extent that the irresponsibility critique targets such attitudes, it does not directly implicate rights as much as lapses in civic responsibility. Indeed, the prominent example offered as a symbol of contemporary attitudes is young people's reported expectation of being tried by a jury coupled with a reluctance to serve on juries.[27] There is no legal right to evade jury service; indeed, it is a civic duty, nonperformance of which the state may legally punish.[28]

This component of the irresponsibility critique is a helpful civics lesson about the role that responsible citizens must play in sustaining a constitutional democracy. In the communitarian view, however, civic education and national or community service cannot fully redress the decline of a responsible citizenry because the roots of the American malaise go deeper. Indeed, the moral or social fabric, the "ecosystems" of society, result significantly from the effects of the choices and conduct of millions of individuals.[29] Echoing Glendon, the "Responsive Communitarian Platform" warns that the most basic institution of civil society—the family—which should be a moral educator schooling the next generation of citizens in the interplay of rights and responsibilities, is in peril and that "the second line of defense"—schools—cannot alone prevent the decline of a responsible citizenry.[30] Moreover, communitarians charge that schools are reluctant to engage in moral education and character formation but must do so to combat the "moral deficit" among young people.[31] (We return to these matters in Chapters 4 and 5.)

Communitarian inventories of the "moral state of the union" indicate that the responsibility deficit in America encompasses not only some conduct protected by legal rights but also lawless behavior that is unprotected by rights and violates the rights of others.[32] Consider, for example, violent crime. What the irresponsibility critique seems to overlook is that although constitutional rights attend persons accused of crimes and limit methods to prevent crime—and communitarians challenge "absolutist" interpretations of such rights—rights do not protect the criminal activity itself.[33] Moreover, notwithstanding the communitarian charge that libertarian interpretations of rights prevent government from addressing violent crime, many liberals argue that providing for the physical security of citizens is the most basic obligation of government.[34]

Communitarians are not alone in focusing on an absence of responsibility as an explanation for many self-destructive and socially costly behaviors. Yet the underlying culprit for a substantial amount of the irresponsible behavior that communitarians target is not rights, but the erosion of qualities like self-control, self-restraint, and respect for others and the law.[35] The communitarians believe, though, that rights have contributed to that erosion, stressing as pivotal the civil rights movement and the broad challenges to authority and tradition during the 1960s.

The Legacy of the 1960s and the Civil Rights Movement: Progress or Pandora's Box?

Out of the new communitarianism emerges a tale of the legacy of the 1960s explaining both the explosion of rights talk and the erosion of morality and civic virtue. We shall attempt a composite, if oversimplified, account.[36] In the 1950s, the moral authority of leaders and community norms were respected; it was possible to talk about what was right and what was wrong. Families were stronger, violent crime rarer, and habits of self-reliance and self-restraint more abundant. This society had some notable failings: racial inequality and segregation, gender inequality (including a male-governed family structure and the exclusion of women from the commercial work world), and the marginal status of certain ethnic and religious groups (like Jews and Catholics). Moreover, the values themselves were somewhat authoritarian. Nonetheless, there was a cultural consensus in America, a traditional morality that was "dominant and effective."[37]

The civil rights movement, the communitarians grant, appropriately criticized injustice and exclusion and rightly sought to realize the ideal of equality for all citizens.[38] But the 1960s proved to be a Pandora's Box: that decade unleashed a dangerous explosion of claims of entitlement, an ideology of personal fulfillment and liberation, and a pervasive challenge to traditional morality and authority.[39] Such a challenge undermined the strong family values that held sway in the 1950s and repudiated a traditional morality that emphasized self-control, self-restraint, and self-discipline. In its place, the challenge of the 1960s left us with eroding moral foundations and institutions, moral relativism, an ideology of liberty as license, and a profound absence of moral consensus on new shared values and new forms of social institutions.[40] Alongside this cultural challenge, the 1980s saw the ascent of economic libertarianism and depiction of the "unbridled pursuit of self-interest" as virtuous.[41] As Etzioni elaborates the contrast, "[i]f the hallmark of the 1950s was a strong sense of obligation, from 1960 to 1990 there was a rising sense of entitlement and a growing tendency to shirk social responsibilities."[42] Today, these developments continue unabated, and we continue to live with their consequences.

The communitarian account is overstated. The assertion of civil rights has no obvious or plausible link to the rise of irresponsible and unlawful behavior, because civil rights do not include "rights," for example, to commit violent crimes or drug offenses.[43] Moreover, many civil rights (such as voting, housing, and education) secure preconditions for responsible citizenship. Communitarians respond that this very expansion of opportunities, benign in itself, inadvertently brought about harmful social changes.[44] But Cass Sunstein put it well when he argued that the posited link between rights talk and a responsibility deficit is exactly backward: rights talk arose because of a deficit of responsibility on the part of society and government.[45] And Michael Schudson is right to argue in *The Good Citizen* that the "rights-bearing citizen," such as Rosa Parks, often sought to redefine rather than reject community, illuminating the inequality and exclusion of existing communities; such citizens appealed to "common American traditions of liberty and equality," often "from the point of view of the people who had been left out of the founders' compact."[46]

Nonetheless, the attempt to link the civil rights movement to a growing social "pathology" and shrinking moral consensus is part of a larger debate over American values that centers on whether society is "defining deviancy down" and becoming too tolerant of behaviors once condemned socially, if not legally.[47] An examination of some of those behaviors traced to the legacy of the 1960s—changes in mores concerning sexuality, greater diversity in family forms, increases in divorce, greater acceptance of pregnancy and parenting outside of marriage, and availability of abortion—suggests that the real targets of the irresponsibility critique are such social changes. Developments in family law and the

Supreme Court's recognition of constitutional rights to liberty and autonomy in the areas of sexuality, reproduction, and marriage also are implicated.[48] Thus, the increasing "constitutionalization" and liberalization of family law, some communitarians argue, impede family law's traditional role in conveying moral messages about the responsibilities of spouses and parents and exalt adult liberty and fulfillment at the expense of children and other dependent persons (including mothers). Pointing to changes in the law of family dissolution, Glendon contends that "the legal system inadvertently fosters irresponsible behavior."[49] In assessing the irresponsibility critique, the critical questions are what messages to draw from these legal developments and whether certain legally protected choices are proxies for irresponsibility.

The Rights Explosion and the Flight from Responsibility

Finally, Glendon and the new communitarians lament the increasing tendency of Americans to express needs and wants in terms of rights, a tendency social critics and popular media describe as "rights inflation" or a "rights explosion." This "vast expansion in the number and scope of rights to which Americans believe they are entitled, and the 'rights culture' this produces," argues Francis Fukuyama (a "Platform" signatory), fosters an "individualism" that seriously threatens community.[50] The attack on "rights culture" seems to target the evidently frivolous or irresponsible assertion of rights. For example, people are said to call for new rights without regard to the obligations that a right creates (e.g., asserting affirmative rights to health care without considering the implications for the fisc). Rather than creating more rights talk—which supposedly makes compromise difficult and devalues rights—communitarians argue for a "return to a language of social virtues, interests, and, above all, social responsibilities [that] will reduce contentiousness and enhance social cooperation."[51]

The rights explosion frequently is said to be accompanied by a corresponding plunge in Americans' sense of personal responsibility, manifested in the tendency to assume the mantle of the victim.[52] To be sure, those who elaborate the victimhood critique offer some absurd examples of rights assertion coupled with denial of personal responsibility. Consider, for example, the lawsuit brought against a refrigerator manufacturer by people injured from running races carrying refrigerators on their backs![53] It is unclear, however, how such refusal to accept responsibility is a legacy of the 1960s or is due to the recognition and enforcement of legal rights.

In sum, all of the components of the irresponsibility critique previously mentioned, understood as a social critique, provide an opportunity
for reflecting on the current state of American society. But for the most
part they are unpersuasive as critiques of legal rights.

Assessing the Irresponsibility Critique as a Jurisprudential Critique

In this section, we argue that the jurisprudential underpinnings of the
irresponsibility critique of rights are flawed. On one reading, the critique
merely seeks to correct some erroneous inferences drawn from certain
features of legal rights, immunity and wrongness. On another reading,
the new communitarians' discontent with these two features and their
impulse to link rights to responsibilities reaches deeper to attack rights
themselves. We need to consider how the new communitarians understand rights and what sorts of rights they would defend.

The Immunity Critique

Rights, Immunity, and Harm   The new communitarians understand legal
rights to protect against legal coercion, preserving a zone of noninterference or immunity: "Rights give reasons to others not to coercively interfere with the [right-holder] in the performance of protected acts." A
consequence is that legal rights may include the freedom to engage in
"morally inappropriate," irresponsible, or even socially harmful conduct
without legal accountability.[54] The social message that people are said to
infer from immunity is that they have a right to be insulated from the
moral claims or scrutiny of others.

Although immunity creates social costs, the irresponsibility critique
appears to accept immunity as a feature of legal rights. Yet its call for a
rhetoric of rights attentive to their social costs suggests ambivalence.
And the critique vigorously rejects any leap from legal immunity to social
unaccountability. In assessing the immunity critique, we should ask
whether legal rights in fact immunize right-holders from liability for
imposing social costs or harms on others.

Wesley Hohfeld's classic account of rights provides a helpful point of
departure. Hohfeld explained legal rights in terms of several possible
pairs of jural relationships.[55] Two are particularly pertinent to the immunity critique. Individual rights against governmental interference—the

constitutional rights often used as examples in the irresponsibility critique—might be understood as taking the form of Hohfeld's first pair, *right/duty:* an individual right to do or not do X correlates with a governmental duty not to interfere with that right (or to provide X). One could also regard constitutional rights as captured by his second pair, *privilege/no right:* an individual privilege or liberty to do or not do X correlates with no right or authority for government to require that an individual do otherwise.[56] In either account, there is a realm of activity or inactivity that is immune from legal interference or sanction.

Jack Balkin argues that on Hohfeld's account "a legal right is a privilege to inflict harm that is either not legally cognizable or is . . . without legal remedy."[57] Similarly, Joseph Singer contends that Hohfeld's analysis demonstrated the limits of the then-prevailing justification for legal rights: John Stuart Mill's harm principle and the distinction between self-regarding and other-regarding acts.[58] It made clear that legal rights protect not merely self-regarding acts but also conduct that harms others. Thus, a consequence of the immunity that legal rights afford may be the imposition of noncompensable harms or costs on others.

The new communitarians do not propose to expand the definition of harm to justify interfering coercively with all activities that impose costs, yet harm does serve as a justification for constraining certain rights. Freedom of speech is the paradigm example of a right that warrants legal protection although it imposes social costs and individual harms.[59] In contrast, in areas of public health and safety, including national security, communitarians reject "absolutist" assertions of rights and emphasize harms and costs.[60] With its imagery of social environments and ecosystems, the irresponsibility critique assumes that a wide range of individual choices have social costs, both for the fisc and the social fabric. When should society use law as a tool to address these costs and when should it rely solely on the community's moral voice? Families and family law are an instructive example. On the one hand, the "Platform" advises that responsibility is "not primarily a legal matter," and that communitarians seek "to affirm the moral commitments of parents" to attend to the moral education of their children. On the other hand, communitarians urge that "the law does play a significant role not only in regulating society, but also in indicating which values it holds dear." Because of the "serious" social costs of divorce, divorce law should "signal society's concern."[61] In other areas, communitarians advance a mix of facilitative, persuasive, and coercive measures to encourage or impose parental, institutional, and governmental responsibility. Thus, although the communitarians accept legal immunity as a feature of some legal rights, they urge a general principle of social accountability for the exercise of rights and argue that legal immunity should not insulate right-holders from such measures.[62]

A comparison with Mill's delineation of the respective spheres of individual freedom and legitimate governmental interference is instructive. Mill argued that an individual is not accountable to society for self-regarding actions (when there is no harm to others), but "for such actions as are prejudicial to the interests of others, the individual is accountable, and may be subjected either to social or to legal punishment, if society [deems] that the one or the other is requisite for its protection." Yet even within the realm of unaccountability, Mill granted that society could use a range of measures, such as "[a]dvice, instruction, persuasion, and avoidance," to signal disapproval of individual action or to attempt to influence such action.[63]

The communitarians seem to reject Mill's nomenclature of a realm of unaccountability because it might send the social message of insulation. In any event, they argue for a narrower understanding of such a realm because the interdependency of contemporary society increases the instances in which the exercise of freedom imposes costs or harms on others.[64] Nevertheless, they might find in Mill support for their argument that a right bestowing legal immunity does not immunize persons from the moral scrutiny or moral claims of others. At the same time, the communitarian quest to link rights and responsibilities poses important questions concerning when persuasive measures rise to the level of social tyranny, coercion, or punishment of the sort that Mill feared and criticized as threatening liberty.[65] We argue that legal immunity does not immunize people from governmental moralizing and the moral scrutiny of others.

Rights as Trumps   In the context of constitutional rights, Ronald Dworkin's conception of rights as trumps has provoked the ire of the new communitarians. They charge that thinking of rights as trumps leads to disregarding any responsibilities to society and any social costs of conduct and shuts down debate about the common good.[66] At bottom, the objection seems to be that this notion has spread from an account of certain fundamental constitutional rights to a conception of legal rights generally, eviscerating moderation of claims by exalting individual desires over social ends.[67] However, the communitarian attack on rights as trumps ignores important limitations on that notion already developed in liberal theory. It reflects a deep discontent with immunity, yet does not offer a clear alternative conception of rights or how social costs should affect their protection.

Many years before Glendon wrote *Rights Talk,* Dworkin observed that "[t]he language of rights now dominates political debate in the United States." In *Taking Rights Seriously,* he defended a "strong sense" of the "old idea of individual human rights." He argued: "Individual rights are political trumps held by individuals. Individuals have rights when, for some reason, a collective goal is not a sufficient justification for denying them what they wish, as individuals, to have or to do, or not a sufficient justification for imposing some loss or injury upon them."[68] Fundamental rights, he argued, trumped the utilitarian calculus of the greatest happiness of the greatest number.

Dworkin contended: "A right against the Government must be a right to do something even when the majority thinks it would be wrong to do it, and even when the majority would be worse off for having it done." To assert that the government has the right to do whatever advances the general welfare or "the right to preserve whatever sort of environment the majority wishes to live in," would "annihilate[ ]" individual rights against the government. It would reduce them to mere interests to be balanced away at the majority's discretion. Dworkin argued that this strong sense of rights marked the "distinctive concept of an individual right against the State which is the heart . . . of constitutional theory in the United States."[69]

Glendon uses Dworkin's idea of "taking rights seriously," even at the expense of the general interest, to illustrate the "illusion of absoluteness" of American rights talk. She states: "[I]t is difficult to imagine any serious contemporary European legal philosopher" asserting, as Dworkin did, that "if someone has a right to something, then it is wrong for government to deny it to him even though it would be in the general interest to do so."[70] Dworkin's account of taking rights seriously clearly conflicts with what Glendon thinks taking the social costs of rights seriously requires.

But an examination of the limits of Dworkin's conception of rights suggests that the illusion of absoluteness may be Glendon's. The first important limit is that the strong rights that Dworkin defended were fundamental constitutional rights, not every constitutional right, much less every right, and certainly not every imaginable "liberty interest." He granted that, with respect to the vast bulk of laws not implicating those strong rights, promoting the general welfare was a sufficient justification for restricting liberty. Even when a strong right against the government was in play, it would overstate the point to say that "the State is never justified in overriding that right." For example, Dworkin acknowledged that the government would be justified in overriding a right of free speech to "protect the rights of others, or to prevent a catastrophe, or even to obtain a clear and major public benefit."[71] Thus, he did not claim that societal welfare never restrains rights or overrides them, merely that fundamental rights are not simply individual "interests" to be balanced against such welfare. Furthermore, a significant ground for limiting rights that Dworkin recognized is the conflicting rights of others, especially conflicts between rights to the state's protection and rights to be free from the state's interference. In such situations, the more important right should prevail over the less important. (In Chapter 6, we address how to resolve such conflicts.) Government could also limit the extension of a right if the values protected by the original right were not at stake or if the costs to society went far beyond "the cost paid to grant the original right."[72]

Finally, Dworkin's account did not presume to answer all questions as to how the moral responsibilities of citizens should guide their lives and exercise of their rights or how government and citizens might attempt in noncoercive ways to shape others' exercise of rights. He addresses such questions in subsequent works in ways that clarify the distinction between responsibility as autonomy and responsibility as accountability. Thus, in elaborating the "principle of personal responsibility" for making the ultimate decisions about our own lives, he distinguishes between permissible—and inevitable—forms of *influence* (such as friends, religion, and culture) and impermissible *subordination* through manipulation or coercion.[73] Government, on his view, may seek to influence or persuade to encourage *responsibility* in making a decision, but it may not insist on *conformity* with its view of the responsible decision[74] (a distinction to which we return in Chapter 3).

Dworkin recognized that a government's taking rights seriously would incur costs: "[T]he majority cannot travel as fast or as far as it would like if it recognizes the rights of individuals to do what, in the majority's terms, is the wrong thing to do." Why take rights seriously if doing so makes it more difficult or costly for a polity to pursue the general benefit? Dworkin argued that, although the "bulk of the law . . . must state, in its greatest part, the majority's view of the common good," the institution of rights is the promise of the majority to the minority "that [its] dignity and equality will be respected." Indeed, ideas of dignity (particularly, the supposition of what it means to treat individuals as full members of the human community) and equality (particularly, the requirement that government treat individuals with equal concern and respect) are

typical grounds for protecting strong rights.[75] As Dworkin elaborates in
Justice for Hedgehogs, principles of dignity feature as the foundation for
this governmental obligation as well as the basis for our special responsibility for our own lives and for what we owe each other.[76]

In sum, the communitarians overlook that Dworkin acknowledged
many limits on the idea of rights as trumps. If they reject his underlying
conception of what a right is, they may reject legal immunity as a feature
of legal rights. If so, we need to know what alternative conception of
rights they would embrace and how they would wed legal, as well as
social, accountability to rights.

The irresponsibility critique appears to grant that a legal right held by
one person generally involves a correlative duty on the part of another,
the Constitution provides a reason for government not to interfere coercively with the exercise of rights guaranteed therein, and the exercise of
legal rights may result in irresponsible or socially harmful conduct. If the
communitarians accept these features of legal rights, it is not clear why
they object to the key component of rights as trumps—that it would be
wrong for government to act coercively to prevent people from exercising rights in order to pursue the general welfare. Glendon, for example,
objects to this claim. Is it therefore right for government to prevent
people from exercising rights in such situations?

Although the new communitarians ask that we talk about rights in a
different way, they offer no coherent alternative to the strong sense of
constitutional rights that Dworkin advances. Perhaps the communitarians object to the peremptory image of a trump, which may send the
social message that a right automatically trumps any consideration of
the impact of rights on the common good, rather than to Dworkin's
particular conceptions. Thus, communitarians may fear that talking
about rights as trumps sends the (mistaken) message that the assertion of
rights cuts off debate. Similarly, Sunstein suggests that too often rights
"masquerad[e] as reasons" and are not conducive to deliberation. In contrast, a more deliberative approach, even if it led to the same protection
of a right, would acknowledge that there are other issues to consider.[77]
But we should observe that the image of rights as trumps itself suggests
that other cards are on the table.

Furthermore, there is reason to doubt that rights operate as trumps in
contemporary constitutional law. It is ironic that the notion features so
centrally in the irresponsibility critique as emblematic of the failings of
contemporary rights talk, given developments in constitutional law since
the publication of Dworkin's initial call to take rights seriously. The
conservative Burger, Rehnquist, and Roberts Courts often have been

criticized for not taking rights seriously. Indeed, James Boyd White has suggested that Glendon's critique of rights tells only part of the story since the "characteristic vice" of the Supreme Court cases of the last few decades is not the assertion of absolute rights of the sort that Glendon decries but "the claim to judge every case by a process of 'balancing' one cluster of interests off against another."[78]

Likewise, other commentators suggest that the metaphor of balancing best describes the identification, valuation, and comparison of competing interests pervasive in adjudication of individual constitutional rights.[79] This metaphor, while consistent with communitarian language of restoring balance and equilibrium, is quite at odds with that of trumps. The defining features of such an age are more likely to be mutual adjustment of conflicting rights or indeed balancing rights away, rather than protecting them absolutely though the heavens fall. We return to such matters in Chapters 6 and 9.

Weighing the Social Costs of Rights   Whether the greater individual accountability that communitarians seek with respect to rights is compatible with a strong conception of rights is not clear. For example, Glendon urges a refined rights rhetoric that is attentive to the social costs of rights and to the question of "the responsibilities, if any, that should be correlative with a given right."[80] The irresponsibility critique warns that strong defenses of individual rights undermine communities and the support on which rights themselves depend.[81]

Glendon unfavorably compares Dworkin's supposedly absolute conception of rights to European declarations explicitly linking rights to duties to serve "the public weal." She offers the Canadian Charter of Rights and Freedoms as a good example of a "strong," though not "absolute," form of rights. It guarantees rights "subject only to such reasonable limits prescribed by law as can be demonstrably justified in a free and democratic society" and subjects a "wide range" of constitutional rights to either a national or local "legislative override procedure."[82] Such comparative models suggest a critique of the immunity that a right affords. And they suggest correctives not merely of social accountability, but also of legal accountability. In Chapter 9, we question whether what American courts do in adjudicating claims of "fundamental" constitutional rights is "absolutist." In Chapter 3, we examine Glendon's analysis of abortion law, one clear example of her rejection of legal immunity in favor of the accountability she finds in European models.

Glendon's appeal to craft a refined rights rhetoric from "indigenous resources"—such as household table talk, models of compromise, attitudes of tolerance and forbearance, and even political deliberation—raises questions as to what sorts of rights she would support and the respective roles of courts and legislatures in enforcing them. First, is Glendon's point that individuals should voluntarily moderate their exercise of rights or that government should restrict such exercise in the general interest of society? Vindication of rights often assumes that there are clear winners and losers, people in the right and people in the wrong. Does government do no wrong when it does not protect people's rights? Moreover, although the mutual forbearance and compromise that go on between family members, neighbors, and business partners may be useful models in certain legal contexts, they are poor models for conceiving the relationship between the rights of individuals and the powers and interests of the government. Thus, we might wonder whether liberalism's commitment to individual freedom could survive the weaker form of rights that Glendon appears to advocate, particularly in the case of vulnerable individuals being asked to moderate their claims against the state.[83]

Second, the communitarian eschewal of rights talk in favor of appeals to social virtues and responsibilities seems to forget the extent to which prior victories in securing civil rights involved challenging the status quo and the ways in which the language of social virtues and the common good (as well as the costs of social change) are typically deployed to reject such challenges. Finally, if a communitarian model of rights would shift responsibility for enforcing rights from courts to legislatures, that move might suggest a less central role for rights and more attention to the costs of rights to the community.

In conclusion, it is not clear how communitarians would factor social costs, virtues, and responsibilities into defining, justifying, and enforcing rights. Is the message of the irresponsibility critique that rights are privileges, to be protected only as long as they are exercised responsibly?[84] A similar concern attends conditioning enforcement of rights on a determination of community approval or interests. One of liberalism's core values is individual liberty, including "the right to be different, the right to pursue ideals one's neighbor thinks wrong. . . ."[85] If responsive communities hold people accountable to some collective notion of responsibility, is there any longer such a right? If recognition of a right is conditioned on whether it imposes costs on others, it may no longer be a right in any meaningful sense.

Which Costs Count?   Let us assume, with the communitarians, that the social costs of rights should factor into the recognition and enforcement of rights in a manner different than they do in liberal accounts. Still, such a communitarian project must determine how to measure social costs relative to the value of rights, as well as when to use legal (versus moral or social) measures for linking rights and responsibility. How would communitarians weigh the costs of protecting rights against the costs of not doing so? What is the cost to individuals of coercion? What is the cost of the risk of governmental error in weeding out costly exercises of rights? An inquiry into which costs count and how much they count will likely yield considerable conscientious disagreement.

One clear example of a near-absolute right that the communitarians defend strongly, and even use to illustrate how rights may license irresponsible and socially harmful conduct, is the First Amendment.[86] (Contrast *Whitney v. California*, where the Supreme Court stated that freedom of speech does not confer a right to speak "without responsibility," for such a right would be an "unbridled license" or "abuse" of freedom.[87]) Communitarians balance the values of the First Amendment and the risks of censorship against the harms of hateful, racist speech quite differently than do critical race theorists and others who argue that the costs of such speech warrant regulating it to pursue equal citizenship for minorities.[88] Communitarians acknowledge that such speech is hurtful but insist on nonlegal remedies, such as raising the moral voice of community against it. Similarly, despite the harms of pornography, it is doubtful whether most communitarians would support civil rights measures advocated by some (though certainly not all) feminists who argue that pornography is not "only words" and contributes centrally to the inequality of women and to violence against them.[89] The very comparative law enterprise that Glendon favors, however, lends support to limits on rights of racist and pornographic expression in view of individual and social harms inflicted by such expression.[90] It is not clear why such a stance is not more communitarian than a strong defense of the First Amendment.[91]

Our point here is that, even though current Supreme Court jurisprudence rejects an "ad hoc balancing of relative social costs and benefits" in particular cases, on the theory that the First Amendment itself "reflects a judgment by the American people that the benefits of its restrictions on the Government outweigh the costs,"[92] one might expect communitarians to urge such balancing. To take a current example of "words that wound,"[93] consider the gulf between the majority and dissent in *Snyder v. Phelps,* in which the Court held that the First Amendment shielded the Westboro Baptist Church from tort liability for intentional infliction of emotional distress on the father of a deceased soldier (Matthew Snyder).

The distress stemmed from Westboro's picketing near the son's funeral with signs like "Thank God for Dead Soldiers," "God Hates Fags," "You're Going to Hell," and "Priests Rape Boys" (reflecting Westboro's "view that the United States is overly tolerant of sin and that God kills American soldiers as punishment").[94] Neither Westboro nor the majority disputed that the deceased soldier's father "suffered 'wounds that are truly severe and incapable of healing themselves.'"[95] Even though the expression of Westboro's views was "particularly hurtful" to Matthew's father, adding to his "already incalculable grief," the majority held that "in public debate [we] must tolerate insulting, and even outrageous, speech in order to provide adequate 'breathing space' to the freedoms protected by the First Amendment." That, Chief Justice Roberts loftily intoned, is the course the United States has chosen "as a Nation," rather than punishing speech that inflicts "great pain."[96]

Justice Alito, the sole dissenter, viewed the costs of rights differently. He concluded (we believe correctly, as does retired Justice Stevens[97]) that the First Amendment does not require that Matthew's father bear such costs: "Our profound national commitment to free and open debate is not a license for the vicious verbal assault that occurred in this case."[98] Matthew was "not a public figure," and all his father wanted was "surely the right of any parent who experiences such an incalculable loss: to bury his son in peace." The First Amendment's commitment to "public debate" would not be undermined by "allowing family members to have a few hours of peace without harassment."[99] Thus, while the majority in *Snyder* concluded that free expression rights "trump," we would think that communitarians (and certainly Glendon) would favor an approach, more akin to that of European jurists, that *would* balance "relative social costs and benefits" and look at the impact of such speech both on Matthew's father and on the community as a whole.[100]

One could foresee similar disagreements over which costs count, and how much, with respect to a wide array of individual rights. Such disagreements raise questions of the relative costs of protecting responsibility as autonomy and promoting responsibility as accountability. To evaluate such costs, we need to consider the justifications for rights. Those justifications implicate the wrongness critique.

The Wrongness Critique

The wrongness strand of the irresponsibility critique of rights involves a feature of legal rights captured by the communitarian slogan, the "gap between rights and rightness": one may have a "right" to do "wrong" acts. As the "Responsive Communitarian Platform" explains, "To say that 'I have a right to do X' is not to conclude that 'X is the right thing for me to do.' . . . [Rights] do not in themselves give a person a sufficient reason to perform [protected] acts."[101] In explaining this gap, Galston states, "Between rights and rightness lies a vast terrain where moral argumentation and (in some cases) forms of public persuasion have a legitimate role."[102] Because the language of rights is morally incomplete, people fail to appreciate the distinction between, and tend to equate, rights and rightness. Moreover, Etzioni asserts, "Many Radical Individualists confuse the right to be free from government intrusion with a nonexistent 'right' to be exempt from the moral scrutiny of one's peers and community."[103]

Positing such a gap, the wrongness critique challenges defenders of legal rights to justify them. We challenge communitarian arguments that rights send the message that rights equal rightness, drawing not only on liberal defenses of rights but also on contemporary debates concerning a number of constitutional rights. Liberal justifications of rights argue that rights protect and call for the exercise of responsibility, although one must differentiate responsibility as accountability from responsibility as autonomy. Liberal responsibility talk emphasizes that rights protect autonomy: they locate in individuals the responsibility to make important decisions in accordance with, or accountable to, conscience. Communitarian responsibility talk, by contrast, stresses that rights require accountability: individuals exercising rights should not be guided primarily by untutored conscience but by the responsibilities, duties, and moral claims laid on them by the moral voice of the community. The deployment of responsibility talk in Dworkin's work offers an opportunity to assess a liberal vocabulary of rights that addresses the issue of responsibility in the senses of both autonomy and accountability. Pressing questions include how that liberal account of rights and responsibilities compares with the proposed communitarian correctives and what role government may properly play in encouraging responsibility.

The Morally Incomplete Language of Rights   The observation of a distinction between rights and rightness is neither a new nor a controversial assertion about the relationship between legal rights and what is morally right. As Dworkin observed in *Taking Rights Seriously*, "[t]here is a clear difference between saying that someone has a right to do something and saying that it is the 'right' thing for him to do, or that he does no 'wrong' in doing it."[104]

What is the significance of this difference? To charge that the language of legal rights is morally incomplete implies that legal rights fail us as a guide to what we ought to do because they do not talk about moral rightness or moral responsibility. Indeed, according to Glendon, this failure matters immensely as legal language migrates beyond its proper sphere and people come to regard law as the primary "carrier" of values.[105] Contemporary liberal rights theorists, however, do not claim that the purpose of declaring individual rights is to signal the requirements for "a fully human and morally satisfactory life" or that the menu of one's legally permissible choices is a full account of one's moral duties and responsibilities.[106]

There may be constraints on rights that are legal, moral, or social and that take the form of responsibilities owed to self, other persons, community, or humanity. Independent of the community's raising its moral voice or laying moral claims, people might consider themselves under moral duties, for example, to engage in benevolence. The communitarians do not typically emphasize such internal convictions of responsibility because they view it as "unrealistic to rely on individuals' inner voices" and to expect them to do the right thing without the moral voice of the community.[107] This suspicion of conscience alone stems in part from communitarianism's diagnosis of a problematic "radical" or "libertarian" American "individualism" that views individuals as self-sufficient, "free-standing agents," rights-bearers with "no inherent duties or obligations unless they choose to embrace them."[108] By contrast, the "Platform" asserts: "While the ultimate foundation of morality may be commitments of individual conscience, it is communities that help introduce and sustain these commitments"; communities should "articulate the responsibilities they expect their members to discharge."[109] Conscience alone may leave us rudderless; "the social pressures community brings to bear are a mainstay of our moral values."[110]

Yet communitarians charge that rights talk so exalts individual autonomy that right-holders view themselves as exempt both from responsibilities and from moral scrutiny or disapproval. Worse still, people shrink from expressing such disapproval or making moral claims on others. We now turn to those charges.

The new communitarians contend that people generally hesitate to use moral suasion because they think that legal rights insulate people from the moral scrutiny of their neighbors and peers.[111] "Liberal virtues" of tolerance, they argue, make people hesitant to judge the choices (and characters) of others.[112] People may refrain out of an attitude of "live and let live," that the choices of others are not our business. Such an attitude might reflect the atomism of contemporary life, the threadbare social fabric that the communitarians lament. Alternatively, not making moral claims on one's neighbor might reflect respect for human moral agency.[113] Do such attitudes stem from an inference of a right to insulation from moral voices and indifference toward the choices of others? Do liberal justifications of rights foster such indifference?

Leading liberal defenses of rights, such as those of Mill and Dworkin, do not advocate indifference by members of society concerning each other's choices and exercise of rights. Mill urged that the harm principle does not entail that people have no interest in each other's actions and well-being.[114] In the realm in which society may not act coercively, he recognized a wide range of acceptable means by which society could attempt to influence individuals in their exercises of liberty and signal disapproval. At the same time, Mill recognized that social disapproval could amount to compulsion or tyranny and praised variation, change, and diversity in lifestyle.

Dworkin envisions liberal citizens who care passionately about what they think is good and argue with and persuade each other concerning the good life. For example, in defending the right to procreative autonomy, he urges that he not be interpreted to counsel indifference toward the decisions of friends, neighbors, and other citizens, because people's choices do have an impact on the moral environment. Citizens must respect others' liberty of conscience, however, and are denied "one weapon": the use of majoritarian power to prohibit individuals from, or punish them for, acting on their view of what life is best for them.[115] Dworkin uses responsibility talk to fortify this argument for restraint: if we accept basic principles of dignity, we must respect the special responsibility of every person to make decisions about ethical values for themselves.[116]

The communitarian concern about indifference appears to stem from worry about liberal "neutrality," or the idea that government should refrain from making substantive moral judgments about the worth of citizens' ways of life.[117] The evident leap from a requirement of governmental neutrality to an inference of citizen neutrality (and indifference) is unwarranted. Communitarians themselves claim to reject the use of public coercion to make citizens embrace a communal vision of the good life.[118] As we discuss in Chapter 3, an important question that the irresponsibility critique raises is what government may do within the realm between coercion and noninterference.

Communitarians contend that the gap between rights and rightness cannot be closed without a richer moral vocabulary invoking principles such as decency, responsibility, and the common good. Notwithstanding recurring images in the irresponsibility critique—picturing rights as knives, guns, porcupine quills, or the like[119]—recognizing and protecting legal rights does not preclude citizens from having views about the right, or responsible, thing to do or communicating those views.[120] Indeed, the launching of various "responsibility" projects and campaigns by civil society and governmental actors[121] challenges Glendon's charge that the "migration" of American rights talk leaves no room for or weakens talk of responsibility and values. There is considerable evidence available in contemporary society that people recognize the distinction between rights and rightness and engage in the sort of moral suasion that the communitarians urge. There is nothing wrong with this behavior in principle, nor anything about it that is necessarily inconsistent with liberalism.[122]

Vigorous debates over a number of constitutional rights, prominently freedom of expression, the right to bear arms, and rights of procreative autonomy, illustrate that citizens often perceive a gap between having a right and doing the right thing and raise their voices to close that gap. Thus, commentary on *Snyder,* the funeral protest case, observed that even though Mr. Snyder lost in court, because "[t]he law says free speech trumps all," he won in the "court of public opinion," because "more people are exercising their free speech to counter [Westboro's] hate" by engaging in "counter-protests."[123] In all these areas, charges of irresponsible use of rights abound, as do campaigns to urge people to behave responsibly and do the right thing. Such campaigns often state the point exactly as the "Platform" does: right-holders confuse a right to do something with doing what is right.[124] They grant that the right-holder has a right to do X, but urge that the right-holder has a responsibility not to do X.[125]

People engaging in such efforts may invoke the social and moral responsibility of a community to create a climate in which exercising rights in certain ways that are harmful to others becomes unthinkable. For example, after the Oklahoma City bombing, President Clinton urged right-wing hate-mongers opposing the federal government to exercise their rights to free expression responsibly.[126] Similarly, after the shooting of Representative Gabrielle Giffords and others at a political rally in Tucson, amidst the decrying of the escalating vitriol in political speech in the United States, President Obama called for "more civility in our public discourse."[127] Former presidents George H. W. Bush and Clinton were named honorary chairmen of a new National Institute for Civil Discourse, which is to address such questions as "How do we nurture robustness on one hand and not in any way chill speech, and keep it in bounds that are not destructive to democracy?"[128] Moreover, right-holders themselves refer to taking responsibility and avoiding social irresponsibility to explain why they have voluntarily refrained—perhaps after the suasion of others—from arguably protected conduct.[129] Tellingly, many conservative proponents of taking responsibility seriously in the area of abortion do not call for responsibility with respect to freedom of speech. Instead, they decry these calls for responsibility as impositions of "politically correct speech," "thought control," and the like.

Of course, when people say that a person ought not to do something, they sometimes mean not simply that it is the wrong thing to do but also that there is not, or should not be, a legal right to do it.[130] (Outside the context of constitutional rights, for example, campaigns against harmful but not-yet-unlawful conduct, such as texting or speaking on cellphones while driving—"distracted driving"—often culminate in laws against such practices.[131]) People may conclude that there is too great a gap between rights and rightness to rely on suasion alone to secure accountability. Most state constitutions, for example, explicitly link free speech rights to responsibility, declaring (in these or similar words): "Every citizen may freely speak, write and publish his sentiments on all subjects, being responsible for the abuse of that right."[132] Thus, discontent with the irresponsibility that certain constitutional rights are said to permit sometimes leads to calls for restricting or regulating those rights, as is evident in the areas of gun control and television violence. With gun control, the issue is sometimes framed in terms of competing rights: pitted against the Second Amendment right to bear arms are people's rights to safety and security, said to be threatened by the proliferation of guns and gun-related violence. At the same time, attempts to regulate the sale of firearms draw charges that regulations would punish citizens who use their rights responsibly and would threaten their safety.

Consider also a pregnant woman's right to decide whether to terminate a pregnancy. Opponents of a legal right to choose abortion not only seek to abolish such a right but also engage in speech or actions designed to persuade individual women not to choose abortion, and physicians not to perform it. The Supreme Court's many rulings about protests by abortion opponents at health care facilities speak of balancing, on one side of the scale, the "right to persuade" exercised by protestors who believe abortion is morally wrong, and, on the other, the right of women seeking medical counseling and treatment to be "let alone" and to avoid "unwanted communication."[133] A recent billboard campaign aimed at persuading African-American women that abortion is a form of racial genocide is another controversial example. Exhortations by political leaders who support reproductive rights that abortion should be "safe, legal, and rare," and calls by both proponents and opponents of abortion rights to pursue common ground on the goal of reducing unwanted pregnancy, are additional examples of efforts to encourage personal and public responsibility.[134] Some acts go beyond suasion and literally prevent women from exercising their rights in the name of serving higher law. The steady attempts by abortion protestors to use various forms of pressure to stop pregnant women from getting abortions and to cut off the availability of legal abortion makes it difficult to accept any claim that abortion rights insulate people from the moral claims or scrutiny of others. Such acts, particularly those directed against physicians, appeal to public shaming by "exposing" physicians within their communities, places of worship, and children's schools as "murderers" and "abortionists." Controversy often ensues, in the aftermath of the killing of doctors who perform abortions, over whether speech condemning such doctors was "irresponsible."[135] Although these illustrations are hardly exhaustive, they suggest that responsibility talk and the use of social suasion concerning the exercise of rights are widespread.

The Messages that Rights Send   The silence of rights talk about responsibility is said to send the message that the existence of a legal right implies the nonexistence of a responsibility or even societal approval of the conduct that the right protects. Justice Scalia states: "There is a perhaps inevitable but nonetheless distressing tendency to equate the existence of a right with the *non*existence of a responsibility," that is, to assume that, if one has a legal right to do something, it is "*proper* and perhaps even *good*" to do it.[136] With respect to abortion, he describes as a "natural," although not "accurate[,] line of thought" the idea that, "[i]f the Constitution *guarantees* abortion, how can it be bad?"[137]

This inference is neither "natural" nor "inevitable." We question the premise that the message is a simple equation of rights with rightness ("how can it be bad?"). Any assumption, like Scalia's, that rights signal rightness stems from an authoritarian view of law: what the law prescribes is right, what it permits is good, and what it forbids is bad. But if a citizen does not believe that law is coterminous with morality, she might conscientiously believe that the acts a law prohibits are morally justified and should be protected by a legal right, or, conversely, that the acts the law permits are unjustified and should be prohibited.[138]

Thus, the existence of a legal right might be read in a number of ways. To take Scalia's example, abortion, a shift from criminalizing it to recognizing a constitutional right to choose it might reflect a changing consensus about what is moral.[139] Of course, there are vexing causal questions about whether changes in law *cause* changes in mores or *reflect* such changes, or some combination of the two. Or, recognizing a right might simply reflect acknowledgment that society will not disintegrate if the protected conduct is not criminally punished or that the social costs of criminal prohibition outweigh the costs of freedom.[140]

Our view is that the existence of a constitutional right signals that this decision and a range of possible choices are protected out of respect for human dignity and autonomy. Allocating decision making responsibility to the individual suggests a societal judgment that it is legally permissible to make such choices and not prudent or appropriate to use law to prohibit them. That there is a range of legally permissible choices, however, does not signal that all choices are equally responsible or equally moral, or even morally permissible. The wrongness critique invites the question whether communitarians hold that certain choices protected by rights are never morally appropriate and always irresponsible.

Is There a Right to Make "Incorrect" or "Irresponsible" Choices? The wrongness critique also raises the issue whether there is a right to make "incorrect" or "irresponsible" choices. Leading liberal justifications of rights derive basic liberties from a conception of persons as having certain moral powers or capacities, for example, the capacity for a conception of justice and the capacity for a conception of the good life.[141] To promote the development and exercise of such capacities, a constitutional liberal regime (we argue in Chapters 4 and 5) properly carries out a formative project, in which both the institutions of civil society and government share responsibility. However, this does not guarantee full development of such capacities or their wisest use.

The wrongness critique implicitly charges that persons are failing to exercise their moral capacities in a responsible way and to appreciate the moral dimensions of rights. A critical question is whether a communitarian corrective would insist on not only social accountability but also legal accountability. In either case, the critique manifests a lack of trust in people as moral agents exercising autonomy and freedom of conscience, capable of acting on their own conceptions of the good life. The communitarians evidently fear that individual conscience is too weak without the reinforcement of the moral voices of others. In that sense, they resemble those critics who charge that people are not good enough for liberalism and fault it for its apparent "fatally flawed assumption . . . that autonomous individuals can freely choose, or will, their moral life."[142]

A common liberal formulation is that rights protect individuals who act in ways thought wrong by society or by others but that reflect their own views of the good. Dworkin uses such a formulation.[143] Similarly, libertarian Roger Pilon argues, "The mere 'irresponsible' exercise of rights, short of violating the rights of others, is itself a right. What else could it mean to be responsible for oneself?" A right to exercise rights irresponsibly, he argues, stems from the acceptance of the notion of individual responsibility to pursue happiness as one sees fit, consistent with the rights of others.[144] Likewise, Stephen Holmes argues that one of liberalism's "core norms or values" is "individual liberty," understood as "a broad sphere of freedom from collective or governmental supervision, including freedom of conscience, the right to be different, the right to pursue ideals one's neighbor thinks wrong, . . . and so forth."[145] In support of that kind of right to be different, Mill argued that individuals have their own well-being most at heart and know best, or better than the majority, what is right for them.[146]

Such liberal themes resonate in our constitutional jurisprudence, which, in justifying rights to liberty and autonomy, observes that there are competing conceptions of the good life (particularly as to matters about which "[m]en and women of good conscience" disagree).[147] That diversity may extend to interpretations of the right and responsible thing to do. Communitarians, liberals, and others may disagree over substantive moral questions such as whether abortion, single parenthood, homosexual sexual conduct, and same-sex marriage are immoral. Liberals who embrace responsibility as autonomy respond that it is the individual's right and responsibility to decide these questions.

Linking protection of rights to the diversity of human moral choices need not stem from moral relativism or skepticism, or denial that there are better and worse, or moral and immoral, choices. It instead appeals to what Rawls calls the "fact of reasonable pluralism"[148]: that it is an inevitable fact (not to be regretted) that, in a society that protects basic liberties such as liberty of conscience and freedom of association, people exercising their moral powers will form and act on divergent conceptions of the good. Moreover, this approach assumes that a stable political order does not require a unitary conception of the good life, a unity that would be possible, if at all, only through the exercise of oppressive state power. (Some communitarians, notably Galston, embrace "value pluralism" (following Isaiah Berlin) and argue for a robust principle of toleration as a restraint on coercive state power.[149]) In Dworkin's account, a liberal society rejects the use of coercive power to compel an individual's adherence to the life others think best for him or her (even if they may be correct) out of the requirements of equal concern and respect and the view that a life lived "against the grain" of one's own conviction is not a good one and has not been improved.[150]

Such defenses of individual freedom, echoed in our constitutional jurisprudence, treat the risk that some people may make incorrect or irresponsible, though legally protected, decisions as a lesser evil than the outright denial to everyone of the right to make decisions profoundly affecting their individual destiny. Allowing people freedom to make decisions with serious consequences for themselves, and to make mistakes in doing so, respects their dignity and autonomy. Developing and exercising personal and moral responsibility require freedom to make judgments. Dworkin argues that the fact that, despite accepting the responsibilities of judgment and of living life well, we may make mistakes is "at the very foundation of our ethical lives."[151] Thus, a legal right securing the opportunity to exercise moral responsibility may protect mistaken, bad, or irresponsible choices.[152] Such a possibility is an implication of securing rights and a cost of preserving freedom.

Rights and Responsibilities in Liberal Justifications of Constitutional Rights   In contrast to the communitarians' wrongness critique, we would argue that the existence of a legal right, far from obscuring the issue of responsibility, calls for the exercise of moral responsibility. Liberal justifications of constitutional rights seek to protect responsibility as autonomy by locating responsibility for making certain important decisions in the right-holder, rather than in the state or other persons. Moreover, in exercising rights, a person may reflect on his or her responsibility to him- or herself and to others, and on the responsible decision to make in those circumstances.

In explaining the tenet that rights do not equate with rightness, Etzioni (invoking Justice Scalia) says that rights protect the freedom to be irresponsible and even socially harmful because "the alternative would sweep away too much good . . . along with the bad."[153] That argument appeals to the risk of governmental error and indiscriminate use of governmental power. But prominent liberal justifications for constitutional rights more directly implicate the individual responsibility of the right-holder. Constitutional rights protect people against governmental coercion within certain zones of thought and conduct out of respect for human personhood, dignity, or autonomy. Such conceptions locate moral responsibility in the right-holder. All these ideas suggest a defense of rights that is rooted in respect for human moral capacity and agency.[154] And all reflect a conception of responsibility as autonomy. Appeals to personhood, dignity, and autonomy are prominent in Supreme Court justifications of constitutional rights to liberty. In Chapter 3, we consider how those justifications and Dworkin's liberal approach attempt to meld responsibility as autonomy with responsibility as accountability in the context of abortion, comparing those efforts with Glendon's communitarian approach.

Conclusion

On close examination, the irresponsibility critique does not establish a strong case against rights as conceived within our constitutional liberalism. The critique reflects ambivalence about core features of rights, immunity and wrongness. There is a corresponding ambivalence about when communitarian correctives to link rights and responsibilities would embody the moral voice of the community through legal coercion and when they would engage solely in moral suasion. We have argued that although the language of legal rights does not offer a full account of moral responsibility, the protection of rights reflects respect for the exercise of individual responsibility as autonomy. That the protection of rights yields some irresponsible conduct is undeniable, yet it is better to bear that cost than to incur the sacrifices of freedom that a communitarian model based primarily on responsibility as accountability would require. In Chapter 3, we examine further the irresponsibility critique, and the tension between responsibility as autonomy and as accountability, in the context of a woman's constitutional right to decide whether to terminate her pregnancy.

CHAPTER THREE

Taking Responsibilities
as well as Rights Seriously

No constitutional right draws the irresponsibility critique more frequently than that of a woman to decide whether to terminate her pregnancy. Critics challenge the *immunity* it provides: a pregnant woman, on this view, should not be insulated from public persuasion against abortion, whether through informed consent laws requiring mandatory ultrasound, counseling at a "pregnancy help center," or statements by her physician about her right to a relationship with her "unborn child." Abortion also illustrates the *wrongness* prong of the irresponsibility critique: the right to choose abortion is a right to do wrong, permitting women to commit an immoral, irresponsible act. Moreover, it "licenses" irresponsibility by others, such as women's male partners and a society indifferent to human life. The right is also the wrong right: society instead should protect the fetus's right to life and the "pregnant mother's" right to a relationship with her "unborn child." To close the gap between rights and rightness, opponents of abortion rights support—and the federal government and many state legislatures have enacted—a wide array of restrictions on the right to choose abortion.

Opponents of legal abortion are not the only critics of rights—and of the right of privacy in particular—for neglecting responsibility. Progressive and feminist theorists who support legal abortion, such as Robin West, argue that constitutional rights have social, moral, and political costs. As against Ronald Dworkin's call for "taking rights seriously,"[1] she calls for "taking responsibilities seriously" by grounding rights such as procreative autonomy in the capacity of women to decide responsibly.

A rights approach, by "insulating" the abortion decision from public scrutiny, "obfuscates the moral quality of most abortion decisions." Under a rights *and* responsibility analysis, support for reproductive freedom would "rest on the demonstrated capacity of pregnant women to decide whether to carry a fetus to term or to abort responsibly." West claims that "the decision to abort is almost invariably made within a web of interlocking, competing, and often irreconcilable responsibilities and commitments."[2] Furthermore, advancing what we call the *negative liberties* critique of rights, she argues that framing the right to choose abortion as a negative right to be free from governmental interference legitimates the government's irresponsibility in failing to provide to women the preconditions for reproductive justice, or positive rights. Such positive rights stem from the public responsibility to meet pregnant women's needs and to address, more broadly, the social and economic conditions leading to unwanted pregnancy and the absence of social supports for parenthood. (Here, progressives and communitarians sound similar themes about how privacy rights insulate women from the help they need.) West also calls for "de-constitutionalizing" abortion and turning from courts to "ordinary politics" to pursue reproductive justice.[3]

In this chapter, we use the contrast between *responsibility as autonomy* and *responsibility as accountability* to assess the irresponsibility critique. Responsibility as autonomy connotes self-governance, that is, entrusting the right-holder to exercise moral responsibility in making decisions guided by conscience and deliberation. Responsibility as accountability, by contrast, connotes being answerable to others for the manner and consequences of exercising one's rights. The irresponsibility critique highlights the tension between pursuing these forms of responsibility. We illustrate that tension by contrasting the critique of abortion rights articulated by communitarian Mary Ann Glendon with the defense of such rights elaborated by liberal Ronald Dworkin. Using these two approaches as foils, we argue (as previewed in Chapter 2) that communitarians like Glendon and liberals like Dworkin emphasize these two different meanings of responsibility. In a surprising move, given his reputation as a champion of rights and the *bête noire* of champions of responsibility, Dworkin himself has turned to responsibility to justify rights and countenances government encouraging responsibility in the exercise of rights. This move parallels the melding of responsibility as autonomy and as accountability in *Planned Parenthood v. Casey. Casey* reaffirmed the right of a woman to decide whether to terminate a pregnancy, yet contemplated that government may undertake a formative project of encouraging, but not coercing, responsibility in making the "ultimate decision."[4]

On Glendon's view, abortion is both a right to do wrong—and it insulates a pregnant woman from public and community persuasion against abortion—and the wrong right—because it fails to protect fetal life. We reject her critique because it advances responsibility as accountability at the expense of responsibility as autonomy: it would permit the government to compel what it holds to be the responsible decision by prohibiting abortion. Instead, we concur with Dworkin that the state may *encourage* responsibility in making decisions such as whether to terminate a pregnancy but may not *coerce* what it thinks is the responsible decision. People live up to the freedom that the right to procreative autonomy protects by exercising their ethical responsibility of reflection in deciding matters of serious moral concern. Dworkin's approach offers a better starting point for thinking about rights and responsibility than does Glendon's.

Governmental persuasion with respect to women's exercise of reproductive rights poses particular problems because debates over such rights involve views about the nature and status of women and motherhood. To a greater degree than Dworkin, and with West, we emphasize the sex equality dimension of these issues. A central premise in *Casey* was that women's ability to participate equally in the life of the nation had been facilitated by the ability to control their reproductive lives.[5] Opponents of legal abortion challenge this premise. They assert that abortion harms women, who naturally want to continue, not terminate, their relationship with their unborn child. In the words of the "Report of the South Dakota Task Force to Study Abortion," for a woman to terminate a pregnancy without suffering "significant psychological trauma and distress" is "beyond the normal, natural, and healthy capability of a woman whose natural instincts are to protect and nurture her child."[6] We assess this *incapability* version of the irresponsibility critique of abortion rights. This critique's premise is that any woman who terminates a pregnancy cannot be *responsible* for her decision in the sense of acting knowingly and freely: she must have done so either because she lacked proper information about what an abortion is or what help is available or because she was pressured or coerced by others. Inevitably, she will suffer regret. Increasingly, this argument features as a rationale for informed consent laws aimed at persuading women against abortion and for laws prohibiting certain abortion procedures (such as the so-called partial birth abortion method). The seeds of this argument were sown in *Casey*'s portrait of abortion as posing psychological peril for women, but *Gonzales v. Carhart* (upholding the "Partial Birth Abortion Ban Act")[7] and a flurry of state restrictions take this argument further in new and disturbing directions.

We criticize this incapability argument, using the distinction between responsibility as autonomy and as accountability. In contrast with West's cogent argument for grounding the right of procreative autonomy in women's capacity to decide responsibly, the incapability argument reflects a lack of trust in, or respect for, such capacity. It also perpetuates problematic stereotypes about women's incompetence and proper roles. When these stereotypes shape laws—aiming to compel women to act as they "naturally" should—they threaten women's reproductive health and their equality and liberty.

We counter with measures that our constitutional liberalism would support to foster women's informed and responsible decision making as well as to show respect for the sanctity of life. We concur with progressive and feminist arguments that the right to terminate a pregnancy hardly exhausts what women need to have reproductive autonomy. We take up West's *negative liberties* critique of rights, agreeing with her call to situate abortion in the broader context of reproductive justice and equal citizenship. But we question her contention that vindicating rights in the courts hinders the pursuit of this broader agenda in legislatures. We explain that our constitutional liberalism lends no support to public irresponsibility but conceives the Constitution as a charter of positive benefits imposing affirmative obligations upon government to secure the preconditions for reproductive justice. It aspires to secure ordered liberty, not liberty without responsibilities.

Responsibility as Accountability versus Responsibility as Autonomy

Planned Parenthood v. Casey in Light of the Irresponsibility Critique

Planned Parenthood v. Casey reaffirmed *Roe v. Wade*'s central holding that, prior to viability, a pregnant woman has the constitutional right to decide whether to continue or terminate her pregnancy. *Casey* stressed the "unique" nature both of pregnancy and the liberty at stake for pregnant women in ways that reflect responsibility as autonomy.[8] Indeed, *Casey* gave a richer account of this liberty than *Roe*, which emphasized the right of the responsible *physician*, in consultation with the pregnant woman, to decide whether abortion was the proper medical resolution of her pregnancy.[9] However, *Casey* departed from *Roe* in giving more latitude to states to promote responsibility as accountability. Because of government's "profound" interest in promoting respect for fetal life, it may, throughout the woman's pregnancy, impose requirements to further this interest, such as waiting periods and informed consent laws, so long as they do not impose an "undue burden" on her right to make the "ultimate decision." *Casey* also justified such regulations as fostering women's health and well-being.[10] Thus, *Casey* sounds in both responsibility as autonomy and as accountability.

According to *Casey*, protecting a realm of individual decision making is compatible with governmental persuasion in favor of one choice (childbirth) rather than another (abortion). This raises the questions of how inviolate the sphere of liberty "promised" by the Constitution is and for what purposes government may seek to steer citizens' exercise of that liberty. The *Casey* joint opinion affirms: "It is a promise of the Constitution that there is a realm of personal liberty which the government may not enter." It speaks of the "right to define one's own concept of existence, of meaning, of the universe, and of the mystery of human life" and states that "[b]eliefs about these matters could not define the attributes of personhood were they formed under compulsion of the State."[11] This anticompulsion rationale in constitutional law resonates with John Locke's famous plea for toleration on the ground that compulsion corrupts belief or choice.[12] *Casey* further states: "The destiny of the [pregnant] woman must be shaped to a large extent on her own conception of her spiritual imperatives and her place in society." It refers to the "urgent claims of the woman to retain the ultimate control over her destiny and her body, claims implicit in the meaning of liberty." Moreover, it explains that matters of human reproduction involve profound beliefs concerning questions of responsibility, about which people of good conscience disagree.[13] Thus far, the joint opinion sounds in responsibility as autonomy.

However, *Casey* does not protect privacy or autonomy as an "insulated" sphere of decision making but presupposes shared sovereignty between a pregnant woman and the government. Prior to *Casey*, the Court struck down informed consent schemes to the extent that the state sought to "wedge" its "message discouraging abortion into the privacy of the *informed consent* dialogue between the woman and her physician."[14] The Court envisioned an inviolate sphere within which women (in consultation with, and as informed by, their physicians) should be free of governmental moralizing against abortion. In contrast, the joint opinion in *Casey* stated:

What is at stake is the woman's right to make the ultimate decision, not a right to be insulated from all others in doing so. Regulations which do no more than create a structural mechanism by which the State, or the parent or guardian of a minor, may express profound respect for the life of the unborn are permitted, if they are not a substantial obstacle to the woman's exercise of the right to choose. . . . Unless it has that effect on her right of choice, a state measure designed to persuade her to choose childbirth over abortion will be upheld if reasonably related to that goal. Regulations designed to foster the health of a woman seeking an abortion are valid if they do not constitute an undue burden.[15]

The state, thus, may encourage a pregnant woman "to know that there are philosophic and social arguments of great weight" in favor of continuing her pregnancy. So long as she is free to make the "ultimate decision" prior to viability, the government may facilitate "wise exercise" of reproductive liberty through measures designed to persuade her in favor of childbirth.[16] The joint opinion overruled progeny of *Roe* affording greater inviolability to a woman's decision making process.[17]

Casey grounds governmental authority to limit women's liberty in the "unique" nature of abortion and its consequences: abortion is not just an exercise of conscience but involves the termination of potential life and has consequences for persons other than the pregnant woman and the fetus. The Court's invocation of such consequences suggests a paternalistic argument for regulation (e.g., negative consequences for the woman, whose decision may be poorly informed because she lacks information about the impact of abortion on the fetus); a moral climate argument (e.g., consequences for medical personnel who perform abortions and members of society who must live with the knowledge that abortions occur); and a harm argument (e.g., "depending upon one's beliefs," the consequences for the fetus).[18] Mapping these consequences onto the two recognized governmental interests, protecting potential life and maternal health, the joint opinion builds into protecting maternal health a governmental concern for women's psychological well-being and for their making "wise" decisions.

Thus, the *Casey* joint opinion concludes that persuasion in favor of childbirth, under the guise of informed consent, protects potential life and fosters women's well-being. Governmental persuasion allegedly helps women not simply to choose, but to choose well. *Casey* appears to build into the undue burden test a requirement that steering against abortion must inform, rather than hinder, women's "free choice."[19] Yet, in equating governmental steering with fostering women's self-government, *Casey* strikingly differs from the model of self-government found in earlier informed consent jurisprudence. Moreover, *Casey*'s depiction of informed consent suggests an underlying vision of abortion as posing psychological peril for women, leading the Court to uphold persuasion against abortion as protecting women against the "devastating consequences" of an ill-informed decision. (In *Carhart*, the Court's concern over such consequences serves as a rationale for banning a "'gruesome'" abortion method, on the premise that physicians cannot be trusted to ensure informed consent.[20])

Is this kind of governmental moralizing compatible with constitutional liberalism? Is it a permissible and attractive way to link rights and responsibility? We take up these questions by examining Glendon's and Dworkin's arguments regarding reproductive rights and responsibilities.

Glendon: Taking Responsibility (as Accountability) Seriously by Coercing Conformity

Glendon advances the irresponsibility critique of rights in her many analyses of American abortion law. We evaluate three strands of that critique: a comparative law argument, a religious/right to life argument, and a harm to women argument. Her famous early works, *Abortion and Divorce in Western Law,* along with *Rights Talk,* criticized the Court's abortion jurisprudence after *Roe* but before *Casey*.[21] In subsequent work, she reiterates much of this criticism even though *Casey* arguably moved the law in her communitarian direction.[22]

The Comparative Law Argument for "Compromise" Abortion Laws   In *Abortion and Divorce in Western Law,* Glendon offered an "anthropological" approach to abortion law to learn about the constitutive message it sends or the "story" it tells about a society. She contrasted America's "extreme and isolating version of individual liberty" (as endorsed in *Roe*) of a pregnant woman who has no responsibilities to others and to whom nothing is owed by society, with Western European laws striking a balance between women's liberty and their responsibilities as members of society who are carrying unborn life. Glendon suggested that America, as well as women's interests, might be better served by a "compromise" abortion law, such as the French law, which guaranteed "the respect of every human being from the commencement of life" but permitted, and paid for, first trimester abortion if a woman stated that (in her sole judgment) she was in "distress."[23]

The French law contained specific regulations—informed consent measures and a waiting period—to promote respect for life. The physician from whom a pregnant woman requested an abortion must provide her with a "brochure" informing her of the "distress" requirement and containing "information about the public benefits and programs that are guaranteed to mothers and children, and about the possibilities of adoption, as well as provide a list of organizations capable of giving assistance." Second, the pregnant woman must "have a private interview, if possible with her partner, with a government-approved counseling service which, in principle, is not to be located in any facility where abortions are performed." This counseling is not neutral, but "is supposed to furnish the woman with assistance and advice, 'especially with a view toward enabling her to keep her child.'" A third requirement is two waiting periods: at least one week from the time of her initial request for an abortion to the consultation, and then at least two days from the time of the consultation to the abortion (with an emergency exemption). Even though Glendon criticizes the U.S. Supreme Court for striking down states' informed consent laws, she makes a telling observation: those state regulations seem "more threatening or anxiety-provoking, while France's are clearly meant to be helpful to the woman while trying to preserve the life of the fetus."[24] In sharp contrast to the United States, France also provided facilities for abortions and funded 70 percent of nontherapeutic abortions and 100 percent of therapeutic ones.

Glendon asks readers on both the pro-life and pro-choice sides to accept that, even if the access to abortion and numbers of abortions were the same in the respective legal systems, a different abortion law would send a different message about respect for life and the seriousness of the abortion decision.[25] The United States, she contends, stands alone among the 20 countries she surveyed in its indifference to unborn life, as evidenced in its allowance of "abortion on demand" and the absence of generous social benefits that might help pregnant women continue their pregnancies.

Glendon has made the often-cited—and often-challenged—argument that, had the U.S. Supreme Court not stepped in and decided the issue for the entire country in *Roe,* the various states likely would have continued working their way toward forms of "compromise legislation" analogous to the laws adopted in the more communitarian legal systems of Western Europe.[26] The great majority of states, she predicted, would end up with "compromise" laws in the "typical middle range of European countries"—treating early abortions leniently but expressing the view that "all abortion is a serious matter." A very few states would have strict laws, and a few might be more liberal, endorsing "early abortion on demand."[27] In a Congressional hearing about an early version of the

"Partial Birth Abortion Ban Act," Glendon contended: "The restrictions on abortion that most Americans support, but which are prohibited from being enacted by *Roe*, are quite similar to those found in Western Europe."[28] Even if her gauging of public opinion is accurate, there are salient differences between the United States and Western Europe: the lack of public funding for most abortions, in most states and under federal law, and the United States' comparatively "laggard" status when it comes to generous social welfare policies for families and for "care-work."[29]

In sum, in her comparativist mode, Glendon argues for a compromise law that would send the right message—abortion is a serious matter—but that, at least early in pregnancy, would permit abortion. Thus, she criticized pre-*Casey* abortion law as affording pregnant women too much immunity from public and private persuasion (because the Court struck down informed consent laws) and too much room for wrongness (because it permitted few restrictions on when and for what reasons women might terminate their pregnancies). One might have expected Glendon to praise *Casey* for moving U.S. law closer to such a compromise law. After all, it permits legislatures to adopt measures, applicable from the earliest stages of pregnancy, to express "profound" respect for fetal life and to shape women's informed consent, so long as they do not place an "undue burden" on women making the "ultimate decision."[30] Although Glendon supports the type of restrictions *Casey* upheld, she sharply criticizes the joint opinion for its protection of the abortion "license." Favorably contrasting European "dignitarian" conceptions of rights, she describes the joint opinion as adding a "postmodern touch" to the "legal portrait of the lone rights-bearer" by advancing "a vision of the self as invented and reinvented through the exercise of the individual's will, limited by nothing but subjective preference."[31] Glendon's criticism also stems from the religious/right to life objection and the harm to women objection.

The Religious/Right to Life Objection to Abortion Rights   In her own writing and in various "pro-life" statements that she has signed, Glendon has advanced a religious/right to life argument against abortion. Abortion rights offend natural truths about human life and dignity. Abortion is a wrong right and diverts attention from collective choice and responsibility. Shortly after the Supreme Court's decision in *Casey*, Glendon's name appeared on "A New American Compact: Caring about Women, Caring for the Unborn."[32] The Compact called for serious moral reflection by the American people, whose voice must be heard through the "normal procedures of democracy." "America," the Compact announced, "does not need the abortion license," which "has ushered in a new era of irresponsibility toward women and children," but instead needs policies that "responsibly protect and advance the interests of mothers *and* their children, both before *and* after birth." Thus, the goal should be the "enactment of the most protective laws possible on behalf of the unborn," ideally prohibiting abortion but recognizing an exception in the "very rare[ ]" cases in which pregnancy poses "a threat to maternal life or health."

The Compact reframes choice: not choice "faced by isolated women exercising private rights" but choice by citizens collectively to determine "[w]hat kind of a people will we be?" and "[w]hose rights will we acknowledge?" It condemns *Roe* for denying "every human being, for the first nine months of his or her life, . . . the most fundamental human right of all—the right to life." It is time "to reconstitute the story of America as a story of inclusion and protection."[33]

The idea that the liberty affirmed in *Casey* perpetuates a wrong right that undermines responsibility, isolates the right-holder from community, and corrodes virtue features in similar statements joined by Glendon.[34] One asserts that *Casey*'s famous declaration, "At the heart of liberty is the right to define one's own concept of existence," is a "sweeping redefinition of liberty" as "nothing more nor less than what is chosen by the autonomous, unencumbered self." The authors contrast the *ordered* liberty "affirmed by the Founders" with such *disordered, "debased"* liberty, which is "utterly disengaged from the concepts of responsibility and community and is pitted against the 'laws of nature and of nature's God.' "[35]

The Harm to Women Objection to Abortion Rights   A third strand of Glendon's irresponsibility critique is that pregnant women do not need abortion rights; to the contrary, such rights harm women, license irresponsibility by men and the larger society, and undermine virtue. This argument, evident in the Compact, challenges the *Casey* joint opinion's claim that abortion rights have helped secure the status of equal citizenship for women. For example, in "The America We Seek: A Statement of Pro-life Principle and Concern," Glendon and other signatories attack the Court for its extreme protection of "the abortion license," which "has helped to erode the moral foundations of the American civic community" and contributed to America's "virtue-deficit." Far from helping women, they charge, "abortion-on-demand" excuses male irresponsibility and marginalizes men who seek to assume responsibility for a child. The autonomy right "enshrined" by the Court gives no "constitutional standing" to any "community" other than the individual and the state, such as husband and wife, or mother and child. A more "responsible" society—in line with the "highest ideals of the Founders"—should "stand for the inalienable right-to-life of the unborn, . . . with women in crisis, and . . . against the abortion license."[36] Here, the religious/right to life and the harm to women objections meld.

In *Rights Talk*, Glendon argues that the right of privacy's "lone rights-bearer," an isolated individual with the "right to be let alone," scarcely resembles and poorly serves the needs of vulnerable pregnant women. She asks whether a better legal approach would envision a woman as "situated within, and partially constituted by, her relationships with others."[37] Her contrasting European example, West Germany's abortion law circa 1991, balanced women's statutory right to free development of their personalities (subject to the limits of the "moral code" and the rights of others) against fetuses' right to life.[38] As Glendon describes it, that law restricted abortion (after compliance with an informed consent procedure aimed at facilitating continuation of the pregnancy) to instances of a medical determination that a pregnancy would pose a serious danger to a woman's physical or mental health that could not otherwise be averted. While this step signaled the "gravity" of the decision, abortion was "relatively easy to obtain" in the first trimester.[39]

Glendon also favorably contrasts German law's "dignitarian" understanding of rights and persons with *Casey*'s "isolating" vision. Her example is *Casey*'s conclusion that "to require a married woman to notify her husband of her intent to have an abortion . . . would violate a woman's liberty." (The Court noted that most women in healthy relationships would tell their husbands, but that this provision put at risk more vulnerable women in abusive relationships.[40]) Glendon charges: "The Court majority's current notion of freedom is thus quite distant from understandings of freedom [such as that of the German Constitutional Court] that stress the dignity of the person as actualized through relations with others and through the development of one's ability to exercise freedom wisely and well."[41]

Assessing Glendon's Irresponsibility Critique   There is a notable absence, in Glendon's comparison, of any acknowledgment of *Casey*'s use of "dignity" in justifying its conception of constitutional liberty. Extrapolating from her critique of Justice Brennan's idea of dignity in earlier abortion cases, the reason may be that the joint opinion's discussion of dignity emphasizes the dignity of the pregnant woman making the decision but does not include that of prenatal life.[42] Even more striking is her silence about *Casey*'s picture of the pregnant woman—hardly a "lone rights-

bearer" insulated from the community, but instead embedded in relationships, such that her decision would have "consequences" for others.
Indeed, one might read *Casey* as communitarian in suggesting that
women have a responsibility to reflect on their decisions because of consequences for others. Particularly baffling is Glendon's reference to the
Court's inattention to exercising freedom "wisely and well." *Casey*
upheld the informed consent scheme to shape the "wise exercise" of a
woman's liberty so she did not make an uninformed decision only to feel
devastated later when she learned about fetal development.[43] The community may reach women by informing them of alternatives to terminating their pregnancies.

Glendon's communitarian critique of *Casey* simultaneously condemns
its rhetoric about autonomy and approves its upholding of the informed
consent scheme before it. Although Glendon and her colleagues ultimately seek a constitutional amendment reversing *Roe* and *Casey* and
their mistaken vision of freedom rooted in "radical autonomy," they support an incremental strategy of state-by-state regulation of, and restrictions upon, abortion.[44] By contrast, some liberal and feminist critics of
Casey praise the joint opinion's rhetoric but criticize it for upholding
such regulations.

In sum, Glendon contrasts the "abortion license"—a wrong right—
with a genuine constitutional right—the right to life of the unborn. The
alternative vision shifts from women's *rights* that allow male and societal irresponsibility to women's *needs,* fetal rights, and society's mutual
responsibility. The abortion battle implicates views about women's roles
as mothers, and so we note here a striking passage, in one declaration,
about the inevitability of sacrifice: members of society have a "mutual
responsibility" to "make sure that all women know that their own physical and spiritual resources, joined to those of a society that truly affirms
and welcomes life, are sufficient to overcome whatever obstacles pregnancy and child-rearing may appear to present. Women intuitively know,
and we should never deny, that this path will involve sacrifice."[45] Men,
they add, must share the sacrifice.

By contrast, in *Casey,* the joint opinion stated that although the sacrifices that "the mother who carries a child to full term" endures—the
anxieties, physical constraints, and pain—have "ennoble[d]" women in
the eyes of the human race and have given a "bond of love" to the infant,
the state may not "insist" that pregnant women "make the sacrifice."
Rather, "the destiny of the woman must be shaped to a large extent on
her own conception of her spiritual imperatives and her place in society."[46]
The vision of mutual responsibility that Glendon and her colleagues

advance would remove women's right to decide not to endure such sacrifice and instead fortify them to know that they *can*—and *must*—do so. This vision echoes a passage Glendon quotes, in *Abortion and Divorce in Western Law,* from the West German Constitutional Court, explaining that legislation must proceed in principle "from a duty of bringing the pregnancy to term" and that "it should be the most eminent purpose of government efforts on behalf of the protection of life to reawaken and, if necessary, strengthen the maternal protective will [in cases] where it has been lost."[47] As we will discuss, a new generation of arguments against abortion contend that it goes against women's very nature to abort their unborn children and, thus, women could do so only if they were misinformed or coerced.

Ironically, notwithstanding Glendon's earlier disavowal of a competing rights model as impoverished, it is precisely the language of rights (i.e., the fetus's right to life) that she employs to justify rejecting women's right to abortion. For pregnant women, responsibility means accountability, the duties that society may reasonably demand of them. Such responsibility should be secured through the coercive power of law, not through mere suasion or exhortation by the moral voice of the community. Glendon's earlier praise of the French scheme might suggest support for responsibility as autonomy (subject to such suasion); however, her later work indicates that responsibility does not entail the exercise of autonomy by a pregnant woman—instead, the only permissible, responsible outcome of a pregnancy is continuation to term. Indeed, the issue is one for societal, not individual, choice. In sum, responsibility requires accountability to communal judgments about protecting fetal life.

Dworkin: Taking Responsibility (as Autonomy) Seriously by Encouraging Reflection

We now turn to the melding of rights and responsibility in Dworkin's work. Both conservative legal scholars like Glendon and progressive legal scholars like West who have called for "taking responsibilities seriously" have used Dworkin as a liberal foil in arguing that "taking rights seriously" has denigrated concern for responsibilities.[48] We begin with a puzzle. It seems reasonable to expect that Dworkin's stance on a pregnant woman's right to terminate her pregnancy would be similar to the Court's earlier abortion jurisprudence, which defended an inviolate sphere of decision making. Given Glendon's criticism that the right of privacy has become "a super-right, a trump" in our constitutional system, she would likely charge that Dworkin's conception of rights as trumps inevitably supports the "paradigm of the lone rights-bearer," insulated from moral scrutiny or governmental persuasion.[49] Further, given the "illusion of absoluteness" in American rights talk and Dworkin's rejection of the "general interest" as a ground for limiting rights, she would likely charge that his model of taking rights seriously excludes taking responsibilities seriously by governmental promotion of the ethical environment.[50]

It is striking, then, that in *Life's Dominion* Dworkin engages in responsibility talk to justify the right to procreative autonomy. He praises the joint opinion in *Casey*, which allows considerable latitude for governmental persuasion of the right-holder. Why? Dworkin advances a conception of ethical liberalism, in which personal responsibility *as autonomy* and the responsible exercise of rights feature centrally. Dworkin's framework is a helpful starting point for a liberal defense of rights against the irresponsibility critique. Giving more explicit attention than he does to the gender dimension of the abortion issue would enrich this liberal defense while illuminating some of the risks of governmental moralizing concerning abortion. Later, we illustrate by analyzing *Carhart* and the flurry of state regulations restricting abortion based on the regret rationale recognized in that case.

Responsibility versus Conformity . Dworkin interprets the Supreme Court's privacy jurisprudence as protecting a realm of decision making critical to the "sense of moral responsibility" from coercion by majoritarian judgments.[51] In *Life's Dominion,* responsibility talk features prominently, not only the responsibility of the individual to make protected decisions reflectively but also that of government to encourage the responsible exercise of rights. "People," Dworkin argues, "have the moral right—and the moral responsibility—to confront the most fundamental questions about the meaning and value of their own lives for themselves, answering to their own consciences and convictions." The constitutional right that protects that moral right is grounded in the liberty protected by the Fourteenth Amendment and in the freedom of conscience secured by the First Amendment.[52] Dworkin describes autonomy as the responsibility to live up to one's freedom by exercising one's rights reflectively.

To say that citizens must answer fundamental questions of conscience for themselves, however, does not mean that states, pursuant to their "responsibility for guarding the public moral space in which all citizens live," may not "encourage their citizens to treat the question of abortion seriously."[53] Decisions about abortion, Dworkin argues, implicate the intrinsic value of the sanctity of life and have an impact on the ethical environment that we share.[54] *Roe* correctly concluded that a fetus was not a constitutional person with "derivative" rights and interests subject to governmental protection but did not address whether a government might constitutionally seek to protect the "detached" value of sanctity by encouraging women to exercise their right to choose abortion responsibly.[55] *Casey*, he concludes, correctly observed that there is no "right to be insulated from all others" in making a decision and that a state may encourage a woman to learn that there are "philosophic and social arguments" in favor of continuing a pregnancy. However, *Casey* erred in upholding the informed consent restrictions before it, because of the burden that they impose, the unlikelihood that they in fact contribute to reflective decision making, and the possibility of encouraging responsibility in more effective and less intrusive ways, such as by providing financial support for poor pregnant women.[56]

Dworkin distinguishes two goals with respect to decision making about matters of conscience: government *encouraging responsibility* in making the decision versus government *coercing conformity* with the majority's conception of the responsible decision.[57] The two goals, he argues, are incompatible: the former encourages individuals to exercise moral responsibility by deciding for themselves, while the latter dictates a result and thus precludes the exercise of responsibility. The Constitution does not prohibit states from pursuing the goal of responsibility, he contends, as long as they "respect the crucial difference between advancing that goal and wholly or partly coercing a final decision."[58] In subsequent work, Dworkin draws a similar line between coercion and manipulation, which are impermissible, and various permissible—indeed, inevitable—forms of influence. The latter include taking the advice of friends, being affected by "the culture in which we all live," or deferring to the judgments of religious texts or religious (or secular) leaders.[59] Dworkin distinguishes these influences from the subordination that responsibility as autonomy condemns.

Immunity and Wrongness   Dworkin argues for legal immunity in the sense of the right to decide free of coercion. He analogizes the abortion controversy to the religious wars of prior centuries and calls for toleration of an individual's exercise of freedom of conscience.[60] Legal immunity, however, does not insulate women deciding whether to have an abortion from state efforts to encourage responsibility in decision making. Moreover, although citizens must adhere to the principle of toleration (e.g., not use the law to enforce conformity with their own view of the right decision), it is understandable and appropriate that citizens care about how strangers, neighbors, and friends make decisions concerning abortion because of the impact on the ethical environment. Thus, in Dworkin's account, a legal right to procreative autonomy does not carry with it a right to be insulated from state encouragement of responsible reflection or from the interests of others in one's decision. In short, he contemplates immunity from coercion, but not insulation from persuasion. As such, his account is not vulnerable to the immunity prong of the irresponsibility critique.

Nor is Dworkin silent on the question of wrongness. Although he rejects coercing exercises of conscience, he is not agnostic on whether or when abortion is the right or responsible thing to do. He maintains (akin to the liberal stance that, he argues, most people share[61]): "Abortion wastes the intrinsic value—the sanctity, the inviolability—of a human life and is therefore a grave moral wrong unless the intrinsic value of other human lives would be wasted in a decision *against* abortion."[62] On that view, there is a range of circumstances in which abortion can be a morally responsible choice.[63]

Does Dworkin Take Responsibility Seriously Enough for Communitarians?

Even if Dworkin takes responsibility seriously enough to disconcert some liberal autonomy or neutrality theorists—those who reject any governmental moralizing about responsible exercise of rights—he does not go far enough to satisfy conservative proponents of responsibility such as Glendon. Conservatives want more than encouraging deliberation and responsible decision making about abortion; they want to be sure that women make the decision they (or, they might say, the majority) think is the responsible decision: protecting the unborn. That is, in Dworkin's terms, Glendon advocates responsibility as conformity or coercion.

Glendon might counter by charging that Dworkin has co-opted the language of responsibility in service of a liberal theory of autonomy. After all, despite *Casey*'s responsibility talk, Glendon faults its supposed exaltation of the liberty of the self "invented and reinvented" through "exercise of the individual's will."[64] She certainly would argue that Dworkin's talk in *Justice for Hedgehogs* of individual responsibility for one's own life, which he ties to dignity,[65] is nothing more than the right to personal autonomy. Put another way, she might argue that encouraging responsibility as Dworkin conceives it is a sham, just another word for encouraging autonomy—which itself was misguided to begin with and is no more justified when dressed up in the garb of responsibility.

There is a nice irony here: Dworkin is saying that government is not promoting responsibility unless it respects the right of the individual ultimately to decide for herself or himself. This is exactly what Glendon would see as licensing irresponsibility.

Does Persuasion Advance a Formative Project for Responsibility as Autonomy?   Dworkin identifies governmental responsibility to undertake what we call a formative project to facilitate autonomous, reflective decision making. His model of liberalism emphasizes ethical individualism, or the idea that persons have the right and nondelegable responsibility to decide for themselves what it means to accept the challenge of living their lives well.[66] Such a model treats reflective self-government as a good that government should foster. The ideal is not simply autonomy in the minimal sense of government leaving persons alone but in a richer sense of government fostering reflective and deliberative self-government, or the ability to "choose well."[67]

Dworkin's identification of a proper governmental interest in encouraging responsibility is cogent and compatible with our constitutional liberalism's model of responsibility as autonomy. Governmental fostering of reflective decision making through making people aware that important, contested values are at stake is consonant with respect for their moral powers. Dworkin's analysis of *Casey*, however, suggests that he also supports a more robust governmental role than facilitation, a hybrid of the coercive role he rejects and the facilitative one he accepts: the government decides through the political process which interpretation of a contestable value is the right one and then *encourages*—rather than *coerces*—everyone to reach the government's conclusion. Government may not force women to "make the decision that the majority, as represented by the legislature, prefers"; however, "the state may reasonably think . . . that a woman tempted to abortion should be at least aware of arguments against it that others in the community believe important and persuasive."[68]

Dworkin's account suggests that equal respect does not rule out governmental moralizing if it is reasonably likely to encourage reflective, responsible decision making. But it would seem more consistent with protecting "finally individual" conviction concerning the best interpretation of a "contestable" value like sanctity to confine government's role to encouraging persons to see that it is a "contestable" value and to encourage them to make the decision conscientiously. If government takes sides, by exposing pregnant women to arguments against abortion in an essentially religious dispute—given that a plurality of Americans cite religious beliefs as the main influence on their opinion about abortion[69]—does this run afoul of the constitutional proscription against even governmental persuasion concerning religion?[70] Would equal respect not be better satisfied by government encouraging citizens to be aware of a range of perspectives concerning a decision for childbirth as well as for abortion?

We hesitate to embrace the idea that government encourages reflective decision making by persuading against the exercise of a protected choice.[71] Admittedly, it is difficult to sort out whether the principle of facilitating autonomy through persuading in favor of one choice is objectionable as a matter of principle, or due to its application in the abortion context.[72] Taken in the abstract, the proposition that governmental persuasion could help people live self-governing lives by facilitating "wise exercise" of their rights and reflection on their responsibilities is plausible—especially if it comes with a set of requirements reasonably ensuring that it would do so. But we have not yet seen an adequate model of such persuasion in constitutional abortion jurisprudence. To the contrary, the plethora of state restrictions on abortion couched as informed consent laws seem more the product of a conscious strategy of incrementally eroding abortion rights. Moreover, such laws are likely to become even less supportive of genuine deliberation, to the extent they are premised upon the incapability argument—that no "normal, natural, and healthy" woman is capable of terminating her pregnancy "without risk of suffering significant psychological trauma and distress."[73] As Carol Sanger observes with respect to mandatory ultrasound as a component of informed consent, such requirements "operate as one last move in the state's refusal to take 'no' for an answer." Rather than aiming to enhance a woman's "deliberative" agency, "[t]he hope is that the fetal image will overwhelm the decision to abort by triggering something like a primitive maternal instinct."[74]

Obviously, one could argue that women who seek abortions do not need persuasion in favor of abortion; to the extent they have not considered the other side, one-sided persuasion in favor of childbirth may enhance their decision making process.[75] But if the goal is reflective decision making, and if abortion may be a morally justifiable and responsible choice, a more balanced presentation of the parameters of responsible reproductive choice could serve that goal and avoid overt governmental side-taking. And while there is clear public support for "persuasive" informed consent schemes,[76] a balanced counseling scheme might also yield greater respect for women's decisions. Of course, for people who believe abortion is always wrong or who accept the incapability argument, any positive discussion of abortion would likely be objectionable.

Indeed, even a *Casey*-type scheme of persuasion would likely fail to garner respect for women's decisions (much less their legal right to abortion) if one accepts the premise that no woman could voluntarily end her relationship with her unborn child.

From the standpoint of responsibility as autonomy, a more defensible approach to informed consent would be balanced counseling encouraging responsible self-determination—more akin to Dworkin's idea of encouraging citizens to reflect upon the best application of a contested value to their lives—rather than governmental steering toward one choice over another.[77] Admittedly, the task of agreeing upon the relevant public values and their proper application to abortion is challenging, given the persistent moral conflict over abortion and what constitutes responsible reproductive choice.[78] A related challenge would be deciding upon the range of views concerning childbirth and abortion that government should present to encourage reflective decision making. This degree of moral conflict, along with continuing contradictions in public policy concerning responsible reproduction, suggest reasons for caution about embracing governmental persuasion in the service of women's reproductive autonomy.

We have used Glendon and Dworkin as foils to elaborate the irresponsibility critique. Strikingly, both theorists have aimed, in their work, to show how the United States could move toward a peaceful resolution or settlement of the abortion controversy—Glendon by emphasizing responsibility as accountability and Dworkin by promoting responsibility as autonomy. The *Casey* joint opinion expressed the hope that its reaffirming but revising *Roe* and reframing the balance between women's liberty and respect for life might contribute to constitutional settlement. Nonetheless, two decades later, the legal right of abortion remains controversial. We believe that this is due in part to deeply held, divergent views of women's proper roles and responsibilities. These come to the fore in the regret or incapability argument for restricting the right to terminate a pregnancy.

Rights, Responsibilities, and Regret: The Incapability Version of the Irresponsibility Critique

"Abortion does cause regret"
—sign on car outside clinic, Brookline, MA

Respect for human life finds an ultimate expression in the bond of love the mother has for her child. The ["Partial Birth Abortion

Ban Act"] recognizes this reality as well. Whether to have an abortion requires a difficult and painful moral decision. *Casey*. . . . While we find no reliable data to measure the phenomenon, it seems unexceptionable to conclude some women come to regret their choice to abort the infant life they once created and sustained. . . . Severe depression and loss of esteem can follow.

—Justice Kennedy, for the majority in *Gonzales v. Carhart*[79]

[T]he Court invokes an anti-abortion shibboleth for which it concededly has no reliable evidence: Women who have abortions come to regret their choices, and consequently suffer from "[s]evere depression and loss of esteem." Because of women's fragile emotional state and because of the "bond of love the mother has for her child," the Court worries, doctors may withhold information about the nature of the intact D & E procedure. . . . The solution the Court approves, then, is *not* to require doctors to inform women, accurately and adequately, of the different procedures and their attendant risks. . . . Instead, the Court deprives women of the right to make an autonomous choice, even at the expense of their safety.

—Justice Ginsburg, dissenting in *Carhart*[80]

Carhart: The Emergence of the Regret Rationale for Restricting the Right to Abortion

The claim that pregnant women who choose to terminate their pregnancies will come to regret their decision features increasingly as an argument not only to engage in private and public persuasion against abortion but also to restrict or eliminate the right to choose abortion. Here, the *incapability* version of the irresponsibility critique of rights is evident: we cannot trust that women really are exercising full moral capacity, and are responsible for their decisions, if they terminate their pregnancies. Their capacity is hindered by a lack of informed consent because physicians do not provide them enough information about abortion methods. Or their natural inclination to have a child may be overborne by coercion, pressure, or influence from their male partners, family members, or friends. Women who choose abortion, on this view, are irresponsible in the sense that they lack the capability to make the decision.

This incapability argument shows vividly how debates over abortion rights continue to involve views about women and motherhood. In *Gonzales v. Carhart*, the Supreme Court upheld the "Partial Birth Abortion Ban Act" (PBABA), a federal criminal ban on so-called partial birth abortions. This marks the first time the Court has upheld a ban on a particular method of abortion and a law restricting abortion that did not make an exception to preserve a woman's health. Justice Kennedy's majority opinion asserts that the mother-child bond is the "ultimate expression" of "respect for human life." He interprets the PBABA as recognizing this bond and, out of concern for women's impaired moral capacity and likely regret if they choose abortion, barring one method of terminating a pregnancy to spare women such regret. The premise for this ban is that, because the abortion decision is "so fraught with emotional consequence," some doctors may not tell pregnant women all the details of the procedure and if the pregnant women later learn of this method, it will worsen their regret:

> The State has an interest in ensuring so grave a choice is well informed. It is self-evident that a mother who comes to regret her choice to abort must struggle with grief more anguished and sorrow more profound when she learns, only after the event, what she once did not know: that she allowed a doctor to pierce the skull and vacuum the fast-developing brain of her unborn child, a child assuming the human form.[81]

A pregnant woman seeking to terminate her pregnancy features, in Kennedy's opinion, as a mother of an unborn child whose natural protective instincts would never have permitted her to consent to a doctor harming her child *had she really known* the method the doctor would use to end her child's life. The presupposition is that the state cannot trust the medical profession to inform pregnant women; therefore it may further women's informed choice by removing that choice.

Justice Kennedy provides no empirical support for this "self-evident" intensification of a "mother's" regret and grief. Indeed, on the proposition that it seems "unexceptionable" that some women come to regret their choice to have an abortion, Kennedy cited to a friend of the court brief filed by Sandra Cano, the plaintiff "Mary Doe" in the early abortion case, *Doe v. Bolton.* That brief presented to the Court narratives (gathered by the South Dakota Task Force) from 180 women answering the question, "How has abortion affected you?" The brief asserts that these narratives reveal, through women's "real life experience," that "abortion hurts women and endangers their physical, emotional, and psychological health" and, therefore, that Congress correctly banned "partial birth" abortion without a health exception.[82] It rejects entirely *Casey's* premise that abortion is within the range of choices that are "central to personal dignity and autonomy" and "to the liberty protected by the Fourteenth Amendment."[83]

With Justice Kennedy's majority opinion, the regret argument for restricting abortion gains legitimacy. In response, Justice Ginsburg, as quoted above, sharply criticizes the majority for invoking this "anti-abortion shibboleth for which it concededly has no reliable evidence." She points out that whereas *Casey* permitted remedying any problem of a lack of information by upholding informed consent laws providing such information, *Carhart* allows depriving women "of the right to make an autonomous choice, even at the expense of their safety." She elaborates: "Eliminating or reducing women's reproductive choices is manifestly *not* a means of protecting them." Instead, "this way of thinking reflects ancient notions about women's place in the family and under the Constitution—ideas that have long since been discredited." Ginsburg reminds the majority of *Casey*'s language that "[t]he destiny of the woman must be shaped . . . on her own conception of her spiritual imperatives and her place in society." She links this constitutional right to "a woman's autonomy to determine her life's course, and thus to enjoy equal citizenship stature."[84] Thus, *Casey* supports responsibility as autonomy, while *Carhart* eviscerates it and promotes responsibility as accountability in its most extreme form: coercing conformity by removing any alternative.

In this powerful dissent, Ginsburg effectively refutes the "abortion harms women" or incapability argument. Unfortunately, the majority's acceptance of it may illustrate the growing power of this new form of the irresponsibility critique of rights. State legislatures have enacted or considered a range of laws ostensibly seeking to protect women from abortion. For example, a new South Dakota informed consent law includes this finding: "It is a necessary and proper exercise of the state's authority to give precedence to the mother's fundamental interest in her relationship with her child over the irrevocable method of termination of that relationship by induced abortion."[85] An earlier South Dakota law included so-called relationship disclosures, requiring a physician to tell a pregnant woman "that the pregnant woman has an existing relationship with that unborn human being and that the relationship enjoys protection under the U.S. Constitution and under the laws of South Dakota" and that "by having an abortion, her existing relationship and her existing constitutional rights with regards to that relationship will be terminated."[86] A federal district court struck down this law as "untruthful and misleading" under current constitutional law (which does not treat the fetus as a "person" or protect a parental relationship with an unborn embryo or fetus).[87] But its enactment is a telling illustration of the attempt to advance a vision of pregnant women as already in a mother-child relationship and to depict the availability of abortion as a threat to that relationship.

Regret and Incapability

How does the regret argument look when viewed as a version of the irresponsibility critique of rights? First, *wrongness:* abortion rights are wrongs for the pregnant woman, who naturally experiences a mother-child bond and wants to continue, not terminate, her relationship with her unborn child. As Reva Siegel documents, at a crucial point, the anti-abortion movement decided that its focus on the right to life of the fetus was not making inroads on abortion rights because proponents of such rights successfully linked them to women's well-being and equality. They launched a new "woman-protective antiabortion argument" that evinced concern for women's well-being by contending that abortion harms women.[88]

Second, *immunity:* privacy rights insulate pregnant women from information they need about what abortion really does to the fetus and about assistance available if they continue their pregnancy. Some states, for example, have "Woman's Right to Know" laws that quote *Casey* on the risk of "devastating psychological consequences" for a woman who learns, after the fact, that her decision was "not fully informed."[89] Moreover, there is a premise that nongovernmental, pro-abortion coercion takes place in that "private," insulated sphere. South Dakota and other states offer the aim of protecting the "pregnant mother" to make sure that her decision is "truly voluntary, uncoerced, and informed" as a rationale for more elaborate informed consent rules. South Dakota's new law requires any woman seeking an abortion to visit a "pregnancy help center," whose mission is to "provide education, counseling, and other assistance to help a pregnant mother maintain her relationship with her unborn child and care for her unborn child." The center is to have a "private interview with her to discuss her circumstances that may subject her decision [to abort] to coercion."[90] The incapability argument views these measures as "help," since it is beyond a woman's capacity voluntarily to terminate the mother-child relationship without serious physical and emotional consequences to herself. Proponents of the law also view it as necessary because physicians cannot be trusted, through the normal informed consent process, to ensure that women act voluntarily. A federal district court issued a preliminary injunction against this law, observing:

Forcing a woman to divulge to a stranger at a pregnancy help center the fact that she has chosen to undergo an abortion humiliates her and degrades her as a human being. The woman will feel degraded by the compulsive nature of [these] [r]equirements, which suggest that she has made the "wrong" decision, has not really "thought" about her decision to undergo an abortion, or is "not intelligent enough" to make the decision with the advice of a physician.[91]

This language recalls Justice Stevens's partial dissent in *Casey*, where he criticized an informed consent law allowing persuasion against abortion as reflecting either "outmoded" assumptions about women's "decision making capacity" or the "illegitimate premise" that "the decision to terminate a pregnancy is presumptively wrong."[92]

Regret and Responsibility: The Responsible Reasons Women Have Abortions

Is the possibility of regret a good reason for restricting a constitutional right? One basic problem is that the "risk of regret is inherent in reaching many moral decisions in individuals' lives," but "this does not justify placing such decisions in the hands of legislators or courts."[93] Why should the decision whether to terminate a pregnancy be different? Indeed, in concluding that a Nebraska informed consent law could have a chilling effect on medical practice, because it allowed women who came to regret their abortion decisions to sue their physicians, a federal district court observed (in an implicit retort to Justice Kennedy's formulation in *Carhart*) that, although there was no "reliable data," unscientific surveys readily indicate high levels of regret by parents at *having* children. This conclusion was buttressed by the streaming into Nebraska of parents from around the nation to drop off their unwanted children after the state passed its "Safe Haven Law" in 2008.[94] As the court concludes: "the most important choices have consequences and no matter how well-reasoned and fully deliberated, those decisions can lead to remorse. That is the price we pay for our freedom."[95]

Furthermore, the regret rationale reflects a lack of trust in women's capacity for responsible moral agency, and a view that women are incompetent decision makers who need protection from their decisions.[96] This argument rests on stereotypes about women's natural and proper role as mothers. Justice Ginsburg, in her *Carhart* dissent, made this point forcefully. Such stereotyping hinders women's responsible self-determination.

Focusing on this gender dimension reveals additional problems with the incapability argument. As evidence that abortion is the wrong right, proponents point to narratives by *some* women who regret their decisions. This cannot suffice to restrict abortion rights for *all* women. Consider another friend of the court brief in *Carhart* (not cited by Justice Kennedy), which offered the stories of women who had second-trimester abortions but, contrary to the women in the Cano brief, asserted that "their ability to obtain safe abortions is fundamental to their lives." Instead of tales of ill-informed choices and regret, these stories stress women's responsible exercise of autonomy: "These women rely upon intimate moral, religious, and personal values to make the right decision for themselves and their families."[97]

Empirical studies of women's abortion decisions indicate the centrality of considerations of responsibility and relationship, challenging the depiction of women as "lone rights-bearers" insulated from family and community or as incapable of responsible decisions. Ever since *Roe,* researchers have asked, "Why do women have abortions?"[98] A recent study concluded: "Women's reported reasons for ending pregnancies have been consistent over time." A "cross-cutting theme" across categories of age, relationship, race, income, and education was "concern for or responsibility to other individuals." Older women, for example, "the large majority of whom were already mothers, regularly cited their responsibility to children or other dependents as a key factor behind the decision to have an abortion." Issues of responsibility also emerge in concerns like lack of economic resources, lack of a partner or a partner's support, and (in the case of younger women with no children) unreadiness to be a parent. "The concept of responsibility is inseparable from the theme of limited resources; given their present circumstances, respondents considered their decision to have an abortion the most responsible action."[99]

Further, ungenerous public policies could influence abortion decisions: "The fact that many women cited financial limitations as a reason for ending a pregnancy suggests that further restrictions on public assistance to families could contribute to a continued increase in abortions among the most disadvantaged women." Concern to avoid single motherhood or a woman's relationship problems were significant factors for many women. These problems included a "partner's drinking, physical abuse, unfaithfulness, unreliability, immaturity and absence (often due to incarceration) or responsibilities to his other children," as well as a partner's denial of paternity and indication that he did not want a child. Abortion opponents might seize on these factors and argue that abortion licenses male irresponsibility, but they would have the causal sequence backward. A male partner's lack of responsibility is a factor leading some women to choose abortion as the most responsible decision; their decisions do not cause that male irresponsibility. In sum, women in these studies spoke of their decision making process as an "intense" and "difficult" one, in which they gave "moral weight" to their responsibilities to "their families, themselves, and the children they might have in the future." Some "described abortion as sinful and wrong," but nonetheless described their abortion as "'the right thing' and 'a responsible choice.'"[100]

While the incapability argument portrays pregnant women as being at the mercy of exploitative abortionists and pressuring partners and families, the study found that women "independently make the decision to have an abortion." Fewer than 1 percent indicated that influence from partners or parents was "their most important reason."[101] These studies support West's call to ground the right to abortion in the capacity of pregnant women to make the decision responsibly. They undercut the incapability version of the irresponsibility critique.

Rights, Responsibilities, and Neglect: The Negative Liberties Critique of Public Irresponsibility

We now explain how our constitutional liberalism would support a right of procreative autonomy as one component of a broader positive program of promoting reproductive justice. We focus on a dimension of the irresponsibility critique evident in Glendon's communitarian arguments and in West's progressive critiques: rights talk obscures public responsibility for meeting women's needs. We engage West's negative liberties critique of the costs of abortion rights—that they legitimate public neglect and irresponsibility—and her call for de-constitutionalizing abortion—turning from courts to legislatures to pursue a robust reproductive justice agenda. Through grappling with her arguments, we sketch a formative project to further reproductive justice.

The Progressive "Negative Liberties" Critique of Abortion Rights

West's negative liberties critique argues that framing a pregnant woman's right to abortion as a "right to be let alone"—as a negative right to be free from governmental interference—has costs. It legitimates the underlying conditions of her pregnancy, including not only the circumstances of the sex leading to pregnancy (which may be unwanted), but also the social and economic burdens parents face in U.S. society (because of the lack of generous social supports for caregiving). A negative right simply legitimates the status quo and, by treating continuing or terminating a pregnancy as women's "choice," resists any public obligation to subsidize women's reproductive choices. Making sure women's choices are "informed"—that they give informed consent—"exhausts the role of the state."[102]

This negative liberties critique erroneously conflates the right to privacy with the idea of the Constitution as a charter of negative liberties. (By "negative liberties," we mean rights that limit what government may do to persons, as distinguished from "positive liberties," or rights that impose affirmative obligations on government to provide certain positive benefits to persons.) On West's view, the right to privacy recognized in *Roe* led to decisions denying rights to positive liberties,[103] such as a right to abortion funding in *Harris v. McRae*[104] and ultimately a right to protection against "private" family violence in *DeShaney v. Winnebago County Department of Social Services*.[105] However, the greatest champions of the right to privacy on the Supreme Court, Justices Blackmun, Brennan, and Marshall, have been the greatest critics of the idea of the Constitution as a charter of negative liberties. All of them wrote or joined in powerful dissents in *Harris* and *DeShaney*.[106] Furthermore, the greatest critics of the right to privacy, Chief Justice Rehnquist and Justice Scalia, have been the greatest champions of the idea of the negative Constitution.[107] We contend that the right of privacy does not entail the idea of the negative Constitution. Progressives and feminists correctly argue that the Constitution, interpreted solely as a charter of negative liberties, does not secure the positive benefits needed fully to guarantee reproductive justice for women and men. But that deficiency is one of a negative Constitution, not a shortcoming of the right of privacy. The right of privacy itself does not license public irresponsibility. Our constitutional liberalism justifies that right in the context of an understanding of the Constitution as a charter of positive benefits, not merely negative liberties.[108]

West argues that the obscuring of public responsibility relates to another cost of rights—the neglect of a broader, aspirational vision of equal citizenship and reproductive justice. This happened with *Roe*, West argues, when it framed the legal right to abortion in terms of a negative right of a physician, in consultation with a patient, to be free from governmental interference, rather than the more robust rights to reproductive justice advanced by the women's movement in early abortion rights litigation. West makes the important observation that when advocates litigate to secure a constitutional right, they do not control the ultimate form that it takes. Moreover, they may have to trim their sails to fit the available framework of constitutional doctrine. The history of the women's movement shows how abortion was one part of a broader reproductive justice and equal citizenship agenda.[109] "The constitutional right to abort a fetus, and the right to be left alone on which it is built, is as hollow as it is in part because it represents just such a truncation of the aspirational feminist vision of reproductive justice from which it was forged."[110]

What would reproductive justice require? West proposes "a state that provides a network of support for the processes of reproduction: protection against rape and access to affordable and effective birth control, healthcare, including but not limited to abortion services, prenatal care, support in childbirth and postpartum, support for breast-feeding mothers, early childcare for infants and toddlers, income support for parents who stay home to care for young babies, and high quality public education for school age children." She does not argue that pro-choice advocates should try to secure this broader positive agenda in the courts. To the contrary: "The Court is not equipped to mandate any of that, and has stated repeatedly that it is not inclined to suggest that a citizen might have a right to a state that does so." Instead, because of the contrast between a judicially recognized and enforced negative right and what might be achieved through more robust "positive legislative schemes," West calls for "de-constitutionalizing" abortion by turning from courts to legislatures and to "ordinary politics," where it might be possible to further reproductive justice. Pro-choice and pro-life advocates might find common ground, given their "common interest in reducing the incidence of abortion, both by minimizing the number of unintended pregnancies and lowering the cost of mothering."[111]

Moreover, West argues that casting abortion rights as negative liberties has "diverted resources" from "forms of social persuasion, including moral argument, that might reduce the number of unwanted pregnancies women experience, whether they result in live births or not." This would reduce "the need for abortion or abortion rights." People, West argues, have moral duties with respect to sex. First, although the constitutionally protected right to use birth control (as in *Griswold v. Connecticut* and *Eisenstadt v. Baird*[112]) is silent concerning any moral duty to do so, government may moralize that heterosexuals have a duty to use birth control if they do not wish to conceive (for example, through sex education curricula for adolescents and public service advertising campaigns). A second moral duty is for a girl or young woman not to engage in sex she does not want, and for a boy or man "not to engage in sex undesired by his partner." Such unwanted sex poses real harms to women, she argues, harms compounded by an unwanted pregnancy. Just as the neglect of these moral duties contributes to the problem of unwanted pregnancy, moralizing in favor of them may lead to behaviors and choices that reduce the need for abortion.[113]

West, in sum, views the defense of a constitutional right to abortion in the courts as hindering the securing of a positive reproductive justice agenda in the legislatures. We do not agree that it is necessary to abandon the first to pursue the second. West powerfully reckons with certain "costs of rights" but may underestimate the benefits. Given the hostility to abortion in a number of states, with legislative enactments openly challenging *Roe* and crossing the lines drawn in *Casey,* courts are one available, if not the best, forum to protect women from further encroachments on reproductive liberty.[114] Her point that rights talk can shrink broader aspirational visions is a useful reminder about the risks of looking only to courts to vindicate rights but is not a compelling reason to give up on courts altogether. Instead, it properly reminds readers of the important responsibilities of the legislative branch, along with the judicial branch, in securing positive benefits. Within our constitutional liberalism, we argue in Chapter 5, government has an affirmative responsibility to secure the preconditions for personal and democratic self-government. Such preconditions include those for reproductive justice. Judicial enforcement of a constitutional right to procreative autonomy does not preclude turning to legislatures and executives to secure the necessary social and economic preconditions for realizing that right. Here is an arena in which all three branches have responsibilities.

Toward a Reproductive Justice Agenda: Personal and Public Responsibility

Women's narratives about why they decide to have an abortion, as well as studies of those decisions, focus attention on the question: Why do women face unwanted pregnancies? What do they need instead of abortion? Communitarians propose a model of mutual responsibility: of what society is willing to do for women and what it may reasonably expect of them. No doubt, if the United States were to move closer to Western Europe in providing generous benefits for pregnancy and parental leave, many financial constraints that make particular pregnancies unwanted might disappear and some women might reconsider the most responsible thing to do under the circumstances. But we do not live in that world, even though many progressives, feminists, and liberals (ourselves included) would like to see the United States move closer to it. Supporting the legal right to abortion does not preclude supporting a generous family policy as part of government's responsibility to facilitate the healthy development of children and to help families carry out their vital tasks of nurture and socialization.

Instructive in this regard is President Obama's speech on an anniversary of *Roe*. He affirmed *Roe* as protecting "women's health and reproductive freedom," and standing for a "broader principle" that government "should not intrude on our most private family matters"; but he also called for finding "common ground" on a broader reproductive health agenda that would "prevent unintended pregnancies, reduce the need for abortion, and support women and families in the choices they make" by expanding "access to affordable contraception, accurate health information, and preventative services." He also urged a recommitment to women's equality.[115] (Unfortunately, the continuing opposition even to one supposed piece of common ground—support for contraception and family planning services—suggests that the "ordinary politics" that West favors is likely to remain quite contentious.[116])

Our constitutional liberalism has much in common with West's vision of reproductive justice. An account of how government could foster reflective reproductive self-determination would attend to the human goods and public values at stake. It would be informed by feminist analysis of the preconditions for and the parameters of responsible sexual and procreative choice. In addition to respect for life, government should advance such public values as the equal citizenship of women, the reproductive health of its citizens (including attention to racial disparities concerning it), and social reproduction (i.e., the importance of bearing and nurturing children and preparing them for citizenship).[117]

Thus, our model of responsibility as autonomy does not understand reproductive rights as solely negative liberties. It conceives reproductive health as a component of positive liberty.[118] Promoting responsibility as autonomy entails governmental responsibility to establish the material and social preconditions for women's equal citizenship, including attention to problems such as sexual violence, other threats to women's bodily integrity, and women's poverty. At present, U.S. public policy emphatically does not foster women's reproductive well-being. The protection of "potential life" and encouragement of women's "responsibility" does not translate into acceptance of public responsibility and a strong commitment of resources to foster the equal citizenship of women as mothers and the well-being of families.[119] All this and more is required if we are to take personal and public responsibilities as well as rights seriously where reproductive freedom and justice are concerned.

Conclusion

To recapitulate our constitutional liberalism's project for taking responsibilities as well as rights seriously: it takes responsibility as autonomy seriously by permitting government to encourage reflective, responsible exercise of rights; it grounds the right to decide whether to terminate a pregnancy in women's capacity to decide responsibly; and it lends no support to public irresponsibility but conceives the Constitution as a charter of positive benefits imposing affirmative obligations upon government to secure the preconditions for reproductive justice.

CHAPTER FOUR

Civil Society's Role in
Cultivating the "Seedbeds of Virtue"

In Chapters 4, 5, and 6, we turn to the neutrality critique. A common critique of liberal theories of rights is that, because they require "neutrality" by government among competing conceptions of the good life, they bar government from cultivating the civic virtue upon which a stable political order depends. Morever, this liberal neutrality, coupled with rights talk's preoccupation with the dyad of the rights-bearing individual versus the state, leads to the neglect of civil society—the realm of intermediate organizations between the individual and the state (including the family, religious institutions, and civic and other voluntary associations) that generate civic virtue and the skills and habits of self-government necessary to secure ordered liberty. The erosion or disappearance of civil society, as well as the "social capital" generated in its institutions, is a common diagnosis of what underlies civic and moral decline in America. Accompanying this diagnosis is the prescription that reviving or renewing civil society—the "seedbeds of virtue"—and shoring up social capital would be a promising remedy for many of the nation's ills.

In this chapter, we consider the critique of liberal theories of rights by proponents of reviving civil society and show that the conception of civil society that our constitutional liberalism supports is not vulnerable to it. We use the term "civil society–revivalists"[1] to evoke how their diagnoses hearken back to an earlier time (whether it be the founding, the nineteenth-century America observed by Alexis de Tocqueville, or the 1950s) when associational life and civic virtue are said to have flourished. We challenge the conclusion that the erosion of civil society and the seedbeds of virtue is a consequence of an excess of liberal virtues, such as tolerance. We also pose some questions for civil society–revivalists about how reviving civil society would cure many of our nation's political, civic, and moral ills. Does civil society cultivate seedbeds of virtue—our foundational "sources of competence, character, and citizenship"[2]—to foster democratic self-government? Or is its more vital purpose to be a buffer against (or enclave of resistance to) the government? Should government attempt to secure "congruence" between democratic values and the values of voluntary associations, or would such an effort offend commitments to pluralism and diversity? Is the decline of civil society due to a flawed liberal conception of the person as an "unencumbered," sovereign self? Do civil society–revivalists ask the right questions or offer the best solutions when they focus on the family and its supposedly weakened capacity to serve as a seedbed of civic virtue? Have gains in equality and liberty contributed to the decline of civil society and civic virtue? Finally, would a revitalized civil society support democratic self-government or supplant it?

Grappling with these questions brings out a basic tension concerning the relationship between civil society and government in cultivating civic virtue: families, religious institutions, voluntary associations, and other institutions of civil society are foundational sources or "seedbeds" of virtues and values that undergird constitutional democracy; and yet these same institutions are independent locations of power that guard against governmental orthodoxy by generating their own distinctive virtues and values.[3] The first idea envisions a comfortable *congruence* or agreement between norms fostered by nongovernmental associations and those inculcated by government. The second idea recognizes the potential for *conflict*. Government's formative project of cultivating good citizenship may clash with the formative tasks of the family, religious institutions, and other voluntary associations.

Negotiating this tension puts liberalism in a double bind. On the one hand, liberalism's critics fault it for doing too little to cultivate civic virtue, because the constraints of liberal neutrality prevent government from promoting a conception of the good life. On the other, critics also charge that it does too much, and flouts liberal neutrality, when it seeks to promote civic virtue and public values; indeed, they charge, it tries to establish a governmental orthodoxy. We illustrate by examining (in Chapter 5) the dual authority of parents and schools to educate children and (in Chapter 6) clashes between governmental promotion, through antidiscrimination laws, of equal citizenship and constitutional rights to freedom of association and the free exercise of religion.

In this chapter, we outline a conception of the roles and regulation of civil society in our morally pluralistic constitutional democracy. Working within the framework of John Rawls's political liberalism, and guided by key feminist commitments, we argue that the associations of civil society play the critical roles of underwriting a stable constitutional democracy and helping citizens to realize the important good of self-respect. Political liberalism distinguishes between the domain of the political and the domain of civil society, yet it posits a relationship of mutual support. We explore the "liberal expectancy" of congruence between these two domains, but illuminate how our constitutional order affirmatively protects discontinuities between them.[4] Throughout, we argue that civil society is as important for securing the capacity for personal self-government as for promoting the capacity for democratic self-government.[5] Our constitutional liberalism, by securing these capacities, pursues ordered liberty, not liberty without virtues.

The Calls for Reviving or Renewing Civil Society

> [Civil society is] a concept rich in historical resonances. . . . With it, . . . we are in the realm of the normative, if not indeed the nostalgic. "Civil society" sounds good; it has a good feel to it; it has the look of a fine old wine, full of depth and complexity. Who could possibly object to it, who not wish for its fulfillment? Fine old wines can stimulate but they can also make you drunk, lose all sense of discrimination and clarity of purpose. What is the case for reviving the concept of civil society?
>
> —Krishan Kumar, "Civil Society: An Inquiry into the Usefulness of an Historical Term"[6]

> The most important development at the end of the twentieth century is the rediscovery of the non-governmental sector of civil society. . . . If the twentieth century was about the neglect, and even the systematic destruction of civil society through statist ideologies and destructive cultural influences, the twenty-first century may represent the era of its restoration.
>
> —Don Eberly, "The Coming Social Renaissance . . ."[7]

The erosion or disappearance of civil society is a common diagnosis of what underlies all manner of discontent, disorder, and irresponsibility in America, and its renewal features prominently as a cure for such problems. In the 1990s, President Bill Clinton invoked a strengthened civil society to address problems that government alone could not solve.[8] First

Lady Hillary Clinton called for building up civil society in order to inculcate values in "our children," and famously argued that "it takes a village" to do so.[9] She characterized civil society as a "pillar" between the marketplace and the government.[10] In the widely discussed book, *Bowling Alone,* Robert Putnam found evidence of the disappearance of civil society and loss of social capital in such phenomena as the decline of bowling leagues and warned of the impact for generating norms of trust and reciprocity.[11] He and his colleagues call for a "sustained, broadbased social movement to restore civic virtue and civic participation in America."[12] And a central premise of a significant book, *Seedbeds of Virtue,* is that America's most serious long-term problem is the weakening of child-raising families and that, accordingly, the challenge of shoring up those seedbeds of virtue should be at the "front and center of American public deliberation."[13]

At the start of the twenty-first century, both Republican President George W. Bush and Democratic President Barack Obama have praised civil society as a vital resource for national renewal and have championed partnerships between government and institutions of civil society, such as religious (or "faith-based") and neighborhood organizations, to address social problems.[14] Obama articulates, as a "fundamental truth" in the twenty-first century, that "strong, vibrant nations include strong, vibrant civil societies."[15] Don Eberly, director of the Civil Society Project and a former White House advisor, contends that the twenty-first century "may represent the era of [the] restoration" of civil society and of a focus not upon "central governments" but upon "social capital, capacity building, philanthropy, and global democratic civil society."[16] Moreover, in American government and international development and charitable organizations, the concept of civil society continues to enjoy a "high profile" as a "democratic miracle worker," even though the evidence on its role in democratization is mixed.[17] In short, interest in reviving civil society is keen.

Broadly speaking, there are two strands of civil society–revivalists: civic revivalists and moral revivalists.[18] We use two notable reports to illustrate these civic and moral strands, respectively: *A Nation of Spectators: How Civic Disengagement Weakens America and What We Can Do about It,* by the National Commission on Civic Renewal,[19] and *A Call to Civil Society: Why Democracy Needs Moral Truths,* by the Council on Civil Society.[20] These strands and reports (and the casts of characters) overlap, but the former emphasizes civic renewal and reinvigorating civic character, the capacity for citizenship, and engagement in shared civic purposes, while the latter stresses moral renewal, nurturing "the seedbeds of virtue," and "rediscovering" the "moral truths" of "the public moral philosophy that makes our democracy possible."[21]

Civil society–revivalists echo themes sounded in prominent critiques of rights talk (addressed in Chapters 2 and 3): there is an imbalance between rights and responsibilities, and the responsible exercise of rights that makes ordered liberty possible requires that persons possess certain virtues.[22] For example, Mary Ann Glendon has analyzed the erosion of civil society as a consequence of a paradox inherent in liberal democracy. The American experiment of liberal democracy and ordered liberty presupposes certain traits of character, but liberalism cannot create or sustain those virtues. This experiment "leaves it primarily up to families, local governments, schools, religious and workplace associations, and a host of other voluntary groups to teach and transmit republican virtues and skills from one generation to the next."[23] The frequently invoked text is The Federalist No. 55: "As there is a degree of depravity in mankind which requires a certain degree of circumspection and distrust, so there are other qualities in human nature which justify a certain portion of esteem and confidence. Republican government presupposes the existence of these qualities in a higher degree than any other form."[24] Because the founders took these seedbeds of virtue for granted as a virtually inexhaustible natural resource, Glendon argues, there was no apparent need for a Constitution that exacted virtue.[25] Nor did the founders establish a regime of government that provided for a national project of character formation.[26]

Another canonical text in this then/now story is Tocqueville's observations of America in the 1830s, Democracy in America, reporting that "Americans of all ages, all stations in life, and all types of dispositions are forever forming associations" for all manner of purposes (including what would be undertaken by government in France or by landed aristocrats in England). He remarked upon the many salutary effects of civil and political associations on sustaining American democracy.[27] Tocqueville, civil society–revivalists claim, recognized how America's voluntary associations "served, often inadvertently, as schools for citizenship."[28] They hail him as a visionary who foresaw the risks posed to democracy and liberty in America by the loosening of associative ties and by the untempered pursuit of individualism and materialism.[29] Nonetheless, Glendon argues, Tocqueville, like the founders, "took for granted" that families—and women, in particular—would inculcate "the requisite habits and beliefs" that could "effectively moderate individual greed, selfishness, and ambition."[30]

The paradox is that liberal democracy depends upon civil society for orderly social reproduction, or creation of good citizens, but it contains the seeds of its own destruction. The argument is that the "absolutist" nature of American "rights talk" and the ascent of a liberal ethic of "expressive individualism" (in contrast with an ethic of self-sacrifice, responsibility, and mutual obligation) have eroded the seedbeds of virtue, undermined civil society, and imperiled our liberal democracy.[31] Americans lack "an adequate linguistic or conceptual apparatus to deal with the intermediate institutions that stand between the individual and the state, [and] we regularly overlook the effects of laws and policies upon the environments within which sociality flourishes, and the settings upon which individuals depend for their full and free development."[32] Liberalism champions individual freedom but separates that freedom from "civic virtue," obscuring freedom's roots in civil society.[33] Moreover, commitment to liberal virtues such as toleration "slides all too easily into the sort of mandatory value neutrality that rules all talk of character and virtue out of bounds"[34] and bars government from shaping character and favoring those seedbeds that foster it. Some civil society–revivalists, such as civic liberal political philosopher William Galston, locate the problem in a *misunderstanding* of the liberal virtue of tolerance as resting on "the relativistic belief that every personal choice, every 'life plan,' is equally good, hence beyond rational scrutiny and criticism" and as barring persuasion in favor of "superior" ways of life.[35]

Clearly, what lies behind many of the calls to revive civil society are serious concerns: how to produce citizens with the virtues, habits, and skills necessary for responsible self-government and how to generate social capital, trust, and social solidarity in a diverse polity. We share these concerns. However, we are critical of many of the claims of the civil society–revivalists, particularly those about liberal neutrality and rights. Moreover, revivalists often look back to the vibrant civil society of an earlier day, but tend to neglect the extent to which earlier conceptions of civic virtue and associational life coexisted with—even depended upon—inequality in civil society and the polity. We concur that there is an important reciprocal relationship between civil society and democracy but argue that it is more complex and indeterminate than many civil society–revivalists evidently believe. After posing some questions for civil society–revivalists, we sketch our own conception of the place of civil society in our constitutional democracy.

Some Questions for Civil Society–Revivalists

How Do the Institutions of Civil Society Serve as Seedbeds of Virtue and Foster Self-Government?

The Claim that Civil Society Is a School for Citizenship   Many civil society–revivalists contend that the institutions of civil society are "seedbeds of virtue"—our foundational "sources of competence, character, and citizenship"—and that they foster self-government.[36] The literature posits a direct relationship between "government of the self" and democratic self-government: "the essence of democracy is self-government, [which] begins with the government *of* the self and moves to the public efforts of citizens whose need for the restraint of law is mitigated by their capacity to restrain themselves."[37]

Many civil society–revivalists claim that a primary function of civil society is preparing children to be good citizens who possess the virtues and traits of character necessary for self-government. The family is "the first and by far the most important" seedbed of virtue, the "cradle of civil society,"[38] but contemporary families have a weakened capacity to perform this function. We agree that families play a vital role in social reproduction. Indeed, our constitutional order locates in parents the fundamental right—and primary responsibility—for the care, custody, control, and education of children.[39] One of us has elaborated a liberal feminist account of the place of families in fostering the capacities for democratic and personal self-government through, for example, providing care and nurture and engaging in the moral and civic education of children.[40] Political liberalism also supports this function of the family. How, according to civil society–revivalists, do families inculcate civic virtue and promote self-government?

Glendon extols "household table talk" as an exemplary discourse countering America's individualist public rhetoric and containing seeds for the renewal of civil society. She envisions a refined rights talk informed by our more nuanced table talk, with its "potentially transform[ative]" insights about "relationships, obligations, and long-term consequences of present acts and decisions" as well as cooperation and compromise.[41] But how does "table talk," with its "recollection and retelling of the family's concrete experiences, and . . . the household's fund of stories about relationships, obligations, and the long-term consequences of present acts and decisions,"[42] shape family members for democratic self-government? It may well build family solidarity and strengthen the family as a community of "memory and mutual aid," but does it instill a broader sense of social solidarity and citizenship? To use a distinction formulated by Putnam, families may foster *bonding* (or exclusive) social capital, but not *bridging* (inclusive) social capital, which generates "broader identities and generalized reciprocity."[43] In his comparative study on trust, Francis Fukayama (a civil society–revivalist) characterizes "familistic" societies as "low trust" societies: with weak voluntary associations, where unrelated people have no basis for trusting one another, and where the state has to play a part to establish social bonds.[44]

Many civil society–revivalists, including Glendon, celebrate the family meal. Social scientists and policymakers concerned about the well-being of children frequently emphasize that this regular family ritual—along with a close parent-child relationship—correlates with numerous positive factors for healthy child and adolescent development and with a reduced risk of numerous negative outcomes.[45] The family meal clearly contributes to children's successful personal self-government and success in life. But it is less clear whether or how it also makes them good citizens.

More generally, there is nothing about families and their moral discourses that insures that they will be seedbeds of virtue rather than "weedbeds of vices" such as parochialism, prejudice, and intolerance, or simply materialism and self-interest.[46] Nor is there any guarantee that families will inculcate *civic* virtues needed for democratic self-government rather than merely imparting *personal* virtues helpful for governing the self. This is one reason why civil society–revivalists stress the role of schools as seedbeds of virtue that teach "civic literacy" and the skills and virtues needed for democratic self-government.[47] So, too, the civic education literature stresses that, while parents may foster children's civic engagement by modeling such engagement themselves and by table talk concerning politics or current events, they may be failing to do so because "parents are themselves the products of recent trends of civic and political disengagement."[48] In short, families may help children develop into good people without helping them to become good citizens. Moreover, while we expect civil society to nurture in children the capacities for democratic and personal self-government, it may hinder those capacities: parents may abuse and neglect children; clergy, coaches, and other trusted adults may sexually abuse them; and institutions responsible for helping and protecting children may fail to do so.

Many civil society–revivalists claim that participation in voluntary associations within civil society fosters the arts and habits of self-government.[49] Our constitutional liberalism likewise harbors a "liberal expectancy" that civil society will support the political order. But there are still empirical questions about whether and how participation in voluntary associations does so.[50] As Yael Tamir observes, "[t]here is no reason to believe that, left on their own, associations will serve as a seedbed of democracy."[51] For example, it is hardly self-evident how participation in bowling leagues nourishes the habits and skills of citizenship, much less civic virtue and democratic self-government.[52] As Amitai Etzioni puts it: "bowling is morally trivial." Bowlers, birdwatchers, and others may formulate minimal norms relevant to their shared activity and share "chitchat," but

> introducing subjects that have a serious moral content—religious differences, sexual conduct, political ideologies—is frowned upon if not tabooed. . . . People who bowl together do not come to new shared understanding as to how far we should let globalism intrude on our lives, how much we should allow inequality to rise, what parents owe to their children and children to their parents, how to deal with the tough issues related to new developments in biotech, when to interfere in the internal affairs of other countries and so on. [I]t seems that good manners, an important part of thin social norms, often entail avoiding such difficult and "divisive" issues.[53]

Along similar lines, Rawls usefully suggests that virtues that are characteristic of certain forms of association in civil society are distinguishable from political virtues.[54] As with families, nothing about associations assures that they will generate virtues rather than vices. Many associations, such as white supremacist and other hate groups, gangs, and organized crime families, offer opportunities for solidarity and shared values but are inimical to civic virtues and democratic self-government.

Many civil society–revivalists concede that "[t]he link between fervent civic participation and generalized social or political trust is not always strong." Group participation, as such, does not automatically generate civic virtue. Some revivalists invoke the idea that "shared civic principles" and certain attitudes (e.g., self-sacrifice, responsibility, and a sense of obligation to the common good) make democracy possible, while their degeneration imperils it. One strategy is to restructure the institutions of civil society better to generate and transmit such virtues, principles, and attitudes. In addition, A Nation of Spectators affirms the important role of schools in fostering "the knowledge, skills, and virtues our young people need to become good democratic citizens" and proposes that schools "reorganize their internal life to reinforce basic civic virtues."[55] It also endorses civic education (to which we turn in Chapter 5) and character education in the school curriculum.

In short, nothing ensures that voluntary associations, including those in which adults participate, will generate democratic values. A Nation of

Spectators acknowledges that some democratic values are "not the goals of associational life, but byproducts." Furthermore, the report asks, "[W]hy should there be such an obvious linkage between free associations and political democracy?" and concedes the possibility that "[t]he goods various groups seek to produce might, in principle, be hostile to the flourishing of other groups and contemptuous of democratic values." Its conclusion is basically to note inconclusiveness on this difficult issue: "Commentators on civil society find themselves in sharp conflict over 'congruence'—the idea that the internal structures and norms of voluntary associations should (or must) be democratic, participatory, and civil if they are to promote broader societal aims of political democracy."[56]

The Personal and Political Uses of Pluralism   Nancy Rosenblum's extensive study of the morality of association and membership in groups, *Membership and Morals: The Personal Uses of Pluralism in America*,[57] identifies the challenges in assessing the relationship between civil society and liberal democracy. Rosenblum deploys the terms "liberal anxiety" and "liberal expectancy" to capture the conflicting set of attitudes that political and legal theorists sometimes adopt concerning this relationship. On the one hand, some accounts of liberal democracy view it as capable of sustaining itself even without civic virtue. One might think of models of interest group pluralism or of the idea in *The Federalist* No. 51 that separation of powers and ambition counteracting ambition, rather than virtue, will check excesses of self-interest.[58] On the other, there is a liberal expectancy of congruence between civil society and democracy—that the values cultivated in civil society will be liberal democratic values and thus will undergird liberal democracy—along with liberal anxiety that such congruence may not develop over time.[59] As we acknowledge later, our own account of the roles of civil society holds this liberal expectancy.

As a number of civil society–revivalists argue, the founders seemed to assume that such a relationship would exist and that a national governmental project of inculcating civic virtue would be unnecessary. But what if, as Rosenblum argues, the virtues of associations are not necessarily congruent with democratic values? Should government seek to achieve such congruence through civic education and other forms of persuasion to cultivate only those associations which instill and sustain democratic values and to weed out those associations which do not?

An alternative conception of civil society does not insist upon congruence but stresses that civil society mediates between individuals and the state. Associations may not generate explicitly democratic values but instead may cultivate a "whole range of moral dispositions, presumptively supportive of political order," such as cooperation or social trust.[60] To use a familiar term, associations may generate social capital. This, Rosenblum observes, is a "more capacious approach to the moral uses of association than the logic of congruence," because "[t]he business of instilling habits of responsibility, reciprocity, cooperation, or trust is compatible with a variety of political orientations and substantive values."[61] This mediating approach is more pluralistic and tolerant, the argument goes, because associations need not be obviously liberal to generate such values. Yet, this approach must grapple with hard questions about the proper scope of freedom of association for illiberal groups that may foster antidemocratic values and indeed may advocate or lead to secession of groups and individuals from the polity.

Both the congruence approach and the mediating approach, Rosenblum argues, rest upon an "airy 'liberal expectancy.'" Both lack an adequate foundation of psychological realism concerning the moralizing or socializing power of groups upon those who join them and the contribution, if any, of such group membership to liberal democracy. These accounts also fail to capture an important aspect of civil society: "the personal uses of pluralism."[62] The reason that the existence of a dense array of associations matters, she contends, is that associations facilitate the experience of pluralism in people's lives. Rather than emphasizing the role of civil society in sustaining democratic self-government, she stresses its role in facilitating personal self-government. Therefore, government should secure the conditions for freedom of association, including protecting rights to exit as well as to enter associations. We find helpful Rosenblum's conclusion that the relationship between group membership and liberal democratic values, beyond the cultivation of a disposition to cooperate, is indirect and indeterminate. We agree that associational life has vital importance for personal self-government.

Rosenblum also finds that the disposition to cooperate, formed in associations, can further the important good of self-respect.[63] This resonates with Rawls's discussion of associative ties as helping members to realize the "primary good" of self-respect, enabling them to "acquire a sense that what [they] do in everyday life is worthwhile."[64] This self-respect, Rosenblum suggests, can be a form of "compensation" for disappointed social, political, or economic expectations.[65] Finally, although some associations may not cultivate virtue, they may confine vice: groups "provide relatively benign outlets for ineradicable viciousness, intolerance, or narrow self-interest" and help contain antidemocratic dispositions from spilling over into violence.[66]

We interpret Rosenblum not as rejecting the idea that associations *can* contribute to democratic self-government and civic virtue, but as calling for greater precision about how they do so. (Thus, in an effort to identify those associations of particular value for democratic public life, Rosenblum has studied the virtues of political parties and the case for "partisanship."[67]) In that spirit, we add two roles of civil society pertaining to democratic self-government.

First, Jane Mansbridge contends that democracies, in practice, produce at best a "rough" or "good enough" legitimacy and need "ways short of civil disobedience and the breakdown of normatively based mutual cooperation to recognize and fight the ongoing injustice of their procedures and their outcomes." They need "deliberative enclaves of resistance" or "counterpublics," whose goals include "understanding themselves better, forging bonds of solidarity, preserving the memories of past injustices, interpreting and reinterpreting the meanings of those injustices, [and] working out alternative conceptions of self, of community, of justice, and of universality. . . ."[68] The civil rights movement and the women's movement offer familiar examples of counterpublics; the contemporary gay and lesbian rights movement is another.

This dimension of civil society illustrates an evidently paradoxical feature of pluralist liberal democracy that we noted above: our constitutional order protects the rights of associations, even though they may be "oppositional" to the state and offer multiple sites of power distinct from the state.[69] What is more, it highlights the efforts of social movements to transform both civil society and the polity better to realize ideals of equal citizenship, justice, and community. Jack Balkin helpfully speaks of social movements as being vital actors in an intergenerational constitutional "project" that recognizes the gap between constitutional ideals and practices and works to bring about the realization of "commitments" or redeem the "promises" in the Constitution.[70] Thus, *A Nation of Spectators* recognizes that "[s]ocial movements frequently arise within civil society, giving voice to new publics and promoting new causes and political identities;" indeed, the movements launched by the "purportedly 'uncivic' generation" that came of age in the 1960s and 1970s "have led to unprecedented advances in rights and social justice."[71]

Second, an adequate account of civil society should recognize that it can provide a multiplicity of sites for public deliberation outside formal political channels. Contending that "[t]he fiction of a general deliberative assembly in which the united people expressed their will belongs to the early history of democratic theory," Seyla Benhabib argues that "today our guiding model has to be that of a medium of loosely associated, multiple foci of opinion formation and dissemination which affect one another in free and spontaneous processes of communication." A plurality of forms of association—ranging from "political parties, to citizens' initiatives, to social movements, to voluntary associations, to consciousness-raising groups, and the like"—can contribute to such deliberation:

> It is through the interlocking net of these multiple forms of associations, networks, and organizations that an anonymous "public conversation" results. It is central to the model of deliberative democracy that it privileges such a public sphere of mutually interlocking and overlapping networks and associations of deliberation, contestation, and argumentation.

Both Benhabib and Mansbridge stress an important dimension of civil society: the public sphere need not be homogeneous and suppress difference; instead, "heterogeneity, otherness, and difference can find expression in the multiple associations, networks, and citizens' forums" that make up public life.[72] As discussed later, political liberalism describes this public sphere as the "background culture" of civil society and recognizes its importance for emancipatory social movements.[73]

Have Liberal Conceptions of the Person Corroded Civil Society and Undermined Self-Government?

Civil society–revivalists, and moral revivalists in particular, relate the breakdown in the capacities necessary for the "government *of* the self" to a "fundamentally flawed" liberal conception of the person. *A Call to Civil Society* describes this flawed conception as follows: "We are self-originating sources of valid claims, essentially unencumbered self-owning and auto-teleological. For short, call it a philosophy of expressive individualism, or a belief in the sovereignty of the self—a kind of modern democratic equivalent of the old idea of the divine right of kings." The report attributes this conception to the liberalism of Rawls. It offers an alternative conception: human beings are "intrinsically social beings, not autonomous creatures who are the source of their own meaning and perfection." Persons are "free, reasonable, and therefore responsible beings with a basic drive to question in order to know;" further, "[o]ur capacity for reasonable choosing and loving is what allows us to participate in a shared moral life, an order common to us all."[74]

We have encountered attribution of this radically autonomous, "unencumbered self" to liberalism in the irresponsibility critique of rights (in Chapter 3) and will see it again in civic republican critiques of rights (in

Chapter 7). Here we respond to the civil society–revivalist critique. First, the report sets up false dichotomies between autonomous beings and social beings, as well as between autonomy and responsibility. A liberal commitment to autonomy does not entail a commitment to atomism, or to the idea that persons can or do exist independently of a web of social relations or influences.[75] Our conception of liberal autonomy is compatible with feminist ideas of "relational autonomy," which recognize, as Jennifer Nedelsky puts it, that "human beings become who they are . . . through the relationships in which they participate" and that "constructive relationships are necessary for autonomy to flourish throughout one's life."[76] Rawls himself speaks of the various institutions of civil society as part of the "background culture" and contends that they play a vital role in nurturing and forming citizens. His political liberalism further conceives of persons as social and situated selves, rather than unencumbered selves. It envisions citizens as "fully cooperating members of society" who are capable of respecting and exercising, not merely the rights, but also the duties, of citizenship.[77]

Second, *A Call to Civil Society* reduces a Rawlsian form of liberalism to an "expressive individualism," and perhaps even to a subjective moral relativism.[78] But recognizing, as Rawls does, that "reasonable moral pluralism" concerning comprehensive moral views is a fact of life in a modern constitutional democracy[79] does not entail such views. Political liberalism would part company with moral revivalists who propose to ground a "common moral life" in the rediscovery of "the existence of transmittable moral truth," a process in which "vigorous communities of faith" are to play a "crucial role" in discovering the "conditions of human flourishing."[80] Nonetheless, Rawls posits that persons with differing comprehensive moral views can reach an overlapping consensus concerning a political conception of justice and, on that basis, endorse fair terms of social cooperation on the basis of mutual respect and trust.[81]

Third, political liberalism's conception of the person does not preclude government from fostering certain "conditions of human flourishing."[82] To the contrary, we argue in Chapters 5 and 6, political liberalism supports a formative project of fostering the capacities of citizens for democratic and personal self-government. Rawls puts forward a political conception of the person with two moral powers: a capacity for a conception of justice and a capacity for a conception of the good.[83] Like Rawls, we express such a project in the language of securing the preconditions for the development and exercise of these two moral powers rather than in the language of human flourishing.[84]

Political liberalism's conception of "reasonable pluralism" differs significantly from the conception of pluralism advanced by moral revivalists. *A Call to Civil Society* states that "pluralism is a fact and freedom is a birthright" but intimates that moral disagreement may largely be overcome through recourse to reason and moral truths. We need "moral truths" in addition to "civic truths," the report states, because the latter "are largely constitutional and procedural, [and] they do not tell us [as the former do] how to pursue happiness or how to live a good life." It acknowledges the likelihood of continuing moral disagreement, but mainly on the ground that "our access to truth is imperfect," not because reasonable moral disagreement is inevitable or desirable in a pluralistic society.[85] This moral revivalist view differs from political liberalism's application of toleration to philosophy itself—which entails the renunciation of seeking the "whole truth" in politics. It also differs from leading accounts of deliberative democracy, which attribute such disagreement not only to "incomplete understanding" (similar to imperfect access to truth), but also to "incompatible values" and "scarcity of resources."[86] And it differs from Michael Sandel's civic republican conception of a process more "clamorous" than "consensual," one that suggests ways of conducting political argument, not transcending it.[87] Notably, Galston, a prominent civic revivalist, advances a conception of liberal pluralism—inspired by Isaiah Berlin's recognition of the inevitability of value pluralism—that seems in tension with this moral revivalist quest for moral truths.[88]

Does the Revivalist Focus on the Family Focus on the Right Problems or Best Solutions?

The family features as "first and most basic" among the seedbeds of virtue in civil society–revivalists' inventory of civil society, and so the endangered state or crisis of America's families prompts great concern.[89] *A Call to Civil Society* diagnoses "the steady break-up of the married couple child-raising unit as the leading propeller of our overall social deterioration and the necessary starting point for any strategy aimed at recovery."[90] Civil and moral revivalists share the conviction that shoring up the "intact," two-parent, marital family and reversing the "trend of family fragmentation"—through divorce and single-parent (mostly fatherless) families—are crucial.[91] A subsidiary claim is that the other institutions of civil society on which the family depends are also failing and that we face a fraying "moral fabric" and a weakened "social ecology."[92]

Family form is of paramount concern to civil society–revivalists because it serves as a proxy for the capacity of families to be "crucial sites for shaping character and virtue."[93] They pay less attention to other factors that shape the capacity of families to carry out what Rawls calls the task of social reproduction, that is, "the raising of and caring for children, ensuring their moral development and education into the wider culture," so that, as citizens, they "have a sense of justice and the political virtues that support political and social institutions."[94] We question whether the revivalists have: adequately assessed the impact of women's changing social and economic roles upon families' roles as seedbeds; sufficiently reckoned with feminist arguments that injustice and inequality within the traditional family hinder families as schools for citizenship; overlooked that promoting equality within marriage might strengthen families; and neglected the fact that diverse forms of family can effectively perform the functions of families.

The Impact of Women's Changing Social and Economic Roles   Discourse on reviving civil society often recognizes that women, particularly mothers, have done the heavy lifting when it comes to moral education of children and preparation of them for citizenship, not only within the family but also through volunteer work in their communities.[95] For much of U.S. history, women's special role as cultivators of civic virtue has coincided with their civic, legal, and social inequality. Tocqueville wrote: "There have never been free societies without mores, and . . . it is woman who shapes those mores. Therefore everything which has a bearing on the status of women . . . is . . . of great political importance." He noted that girls in America are raised with a strong sense of confidence and independence and yet, "[i]n America a woman loses her independence forever in the bonds of matrimony." He also observed that the "American woman is never allowed to leave the quiet sphere of domestic duties."[96]

On Tocqueville's view, women's loss of independence, together with this vision of women and men as having separate spheres and duties, reflected a correct understanding of "democratic equality." This separation of functions allowed the "great work of society" to be "better performed." By contrast, in Europe, "there are people who . . . attribute the same functions to both [sexes], impose the same duties, and grant the same rights," and "have them share everything—work, pleasure, public affairs." This, Tocqueville asserted, is "the sort of equality forced on both sexes" that "degrades them both" and makes "so coarse a jumble of nature's works," producing "nothing but feeble men and unseemly women." Americans have never supposed that "democratic principles should undermine the husband's authority" within the family. This conception of "equal regard" for the different rights and duties of man and woman, Tocqueville concluded, expresses "the true conception of democratic process."[97] With this conception of "democratic equality," Tocqueville explained why "the gradual progress of equality" need not disturb the "great inequality between man and woman which has up till now seemed based on the eternal foundations of nature."[98] His observations illuminate what his feminist interpreters have called the "separate spheres paradox": women shape public life by accepting responsibility for generating civic virtue in the private sphere, so that their "political power derives from their political exclusion."[99]

If prior conceptions of civic virtue assumed sex inequality as part of the natural, social, and legal order, do contemporary conceptions adequately assess how to cultivate civic virtue in an era when constitutional and public norms have repudiated such inequality? And, even in an era of formal equality, do families require role differentiation between the sexes in order to serve as schools for citizenship?

Jean Bethke Elshtain is a prominent, thoughtful civil society–revivalist who acknowledges Tocqueville's analysis of sex roles and democratic equality, relating it to "our own continuing turmoil over what democratic and egalitarian relations between the sexes require." If women "go forth into the world of the economy and polity," just like men, she wonders, what happens to the "domestic hearth"? Egalitarian feminists argue that men should "relent somewhat on their professional commitments and spend more time at home, helping women tend to the smaller world of children, domesticity, and neighborhood and community." "It is a nice theory," Elshtain opines, but one that practice does not support. The upshot, she continues, is: "No one is any longer charged with the singular tasks that Tocqueville had assigned to women: civic and ethical formation within an enlarged domestic sphere." Instead, men and women work longer and harder outside the home, with "no time for family and community." Observing that Tocqueville viewed civil society—particularly the home—as playing a critical role in curbing the American tendencies toward individualism and materialism and restraining equality's excesses, Elshtain worries about the social costs of "unchecked pursuit of egalitarian principles."[100]

Unlike Elshtain, some proponents of focusing on the family as a way of restoring civic virtue embrace a more egalitarian conception. We believe that this is a more defensible approach. Consider the report, *Better Together,* issued by a group directed by Putnam (and including then-state senator Barack Obama), which focuses on strategies for rebuilding social capital. It also includes a then/now story about women's roles: "The movement of women into paid employment has dramatically affected both their lives and the patterns of family and community care. . . . [J]oining the paid workforce places new strains on these women's time, and by extension on the families and community organizations that traditionally have relied on unpaid female labor."[101] The report urges solutions that enlist employers and government to build social capital in families and neighborhoods in ways that recognize these new patterns. It emphatically rejects equating reinvigorating American civic life with an "exercise in nostalgia": "[T]here is little reason to believe that families will, or should, return to the domestic patterns of the 1950s, which drove many women to despair and gave rise to what Betty Friedan labeled 'the problem that has no name.'"[102]

Better Together valuably identifies the need for institutional restructuring—"to replace outdated institutions with new, more relevant institutions and to help existing institutions retool for the 21st century"—as a way to strengthen families' capacity to nurture children and, ultimately, inculcate civic virtue.[103] By comparison, civil society–revivalists are more modest, in exhorting employers to take steps toward more flexible working arrangements "wherever possible."[104] A more robust focus on institutions would stress that law and public policy should address the "disconnect" between the "needs of our families and the demands of our workplace."[105] Addressing that disconnect, as President Obama has expressed it, "reflects our priorities as a society—our belief that no matter what each of us does for a living, caring for our loved ones and raising the next generation is the single most important job that we have."[106] Simultaneously recognizing that these issues disproportionately affect women, while insisting that they are "not just women's issues,"[107] would strengthen civil society without simply rejecting egalitarian feminism as "nice" in theory. Along these lines, many feminist and liberal theorists have argued for greater public responsibility to support care as a basic good upon which all human beings depend.[108] They also have recognized that unequal distribution of responsibility for such care imposes costs on women and burdens their equal participation in society.

The Problem of Injustice within the Family   Thus, when civil society–revivalists focus upon the family as the primary seedbed of virtue, they do not focus enough on the historic problem of inequality within the family and the contemporary vestiges of it. As Mansbridge put it: "Among women, the experience of unequal power is as universal as the experience of connection."[109] How, Susan Moller Okin asked, can the family serve as a school for citizenship (rather than, as John Stuart Mill put it, a "school for despotism") if it is unjust? Okin focused both on problems of violence and domination and on women's disproportionate responsibility for childrearing and household work.[110] A characteristic feature of women's experience in the family, feminists argue, has been care at the expense of self.[111]

From the standpoint of such feminist critiques, revivalists give insufficient attention to the problem of unequal power in civil society and the consequences for women's own self-constitution and status as free and equal citizens. Rights of privacy, religious freedom, and freedom of association—which revivalists assume foster civil society—may undermine women's equality by keeping the state out of the "private" realm.[112] We disagree with this line of feminist critique to the extent that it regards such a state of affairs as a necessary feature of liberalism.[113] Indeed, Okin's critique prompted Rawls to clarify that the principles of justice protect citizens in the domain of civil society, which is not a "private" space beyond their reach.[114] Nonetheless, this critique issues an important challenge to revivalists to focus upon the problems of domination and inequality in civil society and to consider the proper degree of governmental regulation to address those problems. Although we reject any wholesale insistence upon congruence between civil society and democratic values, we believe that it is justifiable for government to take measures to attempt to secure equal citizenship for women, including promoting equality in the family and other institutions of civil society (as we elaborate in Chapters 5 and 6).

The Problem of Unequal Marriages   Turning from the parent-child dimension of family life to that of adult-adult intimate bonds, civil society–revivalists' emphasis on shoring up marriage largely ignores whether promoting greater equality within marriage would strengthen families. To update a question from the *Ladies Home Journal*: "Can marriage be saved?" Or should it? Civil society–revivalists (many of whom are also active in the "marriage movement") condemn divorce and nonmarital family forms as indicia of civic and moral decline and argue for governmental measures to discourage both.[115] In recent decades, state and federal governments have undertaken such measures, aiming to promote "healthy marriage" and "responsible fatherhood" and to deter divorce and mitigate its effects on children through marital and parental education. Civil society proponents might view increases in divorce and decisions to opt out of marriage as evidence of adults selfishly putting their own happiness above the well-being of children.[116] But there is an important gender dimension here: women initiate divorce more frequently than men and are willing to divorce even though doing so often puts them in a worse economic condition. One reason, Margaret Brinig reports, is that "women, unlike men, benefit from good marriages but not from emotionally unsatisfying ones."[117] Women are more sensitive to marriage quality than men, and inequality within marriage impairs marriage quality.[118] Moreover, women's desire for a "partnership of equals" and concerns over whether men will be responsible and faithful marital partners shape their resistance to marrying and willingness to pursue motherhood apart from marriage—even as some affirm their belief in marriage as an institution.[119]

Marriage is an institution in transformation. The hierarchical model of marriage that Tocqueville believed was compatible with "democratic equality" is no longer supported by family law or constitutional law. Some civil society–revivalists do explicitly embrace equality within marriage as a guiding principle. More often, diagnoses overlook egalitarian, or peer, marriage as a promising way to address some sources of discontent within marriage.[120] Moreover, some feminist proponents of extending civil marriage to same-sex couples argue that those marriages may have transformative potential for opposite-sex marriages by calling into question assumptions about the naturalness of hierarchy and gender roles within marriage.[121]

The Problem of Family Forms   Finally, to the extent that civil society–revivalists' prescriptions for the family implicate the war over family forms, we disagree with their common assumption that civic virtue requires one family form, that of a heterosexual, two-parent, married family.[122] Often, this view rests on a premise about a necessary gender complementarity between father and mother and their distinctive contributions to parenting, such that "fatherless" families are less capable of socializing children into "responsible citizens."[123] Some prominent civil society–revivalists oppose extending civil marriage to same-sex couples because it would "require endorsement of the idea that a child does not really need a mother and a father."[124]

We support a functional approach that recognizes that diverse family forms can inculcate civic virtue, accepting *Better Together*'s premise that diverse kinds of families—"whether traditional, non-traditional, blended, or extended"—can be "incubator[s] of social capital."[125] We share Rawls's view that, while government has a legitimate concern with the functions that families perform, "no particular form of the family . . . is required by a political conception of justice so long as the family is arranged to fulfill these tasks [of social reproduction] effectively and doesn't run afoul of other political values."[126] Such a functional approach (we argue in Chapter 7) would support full parenting rights and responsibilities and access to civil marriage for gay men and lesbians. Finally, to the extent that child poverty is a reason civil society–revivalists find the rise in single-parent families troubling, such poverty is not inevitable, as Glendon's own work on the comparatively more generous family policy systems of other nations makes clear.[127]

Have Gains in Equality and Liberty Caused the Decline of Civil Society?

In some calls to revive civil society, a troubling moral accounting seems to juxtapose gains in equal citizenship and the extension of civil rights and liberties to minorities and women against losses in civic virtue, the erosion of civil society, and the emergence of serious moral, civic, or social problems. In such an accounting, the trade-off for the benefits of the civil rights movements in extending full citizenship to African-Americans, women, and other groups has been the breakdown of civil society. We will mention the work of two serious and thoughtful scholars, William A. Galston and James Q. Wilson.

Galston argues that it is a debatable question "whether the cultural revolution of the past generation has left the United States better or worse off," for "[a]lthough the civil rights movement is widely acknowledged to have righted ancient wrongs, epidemics of crime, drugs, and teenage pregnancy have exacted a fearful toll."[128] We certainly concede that the latter are serious problems. But what does the civil rights movement have to do with such problems? Galston claims that society used to have more civic virtue and a "dominant and effective" cultural consensus (namely, one that gave white Anglo-Saxon Protestant men a dominant position in society), while acknowledging that there were some unjust aspects, such as racial inequality and segregation, gender inequality within the household and workplace, and the marginal status of certain ethnic and religious groups. Thus, he grants, the civil rights movements of the 1950s and 1960s properly attacked undeniable injustice toward and exclusion of groups like African-Americans from full membership in society. For Galston, however (as noted in Chapter 2), the civil rights movements in effect opened a Pandora's Box that let loose an indiscriminate attack, in the name of equality and liberty, on all hierarchies and authority that formed part of traditional morality and cultural consensus, and that unleashed a demand for the legitimation of difference, in whatever form, with dire consequences for civil society and the polity.[129]

Similarly, in *Seedbeds of Virtue*, Wilson comments on the difficulty of reckoning up "the balance sheet of [the] sea change in the culture of liberalism." He bemoans a movement away from the traditional morality that "ordinary men and women" lived under for centuries—which included "a firm attachment to the fundamental virtues of daily life, a desire for liberty tempered by moderation, [and] a willingness to judge other people on the basis of standards they thought were universal." He writes:

> I began by recalling the familiar facts of crime, drug abuse, divorce, and illegitimacy, but it is time to recall as well what else has changed. Slavery has been abolished and segregation rolled back; mass higher education has produced a vastly more sophisticated and talented population; and women are less often the victims of a sexual double standard. Against those gains we must measure the increased tolerance of drug experimentation, the social marginalization of religious believers, the heightened skepticism about institutional authority, and a certain confusion over sexual roles.[130]

Wilson's balance sheet either represents a mixed assortment of factors or reflects a questionable etiology of decline.[131] Again, how have gains in racial and gender equality caused such problems, and indeed the decline of civil society?

In any event, Wilson's moral accounting, like Galston's, seems to make the disturbing assumption that more equality and liberty leads to less virtue, and that the trade-off for a more just and inclusive society is a regrettable sacrifice of traditional morality and cultural consensus. These troubling juxtapositions and accountings appear to manifest ambivalence about diversity and the value of individual autonomy,[132] as well as anxiety about the possibility of finding a basis for social stability without moral consensus and hierarchical authority.

Have these changes brought about a decline in civic virtue and an erosion of civil society? Narratives of an earlier time of greater virtue are common in the calls to renew civil society; so, too, is a narrative of progress. But it is problematic to look backwards for a time when virtue was more abundant, for the history of America includes unjust, shameful exclusion of categories of persons from citizenship and full membership in society. Citizenship scholar Rogers Smith challenges the typical narrative of progress that commences with Tocqueville's observations of American society as "shaped by the unusually free and egalitarian ideas and material conditions that prevailed at its founding." This narrative views "[i]lliberal, undemocratic beliefs and practices" along the way, not as essential to American understandings of citizenship and civic ideals, but as "expressions of ignorance and prejudice, destined to marginality by their lack of rational defenses." Smith counters that the "Tocquevillian story" captures important truths, but is too narrow. A more complete account would recognize America's multiple political traditions, which include the powerful hold of "ascriptive forms of Americanism" (such as the unequal status of women, racial minorities, Native Americans, and various immigrant populations) side by side with liberalism and republicanism.[133] Smith demonstrates that the history of U.S. citizenship laws is one "shot through with forms of second-class citizenship, denying personal liberties and opportunities for political participation to most of the adult population on the basis of race, ethnicity, gender, and even religion," reflecting the view of American civic identity that "true Americans were native-born men with Anglo-Saxon ancestors."[134]

There is, however, another type of moral accounting in the discourse about civil society that is less problematic than those implicit in Galston and Wilson, and that may get at part of what concerns them. On this accounting, the trade-off for a more inclusive definition of citizenship (with the content supplied, increasingly, by national norms) is a decline in social solidarity and trust and the loss of civil society, understood as the classical idea of face-to-face interactions in a small republic with a homogeneous people. In *The Idea of Civil Society*, Adam Seligman argues that the basis for membership in society has changed from belonging to particular associations to inclusion in the more universal category of the autonomous, rights-bearing citizen. America has served throughout the world as the "paradigm" of a "truly 'civil society'" precisely because of its idea of moral personhood as the basis for political community and its history of the gradual realization of the category of universal citizenship. (This view should be read against Smith's less benign view of the unfolding dynamic.) Yet, the "paradox of modern society" is that the "very universalization of trust in citizenship . . . undermines th[e] concrete mutuality and shared components of the moral community upon which trust is based. Hence the call for a return to civil society."[135] The problem, Seligman contends, is that universal citizenship affords an inadequate foundation for social solidarity and trust because it is abstract and lacks the face-to-face interactions of the classical idea of civil society. Moreover, although liberal and progressive nationalists attempt to find a model of American citizenship that is not only inclusive but also strong, some scholars contend that inclusive citizenship is inevitably a weak bond as compared with competing stronger membership bonds.[136]

This type of moral accounting usefully identifies the problem of establishing social solidarity and trust amidst difference. What is the glue that holds society together and motivates persons to cooperate? Can there be social solidarity or cooperation in a heterogeneous, diverse society? We will mention three promising paths. First, using as a point of departure the American ideal "E Pluribus Unum" (out of many, one), social capital theorist Putnam argues that "[o]ne of the most important challenges facing modern societies" is "the increase in ethnic and social heterogeneity," which may, in the short term, foster social isolation rather than cooperation and community. Yet this offers "one of our most significant opportunities" for renewing America's "historical identity as a nation of immigrants": by forging "shared identities across ethnic boundaries," generating not only bonding but also bridging social capital.[137] Second, acknowledging the demise of the "informal cultural establishment of the beliefs and mores of white Anglo-Saxon Protestants" and the rise of identity politics, Galston states that "it is clear that no such establishment can or should serve as the basis of national unity."[138] Rather, he suggests, "[t]he alternative to a common culture would seem to be a revitalized understanding of political unity" in the form of a "Constitutional faith."[139] Further, given a highly diverse society, civic education, in which tolerance is a core attribute of citizenship, helps to ensure that "the convictions, competencies, and virtues required for liberal citizenship are widely shared."[140]

Finally, Rawls's political liberalism aims to promote social cooperation on the basis of mutual respect and trust in circumstances of political inclusiveness and moral disagreement. It posits that reasonable pluralism is a permanent feature of a constitutional democracy such as our own, and that achieving uniformity concerning a conception of the good life as the basis of social and political unity is not possible without the use of intolerably oppressive state power.[141] Political liberalism conceives principles of a political conception of justice as establishing fair terms of social cooperation on the basis of mutual respect and trust and even the basis for civic friendship.[142] As we explain later, it assumes that the institutions of civil society will play a formative role in shaping persons to engage in social cooperation (subject to the principles of justice).

Would a Revitalized Civil Society Support Democratic Self-Government or Supplant It?

Is a vital civil society a precondition for vigorous democratic self-government or an alternative to it? Remarkably, many civil society–revivalists, notwithstanding their worries about the decline of virtue and the erosion of trust in our basic political institutions, are ambivalent about the value of government. For all their rhetoric about civil society preparing people for citizenship and democratic self-government, many civil society–revivalists hope that a revived civil society would supplant government (especially the national government) to the extent that the institutions of civil society would reclaim certain functions now performed by government.[143] The reinvigoration of civil society thus would entail the withering away of the state or in any event the shrinking of the national government. (*A Call to Civil Society,* for example, considers "the structures of participatory local government," though not those of the national government, to be among the seedbeds of virtue.[144])

Moral revivalists, in particular, seem to wish to supplant the national government with civil society. An instructive example is Eberly's articulation of the progress made by conservatives in taming a "seemingly untamable welfare state" and defeating the "progressive view" that a "top-down" welfare state could address the "problems of community and human beings." While conservatives have not persuaded the public to abolish the national government, they have succeeded in shifting the focus to enlisting voluntary associations—in particular, "private, faith-based charities"—to address social problems. Eberly insists on the distinctive role of civil society in generating values and fostering moral renewal. Accepting some government as a necessary evil (while trying to "build down bad government"), this approach seeks to "build up the good society" through "replacing more and more of the public sector with a viable social sector." He invokes Tocqueville as describing a people "who thought and acted as though most of the society's work was to be done through voluntary associations."[145]

Civil society–revivalists—both civic and moral—advocate a greater role for civil society in public policy by greater use of public-private partnerships. They also embrace the principle of "subsidiarity"—that the smallest possible unit should be allowed to address a problem and a larger unit should step in to provide aid only if the smaller unit otherwise would fail.[146] Both Republican and Democratic presidents argue that these partnerships are vital, although there are ongoing constitutional concerns about the separation of church and state when governmental funds pay for services with a pervasively religious message.[147] The constitutional liberalism we advance does not rule such partnerships out of bounds. However, while the rhetoric of "compassionate conservatives" is to "unleash" or set free "armies of compassion"—implying that government should fund religious groups as they serve with their distinct religious values and methods—we believe a better model is "harnessing" such armies so that government funds them to pursue public purposes in ways consistent with important public and constitutional values.[148] Despite worries that partnerships with government would destroy the very religious values that make religious groups effective, or

that such groups would become mere "vendors" of governmental programs, religious organizations' actual experience should assuage those
fears.[149] Furthermore, some of the most passionate proponents of these
partnerships caution against the inference that civil society can address
these various social problems without substantial governmental help.[150]

The aspiration that civil society supplant government may belie the
revivalists' claims that civil society is a school for citizenship and democratic self-government. They invoke Tocqueville for such claims. But
Tocqueville observed that participation in "politics" spreads "a general
habit and taste for association," such that "one may think of political
associations as great free schools to which all citizens come to be taught
the general theory of association."[151] In effect, "politics precedes civil
society."[152] Moreover, Tocqueville concluded that the progress of the
idea of equality led inevitably to the concentration of political power in
a single, centralized power, even as he praised political associations as
buffers against such power. He did not envision that civil society alone
could provide all the necessary self-government for the nation or carry
out the functions best suited to a national government.[153]

We should resist taking a "flight from the political," and the related
idea that it is possible to choose civil society alone and escape the power
and coercion of the state.[154] Instead, as Michael Walzer argues, "the
state . . . is unlike all the other associations. It both frames civil society
and occupies space within it. It fixes the boundary conditions and the
basic rules of all associational activity (including political activity)."[155]
Further, while we concur with civil society–revivalists that the institutions of civil society generate and help to maintain values and virtues,[156]
we resist any suggestion that these institutions are the *only* sites that can
generate values and virtues. Finally, we reject the argument that when
government tries to promote public values or to inculcate civic virtues, it
fails to respect pluralism and tramples on the value-generating function
of civil society (a topic we take up more fully in Chapters 5 and 6). Civil
society should support democratic self-government, not supplant it.

The Roles and Regulation of Civil Society within Constitutional Liberalism

We conclude with an outline of the place of associations within our constitutional liberalism, building upon Rawls's political liberalism. Rawls
argues that associations underwrite a stable constitutional democracy

and foster the primary good of self-respect,[157] even as the principles of justice shape associational life. Political liberalism distinguishes between the domain of the political and the domain of civil society, yet it posits a relationship of mutual support, or of reciprocally constituting domains. What implications does this distinction, as well as this relationship, have for the roles and regulation of civil society in a formative project of securing the preconditions for democratic and personal self-government?

The Place of Associations in Underwriting a Stable Constitutional Democracy

Rawls famously argues that it is possible to have a stable political order that rests upon a shared political conception of justice, rather than a shared comprehensive doctrine of the good, such as a religious view. He argues that, given the "fact of reasonable pluralism, constitutional democracy must have political and social institutions that effectively lead its citizens to acquire the appropriate sense of justice as they grow up and take part in society."[158] He maintains that a political conception of justice can be supported by an "overlapping consensus of reasonable comprehensive doctrines." Rawls envisions civil society as featuring in this supporting role:

> Comprehensive doctrines of all kinds—religious, philosophical, and moral—belong to what we may call the "background culture" of civil society. This is the culture of the social, not of the political. It is the culture of daily life, of its many associations: churches and universities, learned and scientific societies, and clubs and teams, to mention a few. In a democratic society there is a tradition of democratic thought, the content of which is at least familiar and intelligible to the educated common sense of citizens generally. Society's main institutions, and their accepted forms of interpretation, are seen as a fund of implicitly shared ideas and principles.[159]

Thus, the "background culture" of civil society with its many associations undergirds a shared political conception of justice. Moreover, Rawls speaks of the "prior and fundamental role" of the "background institutions of civil society" in "establishing a social world within which alone we can develop with care, nurture, and education, and no little good fortune, into free and equal citizens."[160] We shall focus on the tensions inherent in the idea that civil society supports the political order but is distinct from it.

Rawls does not insist upon complete congruence between the values and virtues of the political order and those of civil society. Indeed, he observes that they are not identical and he envisions a division of labor between government and civil society, with each having a set of principles and values appropriate to it.[161] Still, he posits some continuity—or congruence—between the realm of civil society and the political realm, with the former being a "fund of implicitly shared ideas and principles" that make political stability possible. Rawls writes: "[A] freestanding political conception [of justice] does not . . . say that political values are separate from, or discontinuous with, other values." Rather, "citizens themselves . . . view the political conception *as derived from, or congruent with, or at least not in conflict with,* their other values."[162] In other words, there is what Rosenblum describes as a "liberal expectancy" of some congruence.[163] Here we see affinity between Rawls's idea of the place of associations in underwriting constitutional democracy and claims of proponents of civil society that the institutions of civil society are seedbeds of virtue that foster the capacities for democratic self-government.

Political liberalism can harbor such a liberal expectancy because it does not leave the shape of civil society to chance. It holds that a political conception of justice should shape the social world, including the background culture of civil society, so that it will foster free and equal citizenship and support for the political conception of justice. Rawls urges us to think of the principles of justice as "designed to form the social world in which our character and our conception of ourselves as persons, as well as our comprehensive views and their conceptions of the good, are first acquired, and in which our moral powers must be realized, if they are to be realized at all."[164] In a sense, the political domain and the domain of the social world (including civil society) are mutually constituting, but the principles of justice constrain the form the social world may take.

There is a tension between affirming separate domains of the political and of civil society and nevertheless insisting upon the political conception of justice's need to shape the domain of civil society. On the one hand, Rawls argues that associations, such as churches and universities, require principles "plainly more suitable" for their own shared aims and purposes than the principles of justice. On the other hand, he states: "[B]ecause churches and universities are associations within the basic structure, they must adjust to the requirements that this structure imposes in order to establish background justice." For example, these associations "may be restricted . . . by what is necessary to maintain the basic equal liberties (including liberty of conscience) and fair equality of opportunity."[165] (We develop this idea of "mutual adjustment" of basic liberties in Chapter 6.) As Rawls elaborates:

A domain so-called, or a sphere of life, is not, then, something already given apart from political conceptions of justice. A domain is not a kind of space, or place, but rather is simply the result, or upshot, of how the principles of political justice are applied, directly to the basic structure and indirectly to the associations within it.[166]

Rawls offers the example of how principles of justice should shape the family and suggests that a similar analysis would apply to associations. It is a "misconception" to think that the principles of justice "do not apply to the family and hence those principles do not secure equal justice for women and their children." He identifies as one possible source of this misconception the idea that "[t]he principles of political justice are to apply directly to [the basic structure of society], but are not to apply directly to the internal life of the many associations within it, the family among them." The question of how the principles of justice apply to society's basic institutions is "not peculiar" to families, he observes; it "arises in regard to all associations, whether they be churches or universities, professional or scientific associations, business firms or labor unions." For example, it is "[not] desirable, or consistent with liberty of conscience or freedom of association," that the principles of political justice would apply directly to the internal life of churches, just as "[w]e wouldn't want political principles of justice—including principles of distributive justice—to apply directly to the internal life of the family."[167]

Thus, political liberalism does not insist upon complete congruence between principles of political justice and the "internal life" of associations. At the same time, those principles "protect the rights and liberties" of persons even when they are members of associations, and accordingly place certain constraints on associational life. Similarly, "political principles do not apply directly to [the family's] internal life, but they do impose essential constraints on the family as an institution and so guarantee the basic rights and liberties, and the freedom and opportunities, of all its members."[168] Thus, the state to some degree should regulate civil society in order to secure the status of free and equal citizenship for all.

The Place of Associations in Fostering Self-Respect

In political liberalism, associations and associative ties also help members of society to realize the primary good of self-respect. This function of associations relates particularly to aiding persons' development of their capacity to form, act on, and revise a conception of a good life (or their capacity for personal self-government). As Rawls wrote in *A Theory of Justice:*

> It normally suffices [to provide a basis of self-respect] that for each person there is some association (one or more) to which he belongs and within which the activities that are rational for him are publicly affirmed by others. In this way we acquire a sense that what we do in everyday life is worthwhile. Moreover, associative ties . . . tend to reduce the likelihood of failure and to provide support against the sense of self-doubt when mishaps occur. To be sure, men have varying capacities and abilities, and what seems interesting and challenging to some will not seem so to others. Yet in a well-ordered society anyway, there are a variety of communities and associations, and the members of each have their own ideals appropriately matched to their aspirations and talents. . . . What counts is that the internal life of these associations is suitably adjusted to the abilities and wants of those belonging to them, and provides a secure basis for the sense of worth of their members.[169]

Under what conditions will associational life foster self-respect? Let us recall that political liberalism views the political domain and the domain of the background culture of civil society as mutually supporting, and that the principles of justice specify that persons should be accorded the "social bases of self-respect," such as "the equal basic rights and liberties, the fair value of the political liberties and fair equality of opportunity."[170] In other words, the political conception of justice shapes the domain of the background culture of civil society by ensuring that persons within civil society are afforded these social bases of self-respect, including these basic liberties. As noted previously, in explaining the idea of distinct domains, Rawls stresses that "[t]he principles defining the equal basic liberties and opportunities of citizens always hold in and through all so-called domains." As explored more fully in Chapter 5, responding to feminist concern about injustice within families, Rawls clarifies: "The equal rights of women and the basic rights of their children as future citizens are inalienable and protect them wherever they are. Gender distinctions limiting those rights and liberties are excluded."[171] Rawls's clarification applies to associations as well. Thus, to the extent that feminists might criticize political liberalism for ignoring that some associations may hinder, rather than facilitate, women's acquiring the good of self-respect, political liberalism's response would be that the principles of justice shape—and put constraints upon—the background culture of civil society in ways that seek to facilitate persons acquiring self-respect.

Associations also afford a space in which persons may find the self-respect denied them in society's basic institutions. Through membership in associations, citizens may articulate dissenting views about what justice requires and work for change. Political liberalism acknowledges this important transformative aspect of associational life.[172] Our own view of the place of associations recognizes that civil society contributes to liberal democracy by affording oppositional space to "enclaves of protected discourse and action," which allow social actors to seek to correct injustices by bringing about change.[173] Such change may transform the norms and practices of associations, and it may spur passage of new laws and adoption of new interpretations of the Constitution.[174] By doing so, participation in associations may promote self-respect as well as underwrite a stable constitutional democracy.

Conclusion

In this chapter, we have examined the claim by proponents of reviving civil society that liberalism, because of its commitment to neutrality and its preoccupation with the individual's rights against the government, cannot generate or sustain the civic virtues needed to preserve ordered liberty in a liberal democracy. They assert that the realm of civil society is an indispensable—yet neglected—site for the cultivation of those virtues and that certain forms of rights—and rights talk—have eroded the institutions of civil society. In assessing those charges, we have raised some questions for proponents of reviving civil society as a cure for many of our nation's political, civic, and moral ills. Through grappling with those questions, we have explained that our constitutional liberalism shares common ground with civil society–revivalists on the importance of civil society in carrying out a formative project. Moreover, we have sketched our own approach to the roles and regulation of civil society within our morally pluralistic constitutional democracy. We have suggested that civil society is at least as important for securing deliberative autonomy as for promoting deliberative democracy. In the next two chapters, we deepen our examination of the sharing and division of labor between civil society and government for fostering persons' capacities for democratic and personal self-government and show how our constitutional liberalism reckons with conflicts between them.

CHAPTER FIVE

Government's Role in Promoting Civic Virtues

We now turn from civil society's role in cultivating "seed-beds of virtue" to government's role in a formative project of promoting civic virtues, focusing on the shared authority of parents and government in fostering capacities for democratic and personal self-government. We take up the relationships among toleration, autonomy, and this governmental formative project. Discontent with liberal toleration often goes hand in hand with attraction to perfectionist conceptions of the responsibility of government to undertake a formative project of shaping or steering citizens pursuant to a vision of human virtue, goods, or excellence.

Liberal toleration elicits discontent both for being too empty and too robust. Toleration is too empty, some critics charge, because it requires only that government leave persons alone with respect to certain beliefs or conduct, not that other citizens respect or appreciate those persons, beliefs, or conduct. Justice Antonin Scalia's dissent in *Romer v. Evans* illustrates such emptiness (though with approval): so long as government refrains from the use of the criminal law against a disfavored but tolerated minority (such as gay men and lesbians), it may express citizens' moral disapprobation of and hostility toward that minority's conduct through such means as the denial of civil rights.[1]

Other critics of liberal toleration charge that it is too robust because it affords persons too much freedom from government's efforts to cultivate the virtues needed for living good lives. Precisely because prominent liberal conceptions of toleration seek to go beyond empty toleration to respect, they lead to an overly restricted conception of government's proper business. The basic claim of a number of feminist, liberal, and civic republican perfectionist critics is that leaving persons alone is not sufficient to secure the capacities, qualities of character, or virtues necessary for self-government. ("Perfectionism" is the term sometimes given to the idea that government should actively help citizens to live good and valuable lives.[2])

These opposing criticisms stem from competing conceptions of toleration, which we call "empty toleration" and "toleration as respect."[3] Toleration as respect is the more attractive account as a matter of both political morality and constitutional law. It aims to secure more than pale civility or grudging toleration by appealing to the protection of such goods as autonomy and diversity and through seeking to assure mutual respect and civility among citizens. In response to charges that toleration as respect is too robust, we argue that it does not bar government's efforts to foster citizens' capacities for democratic and personal self-government and to promote public values. We use the example of education of children to illustrate the shared jurisdiction of government and families in fostering those capacities. Our constitutional liberalism supports such a formative project.

A Formative Project for Constitutional Liberalism

Fostering Self-Government

Constitution Day is observed each year in the United States on or about September 17, the date of the signing of the Constitution by the delegates to the Constitutional Convention in 1787. Federal law requires that every educational institution receiving federal funds hold an educational program concerning the Constitution every year. The law does not *require* every educational institution to hold such a program; instead, it *conditions* receipt of federal funds upon doing so.

On Constitution Day in 2011, Kent Greenfield published an op-ed piece in the *New York Times* arguing that, "ironically, Constitution Day is probably unconstitutional."[4] First, it imposes an "unconstitutional condition" by making funding conditional upon a waiver of constitutional rights, namely, the right not to applaud the Constitution. Second, it coerces "mandatory patriotism," like a compulsory flag salute, declared unconstitutional in *West Virginia Board of Education v. Barnette* (1943).[5] Greenfield suggests that Constitution Day forces us to celebrate rather than to criticize the Constitution. Neither argument is sound.

First, Constitution Day does not impose mandatory patriotism. No educational institution is compelled to *celebrate* the Constitution or to applaud any particular interpretation of it. An institution would satisfy the federal law by holding a program with a Tea Party Patriot celebrating the original Constitution and condemning twenty-first-century liberal and progressive constitutional practice as unconstitutional—or by having a program criticizing the original Constitution and defending twenty-first-century liberal and progressive constitutional practice as better realizing the ends proclaimed in the Preamble. An institution would satisfy the law if, like Sanford Levinson, its program condemned the Constitution as undemocratic and called for a new Constitutional Convention instead of praising our existing Constitution.[6] Thus, the battle between the Tea Party Patriots and progressives over what to teach about the Constitution on Constitution Day made national headlines.[7] Our point here bears on our argument below that government may try to encourage the liberal virtue of toleration of gays and lesbians through instruction that falls short of compulsory indoctrination.

Second, the argument that Constitution Day imposes an unconstitutional condition would not prevail before the Supreme Court, which has gutted that doctrine in favor of the view that if you want the government's money, you do the government's bidding. You take the bitter with the sweet.[8] While we do not wholly endorse this view, we do argue that the government may encourage, though not compel, individuals and institutions to do good things, including learning about the Constitution, the better to understand and argue about its commitments and to seek to redeem its promises. This bears on our argument in Chapter 6 that government may make funding or other benefits conditional upon not discriminating on the basis of race, sex, or sexual orientation, in order to attempt to secure equal citizenship for all.

The recent Supreme Court has conceived the Constitution merely as a charter of *negative liberties,* protecting people from government but not imposing affirmative obligations upon government to pursue positive benefits. By contrast, we conceive the Constitution also as a charter of *positive benefits:* an instrument for pursuing good things like the ends proclaimed in the Preamble, for which We the People ordained and established the Constitution.[9] The Constitution does not merely protect us from government, notwithstanding the Court and the Tea Party. It constitutes us as a people and as citizens. Despite Madison's famous strategy in *The Federalist* No. 51—"supplying . . . the defect of better motives" by relying upon checks and balances and making "[a]mbition . . . counteract ambition"[10]—the realization of the Constitution's ends and the very maintenance of the constitutional order requires a formative project of cultivating civic virtues in responsible citizens.[11] Such a formative project, with such positive benefits, is necessary to secure ordered liberty.

The U.S. Constitution supports government's role in fostering persons' capacities for democratic and personal self-government. Families and other institutions of civil society also have formative roles. Democratic and personal self-government capture two significant dimensions of self-government protected in the American constitutional order. Our schematic draws on political liberalism, which (as elaborated by John Rawls) posits that free and equal citizens have two moral powers pertaining to self-government: the capacity for a conception of justice and the capacity for a conception of the good.[12] Democratic self-government connotes "deliberative democracy" and implicates a person's capacity to deliberate about his or her conception of justice, including engaging in various forms of political activity and discussion. Personal self-government connotes "deliberative autonomy," and implicates a person's capacity to deliberate about his or her conception of the good, including self-determination and personal decision making with respect to forming, acting on, and revising a conception of a good life.

Our formative project for constitutional liberalism is analogous to Rawls's political liberalism in maintaining that government should not embrace any comprehensive moral doctrine. Nor should government attempt to secure agreement upon an orthodoxy concerning the best way of life. Rawls generalizes the principle of religious toleration to apply to reasonable conceptions of the good, leaving it to citizens themselves to settle questions of religion, philosophy, and morality in accord with views they freely affirm. Instead, in light of the "fact of reasonable pluralism" and "the fact of oppression," we should seek agreement upon a political conception of justice, which is to establish fair terms of social cooperation among citizens on the basis of mutual respect and trust. The basis of social and political unity should not be a comprehensive moral doctrine that could not be endorsed generally by citizens, but principles of constitutional government that all citizens, whatever their comprehensive views, can reasonably be expected to endorse.[13]

Does Political Liberalism Rule out a "Formative Project" of Promoting Self-Government?

Does renouncing a government-fostered comprehensive moral doctrine mean that government may not play any role in shaping citizens and promoting values? Perfectionist civic republican Michael Sandel contends that liberalism, in contrast to civic republicanism, lacks the resources to carry out a "formative politics" of shaping persons into self-governing citizens.[14] Similarly, perfectionist liberal critics such as Joseph Raz depart from such liberalism because of its supposed requirement of "neutrality" and narrow conception of government's role in shaping citizens and promoting values. They charge that government should promote the well-being of its citizens.[15] Feminist critics fault political liberalism for its supposed inattention to the preconditions for women's self-government as well as the supposed limits that it places upon using government to secure equality for women. Political liberalism, feminist Susan Moller Okin claims, puts liberal toleration squarely in conflict with sex equality, for it requires toleration of comprehensive moral doctrines (such as those of religious fundamentalists) that espouse or require a sexist division of labor between women and men.[16]

The gap between political liberalism and its critics as to government's authority to foster citizens' capacities for self-government is not as great as is commonly assumed. Our constitutional liberal formative project builds upon the common ground between political liberalism and its perfectionist critics. First, it recognizes a proper role for government in helping to develop the moral powers (or capacities) of citizens, to prepare them for self-governing citizenship. Indeed, what separates perfectionism from political liberalism is that perfectionists appeal to furthering human goods, while political liberals generally appeal to fostering the preconditions for free and equal citizenship and the capacities for democratic and personal self-government.[17] But there is unquestionable overlap here.

Second, constitutional liberalism would support governmental persuasion in the form of promoting political (or public) values such as the equal citizenship of women and discouraging beliefs or conduct that undermine such values. Contrary to Sandel's stark dichotomy between liberalism and republicanism, constitutional liberalism and republicanism are compatible with respect to the idea that citizens should have political virtues and be willing to take part in public life. Moreover, society may affirm the superiority of certain forms of moral character and affirm moral virtues linked to self-government and responsible citizenship, for example, the virtues of tolerance, civility, reciprocity, and cooperation. The key distinction with respect to appropriate and inappropriate governmental persuasion is between promoting virtues (or values) characterizing the ideal of the good citizen and promoting virtues (or values) characterizing ways of life belonging to particular comprehensive moral doctrines.[18] Subject to this limit, constitutional liberalism would allow government to encourage compliance with law, acceptance of the principles of justice and political virtues, and development of citizens' capacities for self-government.

Although constitutional liberalism is not coextensive with feminist perfectionism, many feminist goals can be pursued within a constitutional liberal framework through the appeal to the political value of equal citizenship. Government need not be neutral as between the equality of women and their subordination. Liberal toleration does not extend to unreasonable comprehensive moral doctrines, for example, those that seek to use government to deny or violate the basic rights and liberties of women or other groups of citizens.[19] Government may use coercion to secure women's equal citizenship and basic liberties. Thus, antidiscrimination laws such as Title VII appropriately reach private power by limiting freedom of employers and employees to discriminate for the sake of securing the equality of citizens. Government may enlist public support for the political value of the equal citizenship of women, such as campaigns against domestic violence or employment discrimination. Indeed, invoking Rawls's statement that "[t]he same equality of the Declaration of Independence which Lincoln invoked to condemn slavery can be invoked to condemn the inequality and oppression of women," Okin suggested that political liberalism could—and should—embrace an anticaste or antisubordination principle to advance the substantive equality of women.[20] Our constitutional liberalism does embrace such a principle.

Third, the principle that government should not promote one comprehensive moral doctrine over others does not mean that it may not regulate the basic institutions of society in which personal or "private" life is lived. Political liberalism does not require that the political principles of justice directly regulate the internal life of families, but they do impose constraints upon the family. Responding to Okin, Rawls granted that his account of liberalism in A Theory of Justice paid insufficient attention to the question of justice within the family, but clarified (as we noted in Chapter 4) that "[i]f the so-called private sphere is alleged to be a space exempt from justice, then there is no such thing" within political liberalism: "The equal rights of women and the basic rights of their children as future citizens are inalienable and protect them wherever they are." Thus, the argument for toleration of reasonable moral pluralism does not entail that redressing private violence and subordination are not the proper business of government. So, too, if injustices within the family "undermine children's capacity to acquire the political virtues required of future citizens in a viable democratic society," then "the principles of justice enjoining a reasonable constitutional democratic society can plainly be invoked to reform the family."[21]

In sum, political liberalism does not bar government from undertaking a formative project of helping citizens attain the preconditions for self-government, nor does it tie government's hands from addressing private sources of injustice threatening such self-government. Our constitutional liberalism posits the responsibility of government to help persons develop their moral capacities for self-government and, in that sense, live good lives. To that extent, it is a mild form of perfectionism.

The Role of Education in Preparing Children for Citizenship and for Success in Life

Education of children is one of government's most significant formative responsibilities. Constitutional liberalism supports compulsory education of children to prepare them for responsible citizenship. The state has an immediate interest in protecting children, as "immature citizens,"[22] and facilitating their healthy development as well as a longer-term interest in preparing children to be fully participating and cooperating members of their communities and the polity. We express these ideas by referring to the dual purpose of education to foster "success in life" along with responsible citizenship (paraphrasing *Brown v. Board of Education*).

Civic education, the *National Standards for Civics and Government* declare, "is essential to the preservation and improvement of American constitutional democracy." Many state constitutions explicitly declare that education maintains the "stability of a republican form of government" and is the "safeguard of liberty."[23] Even William Galston's liberal pluralism, with its robust defense of minimal governmental regulation of civil society, recognizes that the government has a "legitimate and compelling interest in ensuring that the convictions, competences, and virtues required for liberal citizenship [such as tolerance] are widely shared." Thus, he supports a "parsimonious but vigorous system of civic education," in which teaching tolerance plays a central role.[24]

Needless to say, there is tension between pursuing the goals of preparing children to live in a diverse, morally pluralistic society, in which toleration is a virtue, and respecting the rights of parents to instruct their children in a particular way of life that rejects such "modern" virtues as toleration.[25] We illustrate this tension by examining several cases in which religious parents and students objected to school curricula or programs aimed at teaching tolerance. In resolving these controversies, it is important to remember that our constitutional order does not allocate absolute authority over children either to parents or to the state. It recognizes both the fundamental—but not absolute—rights and responsibilities of parents to direct the education of their children as well as the state's substantial—but not absolute—authority to foster the healthy development of children and to prepare them for citizenship. Such divided authority is important for securing the capacities of children for self-government and recognizing that they are "independent persons-in-the-making with their own basic interests and their own lives to lead."[26]

This divided authority bears on the issue of congruence introduced in Chapter 4. As Galston recognizes, there is no guarantee that families will "reinforce liberal democratic virtues and beliefs."[27] For this reason, many education theorists speak of schools as serving a complementary or "compensatory" role in teaching civic knowledge, skills, and virtues that children may not learn elsewhere.[28] Thus, Nancy Rosenblum contends that "incongruent families" are not "fatal to democratic education if we credit the formative effects of other institutions of civil society."[29] Indeed, to the extent that schools may be uniquely situated to carry out certain forms of civic learning, retaining this shared authority is important.

The Dual Authority of Families and Schools for Fostering Children's Capacities

How might we envision the dual authority of families and schools for fostering the capacities for self-government, in the sense of preparing children both to be good citizens and to live good, successful lives? It is tempting to posit a simple division of labor: parents teach children how to be good people and schools teach them how to be good citizens. This schematic is too neat, but there are elements of truth in it. First, as the Supreme Court put it in *Troxel v. Granville,* our constitutional order recognizes "the fundamental right of parents to make decisions concerning the care, custody, and control of their children." It quoted a famous precedent, *Pierce v. Society of Sisters:* "[t]he child is not the mere creature of the State; those who nurture him and direct his destiny have the right, coupled with the high duty, to recognize and prepare him for additional obligations."[30]

Second, it is often argued that "schools . . . bear a special and historic responsibility for the development of competent and responsible citizens."[31] The movement to establish common public schools aimed to use education to shape children from diverse ethnic backgrounds and national origins into citizens unified around a shared set of political ideals.[32] *Brown* referred to education as "the very foundation of good citizenship,"[33] and the Court subsequently has characterized the objectives of public education as the "inculcat[ion of] fundamental values necessary to the maintenance of a democratic political system."[34]

However, this division of labor between families molding the good person and schools the good citizen cannot hold. For (as we saw in Chapter 4) the idea that families play an indispensable role in forming good citizens has a long history. And schools today aim for more than preparation for citizenship. In *Brown*, the Court stated: "In these days, it is doubtful that any child may reasonably be expected to succeed in life if he is denied the opportunity of an education."[35]

The literature on civic education similarly regards education as vital not only to democracy but also to success in life generally. Indeed, a recent report by the American Enterprise Institute contrasted the historical emphasis on schools' *public* purposes in molding "republican machines" (quoting founder Benjamin Rush) to support and defend the nation with the contemporary focus on the "private purposes" of schooling to make students ready for college and career.[36] An examination of state constitutions that set out the aims of public education confirms the dual goals of preparing children for citizenship and for success in life.[37] As this literature maintains, there is considerable spillover between the skills required for these different domains.

Thus, in our constitutional order, both families and schools generate the capacities for democratic and personal self-government. Children are neither, as *Pierce* famously expressed it, "mere creatures of the state" nor, as Stephen Macedo puts it, "simply creatures of their parents." Macedo explains: "the child can rightfully be subjected to parental or public efforts to inculcate their visions of good character so long as these efforts are not repressive, and so long as the child is also presented with information about alternative ways of life." The goal is that neither parents nor the democratic community should "be allowed to confine children's options within narrow limits, or deny any child the right to pursue his or her own path in life."[38] We support this model of divided authority.[39] It is consistent with a premise that the lessons learned at home and in school may or should reinforce or complement each other.[40] Further, schools may play a compensatory or ameliorative role: some arguments for both civic and character education in schools stress that they are all the more important because families are neglecting—or even failing in—their duty to provide such education to children.[41]

This model of shared authority holds promise but runs into tensions when parental and school values conflict, and when instruction at home conflicts with inculcation of democratic values at school. We explore these tensions by analyzing the civic mission of schools along with teaching tolerance and respect for diversity as a component of that mission.

How Should Schools Carry Out Their Civic Mission?

We here sketch the civic mission of schools in instructing about rights, responsibilities, and virtues. We emphasize several themes: the role of civic education in the "preservation and improvement of American constitutional democracy"[42] and the historic role and unique capacities of schools to provide it; the aims and scope of civic education and the basic agreement between teachers and parents on what civic education children should receive; the spillover between civic education and education for "success in life"; and the emphasis upon tolerance and equality as "core" elements of civic education.[43]

The Historic Role and Unique Capacities of Schools for Carrying Out Civic Education   A basic rationale for civic education is that "[i]ndividuals do not automatically become free and responsible citizens but must be educated for citizenship." A recent consensus statement, *The Civic Mission of Schools,* finds the vision "that all education had civic purposes and every teacher was a civics teacher" reflected in the establishment, in the nineteenth century, of public schools in America. Further, "40 state constitutions . . . mention the importance of civic literacy among citizens, and 13 of [them] state that the central purpose of their educational system is to promote good citizenship, democracy and free government."[44]

Like the civil society narratives, the civic education narratives see a crisis requiring remedy: young people, like "increasing numbers of Americans," have "disengaged from civic and political institutions and from political and electoral activities such as voting and being informed about public issues." The remedy is reinvigorating the civic mission of schools: "It is crucial for the future health of our democracy that *all young people,* including those who are usually marginalized, be knowledgeable, engaged in their communities and in politics, and committed to the public good."[45]

Why are *schools* critical to carrying out civic education? The reasons are pertinent to understanding the division of labor between the institutions of civil society (and families, in particular) and public institutions (schools, in particular) for the formative responsibility of preparing children for responsible citizenship. *The Civic Mission of Schools* states: "Schools are the only institutions with the capacity and mandate to reach virtually every young person in the country. Of all institutions, schools are the most systematically and directly responsible for imparting citizen norms" and "best equipped to address the cognitive aspects of good citizenship." Another claim is that schools create a community that is a microcosm of the broader society and take on the challenge of forging unity out of diversity: "Schools have the capacity to bring together a heterogeneous population of young people—with different backgrounds, perspectives, and vocational ambitions—to instruct them in common lessons and values."[46] Moreover, the *National Standards for Civics and Government* argues that the schools' "informal curriculum"—the "governance of the school community and relationships among those within it"—"should embody the fundamental values and principles of American constitutional democracy."[47]

There is also an ameliorative argument about the civic mission of schools: "many non-school institutions that used to provide venues for young people to participate in civil and political affairs (such as political parties, unions, nonprofit associations, and activist religious denominations) have lost the capacity or will to engage young people." Moreover, while civil society–revivalists stress the civic role of families, *The Civic Mission of Schools* worries that "families may not be doing as much to encourage their children's civic involvement as in the past—partly because parents are themselves the products of recent trends in civic and political disengagement." Schools can help "reverse these trends" and have a positive impact on other institutions. Finally, proponents of civic education point to a disturbing civic empowerment gap (based on race, income, and other factors) in civic and political knowledge between the best and worst prepared students and contend that "[s]chools can address troubling *inequalities* in civic and political engagement."[48] These arguments about the unique capacities of schools for carrying out civic education are germane to the questions of homeschooling: the extent to which parents should be able to opt their children out of the school curriculum and whether the states should require home-schooled children to participate in a school curriculum about civics.

The Aims and Scope of Civic Education   Civic education aims to instruct young people in the "knowledge, skills, and virtue" vital for competent and responsible citizenship and "essential to the preservation and improvement of American constitutional democracy."[49] *The Civic Mission of Schools* states: "competent and responsible citizens . . . have moral and civic virtues such as concern for the rights and welfare of others, social responsibility, tolerance and respect, and belief in the capacity to make a difference." Such citizens are informed and thoughtful, understand the history and processes of American democracy, "think critically, and enter into dialogue among others with different perspectives." Moreover, they participate in civil society and "act politically by having the skills, knowledge, and commitment needed to accomplish public purposes, such as group problem solving, public speaking, petitioning and protesting, and voting."[50]

The literature on civic education rejects a model of indoctrination or "rote education" in favor of stressing active learning, participation, and critical reflection on America's ideals as well as disparities between those ideals and reality.[51] A recent survey by the American Enterprise Institute, *High Schools, Civics, and Citizenship,* reported an encouraging congruence between civics teachers and the general public as to what the basic content of civic education should be. (The report also notes "remarkably similar views" shared by public and private school teachers on "what it means to be an American and what students should learn about citizenship.") In brief, educators and the public believe that children should be taught that America is a "unique country that stands for something special in the world" and that it is important for students to "respect and appreciate their country but know its shortcomings." The report calls this a "warts and all" approach to teaching American history.[52]

A similar emphasis on critical thinking about "disparities between ideals and reality in American political and social life" pervades the government-funded *National Standards for Civics and Government.*[53] Texts and teachers should cover "the constitutional rights that individuals and groups have to promote change."[54] "Active" learning should help students analyze conflicts among basic values and apply those values to contemporary issues. "Teach the conflicts" or "don't avoid the controversy" are other ways to characterize these methods.[55]

Civic education is essential to the "preservation *and improvement* of American constitutional democracy."[56] Teaching students to think critically about political institutions aids in pursuing these goals. In the words of one expert on civic learning: "We must prepare citizens for politics, but also improve politics for citizens."[57] Not all proponents of civic education agree with the "warts and all" approach. Some charge that it promotes "an adversary culture that emphasizes the nation's warts and diminishes its genuine accomplishments." They worry that too much emphasis upon diversity and multiculturalism comes at the expense of a proper focus on America's "value-based identity" and the need to forge "one out of many" ("E pluribus unum").[58]

Spillover between Civic Education and Education for Success in Life   There is spillover between schools' civic mission and their task of preparing students for success in life. As one report stresses: "[T]he same skills that people need to be effective, responsible citizens . . . are also essential in the workplace." Moreover, effective civic leadership is necessary for "sustaining a robust local economy" and generating social capital.[59]

Civics teachers focus on the "implicit curriculum" of citizenship "because they want their students to carry values and habits into the outside world that will allow them—and their communities—*to succeed*." A majority believe it "absolutely essential" to teach students "to have good work habits such as being timely, persistent, and hardworking" and "to follow rules and be respectful of authority."[60] Even the *National Standards for Civics and Government,* which sharply distinguishes "civic life" ("concerned with the affairs of the community and nation") and "private life" ("individual devot[ion] to the pursuit of private interests"), favorably views as civic goals promoting personal responsibility and preparing students for "further learning and productive employment."[61] Many view good work habits as an essential virtue of citizenship, evident in the idea that being an American means "working hard and playing by the rules" and being independent.[62]

Tolerance and Equality as Essential Elements of Civic Education   Finally, civic education should focus not only on constitutional rights and the responsibilities of citizenship, but also on virtues. Notably, "to be tolerant of people and groups who are different than themselves" ranks very high among the "absolute essentials" that schools should teach.[63] Tolerance is a core liberal virtue, particularly in a society characterized by "reasonable pluralism."[64] What teaching tolerance requires, however, is controversial. Furthermore, having students internalize equality as a "core value" is a high priority for civics teachers.[65] Yet equality, too, is hardly free from controversy, and understandings of our constitutional commitments to equality and social norms concerning it change over time.

Clashes between Schools and Parents over the Civic Mission of Schools

Conflicts arise when government, pursuant to the civic mission of schools, seeks to inculcate conceptions of citizenship and civic virtue that families do not foster. We offer two examples: parental objection to a curriculum that stresses the importance of critical thinking and parental and student objection to teaching tolerance and respect for different ways of life. We begin with the famous *Mozert* case and then discuss three cases from a newer generation of challenges. With each case, we consider the claim that such education threatens parents' fundamental right—and responsibility—to instill values in their children.

Developing the Capacity for Critical Thinking and Promoting Civil Tolerance

On prominent accounts of civic education, critical thinking is a capacity necessary for democratic self-government.[66] Cultivating that capacity, some contend, has salutary effects on children's capacities to be good citizens and to live good lives.[67] But others warn of the "corrosive" effects of doing so.[68] Parents may fear that cultivating critical thinking in political life may lead to critical reflection by children on their own way of life. The most famous case involving the clash between the values of fundamentalist families and the imperatives of public education is *Mozert v. Hawkins County Board of Education.*[69] That case involved a Tennessee "character education" statute, which, like civic education programs, aimed "to help each student develop positive values and improve student conduct as students learn to act in harmony with [such] values and learn to become good citizens in their school, community and society."[70] Fundamentalist parents objected to a "critical reading" curriculum. One parent said "she did not want her children to make critical judgments and exercise choices in areas where the Bible provides the answer." The parent also objected to the curriculum of teaching tolerance: "We cannot be tolerant in that we accept other religious views on an equal basis with our own." Invoking the Supreme Court's affirmation that public schools teach "fundamental values 'essential to a democratic society,'" the court concluded that the reading material promoted the important virtue of "*civil* tolerance," or the idea that "in a pluralistic society we must 'live and let live.'"[71] Given the importance of the capacity for critical thinking to democratic self-government and to participation in other domains of life, a strong case can be made that fostering it is part of government's formative responsibilities.

More was at stake than cultivating good citizenship. As the concurring opinion pointed out, the curriculum aimed to "prepare students for life in a complex, pluralistic society."[72] Many liberals fear that children instructed only in their parents' way of life will not be exposed to alternative possibilities or develop independent judgment about how to live their own lives as they mature.[73] Accordingly, some are critical of the Supreme Court's decision in *Wisconsin v. Yoder*, which held that compulsory school attendance of Amish children beyond the eighth grade violated their parents' right to free exercise of religion. In his famous dissent in *Yoder*, Justice William O. Douglas feared that the Amish children who failed to get a complete formal education (receiving only "continuing informal vocational education") would be "harnessed to the Amish way of life" and be "forever barred from entry into the new and amazing world of diversity that we have today."[74] Education about diverse ways of life, Macedo contends, is needed not only for good citizenship—to foster virtues such as respect for the rights of others, toleration of reasonable pluralism, and mutual respect—but also for a good life—to help children make "informed and independent decisions" about how they wish to live their own lives.[75]

Fundamentalist parents fear that teaching their children the liberal virtues of critical thinking and toleration and respect for diversity directly threatens the survival of their way of life.[76] Some liberals, for example, Galston, have defended a right to live an unexamined life and rejected the idea that liberalism's legitimate civic purposes extend to developing in children critical ("corrosive") reflection on ways of life. It should have been possible, he argues, to offer some kind of accommodation to the fundamentalist parents in *Mozert* to keep their children in the public school system without "erod[ing] the essential conditions of civic unity." Galston wisely draws attention to the prudential concerns at issue: what if the lack of accommodation drives parents to remove their children from the public school system entirely? However, even if, as he argues, parents have an "expressive liberty" interest in instructing their children in their values and way of life,[77] schools have an interest in the healthy development of children. Further, exposure by children to a curriculum teaching critical thinking and toleration and respect for diversity does not preclude parents from carrying out their own formative responsibilities as they see them.

The Missing Dimension of Sex Equality

The extensive literature on conflicts between school curriculum and fundamentalist families tends to neglect that in many instances promotion of sex equality is part of what those families find objectionable.[78] Religious fundamentalists typically assume a scriptural foundation for a patriarchal family structure of husband as "head" of the household, both as breadwinner and as authority, and wife as caregiver/homemaker and as submissive to that authority.[79] Fundamentalist families may socialize their children into gender roles that replicate this division of labor and authority/submission model. Due to the gender revolution in constitutional law and family law, the public repudiation of coverture and the erosion of separate-spheres ideology stand in tension with private orderings and worldviews that reinforce traditional gender roles. The capacity for critical reflection is important for inculcating sex equality as a public value, for that capacity might counter socialization into such roles and patriarchal authority. Moreover, the capacity for critical reflection enables persons to reflect on current institutional arrangements and to perceive gaps between ideals and practices. Indeed, the story of the emergence of sex equality as a constitutional principle and public value includes a history of critical reflection, dissident citizenship, and reconstruction of national commitments to include women's liberty and equality.

The fundamentalist parents in *Mozert* objected to a curriculum that seemed to challenge traditional gender roles by teaching "role reversal or role elimination, particularly biographical material about women who have been recognized for achievements outside their homes."[80] And yet government's interest in promoting sex equality played no role in the court's analysis of the justifications for the curriculum. Principles of toleration and parental liberty preclude government from compelling families to reject certain traditional gender roles. However, it is consistent with the model of divided authority over children that schools, playing an ameliorative or compensatory role, may use curriculum to model sex equality to boys and girls in ways that might "eliminate differences in their basic liberties and opportunities."[81]

Our approach is to examine places in the existing curriculum where sex equality might be featured. These places include civic education, character education, family life and health education, and sex education. Fostering civic literacy about sex equality, for example, would include relevant federal constitutional law and civil rights statutes, as well as the history of dissident citizenship that has developed national commitments to securing women's liberty and equality.[82] Equality is among the core national commitments in prominent accounts of civic education;[83] we propose incorporating a more robust focus on sex equality. The lesson of women's exclusion from full citizenship and their gradual inclusion should be part of education about the " 'fundamental values necessary to the maintenance of a democratic political system.' "[84] Undeniably, conflicts exist over the meaning and scope of our commitments to equality. As we have seen, however, teaching the conflicts is an important component of effective civic education.[85]

Conflicts over Teaching Tolerance and Respect for Diversity

If *Yoder* is the paradigm case of a court protecting religious parents' way of life by allowing them to remove their children from high school, then *Mozert* is the paradigm case of a court not permitting parents who wished to keep their children in the public school to exempt them from exposure to an objectionable curriculum. An important principle at work here is that, while parents have a constitutional right to direct the education of their children (and may select private rather than public education), that right does not include the right to dictate the curriculum.

In recent years, one area of conflict concerns school curricula and school-sponsored programs that aim to teach tolerance and respect for diversity. Schools justify such instruction on grounds of promoting mutual respect, civility, and safety as well as combating stereotyping. Sexual orientation and family diversity are particular sources of controversy. Religious parents—and sometimes religious students—object that messages about tolerance and respect concerning homosexuality and families formed by gay men and lesbians threaten their parental liberty and religious freedom.

Tolerance is a "core attribute" of citizenship in the diverse society likely to result from "liberal pluralist institutions." If tolerance is necessary to sustain the political order, it should be among those civic virtues that civic education inculcates. Tolerance as a civic virtue, Galston contends, is "a principled refusal to use coercive state power to impose one's views on others, and therefore a commitment to moral competition through recruitment and persuasion alone."[86] However, not all agree, particularly when teaching tolerance seems to entail intolerance toward religious viewpoints. And many conceive it as "empty toleration" rather than "toleration as respect." A more prudent course, some argue, would be to keep controversial issues such as tolerance of homosexuality out of the schools.[87] Galston, who insists that civic education should include tolerance, recognizes that "[c]lashes with faith and conscience cannot be avoided," but insists that "they can be minimized."[88]

We will analyze three cases to illustrate how our constitutional liberalism supports teaching tolerance as part of schools' formative responsibilities. A political liberal regime is tolerant toward the intolerant to the extent that it does not insist upon congruence between democratic principles, virtues, and values and those of the institutions of civil society, including families. When schools teach tolerance, they aim for civil tolerance, not to persuade students about the merits of particular religious points of view. To be sure, teaching tolerance is often paired with teaching respect for difference or diversity. This suggests, at a minimum, teaching students to live and let live, but may also imply cultivating appreciation, or "toleration as respect."

How might schools seem to be "intolerant" in promoting tolerance? They might limit student speech and behavior in the school environment because of the impact on other students, interference with the school's civic mission, or other pedagogical concerns. Examples include "zero tolerance" for bullying and harassment. Further, some religious parents assert that schools are "intolerant" when they promote a message about tolerance that conflicts with their beliefs and will not exempt their children from hearing it.

Parents' Challenges to School Curricula about Family Diversity   From the perspective of religious parents and students who challenge curricula or programs designed to teach tolerance, enduring lessons or assemblies they perceive as offensive indoctrination infringes deeply upon their freedom of speech and free exercise of religion, as well as upon parental liberty. Schools seem to be taking sides in controversial matters. Thus, conservative Christian parents in a Minnesota school district successfully fought for a policy that public school teachers must remain "neutral" on homosexuality, forbidding any description of homosexuality or same-sex marriage as normal.[89]

However, if we shift the perspective to those of gay and lesbian students or students with gay or lesbian parents, school may not feel like a safe environment. Indeed, in the Minnesota school district with the "neutrality" policy, several gay and lesbian students sued school officials, contending that the policy "fostered oppressive silence and corrosive stigma," and that the officials had done nothing to address "relentless" antigay bullying of students who were—or were perceived to be—gay or lesbian.[90] Further, antigay bullying may have been a factor in the recent rash of teen suicides (or "bullycides") in the school district.[91] Shocking instances of young people taking their own lives because of bullying or harassment over their sexuality have propelled tough new antibullying laws and prompted many schools to redouble efforts to protect students and to design curricula to foster mutual respect and civility and to create a "safe" learning environment.[92] State antidiscrimination and antibullying laws often require such instruction.[93]

Proponents of civic education warn that bullying (including cyberbullying) and harassment "undermine democratic norms."[94] Both safety and civic education are strong rationales for a teaching tolerance curriculum. Difference—or perceived difference—is often the basis for bullying.

Gender and sexual identity are two common reasons students say they are bullied or harassed.[95] Further, in states like Massachusetts, which permit same-sex couples to marry, including families formed by gay men and lesbians in curriculum about family life is a logical extension of existing pedagogical goals of fostering mutual respect and learning about difference.

In *Parker v. Hurley*,[96] two families asserted that a Lexington, Massachusetts school systematically indoctrinated their children about homosexuality and same-sex marriage in ways contrary to their religious beliefs. They asserted their Due Process right to parental liberty as well as their own and their children's rights to free exercise of religion. They objected not to the "nondiscrimination curriculum" as such, but to the school district's refusal to provide them notice of that curriculum and exemption of their children from instruction in it.

One family objected to giving children in kindergarten and first grade a "Diversity Book Bag," which included two books that portray diverse families, including families in which both parents are the same gender. The family also objected to books in the classroom, such as *Molly's Family*, in which a girl "who is at first made to feel embarrassed by a classmate because she has both a mommy and a mama . . . learns that families can come in many different varieties." The other family objected when their son's second grade teacher read the class *King and King*, a book "that depicts and celebrates a gay marriage." In the story, a prince, ordered by his mother to marry, rejects various princesses and finally falls in love with and marries another prince. The parents argued that these books were "indoctrination" of their children contrary to their religious beliefs and taught that "homosexuality and homosexual relationships or marriage are moral and acceptable behavior." The principal refused their requests for notice and an exemption.[97]

Why did the school introduce young students to these books? A Massachusetts law specified that academic standards were to be "designed to inculcate respect for the cultural, ethnic, and racial diversity of the commonwealth" and to "avoid perpetuating gender, cultural, ethnic or racial stereotypes." This statute, passed in 1993, does not specifically name sexual orientation, but the subsequent comprehensive health curriculum included a "Family Life" component, which stated that children should be able to "describe different types of families." Young school children should also be able to "describe the concepts of prejudice and discrimination."[98]

Pointing to the "important influence teachers have on this age group," the parents feared "their own inability . . . to counter the school's approval of gay marriage," particularly if they lacked advance notice. Their children were "essentially" required "to affirm a belief inconsistent with and prohibited by their religion." The parents also asserted: "it is ironic, and unconstitutional under the Free Exercise Clause, for a public school system to show such intolerance towards their own religious beliefs in the name of tolerance."[99]

The First Circuit ruled against the parents, concluding that "the state's interest in preventing discrimination, specifically discrimination targeted at students in school, justified the policy." The court invoked the Supreme Court's precedents about "the role of public education in the preparation of students for citizenship." It added: "[g]iven that Massachusetts has recognized gay marriage under its state constitution, it is entirely rational for its schools to educate their students regarding that recognition."[100] (Fears concerning the implications of legalizing same-sex marriage for the curriculum were exploited by proponents of Proposition 8 in California.[101])

The parents relied on *Yoder,* and the court stated: "To the extent that *Yoder* embodies judicial protection for social and religious 'sub-groups from the public cultivation of liberal tolerance,' plaintiffs are correct to rely on it."[102] However, the court observed, *Yoder* "emphasized that its holding was essentially sui generis," since compulsory attendance at *any* school would prevent Amish parents from "making fundamental decisions about their children's religious upbringing and effectively overrode their ability to pass their religion on to their children, as their faith required." By contrast, the Massachusetts parents challenging the school curriculum decided to place their children in the public schools and were not living in a "largely separate culture." Moreover, "[e]xposure to the materials in dispute here will not automatically and irreversibly prevent the parents from raising [their children] in the religious belief that gay marriage is immoral."[103]

The parents asserted that their curriculum claim was "a logical extension" of their "fundamental" parental liberty. The court found more persuasive the school district's argument that such a claim "runs afoul of the general proposition that, while parents can choose between public and private schools, they do not have a constitutional right to 'direct *how* a public school teaches their child.'"[104]

The parents did not dispute the school's interest in "promoting tolerance, including for the children (and parents) of gay marriages." They conceded that "the school system has a legitimate secular interest in seeking to eradicate bias against same-gender couples and to ensure the safety of all public school students" (an important concession given reports of high rates of harassment and bullying of gay and lesbian students). However, they countered that they have "an equally sincere interest in the accommodation of their own religious beliefs and of the diversity represented by their contrary views." They sought not to control the curriculum, but to have "notice" of it and "an exemption . . . up to seventh grade" (when they would be protected by the state law opt-out provision). The court rejected the parents' allegation of "indoctrination," that the "state has put pressure on their children to endorse an affirmative view of gay marriage and has thus undercut the parents' efforts to inculcate their children with their own opposing religious views." The court found the closest parallel in *Barnette*—we think correctly—in which the Supreme Court drew a line between the state compelling the recital of the Pledge of Allegiance, which was constitutionally impermissible, and attempting to "inculcate values by instruction," which was constitutionally permissible. The *Parker* court concluded that occasional exposure to the diversity curriculum was not a "viable case of indoctrination." Such exposure "does not inhibit the parent from instructing the child differently." Parents did not receive advance notice of the particular books but had "notice" of the school's "overall intent to promote toleration of same-sex marriage" and "retained their ability to discuss the material and subject matter with their children."[105]

What about the children's free exercise claim? The student receiving the Diversity Book Bag was not required to read the books made available to him. The books themselves do not "endorse" same-sex marriage, but merely "describe how other children might come from families that look different from one's own." A "more significant claim" was made by the child who "was required to sit through a classroom reading of" *King and King*, which "affirmatively endorses homosexuality and gay marriage." Nonetheless, the court drew a pertinent line between attempting to "influence the listening children toward tolerance of gay marriage" and "systemic indoctrination." Even assuming, the court observes, "a continuum along which an intent to influence could become an attempt to indoctrinate," this case "is firmly on the influence-toward-tolerance end." What is more: "There is no allegation that [the child] was asked to affirm gay marriage. Requiring a student to read a particular book is generally not coercive of free exercise rights."

Some dissatisfied parents respond to the proposition that "parents simply do not have a constitutional right to control each and every aspect of their children's education" by electing to homeschool their children. This raises a practical problem: if a consequence of refusing to allow parents to opt their children out of an objectionable curriculum is that they opt out of the public school system entirely—by choosing private schools or homeschooling—that limits schools' ability to pursue their educational mission and inculcate civic virtues. Are there prudential arguments for giving exemptions—even if schools are not constitutionally required to do so—in order to keep such children in the schools? Some liberal theories, like Galston's "parsimonious" approach to civic education, say yes. He supports the outcome in *Yoder* and would have found a way to accommodate the parents in *Mozert*. At the same time, if one takes seriously Galston's argument that tolerance is a core virtue in a society with a "high degree of social diversity," it would seem that schools' efforts to inculcate tolerance toward family forms made possible by evolving understandings of liberty and equality would be part of even a parsimonious civic education. Massachusetts's curriculum was not trying to instruct children that their religious understandings of marriage were wrong, but rather to encourage civil tolerance toward diverse families, including those lawfully formed by civil marriage under the laws of the state. That civic aim is eminently defensible.

What Space Exists for Religious Dissent in School from the Promotion of Tolerance? Are Schools Promoting Tolerance by Intolerance?   Conflicts also arise when schools attempt to promote tolerance and respect for diversity and students seek to dissent because of their religious beliefs. Do school efforts to foster appreciation of diversity amount to "one-way diversity," with government taking sides by being intolerant of religious beliefs that conflict with its vision of diversity? We discuss two cases reaching contrasting results as to whether a school properly restricted a religious student's dissent. We believe the courts correctly decided each case.

Hansen v. Ann Arbor Public Schools[106]   A religious student who believed homosexuality was immoral sought to express her views during Pioneer High School's celebration of "Diversity Week," which traditionally included a school assembly; panel discussions on race, religion, and sexual orientation; and various multicultural activities. Generally, the student council organized the panels; this particular year, it invited other student organizations to help. The Gay/Straight Alliance (GSA) (the only club that responded) proposed a panel on "religion and homosexuality" to bring in adult religious leaders to address objections to homosexuality rooted in religious beliefs.

Betsy Hansen, a member of the student organization Pioneers for Christ, sought to have a clergy member on the panel who would bring a different point of view. This posed a dilemma, in the view of the GSA's faculty advisor, who took an active role in organizing the panel: Betsy's group members "have a legal right to be on the panel" and "to say that homosexuality is not a valid lifestyle," but to let them speak would "fly in the face of the panel's intent and potentially cause hurt feelings all around." Betsy's request was denied, although on the Friday before the Monday event, she was given the unrealistic option of organizing her own panel. Then, as an "offer of good will," the faculty advisor gave her an "opportunity to give a two-minute speech" about "what diversity means to me." However, the advisor required her to submit her speech in advance and then recommended that she change a part of it. Betsy felt that she had to comply and removed this "objectionable content":

> One thing I don't like about Diversity Week is the way that racial diversity, religious diversity, and sexual diversity are lumped together and compared as if they are the same things. Race is not strictly an idea. It is something you are born with; something that doesn't change throughout your life. . . . It involves no choice or action. On the other hand, your religion is your choice. Sexuality implies an action, and there are people who have been straight, then gay, then straight again. I completely and whole-heartedly support racial diversity, but I can't accept religious and sexual ideas or actions that are wrong.

Meanwhile, the panel took place with six "pro-homosexual adult clergy and religious leaders," and no representatives from Pioneers for Christ. The panel's theme was that passages of scripture "referring to homosexuality had been misunderstood or mistranslated by others to mean that homosexuality was immoral or sinful or incompatible with Christianity."[107]

Betsy prevailed in court on her free speech and establishment claims. The court concluded that, in helping organize a panel on religious perspectives on homosexuality, the school was promoting a particular religious view. The court remarked upon "the ironic, and unfortunate, paradox of a public high school celebrating 'diversity' by refusing to permit the presentation to students of an 'unwelcomed' viewpoint on the topic of homosexuality and religion, while actively promoting the competing view." It found this practice of "one-way diversity" troubling because the approved viewpoint was "presented to students as religious doctrine" by religious clergy "quoting from religious scripture." At the same time, school administrators attempted to censor a speech by a student whose view of "what diversity means to me" represented "the unapproved viewpoint."[108]

Is the school barred from taking sides on the question of what respect for diversity means? Not at all, the court correctly said: provided it does not violate the Establishment Clause, "[a]n arm of local government—such as a school board—may decide not only to talk about gay and lesbian awareness and tolerance in general, but also to advocate such tolerance if it so decides, and restrict the contrary speech of one of its representatives." However, when a school sponsors student speech, it may exercise editorial control over that speech only if the restrictions "are reasonably related to pedagogical concerns" and are "viewpoint-neutral."[109] The restriction on Betsy's speech and the exclusion of the Pioneers for Christ point of view from the panel were, instead, motivated by the inconsistency of her message with the view that homosexuality and religion were compatible. As stated previously, the court makes much of the irony that the school sought to promote *tolerance* by being *intolerant* of Betsy's viewpoint.

The school claimed that not allowing Betsy or clergy she proposed to deliver a message was motivated by its commitment to "provide a safe and supportive environment for gay and lesbian students." However, it did not show how allowing either would threaten gays and lesbians or make them feel less safe: "the testimony of the PHS administrators was that there had been no reports, surveys, or complaints about harassment or victimization because of a student's sexual orientation."[110]

The court concluded that the school's "level of involvement . . . in selecting the clergy for the panel, vetting the religious beliefs of the chosen clergy, . . . and providing school facilities and a captive audience of students for the clergy, and censoring and editing Betsy Hansen's speech based on its religious viewpoint" constituted "excessive entanglement with religion." Because of the unique role of public schools, in Justice Frankfurter's words, "as perhaps the most powerful agency for promoting cohesion among a heterogeneous democratic people," they must "keep scrupulously free from entanglement in the strife of sects."[111] Frankfurter's language reinforces our discussion earlier about schools' unique capacity to carry out civic learning and further unity amidst diversity or pluralism.

Betsy's parents unsuccessfully argued that their rights to control their child's education and religious upbringing were violated. *Meyer v. Nebraska* and *Pierce v. Society of Sisters*'s declarations about guarding against state standardization of children, the court held, do *not* encompass "a fundamental right [of parents] to dictate the curriculum at the public school to which they send their children." As did *Parker, Hansen* distinguished *Yoder,* finding that a 50-minute panel discussion, from which students could opt out, did not equate with " 'a *Yoder*-like clash' " between "the essence of a religious culture of an entire community and the beliefs espoused by the panelists."[112]

Harper v. Poway Unified School District[113]   Student dissent was also the subject in this case, in which the majority and dissenting opinions clash over whether it is appropriate for schools to teach tolerance with respect to controversial matters such as sexual orientation. By contrast to Betsy Hansen's school, this California high school had "a history of conflicts among its students over issues of sexual orientation," including anti-homosexual speech during the annual "Day of Silence," which the school allowed the Gay-Straight Alliance to hold "to teach tolerance of others, particularly those of a different sexual orientation."[114]

A student, Tyler Harper, filed a lawsuit after he was asked by school officials to remove a homemade T-shirt with religious messages condemning homosexuality that he wore on the "Day of Silence." The front of the shirt stated: "I WILL NOT ACCEPT WHAT GOD HAS CONDEMNED," and the back read: "HOMOSEXUALITY IS SHAMEFUL. Romans 1:27." On the next day, the front of the shirt read: "BE ASHAMED, OUR SCHOOL HAS EMBRACED WHAT GOD HAS CONDEMNED." The student refused to remove his shirt, was given a dress code violation, and was sent to the principal's office. The assistant principal explained to Tyler that the "Day of Silence" was "not about the school promoting homosexuality but rather it was a student activity trying to raise other students' awareness regarding tolerance in their judgment of others." Further, his shirt "was inflammatory under the circumstances and could cause disruption in the educational setting." The assistant principal also discussed with Tyler ways that "he and students of his faith could bring a positive light onto this issue without the condemnation that he displayed on his shirt." Tyler refused to remove the shirt and return to class; he repeatedly asked to be suspended. The school did not suspend or discipline him in any way, and he received attendance credit for the day.[115]

The student asserted that the school's actions violated his rights to free speech and free exercise of religion, as well as the Establishment Clause. The Ninth Circuit disagreed. It expressed serious doubt that the prohibition of his T-shirt was impermissible "viewpoint discrimination," countering: "a school has the right to teach civic responsibility and tolerance as part of its basic educational mission; it need not as a quid pro quo permit hateful and injurious speech that runs counter to that mission." Thus: "A school need not tolerate student speech that is inconsistent with" that mission, "even though the government could not censor similar speech outside the school." It drew analogies between intolerance based on sexual orientation and religious and racial intolerance:

> [P]ublic schools may permit, and even encourage, discussions of tolerance, equality and democracy without being required to provide equal time for student or other speech espousing intolerance, bigotry, or hatred. . . . [B]ecause a school sponsors a "Day of Religious Tolerance," it need not

permit its students to wear T-shirts reading "Jews are Christ Killers" or "All Muslims are Evil Doers." Such expressions would be "wholly inconsistent with the 'fundamental values' of public school education." Similarly, a school that permits a "Day of Racial Tolerance" may restrict a student from displaying a swastika or a Confederate Flag.[116]

This line of reasoning about teaching tolerance is relevant to the educational missions of universities, as we discuss in Chapter 6.

The court employed a clash of rights analysis, drawing on the Supreme Court's holding in *Tinker v. Des Moines* that schools may properly restrict student speech that interferes or collides with the rights of others or causes substantial disruption.[117] There was a "fundamental" collision between Tyler's asserted right to wear his T-shirt and other students' rights "to be secure and to be let alone" at school. Moreover, California's education law protects the right of pupils to "participate fully in the educational process, free from discrimination and harassment." The court stressed the injuries that minority groups experience from certain kinds of speech—verbal assaults on the basis of a core identifying characteristic such as race, religion, or sexual orientation—and the authority of schools to prohibit such speech:

> Speech that attacks high school students who are members of minority groups that have historically been oppressed, subjected to verbal and physical abuse, and made to feel inferior, serves to injure and intimidate them as well as to damage their sense of security and interfere with their opportunity to learn. . . . Those who administer our public educational institutions need not tolerate verbal assaults that may destroy the self-esteem of our most vulnerable teenagers and interfere with their educational development.

The court supported this harm argument with statistics about the relationship between antigay discrimination and decline in school performance and the impact of harassment on gay and lesbian students. The court clarified that it was not ruling that schools may "'define civic responsibility and then ban opposing points of view,'" but only that schools may prohibit wearing of T-shirts in high school classes "that flaunt demeaning slogans, phrases, or aphorisms relating to core characteristics of particularly vulnerable students and that may cause them significant injury."[118]

Tyler argued that when school officials challenged him about and punished him for wearing his T-shirt, they unconstitutionally burdened his free exercise of religion. However, the court emphasized that the right to free exercise does not relieve Tyler of the obligation to comply with a "valid and neutral law of general applicability"—in this case, a dress code prohibition on wearing clothing with demeaning messages about particular groups.[119]

Furthermore, the court concluded, the school "has a compelling interest in providing a proper educational environment for its students" and its actions were narrowly tailored to that end. The court reiterated the Supreme Court's teaching that inculcation in fundamental democratic values and virtues is "truly the 'work of the schools'": "school officials' statements and any other school activity intended to teach [Tyler] the virtues of tolerance constitute a proper exercise of a school's educational function, even if the message conflicts with the views of a particular religion." Moreover, "a public school's teaching of secular democratic values does not constitute an unconstitutional attempt to influence students' religious beliefs. Rather, it simply reflects the public school's performance of its duty to educate children regarding appropriate secular subjects in an appropriate secular manner." The emphasis on appropriate *secular* instruction in *secular* democratic values puts it, we believe, just right. As the court explains: "the school acted in order to maintain a secure and healthy learning environment for all its students, not to advance religion."[120]

In dissent, Judge Kozinski favorably cited the *Hansen* case to argue that the majority upheld "promoting diversity by means of intolerance and suppression of speech." He raised the threshold question: is tolerance a virtue that schools should promote? In a pluralistic society, he observed: "Tolerance is a civic virtue, but not one practiced by all members of our society toward all others." In particular, "tolerance toward homosexuality and homosexual conduct is anathema to those who believe that intimate relations among people of the same sex are immoral or sinful." If schools keep "the subject . . . out of the school environment," then "these differences of opinion need not clash." If schools do not, "a visible and highly publicized political action by those on one side of the issue will provoke those on the other side to express a different point of view, if only to avoid the implication that they agree." He contended: "[O]ne man's civic responsibility is another man's thought control. . . . Having public schools, and those who fund them, define civic responsibility and then ban opposing points of view, as the majority seems willing to do, may be an invitation to group think."[121] With all due respect, Kozinski's overblown dissent misunderstands that the court's contextual holding concerning the school's dress code was a "far cry" from supporting a ban on opposing points of view. [122]

The problem that we see with Judge Kozinski's argument is that it suggests that governmental opposition to hateful speech directed at a group protected by antidiscrimination laws is just one "side" of an issue rather than expression of an important public value, rooted in constitutional norms. As we discuss in Chapter 6, the Supreme Court has recognized a "firm national policy" of ending racial segregation in education and described the eradication of sex discrimination as a governmental interest "of the highest order."[123] The commitments to racial and sex equality are not mere sectarian points of views, but public and constitutional values. Public policy with respect to sexual orientation is less uniform— indeed, it is evolving—at the national level, but some states include sexual orientation as a prohibited basis of discrimination. Finally, as a practical matter, as shown above, the Minnesota school district's experiment with "neutrality" and keeping "the subject . . . out of the school environment" hardly led to civic peace.

Homeschooling

We turn now to homeschooling as a test case for how our constitutional liberalism would reconcile the dual authority of parents and schools to educate children. As of 2007, parents were homeschooling approximately 1.5 million children in the United States, nearly double the estimated number in 1999.[124] Is homeschooling consistent with our constitutional order's model of divided authority over children? Some proponents of homeschooling hold an absolutist view of parental rights: homeschooling flows naturally from parents' "fundamental, God-given constitutional right" (and responsibility) to direct the education of their children.[125] According to the Home School Legal Defense Association (HSLDA), "fundamental" means absolute and exclusive: parents alone should control their children's education, free (or nearly free) of governmental regulation. As homeschooling parents (represented by HSLDA lawyers) expressed this position, in a sweeping challenge to Pennsylvania's regulations concerning homeschooling: "the Lord has established jurisdictional boundaries between the family and the State," such that "subjecting their home education program to the authority, oversight and discretionary review of the State violated Biblically-ordained jurisdictional lines. . . ."[126]

For many parents (whether conservative or progressive), the turn to homeschooling is an act of political *protest* against public education.[127] For religious parents, it is often a deliberate decision to shield their children from what they consider to be harmful secular values (indeed, an "orthodoxy") that threaten religious values inculcated in the home. As HSLDA Chairman Michael Farris articulates the values that Christian homeschooling parents are "effectively transmitting": "Homosexuality is a sin. Men should be the leaders of their families. Jesus is the only way to God. All other religions are false."[128] For such parents, civic education aimed at inculcating "mandatory tolerance" violates parental rights that are "prior to any government claims over our children."[129]

A contrasting view is that the state has paramount authority to ensure the healthy development of children and to prepare them for full citizenship as adults and therefore it should ban homeschooling, or restrict it after a certain age. If parents can shield their children entirely from a common, public education—or even a private education influenced by public norms—the state loses a vital avenue for instilling important civic virtues and public values. Thus, Vivian Hamilton argues for "obligatory out-of-home comprehensive education" for adolescents to safeguard "immature citizens' future liberty" and ensure "the citizenry's ability to perform functions essential to the state's preservation." Moreover, students who "are channelled into a life course that is consistent" with their parents' values and who know nothing of "the alternatives available to them make no choice at all."[130] In many states, homeschooling is so unregulated that it is taking place, as Kimberly Yuracko puts it, "off the constitutional grid." States are not living up to their obligations (under state constitutions) to provide children with an education to prepare them for democratic citizenship. Gender inequality is another concern: some religious parents who believe girls are destined for different roles in society than boys may include such messages in homeschooling and provide girls different substantive education than boys.[131]

Our constitutional liberalism rejects both the absolutist interpretation of parental liberty and the view that homeschooling should never be permitted. We agree with liberal theorist Rob Reich that homeschooling can pose a "civic peril" by allowing parents to insulate their children entirely from the civic learning that schools attempt to carry out and from "exposure to diverse ideas and people."[132] Schools have a historic role and unique capacities in carrying out a civic mission and forging "E pluribus unum." A healthy constitutional democracy "relies upon citizens who share core values, including tolerance for diversity"; if parents who reject such values "withdraw their children entirely from the public sphere," children are "sheltered from any countervailing messages."[133] We also agree with Yuracko and other feminist theorists that highly sexist homeschooling poses constitutional and practical problems.[134] Another form of peril is to the safety and welfare of children: when homeschooling parents neglect or abuse their children, sometimes pursuant to extreme views of child "discipline."[135]

Nonetheless, we conclude that the dual authority of parents and government for the education of children is compatible with homeschooling under certain conditions: state regulation is necessary to ensure that homeschooling is providing children an adequate education; and home-schooled children should have mandatory participation in civic education in a school setting.

The guiding principles we apply here include the proposition that education in schools helps to prepare children both for good citizenship and for success in life. As the literature on civic education indicates, the knowledge, habits, and skills important for sustaining our constitutional order are often of critical importance for flourishing in other realms of life such as work and relationships. Schools carry out their mission through inculcating critical thinking and engaging students in a process of active learning with peers to consider how values and principles relate to contemporary issues, how to address conflicts of rights and values, and the like. Thus, a model that would allow parents to insulate their children entirely from schools' civic mission and to control completely the curriculum their children are taught would put children at risk of not acquiring this knowledge or these habits and skills. Unregulated home-schooling prevents this process of civic learning and peer interaction. Given contemporary accounts of how civic learning best occurs, there is sufficient justification to require that homeschooled children above a certain age participate, with other children, in a civics curriculum.

A second guiding principle is that our constitutional order disperses power. Diverse writings about education of children converge on a basic point: no one entity—parents or government—should have absolute power over children.[136] Shared power allows for checks and balances so one domain may compensate for the other and no one formative context is determinative. Children also possess constitutional rights and, as Martha Fineman observes, too often "the independent interests of the child" are "submerged as we slip into a consideration of the competing claims of authority over children made on behalf of parent and state."[137]

The Supreme Court has explained that our constitutional order is not that of Sparta or Plato's republic, regimes with governmental formative projects that eliminated or greatly reduced parental responsibility for socializing children. However, it has also declared that the state's power to shape citizens goes "very far indeed" and that parents are free to make martyrs of themselves, but not of their children.[138] Allowing home-schooling but regulating it respects parental liberty while also protecting the state's interest in the healthy development of children. Requiring children to participate in civics instruction in schools respects the state's authority to teach lessons "plainly essential to good citizenship."[139]

Parents choose homeschooling for three common reasons: "desire to provide religious or moral instruction" to children; "concern about the school environment" and protection of children from negative features, such as peer pressure, safety, and drugs; and, a distant third, "dissatisfaction with academic instruction available at other schools," coupled with the belief that parents can provide their children a superior education in the home.[140] Our constitutional liberalism takes these parental concerns seriously, while also reckoning with the needs and rights of children as well as the state interests at stake.

With regard to the first (and by far most common) reason—providing religious or moral instruction—we have argued that commitment to divided authority entails rejecting a model of homeschooling that would enable parents completely to isolate children from governmental attempts to inculcate values. A primary function of education is preserving democracy; thus, government has a strong interest in children developing the capacities for democratic self-government. We agree with Catharine Ross that "the needs of a pluralist democracy trump parental preferences" when the issue is teaching "the core value of tolerance," which advances "civic equality, liberty, and opportunity."[141]

With respect to the second reason—concern for the school environment—ensuring the safety of children is a legitimate parental concern. As Justice Alito observes: "Experience shows that schools can be places of special danger," and "[d]uring school hours . . . parents are not present to provide protection and guidance" and their children "may be compelled on a daily basis to spend time at close quarters with other students who may do them harm."[142]

However, unregulated homeschooling may pose serious dangers to children, not only to the quality of their education but also to their health and safety. When children simply drop off the map (as in states where parents are not even required to inform public authorities that they are homeschooling them[143]), parental claims to be homeschooling may shelter child abuse and neglect. A New Jersey court asked: "In today's threatening world, . . . how can we *not* monitor the educational welfare of all our children?" It offered graphic examples of abused and neglected children whose abuse went "undiscovered" because they were "allegedly 'homeschooled' and because no one, such as a teacher or nurse, was able to observe any abuse in a school setting."[144]

Homeschooling parents often assert an absolute right to shield their children from such scrutiny, but this dangerous view ignores—if not rejects—the compelling interest of states in the safety and healthy development of children. For example, in *Jonathan L. v. Superior Court of Los Angeles County,* a homeschooled teenage daughter who had been sexually abused by her father wished to attend public school; the attorney for her younger siblings sought an order that they attend public school, rather than be homeschooled, "so that they would be in regular contact with mandatory reporters of abuse and neglect." The parents asserted religious motivations for homeschooling. The trial court declined to issue the order, "based on its view that parents have an absolute constitutional right to homeschool their children." No such absolute right exists, the reviewing court correctly countered. It explained that parents' right to "direct[] the education of their child . . . must yield to state interests in certain circumstances." In this case, California has a "compelling" interest in the safety of children, and "the safety of the child cannot be guaranteed when the child is shielded from all mandated reporters of child abuse." "Restricting homeschooling," the court concluded, was the "least restrictive means" of furthering child safety: rather than removing the children entirely from the custody of their parents, the children's "educators would change in order to provide them an extra layer of protection."[145]

Such an "extra layer of protection" is critical when homeschooling parents adhere to extreme beliefs about child "discipline," claiming they are following Biblical precepts. A series of deaths of homeschooled children evidently caused by parents inflicting corporal punishment and other "discipline" (guided, they say, by a popular Christian ministry book, *To Train Up a Child*), shockingly illustrates the perils for vulnerable children in such households.[146]

What of the third reason—the quality of education argument for homeschooling? Ideal theory about the role of education should not divert attention from the inadequacies of many public schools in giving students an education that prepares them for success in life. Further, faced with court rulings that parental rights to direct children's education do not entail that they may dictate the particular curriculum, parents may elect to do so through homeschooling. To the extent that homeschooling aims at providing the best possible education for a particular child, it reflects a culture of "intensive parenting," aimed at unlocking the unique potential of every "precious" child.[147] It may also reflect a model of intensive *mothering*: conservative defenses of homeschooling argue for a return to the home as the proper site of education; within the home, mothers resume their traditional role of educators.[148]

Unlike remedies that aim to strengthen public education, homeschooling is a self-help, opt-out remedy, perhaps "the ultimate form of privatization."[149] There is a troubling inequality in this way of "fixing" the problem of bad schools: homeschooling is not a realistic option for every family, since a family must be able to afford to have a parent provide uncompensated labor as an educator in the home.[150] Because education is a critical responsibility of government, government may properly impose regulations upon homeschooling to ensure that children are, in fact, receiving an adequate education. Looking to state constitutions and their interpretations, Yuracko argues that parents must provide at least the constitutional minimum of education.

We do not take a position as to the exact type of regulation that should apply to homeschooling. However, at present, as a result of concerted efforts by groups such as HDSLA, the pendulum has swung too far, in a number of states, toward deregulation or minimal regulation.[151] We make four proposals. First, at a minimum, homeschooling parents should have to comply with normal, standardized achievement testing to make sure their children are achieving basic benchmarks. And it seems reasonable to require homeschooling parents, as some states do, to communicate their yearly educational plans to the public school authorities and provide examples of student work.[152]

Second, homeschooling is an area where fruitful partnerships between school districts and parents may be possible, as is evident in the approaches taken by some states that allow, and even encourage, homeschooling parents to use the schools, or opt-in, selectively. Developing ways that schools, without suffering financial hardship, could allow selective opting in could address concerns about children being entirely insulated.[153]

Third, all children, including homeschooled children, should participate in civic learning in schools. While parents who view parental rights as absolute will object, we believe that the state's strong interest in children as future citizens amply supports such a requirement. Parents still have the authority to promote their own way of life. True, this requirement may lead parents who strongly object to negate the messages taught at school, but at least students will get exposure to civic education and have a chance to acquire this knowledge and to develop these skills and habits.

We see problems with simply requiring parents to include a civics unit in their homeschool curriculum and then testing children on it.[154] The state hardly has the resources to monitor the teaching of such lessons, and parents who disagree with the substantive messages may simply refuse to conduct them or make clear that they find them repugnant and wrong. Even if parents willingly conduct such lessons, homeschooled children will lack the opportunity to hone skills of critical thinking through studying civics in the context of a classroom and, together with other students, working out how ideals and principles apply to particular contemporary problems.

Critics of our proposal might object that homeschooled children do not need exposure to a public curriculum on civic education because families who homeschool, as a group, "demonstrate higher levels of participation at almost every level of civic activity than do families who send their children to public schools." Through groups like HSLDA, homeschooling families mobilize and engage in "concerted political action . . . whenever and wherever their interests are at stake."[155] Homeschoolers and their children have been "foot soldiers" in campaigns by conservative Republican candidates.[156] Teaching children (as HSLDA aims to do) how to use the political process to achieve one's ends is an important skill for democratic self-government,[157] but does not vouchsafe good citizenship. Learning to work cooperatively with people who are different in order to achieve common political ends is an important component of good citizenship, which civic education of the sort we advocate would teach. Another is learning how to engage in democratic deliberation with those with whom we disagree according to norms of civility and mutual respect.

Finally, courts may properly order homeschooled children to attend public school where there is a problem of neglect or abuse in the home.[158] School officials should have authority to decline a parental request to homeschool, or at least require regular contact between the children and some public official, where they have reason to believe children might be subject to extreme corporal punishment or other forms of abuse. As noted above, one form of peril homeschooled children face occurs when their isolation shields them from routine, regular contact with school teachers and other officials who have an obligation, under state laws, to report suspected child abuse or neglect. However imperfect child protection systems are, they provide some opportunities to detect and prevent harm to children.

Conclusion

We have examined the shared responsibility of parents and government in fostering capacities for democratic and personal self-government, for good citizenship, and for success in life. We have focused on the role of civic education in such a formative project, illustrating conflicts between governmental efforts to forge "one out of many" ("E pluribus unum") and to prepare children to live in a diverse, morally pluralistic society, on the one hand, and respect for the rights of parents to bring up children pursuant to their own conceptions of the good life, on the other. In Chapter 6, we turn to conflicts between the formative projects of government and the associations of civil society.

CHAPTER SIX

Conflicts between Liberty and Equality

s shown in Chapters 4 and 5, there is a basic tension in the
U.S. constitutional order between two important ideas
about the relationship between civil society and government: families, religious institutions, and the many voluntary associations of civil society are foundational sources or "seedbeds" of virtues
and values that undergird constitutional democracy, and yet these same
institutions are independent locations of power and authority that guard
against governmental orthodoxy by generating their own distinctive virtues and values. The first idea envisions a comfortable *congruence* between
norms fostered by nongovernmental associations and those inculcated
by government.

What happens, however, when values and virtues generated by nongovernmental institutions *conflict* with political values and virtues? The
second idea about the relationship between civil society and government
recognizes this potential for conflict. Government's formative project of
cultivating good citizenship may clash with the formative tasks of religious institutions and voluntary associations, just as it may clash with
that of families. Our constitutional order reflects this tension between
civil society as congruent with, versus buffering against, the government.
For it recognizes the fundamental right—and responsibility—of parents
for the care, custody, and education of their children, even as it recognizes education of the young as perhaps the most important function of
government. Classic parental liberty cases affirm that the state may go
"very far indeed"[1] in inculcating good citizenship in children but may
not rely on measures that coercively impose a governmental orthodoxy.

The possibility of conflict invites the question of how much pluralism a healthy constitutional democracy can sustain in a system in which there coexist multiple sites of sovereignty (or authority)[2] alongside the ideal of unity amidst diversity. What limits must government respect, for example, when it regulates or encourages behavior to advance political virtues or values?

In this chapter, we analyze such conflicts and show how constitutional liberalism justifies the use of antidiscrimination law to secure the status of equal citizenship for everyone.[3] In doing so, we tell two stories about clashes of rights: the first about clashes between freedom of association and equal protection, and the mutual adjustment of conflicting basic liberties to secure the family of basic liberties as a whole, and the second about congruence and conflict between protecting freedom of religion and association, on the one hand, and protecting against discrimination on the basis of race, sex, and sexual orientation, on the other. The second story looks backward to our analysis in Chapters 4 and 5 of civil society's and government's formative projects, while the first looks forward to our analysis in Chapter 9 of the "absolutism critique" of liberal theories of rights. We also use these stories to illustrate two tools that government may use in a formative project of securing the status of equal citizenship for all: outright prohibition of discrimination or exclusion upon certain bases such as race, sex, or sexual orientation and conditioning benefits or subsidies upon a group's not discriminating on such bases.

To advance the first story, we focus on *Roberts v. United States Jaycees*[4] (forbidding the Jaycees to exclude women) and *Boy Scouts of America v. Dale*[5] (permitting the Boy Scouts to exclude homosexuals). We use these cases to illustrate the tool of outright prohibition of discrimination on certain bases.

To tell the second story, we focus on *Bob Jones University v. United States*[6] (upholding the Internal Revenue Service's revocation of a fundamentalist Christian university's tax-exempt status because of its racially discriminatory policies) and *Christian Legal Society v. Martinez*[7] (upholding a public university's enforcement of antidiscrimination norms by tolerating but not subsidizing a student religious organization's freedom to exclude homosexuals). Our analysis of these cases also illustrates the tool of conditioning benefits or subsidies upon a group's not discriminating on certain bases.

Both stories—and all four cases—illustrate the struggles between the formative projects of civil society and government and between competing visions of diversity and pluralism. We conclude this chapter by examining a new generation of conflicts of rights: arguments for religious exemptions concerning same-sex marriage. Our constitutional liberalism provides a framework for resolving clashes of rights so as to promote ordered liberty and equal citizenship for all, not the absolutism of one liberty to the exclusion of other constitutional commitments.

The Mutual Adjustment of Basic Liberties to Secure the Family of Basic Liberties as a Whole

What is to be done when basic liberties conflict with one another? How should we address clashes of rights, or more precisely, clashes of higher order values or interests that underlie rights?[8] Our constitutional liberalism, like John Rawls's political liberalism, accords priority to the family of basic liberties as a whole over the pursuit of conceptions of the public good or the imposition of perfectionist values rooted in a comprehensive conception of the good.[9] This understanding of priority entails that it may be permissible to regulate certain basic liberties for the sake of securing others or the whole family of such liberties. No single basic liberty by itself is absolute. In this section, we illustrate how our constitutional liberalism's guiding framework might help frame and ultimately resolve such clashes. We focus on two important Supreme Court cases that involve clashes between the First Amendment's protection of freedom of association and the Equal Protection Clause's concern for equal citizenship. Our constitutional liberalism is committed, not to protecting an absolutist First Amendment to the exclusion of equal citizenship, but to securing a fully adequate scheme of the basic liberties as a whole.

The Priority of the Basic Liberties, or Taking Rights Seriously

Let us recall two familiar refrains within liberal political philosophy and constitutional theory about the status of basic liberties or rights. One, associated with Rawls, is about the "priority of the basic liberties."[10] The other, associated with Ronald Dworkin, is about "taking rights seriously."[11] These two formulations arose in part in response to concerns that utilitarians, communitarians, and balancers of all stripes do not appreciate or honor the nerve or force of claims of basic liberties or rights. To generalize, there is a twofold worry: these balancers reduce stringent claims of basic liberties or rights of individuals to mere claims of interests, and they elevate mere claims of interests of the government and the community into stringent claims of rights.

Justice Felix Frankfurter—balancer *par excellence* and *bête noire* of any serious proponent of "taking rights seriously"—famously illustrated both moves in cases involving the First Amendment. In concurrence in *Dennis v. United States*,[12] which upheld convictions of leaders of the Communist Party under the Smith Act during the Cold War, he reduced the freedom of expression of individuals to a mere interest that Congress may balance against the claims of the whole nation to national security. And in the two cases involving compulsory flag salutes, *Minersville School District v. Gobitis* (for the majority upholding such salutes)[13] and *West Virginia Board of Education v. Barnette* (in dissent from the majority opinion invalidating such salutes),[14] he illustrated the second move by framing the clash between Jehovah's Witnesses' freedom of religion and expression and the government's interest in inculcating patriotism through compelling students to salute the flag as a "clash of rights."[15]

Frankfurter was criticized in both instances. In *Dennis,* Justice Hugo Black did so in dissent, powerfully arguing that the First Amendment is an absolute right that is not simply to be balanced away out of concern for national security. Black lamented that the Court's (and Frankfurter's) approach "waters down the First Amendment so that it amounts to little more than an admonition to Congress" that is likely to protect only "'safe' or orthodox views." He further expressed the "hope" that "in calmer times" the Court would "restore the First Amendment liberties to the high preferred place where they belong in a free society."[16]

In *Barnette,* Justice Robert Jackson for the majority (over Frankfurter's dissent) pointedly argued that there was no clash of rights at issue. Instead, the "sole conflict" was between the individual rights of the Jehovah's Witnesses to "self-determination" and the claims of governmental authority to inculcate orthodoxy.[17] Jackson famously added: "If there is any fixed star in our constitutional constellation, it is that no official, high or petty, can prescribe what shall be orthodox in politics, nationalism, religion, or other matters of opinion or force citizens to confess by word or act their faith therein."[18]

Both of these cases involved the First Amendment, and constitutional and political theorists who give "priority" to basic liberties or who "take rights seriously" are rightly proud to take their stand with Black and Jackson and against Frankfurter in these battles.[19] But all this should not blind us to the possibility of there being genuine clashes of rights—unlike Frankfurter's wrongheaded conception of a clash of rights—in which giving priority to the family of basic liberties as a whole may preclude according "absolutist" protection to First Amendment freedoms. Put another way, in rightly being "anti-balancing," we may have overlooked the possibility of such genuine clashes and failed to provide a framework for thinking about how to address them.

Mutual Adjustment of Basic Liberties to Secure the Family of Basic Liberties as a Whole

How would constitutional liberalism, by analogy to Rawls's political liberalism, accord priority to the basic liberties while also addressing conflicts among them? Rawls argues that it is appropriate to engage in mutual adjustment of basic liberties to secure a fully adequate scheme of the whole family of basic liberties: because "the various basic liberties are bound to conflict with one another, the institutional rules which define these liberties must be adjusted so that they fit into a coherent scheme of liberties." Thus, he concedes that "[t]he public use of our reason must be regulated" as distinguished from restricted. However, the priority of the basic liberties requires that such regulation be done, so far as possible, to preserve "the central range of application" of each basic liberty. Further, "[t]he priority of these liberties is not infringed when they are merely regulated, as they must be, in order to be combined into one scheme."[20]

Notwithstanding such regulation or mutual adjustment of the basic liberties, Rawls's framework entails a form of absolutism. For "the priority of liberty means that the first principle of justice assigns the basic liberties, as given by a list, a special status": "They have an absolute weight with respect to reasons of [utilitarian] public good and of perfectionist values." Hence, the priority of the basic liberties implies in practice that "a basic liberty can be limited or denied solely for the sake of one or more other basic liberties, and never . . . for reasons of [utilitarian] public good or of perfectionist values."[21] That is, utilitarian pursuits of the greatest happiness of the greatest number and perfectionist aspirations to inculcate a comprehensive conception of the good life do not justify overriding or limiting basic liberties.

The "mutual adjustment" of the basic liberties, Rawls contends, "is markedly different from a general balancing of interests which permits considerations of all kinds—political, economic, and social—to restrict these liberties, even regarding their content, when the advantages gained or injuries avoided are thought to be great enough." Rather, it "is grounded solely on their significance as specified by their role in the two

fundamental cases" of what we call deliberative democracy and deliberative autonomy. Furthermore, this adjustment is guided by the aim of
specifying a fully adequate scheme of these liberties.[22]

In assessing absolutist protection for freedoms under the First Amendment, we should bear in mind Rawls's suggestion concerning the priority
of the basic liberties: "Whenever we enlarge the list of basic liberties we
risk weakening the protection of the most essential ones and recreating
within the scheme of liberties the indeterminate and unguided balancing
problems we had hoped to avoid by a suitably circumscribed notion of
priority."[23] Similarly, whenever we enlarge or overextend the protection
of one basic liberty such as freedom of association or religion, we risk
weakening the protection of other basic liberties or values such as equal
protection. Or vice versa, as critics of the extension of antidiscrimination law allege.

The Priority of the Family of Basic Liberties as a Whole

We need a framework that will enable us to take freedom of association
and religion together with equal protection seriously, at least to the
extent of securing the core or central range of application of each. Yet we
also must rethink how to do this in order to avoid absolutism of one or
the other, as well as to avoid sliding into the morass of balancing generally. In short, we need an architecture or structure of basic liberties that
promises to do both.

Our constitutional liberal guiding framework provides such an architecture and helps frame our judgments regarding what to do when con-
fronting clashes between protecting freedom of association or religion
and securing equal citizenship. Within this framework, we give priority
to the whole family of basic liberties over utilitarian, communitarian,
and perfectionist conceptions of general welfare or common good—not
priority or absolutism to any particular basic liberty over others. Furthermore, according priority to the whole family of basic liberties does
not preclude regulating or adjusting one basic liberty to secure the central range of application of another. This adjustment may be acceptable
so long as we also secure the central range of application of the former
basic liberty. But note that this idea does not open the door generally to
balancing rights against governmental interests for all kinds of reasons:
the only permissible type of regulating or adjusting of one basic liberty
is to secure another basic liberty, not to pursue utilitarian, communitarian, or perfectionist conceptions of the general interest, the common
good, or other ends.

We sketch how such a guiding framework might apply to *Roberts* and *Boy Scouts*. Our aim is architectural: to illustrate how we might use the guiding framework to structure the inquiry in such cases.[24] We show how we might pursue the aims of antidiscrimination law without ignoring the "fixed star" that government may not impose an orthodoxy concerning beliefs.

Roberts v. United States Jaycees   In the Supreme Court's decision in *Roberts*, unlike its decision in *Buckley v. Valeo*, the Court did not view it as "wholly foreign to the First Amendment"[25] to regulate freedom of association on the basis of concern for equal protection. *Roberts* held that men's rights to associate with one another (and not to associate with women) in the U.S. Jaycees, or Junior Chamber of Commerce, a commercial and civic organization, were overridden by women's rights not to be discriminated against in places of public accommodation.[26] The Court held that the state of Minnesota had a compelling governmental interest in eliminating gender discrimination in public accommodations.

Constitutional liberalism embraces such a holding as necessary to secure for women and men alike the common and guaranteed status of equal citizenship. *Roberts* illustrates how our constitutional liberal guiding framework might apply in a situation involving a clash between freedom of expressive association and equal protection for women. Notably, the Court did not simply say that freedom of association is well-nigh absolute, and that it is "wholly foreign to the First Amendment"[27] or "thought control"[28] for government to take measures that express the view that women are equal citizens. Nor did Justice Brennan's opinion for the Court in *Roberts* do what Chief Justice Rehnquist's opinion for the Court subsequently did in *Boy Scouts:* simply defer to the Jaycees' claims that being forced to admit women would impair their expression or impede their ability to disseminate their views or message.[29] Instead, the Court recognized that the state was furthering a compelling governmental interest and that it was doing so through "the least restrictive means of achieving its ends." The Court relates Minnesota's protection of its citizens "from a number of serious social and personal harms" flowing from gender discrimination to its own recognition, in its Equal Protection opinions, about why such discrimination is wrong and harmful.[30]

At the same time, the Court gave due regard to the Jaycees' claims to freedom of association. It concluded that "the Jaycees has failed to demonstrate that the Act imposes any serious burdens on the male members' freedom of expressive association." In particular, the Court, observing that the Jaycees already admitted women as junior members and invited them to participate in their training and community activities, held that there was "no basis in the record for concluding that admission of women as full voting members will impede the organization's ability to engage in these protected activities or to disseminate its preferred views."[31] We should treat *Roberts* as an archetype of how the Court might frame clashes between freedom of association and equal protection and of how it might secure the core or central range of application of both freedoms, rather than privileging the former to the exclusion of the latter.

Not all liberals agree with this approach to mutual adjustment of freedom of association and equal protection. Some see *Roberts* as undermining pluralism. For example, Nancy Rosenblum and William Galston see it as enforcing congruence between the democratic values that should be affirmed in public life and the diverse values that may be pursued by associations in civil society.[32] They argue against the appropriateness of governmental intervention to enforce the democratic value of gender equality throughout civil society.

But it is certainly possible to believe that *Roberts* was rightly decided as a matter of constitutional law, on the ground that prohibiting gender discrimination in "places of public accommodation" like the Jaycees is a compelling governmental interest, without thinking that it is appropriate for the government to intervene to enforce gender equality throughout civil society. For one thing, most institutions in civil society are not "public accommodations" as a matter of statutory and constitutional law and therefore are beyond the reach of the *Roberts* decision. For another, it is appropriate and justifiable in some circumstances for the government to regulate freedom of association in order to attempt to secure equal citizenship for all, including women and racial minorities. Thus, the Court noted the importance of "removing the barriers to economic advancement . . . that have historically plagued certain disadvantaged groups, including women." It concurred with the Minnesota Supreme Court's observation that the Jaycees local chapters were "places" under the Minnesota statute, offering members "leadership skills," "business contacts and employment promotions," and that "[a]ssuring women equal access to such goods, privileges, and advantages clearly furthers compelling state interests."[33] Rosenblum has acknowledged that the workplace is an important exception to the autonomy of group life and has fully endorsed, for example, Title VII (which prohibits employment discrimination on the basis of race, color, religion, sex, or national origin).[34] Accordingly, to reject her conclusion regarding *Roberts* is not necessarily to reject her overall position against enforcing congruence between democratic values in public life and the values pursued by associations in civil society.

Boy Scouts of America v. Dale   The Boy Scouts of America, asserting that homosexual sexual conduct was inconsistent with the values they seek to instill, revoked the adult membership of James Dale, an Eagle Scout who was "an avowed homosexual." The Supreme Court's decision in *Boy Scouts* held that it would violate the Boy Scouts' freedom of expressive association to require them to admit homosexuals because doing so would "materially interfere with the ideas that the organization sought to express."[35] *Boy Scouts* did not follow the example of *Roberts* by upholding New Jersey's attempt to regulate freedom of association in order to further the compelling governmental interest of prohibiting discrimination in public accommodations on the basis of sexual orientation. (The New Jersey law lists sexual orientation along with race and gender as prohibited bases of discrimination.)[36]

What could account for the different outcomes in *Roberts* and *Boy Scouts*? First, one might argue that there is a difference in the character of the freedom of association: the Jaycees were engaged in commercial association, while the Boy Scouts were involved in civic association.

Second, one might argue that the Boy Scouts really were trying to communicate a message about moral straightness that required exclusion of homosexuals—Rehnquist's opinion in *Boy Scouts* granted that the Scout Oath and Scout Law did not expressly mention sexual orientation but emphasized that they did use the terms "morally straight" and "clean," which the Boy Scouts now say requires exclusion of homosexuals—whereas the Jaycees had no such message that required exclusion of women. But what if in *Roberts* the male Jaycees had said that their message was not simply that "commerce is good," but that "commerce by men is good, and commerce by women is bad, because men by nature belong in the marketplace, and women by nature belong in the home"? The Court's reasoning in *Boy Scouts* suggests that the male Jaycees should have prevailed in that case on the ground that forcing them to admit women would "materially interfere with the ideas that the organization sought to express."[37]

Third, one might argue that there is a difference in the governmental interests that could be invoked to justify the regulation of freedom of association in the two cases. The majority opinion in *Boy Scouts* stated that "[w]e recognized in cases such as *Roberts* . . . that States have a compelling interest in eliminating discrimination against women in public accommodations." But in *Boy Scouts*, the legislature and Supreme Court of New Jersey (drawing on *Roberts*) had adopted the view that the state has a compelling interest in eliminating discrimination on the basis of sexual orientation in public accommodations. The U.S. Supreme Court's decision acknowledged that view but conclusorily dismissed it.[38]

Even if the Court were not ready to go all the way with *Roberts* and hold that a compelling governmental interest was present in *Boy Scouts*, it should have taken at least a few steps in that direction, given its decisions in *Romer v. Evans*[39] (invalidating a state constitutional amendment "bar[ring] homosexuals from securing protection" against discrimination that had been justified in part to protect freedom not to associate with homosexuals) and *Lawrence v. Texas*[40] (striking down a state statute making it a crime for two persons of the same sex to engage in certain intimate sexual conduct not forbidden to two persons of the opposite sex). These two cases held that governmental aims reflecting "animus" against or a "bare desire to harm" a politically unpopular group like homosexuals do not constitute legitimate governmental interests.[41] And they also suggested that government may not take measures that "demean" the lives of homosexual persons.[42] Together, *Romer* and *Lawrence* manifested some concern for government's securing the status of gays and lesbians as free and equal citizens.[43] Therefore, in adjusting the clash between the concerns for freedom of association of the Boy Scouts and for equal citizenship of homosexuals, the Court should have recognized the latter as a more substantial concern than it did.

The place of the Boy Scouts of America as not only "the largest civic youth organization in the United States," but also, as Andrew Koppelman and Tobias Barrington Wolff explain, "the only boys' organization with quasi-official status," fortifies our conclusion that *Boy Scouts* resolved this clash wrongly. As Koppelman and Wolff point out, the Boy Scouts has a Congressional charter; "every president since William Howard Taft has been the BSA's honorary president"; and it has special permission to use military equipment. Given how "deeply entwined with the state" the Boy Scouts is, and its many representations of itself as inclusive, "nonsectarian," and open "to all creeds, races, and classes," its exclusion of homosexual boys "publicly stands for the proposition that gay people are inherently defective and contaminating."[44]

The Court might say that *Lawrence* and *Romer* are different because *Boy Scouts* involved diversity within civil society, and freedom not to associate has greater force there than when government has passed laws relating to homosexual sexual conduct or to homosexuals' status in the community (as was the case in *Lawrence* and *Romer*). But under New

Jersey law, the Boy Scouts constitute a "public accommodation," just as under Minnesota law the Jaycees do (though the Court in *Boy Scouts* questioned the expansive reach of New Jersey's definition of "public accommodation"). So the difference between *Roberts* and *Boy Scouts* could come down to the difference between the Court's view of the interests in eradicating gender discrimination and sexual orientation discrimination. On this matter, we believe that the New Jersey Supreme Court correctly stressed the *similarity* between these two forms of discrimination and the harms of stereotyping and was right (as Justice Handler's concurrence put it) to "emphatically reject the use of stereotypical assumptions about homosexuals"—such as their immorality—to justify discrimination based on sexual orientation.[45]

We should acknowledge that, had it been the Jaycees rather than the Boy Scouts excluding homosexuals, the case might have come out differently. We allude to the fear about homosexual scout leaders seducing boys or inspiring them—through their positive role models—to become more tolerant of homosexuals or indeed to become homosexuals (if one becomes a homosexual as distinguished from being homosexual). Presumably there would be no analogous fear about adult Jaycees.

Finally, the majority opinion in *Boy Scouts* stated that "we must . . . give deference to an association's view of what would impair its expression" and that "Dale's presence in the Boy Scouts would, at the very least, force the organization to send a message, both to the youth members and the world, that the Boy Scouts accepts homosexual conduct as a legitimate form of behavior."[46] The Court in *Roberts* was not bowled over by analogous arguments of the Jaycees, for it held: "[A]ny claim that admission of women as full voting members will impair a symbolic message conveyed by the very fact that women are not permitted to vote is attenuated at best."[47]

In dissent in *Boy Scouts*, Justice Stevens insightfully included concerns for equal citizenship in the analysis. He argued that "[u]nder the majority's reasoning, an openly gay male is irreversibly affixed with the label 'homosexual.' That label, even though unseen, communicates a message that permits his exclusion wherever he goes. . . . [R]eliance on such a justification is tantamount to a constitutionally prescribed symbol of inferiority."[48] Rehnquist's majority opinion did not even attempt to answer Stevens's powerful critique. Furthermore, Stevens saw the analogy between this symbol of inferiority and that involved in the prohibition of miscegenation struck down in *Loving v. Virginia*[49] (and racial prejudices more generally).[50] An anticaste principle of equal citizenship would condemn both alike. It is well to recall that the whites in *Brown v. Board of Education* asserted a freedom of association claim—freedom not to associate with blacks in public schools[51]—yet the Court protected blacks' rights to equal protection over and against that claim. Rehnquist may have failed to see the analogy or may have rejected it.[52] In any case, his opinion did not face up to it or otherwise acknowledge concerns for securing equal citizenship together with freedom not to associate.

Religious and Political Virtues and Values in Congruence or Conflict?

When the issue is conflict between religious and political values, one obvious constitutional limit upon government's formative project is that it may not compel religious belief. Doing so would offend the principle of toleration, reflected in the First Amendment's protection of the free exercise of religion. Our constitutional liberalism, like Rawls's political liberalism, maintains that, given the "fact of reasonable pluralism" that results when persons are free to exercise their moral powers, uniformity of belief—or orthodoxy—would be possible only by the exercise of "intolerable" governmental power (the "fact of oppression").[53] A second constitutional limit is that government may not favor one religious message over another or become entangled with religion. This would violate the First Amendment's prohibition of the establishment of religion. The robust protection of religious belief, however, does not cover all religious practice, or religiously motivated conduct. The government may regulate religiously motivated conduct in order to secure the status of equal citizenship for all; doing so would involve what we have called mutual adjustment. In doing so, government may promote congruence in circumstances of conflict between religious values and political values. Here, to avoid compelling religious conduct or belief, government may refrain from using the tool of outright prohibition of religious groups from discrimination in favor of using the tool of conditioning of benefits upon not discriminating.

We illustrate with two cases involving the application of antidiscrimination norms in institutions of higher learning. In the first, a Christian school had internal policies in conflict with national antidiscrimination norms. In the second, a public university sought to inculcate antidiscrimination norms, including in student organizations enjoying university support. Both cases highlight significant disagreements over how government may pursue a formative project in a manner respectful of pluralism and the prohibition against imposition of a governmental orthodoxy.

Bob Jones University v. United States: Promoting Congruence

In *Bob Jones University v. United States,*[54] the U.S. Supreme Court rejected a challenge brought by Bob Jones University, a fundamentalist Christian school, to the Internal Revenue Service's ("IRS") denial of §501(c)(3) tax-exempt status to the university because of its racially discriminatory practices. It is read instructively as a case about *congruence.*

Congruence between Public and Civil Society Purposes   A central reason that the Court affirms the IRS's denial is that prior decisions "stated that a public charitable use must be 'consistent with local laws and public policy.'"[55] Here, according to Chief Justice Burger's majority opinion, the relevant public policy is "a firm national policy to prohibit racial segregation and discrimination in public education."

> [T]here can no longer be any doubt that racial discrimination in education violates deeply and widely accepted views of elementary justice. Prior to 1954, public education in many places still was conducted under the pall of *Plessy v. Ferguson*; racial segregation in primary and secondary education prevailed in many parts of the country. . . . This Court's decision in *Brown v. Board of Education* signaled an end to that era. Over the past quarter of a century, every pronouncement of this Court and myriad Acts of Congress and Executive Orders attest a *firm national policy* to prohibit racial segregation and discrimination in public education.[56]

The very fact that this nation struggled with and repudiated racial segregation fortifies the Court's conviction that current practices of discrimination are not congruent with public values and, therefore, not a "public charitable use."

How do Bob Jones University's practices clash with this fundamental national policy? The University's sponsors "genuinely believe that the Bible forbids interracial dating and marriage," leading it, initially, to exclude "Negroes" from admission; then to admit only Negroes married within their race; and later, to admit Negroes subject to a disciplinary rule prohibiting interracial dating and marriage.[57] The University's argument recalls the statement of the trial judge in *Loving v. Virginia*: "Almighty God created the races white, black, yellow, malay and red, and he placed them on separate continents. . . . The fact that he separated the races shows that he did not intend for the races to mix."[58]

The Court rejects the University's free exercise of religion claim. It observes that "[n]ot all burdens on religion are unconstitutional. . . . The state may justify a limitation on religious liberty by showing that it is essential to accomplish an overriding governmental interest."[59] Government, the Court continues, may not accommodate the University's interest consistent with pursuing the compelling governmental interest in eradicating racial discrimination in education. To the University's argument that it allows all races to enroll but just restricts their interracial association, the Court counters that precedents, such as *Loving,* "firmly establish that discrimination on the basis of racial affiliation and association is a form of racial discrimination."[60]

The Court also observes that the case does not involve an outright prohibition of religious conduct, but the denial of a tax exemption. The Court states: "Denial of tax benefits will inevitably have a substantial impact on the operation of private religious schools, but will not prevent those schools from observing their religious tenets."[61] In other words, the Court distinguishes outright prohibition of their racially discriminatory conduct from conditioning benefits upon their refraining from racial discrimination.

Bob Jones University may continue with its discriminatory practice, the Court points out, but as long as it does it may not be accorded the status of a tax-exempt charity. In effect, government must tolerate, but need not subsidize religious practice that offends fundamental national policies. Charitable trust laws, or common law standards of charity, require "that an institution seeking a tax-exempt status must serve a public purpose and not be contrary to established public policy." The Court explains the place of charities in the political order:

> Charitable exemptions are justified on the basis that the exempt entity confers a public benefit—a benefit which the society or the community may not itself choose or be able to provide, or which supplements and advances the work of public institutions already supported by tax revenues. . . . [T]o warrant exemption under §501(c)(3), an institution must fall within a category specified in that section and must demonstrably serve and *be in harmony with the public interest.* The institution's purposes must not be so at odds with the common community conscience as to undermine any public benefit that might otherwise be conferred.[62]

Striking here is the Court's notion of tax-exempt charities as filling gaps—by providing benefits not supplied by "society or the community"—and as supplementing the work of public institutions. Today, national political leaders champion the place of faith- and community-based institutions in filling such gaps and being partners with government in providing important public services and advancing public policies.[63] Also noteworthy is the Chief Justice's alternating between "harmony with the public interest" and not being "at odds with the common community conscience." Both of these expressions not only reiterate the importance of congruence with public values but also imply a "deeply and widely accepted," rather than pluralistic, view of the public interest or conscience.

Justice Powell's Competing Vision of Pluralism and the Public Good   Justice Powell's concurring opinion in *Bob Jones University* articulates a competing vision of the functions of the institutions of civil society: as buffering or guarding against governmental orthodoxy, an idea in tension with the "liberal expectancy" of congruence between civil society and the political order. His view of the proper understanding of pluralism is that a lack of congruence is a salutary check on state power:

> Far from representing an effort to reinforce any perceived "common community conscience," the provision of tax exemptions to nonprofit groups is one indispensable means of limiting the influence of governmental orthodoxy on important areas of community life. Given the importance of our tradition of pluralism, "[t]he interest in preserving an area of untrammeled choice for private philanthropy is very great."[64]

Governmental tolerance of diversity animates Powell's emphasis on civil society's buffering role. This vision is in sharp contrast with the majority's interpretation of the tax exemption laws as requiring congruence between associational ends and a firmly and widely shared view of the public interest and community conscience. Powell remarks upon the enormous diversity among the thousand-page list of tax-exempt organizations, names a few dozen (including the American Friends Service Committee, the Jehovah's Witnesses in the United States, Union of Concerned Scientists Fund, Inc., and both the National Right to Life Educational Foundation and the Planned Parenthood Federation of America), and concludes:

> It would be difficult indeed to argue that each of these organizations reflects the views of the "common community conscience" or "demonstrably . . . [is] in harmony with the public interest." . . . Rather, they illustrate the commendable tolerance by our Government of even the most strongly held divergent views, including views that at least from time to time *are* "at odds" with the position of our Government."[65]

Powell also quotes his own dissent in *Mississippi University for Women v. Hogan,* in which the Court struck down a university's policy of admitting only women to its nursing school.[66] There, he observed: "A distinctive feature of America's tradition has been respect for diversity. This has been characteristic of the peoples from numerous lands who have built our country. It is the essence of our democratic system."[67] He adds that sectarian schools make an "important contribution" to this tradition, by providing an "educational alternative for millions of young Americans" and "often afford[ing] wholesome competition with our public schools."[68] This notion of civil society's institutions competing with governmental ones is a salient idea in contemporary debates over the proper reach of public norms and antidiscrimination laws, where scholars inclined to Powell's view of diversity and pluralism call for a "moral marketplace" in which government is one actor, not a monopolist.[69]

Is there no place, on this view, for governmental promotion of "firm national policies" or basic constitutional commitments? Must government fund—or permit a subsidy through a tax exemption—regardless of how sharp the conflict between public and private values? Powell acknowledges that these considerations about diversity may not always be dispositive and that, sometimes, "governmental orthodoxy" should prevail. Indeed, with respect to Bob Jones University, he agrees with the Court that "Congress has determined that the policy against racial discrimination in education should override the countervailing interest in permitting unorthodox private behavior."[70]

Powell's concurrence contains the seed of an idea that features in contemporary debates between two competing conceptions of the U.S. constitutional order's commitments to diversity and pluralism. Are these commitments best served by requiring that all institutions be open to all and practice no discrimination in membership, so that every group is a microcosm of the diverse whole? Or, are diversity and pluralism better served by allowing groups to pursue their own distinctive goods and purposes, including exercising discrimination concerning who may be members, so that the macrocosm is diverse in the sense that it is made up of many distinct groups?[71] Side-by-side with these questions is that of the role of government in subsidizing, or supporting, diversity and pluralism. The majority's distinction between tolerating and subsidizing associations whose values are not congruent with national commitments clashes with Powell's vision of a form of toleration that includes subsidies for unorthodox associations because of their contribution to pluralism. The recent case of *Christian Legal Society v. Martinez* revisits such questions.

Christian Legal Society v. Martinez: Antidiscrimination Law as a Vehicle for Teaching Social Cooperation amidst Diversity

What might *Bob Jones University* portend for contemporary challenges to governmental efforts to protect against discrimination on the basis of sex and sexual orientation? One view is that racial discrimination is a special case, manifested by a "firm national policy" of rectifying a shameful past practice of segregation, distinguishable from other anti-discrimination policies. However, in *Roberts,* in upholding Minnesota's public accommodations law barring sex discrimination against the freedom of association claim of the Jaycees, the Supreme Court analogized the stigmatic injuries and denial of dignity stemming from denial of access to public accommodations based on race to dignitary injuries due to denials based on sex.[72] It cited *Heart of Atlanta Motel v. United States,* upholding Title II of the Civil Rights Act of 1964, the "object" of which "was to vindicate 'the deprivation of personal dignity that surely accompanies denials of equal access to public establishments.'"[73] The Court characterized Minnesota's "historical commitment to eliminating discrimination and assuring its citizens equal access to publicly available goods and services" as "compelling state interests of the highest order."[74]

Jonathan Turley finds the ruling in *Bob Jones University* incompatible with "the pluralistic ideals of our society," and foresees that "gay rights and same-sex marriage" will "reignite" this "controversy over tax-exempt status." Society will "have to choose between the ideals of pluralism and equal treatment." He grants that racially discriminatory policies of the sort followed by Bob Jones University are "bad for society," and "[t]hankfully," followed by "relatively few organizations." By contrast, "[i]t is far more common for mainstream religious and civil groups to discriminate on the basis of sexual orientation." The potential for those groups to be "disenfranchised" (i.e., have their §501(c)(3) status challenged), applying the logic of *Bob Jones University,* is "quite large."[75] However, according to Douglas Kmiec, "the IRS has refused explicitly to push *Bob Jones* beyond the topic of race."[76]

In contrast with the firm national policies in favor of ending racial discrimination and sex discrimination, no such firm national policy *yet* exists with respect to prohibiting discrimination based on sexual orientation. Indeed, certain federal laws (such as the Defense of Marriage Act) explicitly require such discrimination, and federal law in general lags behind the law of many states in this area, as it did with both racial and sex discrimination. When the Supreme Court, in *Dale,* upheld the Boy Scouts' claim that compelling it to admit a homosexual scoutmaster pursuant to the "public accommodations" provisions of New Jersey's antidiscrimination law violated its constitutional rights to freedom of association, the Court simply stated, without elaboration: "The state interests embodied in New Jersey's public accommodations law do not justify such a severe intrusion on the Boy Scouts' right to freedom of expressive association."[77] However, with the recent repeal of the Don't Ask, Don't Tell policy regarding homosexuals in the military, the Obama Administration's announcement that it will no longer defend the Defense of Marriage Act (DOMA) in litigation challenging its constitutionality, Congress's holding hearings on a bill to repeal DOMA, and, most recently, President Obama's statement that he thinks that same-sex couples "should be able to get married," federal policy may be in a state of transition.[78] Proponents of the Respect for Marriage Act (the bill to repeal DOMA) argue that "the issue of civil rights is" not "merely one for the history books," and that Congress needs "to keep our Nation moving toward equality in our efforts to form a more perfect union."[79] Supporters link earlier forms of state-supported discrimination (such as racial segregation) to DOMA's creation of a "tier of second-class families" and denial of "dignity": the law of several states now permits or recognizes marriages by same-sex couples, but the federal government fails to respect those families or those states.[80] And the Court's own jurisprudence, in *Romer* and *Lawrence,* central to the DOMA litigation, reflects an evolution toward finding the singling out of persons for disfavored treatment on the basis of sexual orientation constitutionally problematic.[81]

The University's Educational Mission and the Distinction between Carrots and Sticks In *Christian Legal Society v. Martinez,*[82] the Supreme Court, by a 5–4 margin, upheld a public university's antidiscrimination policy against a challenge that it violated a student group's rights to free speech, expressive association, and free exercise of religion. The Court had occasion to consider the relationship among various forms of discrimination, as well as the import of *Bob Jones University* for a public university's efforts to advance its educational mission through an antidiscrimination policy. The majority, concurring, and dissenting opinions offer sharply contrasting visions of the importance of congruence between democratic and associational values and of the best understanding of diversity and pluralism.

Justice Ginsburg, writing for the majority, begins by stating that "the First Amendment generally precludes public universities from denying student organizations access to school-sponsored forums because of the groups' viewpoints." But the "novel question" presented in this case was: "May a public law school condition its official recognition of a student group—and the attendant use of school funds and facilities—on the organization's agreement to open eligibility for membership and leadership to all students?"[83]

Hastings Law School had a Nondiscrimination Policy, to which all registered student organizations ("RSOs") were subject. It stated, in relevant part:

> [Hastings] is committed to a policy against legally impermissible, arbitrary or unreasonable discriminatory practices. All groups, including administration, faculty, student governments, [Hastings]-owned student residence facilities and programs sponsored by [Hastings] are governed by this policy of nondiscrimination. [Hastings's] policy on nondiscrimination is to comply fully with applicable law.
>
> [Hastings] shall not discriminate unlawfully on the basis of race, color, religion, national origin, ancestry, disability, age, sex or sexual orientation. This nondiscrimination policy covers admission, access and treatment in Hastings-sponsored programs and activities.[84]

Hastings interpreted this policy to mandate an "acceptance of all comers" by RSOs. School-approved groups must "allow any student to participate, become a member, or seek leadership positions."[85]

The Hastings chapter of the Christian Legal Society ("CLS"), an association of Christian lawyers and law students that charters chapters at law schools throughout the county, sought an exemption from this policy. The source of the conflict was that the chapters must adopt bylaws requiring members and officers to sign a "Statement of Faith" and to conduct their lives in accord with prescribed principles, including the tenet that "sexual activity should not occur outside of marriage between a man and a woman." CLS interpreted this principle to exclude from the group anyone who engages in "unrepentant homosexual conduct" and who holds religious convictions different from those in the Statement of Faith.[86] (Notably, by contrast to the Boy Scouts of America's "secret" policy opposing homosexuality as contrary to its mission, CLS's policy is very public and very clear.[87])

Hastings rejected CLS's request for an exemption, concluding that if it wished to operate within Hastings's program of student groups, it must "open its membership to all students irrespective of their religious beliefs or sexual orientation." The benefits attendant upon being an RSO included seeking financial assistance from the school, "which subsidizes their events using funds from a mandatory student-activity fee imposed on all students." RSOs could also use Law School channels to communicate with students (such as a weekly newsletter, advertising on bulletin boards, and an annual student organization fair) and apply to use Law School facilities for meetings and office space and use the Law School's name and logo.[88]

When Hastings denied CLS's request for an exemption, it indicated that if the group chose to operate outside the RSO system, it could still use Hastings facilities for meetings and activities and use chalkboards and campus bulletin boards to announce its events. "In other words, Hastings would do nothing to suppress CLS's endeavors, but neither would it lend RSO-level support for them."[89] As this line-drawing noted by Justice Ginsburg indicates, this case illustrates a way, other than outright prohibition or compulsion, that government may try to promote democratic values by persuading a religious group not to discriminate: denial of a status to which benefits attach. In this sense, it is a subsidy case (like *Bob Jones*), not a prohibition case.

CLS declined to alter its bylaws and, operating without RSO status, held weekly meetings and sponsored several events. It sued Hastings for violation of federal constitutional rights to free speech, expressive association, and free exercise of religion, losing on all claims in the federal district court and, on appeal, in the Ninth Circuit.[90] CLS might well have expected, given the Supreme Court's precedents on religious freedom in universities and freedom of association, that victory was likely in that court. How, after all, can Hastings's open membership rule be squared with protection of freedom of expressive association? How can a group "stand for" particular values, if it must admit as members persons who disagree with those values? What goals could Hastings be furthering that outweighed this expressive freedom?

Nonetheless, the Court ruled against the student organization. Justice Ginsburg looks to the Court's public accommodations decisions, such as *Roberts* and *Dale*, stating that regulations of associational freedom are permitted if they serve "compelling state interests" that are "unrelated to the suppression of ideas," and cannot be advanced by "significantly less restrictive [means]."[91] *Roberts*, Ginsburg acknowledges, recognized that "[f]reedom of association . . . presupposes a freedom not to associate." That recognition shaped the Court's reasoning in favor of the Boy Scouts in *Dale*. "Insisting that an organization embrace unwelcome members," the precedents teach, "directly and immediately affects associational rights."[92]

CLS relied on *Dale* to support its case, but Justice Ginsburg distinguishes between *compelling a group to include unwanted members*, "with no choice to opt out" (the public accommodations law at issue in *Dale* would have forced the Boy Scouts to accept members it did not desire), and *denying a group a "state subsidy" if it did not do so*. The line between coercion and persuasion is critical: "CLS, in seeking what is effectively a state subsidy, faces only indirect pressure to modify its membership policies; CLS may exclude any person for any reason if it foregoes the benefits of official recognition."[93]

Relevant here are both the distinction between carrots and sticks and the distinction between tolerating and supporting discrimination. Requiring someone to take action, the Court states, is different from withholding benefits if they do not. For this proposition, Ginsburg cites both *Bob Jones University* and *Grove City College v. Bell*,[94] where the Court held that a private religious college's receipt of federal financial aid made it subject to compliance with Title IX's prohibition of sex discrimination. Hastings is "dangling the carrot of subsidy, not wielding the stick of prohibition."[95] Ginsburg explains the constitutional significance of the distinction: "'That the Constitution may compel toleration of private discrimination in some circumstances does not mean that it requires state support for such discrimination.'"[96] (The majority's reasoning here is consistent with an idea discussed in Chapters 3 and 5: toleration forbids the government to *compel* but leaves room for it to *persuade* by supporting conduct it seeks to promote and declining to support disfavored conduct.)

Justice Ginsburg acknowledges that once a public university has opened up a limited public forum, it "may not exclude speech where its distinction is not reasonable in light of the purpose served by the forum ... nor may it discriminate against speech on the basis of ... viewpoint."[97] Given the function of the RSO forum, is the "accept-all-comers" rule reasonable? The Court concludes that it is, emphasizing a university's authority to advance its educational mission and insisting that courts should not substitute their own notions of sound educational policy for those of school authorities.

Hastings justified its policy on several grounds. Most relevant here are two. First, it made a *tolerance amidst diversity* argument concerning the preparation of young people for participation in the democratic process and for citizenship:

> [T]he Law School reasonably adheres to the view that an all-comers policy, to the extent it brings together individuals with diverse backgrounds and beliefs, "encourages tolerance, cooperation, and learning among students." ... And if the policy sometimes produces discord, Hastings can rationally rank among RSO-program goals development of conflict-resolution skills, toleration, and readiness to find common ground."[98]

Second, Hastings defended its policy as conveying its decision "to decline to subsidize with public monies and benefits conduct of which the people of California disapprove."[99] The voice of the people of California is embodied in the state's educational code, which forbids discrimination on the basis of sexual orientation. As Toni Massaro observes, "the choice made here—to prevent RSOs from discriminating on the basis of characteristics that are commonly listed in nondiscrimination laws nation-wide—is *exceedingly* hard to characterize as constitutionally suspect," and "is easier . . . to characterize as constitutionally *required*. . . ."[100] Although the Court does not cite *Bob Jones University* here, and this case involves a firm *state* policy, the Hastings case recalls that earlier case's distinction between permitting discriminatory conduct that conflicts with public policy and subsidizing it.

Justice Ginsburg's majority opinion accepts these justifications. In addition, it concludes that Hastings's "accept-all-comers" policy aims at conduct, not belief: "rejecting would-be members." The Court stresses that the policy aims to avoid the harms of exclusionary membership policies, drawing analogies to harms inflicted by racial and sex discrimination. Thus, CLS's conduct, not its Christian viewpoint, stands "between the group and RSO status."[101]

Justice Stevens's Concurrence: The University's Educational Mission   Justice Stevens in concurrence similarly argues that the educational mission of Hastings, a public university, justifies its antidiscrimination policy. He brings out that educational policies like the RSO policy reflect and promote values, including tolerance and respect:

> Academic administrators routinely employ antidiscrimination rules to promote tolerance, understanding, and respect, and to safeguard students from invidious forms of discrimination, including sexual orientation discrimination. Applied to the RSO context, these values can, in turn, advance numerous pedagogical objectives.

Religious organizations, like all other organizations, "must abide by certain norms of conduct when they enter an academic community."[102]

Is a public university, on this view, more like an institution of civil society, or more like an arm of government? On the one hand, rhetoric about freedom of speech refers to schools—academic communities—as important marketplaces of ideas, suggesting an absence of direction about norms and values. On the other hand, Stevens states that, by contrast to the government's role in the public square in general, "[p]ublic universities serve a distinctive role in a modern democratic society" that justifies their formative role of inculcating certain norms and values:

> Like all specialized government entities, they must make countless decisions about how to allocate resources in pursuit of their role. Some of those decisions will be controversial; many will have differential effects across populations; virtually all will entail value judgments of some kind. As a general matter, courts should respect universities' judgments and let them manage their own affairs.[103]

Thus, like the majority, Steven urges judicial deference to a university's understanding of its own mission and attendant values.

Furthermore, Stevens presses an analogy between exclusion on the basis of sexual orientation and exclusion or mistreatment of other groups historically subjected to discrimination but now protected by antidiscrimination laws (such as Jews, blacks, and women):

> In this case, petitioner excludes students who will not sign its Statement of Faith or who engage in "unrepentant homosexual conduct." . . . The expressive association argument it presses, however, is hardly limited to these facts. Other groups may exclude or mistreat Jews, blacks, and women—or those who do not share their contempt for Jews, blacks, and women. *A free society must tolerate such groups.* It need not subsidize them, give them its official imprimatur, or grant them equal access to law school facilities.[104]

This passage calls to mind classic racial discrimination cases like *Shelley v. Kraemer*[105] and *Palmore v. Sidoti*,[106] and the more recent sexual orientation discrimination case of *Romer*,[107] all of which offer similar statements about the Constitution or government not supporting or giving effect to private prejudice. Also notable is Stevens's reference to religious, racial, and sex discrimination as things that government must tolerate in civil society but need not support or subsidize. The implication is that government may seek to promote congruence with public goals and values.

Justice Alito's Dissent: How Not to Promote Genuine Tolerance, Diversity, and Pluralism   Justice Alito's lengthy and impassioned dissent, joined by Chief Justice Roberts, Justice Scalia, and Justice Thomas, casts the majority opinion as a departure from protection of "the freedom to express 'the thought that we hate'" to suppression of speech that offends "prevailing standards of political correctness in our country's institutions of higher learning."[108] We focus on his arguments that join issue with the majority and concurrence over congruence, toleration, and the best understandings of diversity and pluralism. *Bob Jones University* does not appear in his dissent, although the Court's freedom of expressive association precedents, such as *Roberts* and *Dale*, feature prominently.

Where the majority and concurring opinions stress the authority of a university to carry out an educational mission that entails value judgments, Justice Alito invokes *Roberts* and *Dale*, arguing that "[t]he forced inclusion of an unwanted person in a group infringes the group's freedom of expressive association if the presence of that person affects in a significant way the group's ability to advocate public or private viewpoints."[109]

He argues that the "accept-all-comers" policy—leading to such "forced inclusion"—is antithetical to fostering diversity and pluralism.

What of Hastings's argument that the policy, "by bringing together students with diverse views, encourages tolerance, cooperation, learning, and the development of conflict-resolution skills"? Alito counters that these are "obviously commendable goals, but they are not undermined by permitting a religious group to restrict membership to persons who share the group's faith." As he sees it, many religious groups impose such restrictions (e.g., "regularly differentiate between Jews and non-Jews") and "[s]uch practices" (contra Justice Stevens's rhetoric about contempt for Jews, blacks, and women) are not manifestations of "'contempt' for members of other faiths" and do not "thwart the objectives that Hastings endorses." Strikingly, Alito asserts that CLS's restrictive practices and Hastings's goals are in harmony in the sense that the former will not undermine the latter:

> Our country as a whole, no less than the Hastings College of Law, values tolerance, cooperation, learning, and the amicable resolution of conflicts. But we seek to achieve those goals through "[a] confident pluralism that conduces to civil peace and advances democratic consensus-building," not by abridging First Amendment rights."[110]

This conclusion stems from his vision of pluralism, which allows diverse groups to flourish by controlling their own memberships.

Thus, Alito's model of diversity and pluralism, like Powell's vision in his *Bob Jones University* concurrence, entails that we do not need congruence to support democracy. On his model, each group may form around its own distinctive views and exclude those who do not share such views, thus creating a diverse whole out of distinct parts. Furthermore, Alito's concerns here accord with the worry that, as the reach of antidiscrimination law expands, the potential for conflict with religious and associational freedom expands as well.[111] That worry receives its clearest expression to date in a new generation of conflicts arising as states legalize marriage or civil unions for same-sex couples.

A New Generation of Conflicts of Rights: Religious Exemptions Concerning Same-Sex Marriage

Prominent religious leaders and scholars assert that, as states afford more protection to gay men and lesbians through civil rights laws and give official recognition and support to their intimate and family relationships through amending civil marriage laws or creating civil union and domestic partnership laws, the clash between such protections and the protection of religious liberty becomes acute.

When government does not exempt religious institutions and persons from the reach of public accommodations laws, the argument goes, it compels them to obey unjust laws and undermines the role of civil society as a buffer against overweening state power. These "emerging conflicts"[112] implicate both of the frameworks we use in this chapter: congruence and conflict between the values and virtues of civil society and public values and virtues and mutual adjustment of basic liberties to secure the status of equal citizenship for all. We sketch how our constitutional liberalism addresses these conflicts.

The Manhattan Declaration: A Call of Christian Conscience

On November 20, 2009, a group of prominent Christian clergy, religious leaders, and scholars released "The Manhattan Declaration: A Call of Christian Conscience."[113] Drafted by Professor Robert P. George (a prominent political and constitutional theorist at Princeton University), Professor Timothy George (Beeson Divinity School, Samford University), and Chuck Colson (Chuck Colson Center for Christian Worldview), and signed by "more than 125 Orthodox, Catholic and evangelical Christian leaders,"[114] the Declaration addresses three areas under threat: Life, Marriage, and Religious Liberty. On the website announcing the Declaration, three images alternate: a hand cradling tiny human feet; the Holy Bible cushioned on an American flag; and a bride and groom joining hands before an officiant at their wedding. This iconography of Bible and flag clearly implies a basic congruence between biblical and proper political values.

The Declaration insinuates congruence when it articulates the religious roots of the correct "objective" understanding of marriage. Citing biblical verses, it contends that "marriage . . . is the first institution of human society," the foundation of all other institutions.[115] The "impulse to redefine marriage" to recognize same-sex marriage, the Declaration states, "reflects a loss of understanding of the meaning of marriage as embodied in our civil and religious law and in the philosophical tradition that contributed to shaping the law."

It is a mistake, the Declaration contends, to believe, as a matter of "equality or civil rights," that homosexual relationships should be recognized as marriage: "No one has a civil right to have a non-marital relationship treated as a marriage." Although those disposed toward homosexual sexual conduct are entitled to compassion and respect as human beings "possessing profound, inherent, and equal dignity," they simply are not capable of marriage. This is because of the "objective reality" of marriage as a "covenantal union of husband and wife," and the role of "sexual complementarity" in marriage: the union of one man and one woman is "sealed, completed, and actualized by loving sexual intercourse in which the spouses become one flesh, not in some merely metaphorical sense, but by fulfilling together the behavioral conditions of procreation."

Thus, the Declaration maintains, it is not "animus" or "prejudice" that leads them to "pledge to labor ceaselessly to preserve the legal definition of marriage," but "love" and "prudent concern for the common good." This statement no doubt is aimed at findings and conclusions in some state and federal court opinions rejecting traditional rationales for excluding same-sex couples from civil marriage as, in fact, manifestations of constitutionally impermissible prejudice or animus.[116]

When new definitions of marriage in civil law disturb this congruence between religious and civil law, the Declaration contends, "genuine social harms follow," including threats to religious and parental liberty.[117] It identifies, as one such threat to religious liberty, "the use of antidiscrimination statutes to force religious institutions, businesses, and service providers of various sorts to comply with activities they judge to be deeply immoral or go out of business." It offers two examples. The first is the often-discussed controversy over Massachusetts's refusal to give Catholic Charities a religious exemption so that it could decline to place children for adoption in homes with gay and lesbian parents.[118] The Declaration states that Catholic Charities "chose with great reluctance to end its century-long work of helping to place orphaned children in good homes rather than comply with a legal mandate that it place children in same-sex households in violation of Catholic moral teaching."[119] The second example involves the loss of tax-exempt status of "a Methodist institution" in New Jersey when "it declined, as a matter of religious conscience, to permit a facility it owned and operated to be used for ceremonies blessing homosexual unions." (The word "blessing" here is misleading. The "institution" enjoyed exemption from state real estate taxes based on a representation that the facility (a boardwalk pavilion and other property) would be "open to the public on an equal basis." It lost the exemption when it declined to allow a same-sex couple to rent the pavilion for a civil union ceremony although it permitted rentals for weddings.[120]) The Declaration links these developments to the "disintegration of civil society," imperiling religious institutions as the "intermediate structures of society," the "essential buffer against the overweening authority of the state, resulting in the soft despotism Tocqueville so prophetically warned of."[121]

The Declaration draws a striking analogy between Christian civil disobedience in the face of unjust racist laws and that in the face of contemporary civil rights laws. Drawing on Dr. Martin Luther King Jr.'s "exemplary and inspiring" example, the Declaration warns that its signatories will not "bend to any rule purporting to force us to bless immoral sexual partnerships, treat them as marriages or the equivalent, or refrain from proclaiming the truth, as we know it, about morality and immorality and marriage and the family." Thus, the Declaration claims that religious people who fight *against* contemporary civil rights laws are like heroic civil rights leaders of King's day fighting *for* civil rights laws.[122]

Mutual Adjustment of Basic Liberties: Religious Exemptions Concerning Same-Sex Marriage

The signatories to the Manhattan Declaration, along with many other opponents of same-sex marriage, would resist our framework for the mutual adjustment of basic liberties, for they deny that the antidiscrimination claims of homosexuals are of sufficient weight to warrant any adjustment of religious liberty. Robin Fretwell Wilson, though not a signatory to the Manhattan Declaration, argues for developing freedom of conscience clauses for religious institutions and persons refusing to provide goods and services to same-sex couples, by analogy to existing conscience clauses in the context of certain health care services. Addressing the argument that being turned away on the basis of sexual orientation would do "harm to one's dignity," inflicting "the same harm as racial discrimination does," she contends:

> While the parallels between racial discrimination and discrimination on the basis of sexual orientation should not be dismissed, it is not clear that the two are equivalent in this context. The religious and moral convictions that motivate objections to refuse to facilitate same-sex marriage simply cannot be marshaled to justify racial discrimination.[123]

This line of argument suffers from amnesia. Historically, religious convictions have been marshaled to justify racial discrimination and bans on interracial marriage. (This is not to deny that some religious denominations came to oppose such bans.[124]) The racially discriminatory policies forbidding interracial dating and marriage at Bob Jones University were based on religious and moral convictions. Moreover, the trial judge in

Loving justified bans on interracial marriage on biblical grounds. Lest one think such religious objections to interracial marriage were confined to the South, we quote former President Harry S Truman, the "man from Missouri" who issued an executive order that initiated racial integration of the military. Asked in 1963 whether he thought racial integration would lead to "inter-marriage," he said: "I hope not. I don't believe in it. The Lord created it that way. You read your Bible and you'll find out."[125]

We believe the better approach is to recognize that, when a religious group seeks to discriminate on the basis of race, gender, or sexual orientation, society faces a "head-on clash" of civil rights—between freedom of religion and freedom from discrimination.[126] Like Chai Feldblum, we might express "sympathy" for those religious persons providing goods and services who object to providing them to unmarried and homosexual couples, but we must recognize that "an inevitable choice between liberties must come into play." Asserting the dignitary interests at stake for LGBT people, and their interests in living "honestly and safely in all aspects of their social lives," she argues that society "should come down on the side of" protecting their "identity liberty" through affording a "baseline of nondiscrimination" (or, as we would put it, securing the status of equal citizenship for everyone). Like Feldblum, we would argue that, when individuals (or organizations) "choose to enter the stream of economic commerce by opening a commercial establishment, . . . it is legitimate that they play by certain rules."[127] Justice O'Connor made a similar point in concurrence in *Roberts:* "An association must choose its market. Once it enters the marketplace of commerce in any substantial degree it loses the complete control over its membership that it would otherwise enjoy if it confined its affairs to the marketplace of ideas."[128] And Congress used similar reasoning in defending Title II of the Civil Rights Act.[129] Furthermore, we hope that the forces of our large commercial republic in due course will moderate religious claims like those made in the Manhattan Declaration.[130]

Mutual adjustment of conflicting basic liberties need not occur within constitutional doctrine itself. It can occur through partnerships between courts interpreting constitutions and legislatures devising remedies by enacting laws that embody such mutual adjustments. Some states that have passed laws recognizing same-sex marriages or civil unions have attempted to resolve the clash with religious freedom by permitting religious exemptions. The Illinois law encapsulates the conflict—along with the mutual adjustment—in its very title: "The Illinois Religious Freedom Protection and Civil Union Act."[131] The statute recognizes civil unions between not only same-sex couples but also opposite-sex couples and provides, in §20, for the "same legal obligations, responsibilities, protections, and benefits as are afforded or recognized" for marriages. In §15, entitled "Religious Freedom," the Act states: "Nothing in this Act shall interfere with or regulate the religious practice of any religious body." It continues: "Any religious body, Indian Nation or Tribe or Native Group is free to choose whether or not to solemnize or officiate a civil union." (Of course, the First Amendment would protect that freedom not to solemnize even without an explicit declaration.) The New Hampshire law likewise embodies the mutual adjustment in its title: "An Act affirming religious freedom protections with regard to marriage."[132] The statute recognizes same-sex marriages and provides for exemptions from requirements of providing "services, accommodations, advantages, facilities, goods, or privileges to an individual . . . related to the solemnization of a marriage . . . in violation of his or her religious beliefs and faith."

When the New York legislature passed the Marriage Equality Act in 2011, it included expansive exemptions for religious organizations and benevolent orders, which were critical to certain religious lawmakers supporting the bill (as we elaborate in Chapter 7). The supporting statement for the Act explained: "this bill grants equal access to the government-created legal institution of civil marriage, while leaving the religious institution of marriage to its own separate, and fully autonomous sphere."[133] Religious clergy continue to enjoy constitutional freedom not to perform marriages that offend their religious beliefs. In addition, religious institutions and benevolent organizations enjoy exemptions (similar to those in New Hampshire) from providing "accommodations, advantages, facilities or privileges related to the solemnization or celebration of a marriage."[134] What these exemptions properly did *not* do was relieve public servants of their duty to provide a license to applicants of the same sex who meet New York's eligibility requirements on the ground that such marriages offend their religious beliefs. (As Governor Cuomo put it: "When you enforce the laws of the state, you don't get to pick and choose!"[135]) Nonetheless, the refusal of an elected town clerk to comply with her obligation to issue a marriage license to same-sex couples because "God doesn't want me to do this"—and one couple's formal objection to this refusal—feature in warnings of how redefining marriage threatens religious liberty.[136]

Religious exemptions, whether or not the federal or state constitutions require them, may be justifiable as a prudential mutual adjustment of conflicting basic liberties in circumstances of moral disagreement and flux, at least as an interim remedy. To be sure, this mutual adjustment will likely be unsatisfactory both to some proponents of marriage equality and to some opponents, particularly those who insist on congruence between civil and religious definitions of marriage, lest government undermine marriage and the family.[137] Here we shall draw an analogy to Chief Justice Amestoy's opinion for the Vermont Supreme Court in *Baker v. State*,[138] which led to (what proved to be) the interim legislative remedy of recognizing same-sex civil unions. The court held that a law limiting marriage to opposite-sex couples violated the Common Benefits Clause of the Vermont Constitution. But instead of ordering the state to permit same-sex marriage, the court left it to the Vermont legislature to remedy the constitutional violation by devising a statutory scheme to afford common benefits to same-sex couples.

Soon after the decision in *Baker,* the Vermont legislature enacted a statute recognizing same-sex civil unions but not same-sex marriage.[139] It reserved "marriage" for opposite-sex couples. Nonetheless, it afforded all of the benefits of marriage (except the expressive value of the name "marriage") to such civil unions. But that is not the end of the story. In 2009, Vermont enacted a law recognizing same-sex marriage.[140] After living with civil unions for nine years, the good people of Vermont had seen that the skies did not fall. Moreover, the Vermont legislature came to see that civil unions did not afford full equality.[141]

Recognizing same-sex civil unions and permitting religious exemptions concerning same-sex marriage are both prudential remedies, rooted in recognition of religious and moral objections to extending marriage to same-sex couples. Each stops just short of affording full, equal citizenship to gays and lesbians, for the time being, out of respect for and deference to those religious objections. As Martha Minow sensibly observes, such respect, along with prudential concerns over "backlash"— mobilizing religious groups to "fight against civil rights reforms" instead of working out "practical accommodations"—counsels against too strong an insistence on congruence.[142] We return to the subject of backlash in Chapter 8.

But we tender the hope that the prudential, mutual adjustment by granting religious exemptions concerning same-sex marriage will follow the path of same-sex civil unions in Vermont, if not within a decade, perhaps within a generation: that religious exemptions will prove to be a ladder to full, equal citizenship through acceptance of same-sex marriage. We should note that the generational divide concerning same-sex marriage could not be clearer[143]—nor could it be clearer that time is on the side of the proponents of same-sex marriage eventually winning full acceptance.

We can think of no better coda to this discussion of religious convictions supporting discrimination than to observe what happened when Bob Jones University finally ended its racially discriminatory policy forbidding interracial dating and marriage in 2000. The leading representative of the next generation of the Jones family—President Stephen Jones—said that he had never been more proud of his father—Bob Jones III—than when he ended the policy after long defending it.[144] Indeed, in 2008, the University issued an apology for its "racially hurtful" discriminatory policies.[145]

We wish to invoke the exhortation from Justice Greaney's concurring opinion in *Goodridge v. Department of Public Health,* the Massachusetts same-sex marriage decision. Greaney expresses the hope that the court's decision "will be accepted by those thoughtful citizens who believe same-sex unions should not be approved by the State." Greaney does not mean "grudging acknowledgment of the court's authority to adjudicate the matter." Instead, he argues that commitment to "common humanity" and "[s]imple principles of decency" require that "we extend to the plaintiffs, and to their new status, full acceptance, tolerance, and respect. We should do so because it is the right thing to do."[146] Justice Greaney's exhortation to move from "grudging acknowledgment" to full acceptance and respect sets the stage for our next chapter: the grounds on which to justify constitutional rights.

CHAPTER SEVEN

Autonomy versus Moral Goods

In Chapters 7 and 8, we take up two diametrically opposed republican challenges—perfectionism and minimalism—to liberal justifications of constitutional rights of the sort John Rawls, Ronald Dworkin, and we propound. On the one hand, to be discussed in this chapter, Michael Sandel charges that such theories are too thin: they represent a "minimalist liberalism" and an impoverished vision of freedom and justice that exalts choice without regard for the moral good of what is chosen.[1] He exhorts us to embrace a robust civic republican perfectionist conception of freedom and justice. Sandel argues that in interpreting constitutional rights like privacy, courts should move beyond liberal autonomy arguments about protecting individual choices to perfectionist moral arguments about fostering substantive human goods or virtues. For example, in *Lawrence v. Texas*,[2] the Court should have justified protecting homosexuals' right to privacy not on the basis of homosexuals' freedom to make personal choices, but on the ground of the goods or virtues fostered by homosexuals' intimate associations.

On the other hand, to be discussed in Chapter 8, Cass Sunstein objects that liberal theories like ours are too thick: they sponsor "maximalist," "perfectionist" constitutional interpretation by the judiciary that intrudes too deeply on the political processes, ignores the risks of backlash, and exaggerates the institutional capacities of courts to the detriment of democratic capacities.[3] He develops a "minimalist" republican constitutional theory, with narrow and shallow justifications for constitutional rights. He contends that courts should eschew both autonomy arguments about choices (such as those liberals like us make) and moral arguments about goods (such as those perfectionists like Sandel make) in

favor of seeking "incompletely theorized agreements" on particular outcomes and "leaving things undecided" in order to allow democratic deliberation to proceed. Thus, in *Lawrence,* the Court should have avoided
deciding whether homosexuals, like heterosexuals, have a right to privacy or autonomy and instead struck down the law banning same-sex
sodomy (but not opposite-sex sodomy) on the ground of desuetude:
"Without a strong justification, the state cannot bring the criminal law
to bear on consensual sexual behavior if enforcement of the relevant law
can no longer claim to have significant moral support in the enforcing
state or the nation as a whole."[4]

We argue that our constitutional liberalism, despite Sandel's criticisms, can justify constitutional rights on the basis of both respecting
autonomy and cultivating virtues: both are essential to ordered liberty. It
is a mild civic liberal perfectionism (as we explained in Chapter 5). In
Chapter 8, we argue that our constitutional liberalism, notwithstanding
Sunstein's criticisms, is not too intrusive on the political process, is not
undercut by exaggerated fears about backlash, and does not presuppose
the exaggerated capacities of philosopher judges living on Olympus. All
that it requires is that judges be capable of doing what they have been
doing all along. We substantiate these arguments in Chapter 9.

Perfectionist Civic Republican versus Liberal Conceptions of Justice

Our constitutional liberalism builds upon and is analogous to Dworkin's
and Rawls's liberal conceptions of justice.[5] Sandel interprets such liberals as thinking about justice in terms of *respecting freedom* as distinguished from *maximizing welfare* or *cultivating virtues.* Sandel is the
leading critic of such liberal conceptions, interpreting them as holding
that law should be neutral concerning competing conceptions of virtue
or the best way to live, and that "a just society respects each person's
freedom to choose his or her conception of the good life."[6] He is also the
most prominent perfectionist civic republican proponent of conceiving
justice in terms of cultivating virtues. Nonetheless, the distance between
his conception and our constitutional liberalism is not as great as his
formulations might suggest.[7]

First, we argue that government should undertake a formative project
of securing the capacities for democratic and personal self-government,
including cultivating the civic virtues necessary for responsible citizen-

ship. Second, we reject the idea that rights insulate right-holders from moral judgments about their exercise and argue that the state may encourage people to exercise their rights responsibly, short of compelling them to do what the government thinks is the responsible thing.

In what follows, we suggest that the contrasts between justice as respecting freedom and justice as cultivating virtues are not as stark as Sandel has put them. Thus, prominent liberal political theorists such as William Galston and Stephen Macedo have developed attractive conceptions of civic liberalism, arguing persuasively that liberalism has a proper concern with cultivating civic virtues.[8] We too are working on this terrain of civic liberalism in this book.

We situate Sandel's most recent work on the grounds for justifying constitutional rights in the context of his prior writings. We elaborate his various critiques of liberal justifications for rights and how our constitutional liberalism is not vulnerable to those critiques, using *Lawrence* as an example. We explicate his distinction, in *Justice,* between the Aristotelian, virtue-based justification for rights he favors and the liberal, freedom-based justification he critiques. We find powerful his contention that arguments about virtue and moral worth are at the heart of the debate over opening civil marriage to same-sex couples and, thus, that it is impossible to avoid substantive moral argument. However, we challenge his dichotomy between cultivating virtue and respecting freedom as grounds for justifying rights. We do this by showing how both strands of argument feature in opinions by the high courts of Massachusetts (*Goodridge*) and California (*In re Marriage Cases*) extending the right to marry to same-sex couples. We then turn to a legislative example of how virtue-based arguments (appeals to moral worth and the goods of marriage) and freedom-based arguments (appeals to choice, equality, and fairness) both played a part in the New York legislature's enacting a law opening up civil marriage to same-sex couples. We highlight the role of religious arguments—for and against the law—and differing understandings of the relationship between civil and religious marriage in the legislative debate.

The Right of Privacy in Sandel's Prior Work

In previous writings, we have engaged with Sandel's prior work concerning the form that constitutional interpretation should take in the face of moral disagreement and political conflict about basic liberties, such as the right to privacy or autonomy.[9] Sandel argued that courts should move beyond liberal autonomy arguments about choices to republican moral arguments about substantive human goods or virtues.[10] For this reason, Sandel criticizes the majority opinion in *Bowers v. Hardwick*[11] for refusing to recognize homosexuals' right to privacy in their intimate associations and the dissenting opinions by Justices Blackmun and Stevens for making liberal arguments sounding in choice and toleration rather than republican arguments sounding in moral goods.[12] Such toleration arguments, Sandel argues, bracket the issue of the morality of homosexual intimate association and avoid addressing the "wrongness" critique of rights: that rights license immoral conduct. Consequently, homosexual intimate association is defended wholly independent of its moral worth and, worse yet, is demeaned as a "base thing that should nonetheless be tolerated so long as it takes place in private."[13] Furthermore, Sandel argues that, in *Lawrence,* the Supreme Court should have justified protecting homosexuals' right to privacy not on the basis of homosexuals' freedom to make personal choices, but on the ground of the goods or virtues fostered by homosexuals' intimate associations.[14]

Unlike some liberals, who reject out of hand Sandel's call for a civic republicanism that engages in substantive moral argument, we argued that in a liberal republican constitutional democracy such as our own it is appropriate to make both liberal autonomy arguments and civic republican virtue arguments. Sandel, we argued, overstates the supposed dichotomy between the liberal appeal to choice and the republican appeal to moral goods. We cautioned against his call for substantive moral argument to the extent that it, on the one hand, would jettison liberal commitments to toleration and autonomy and, on the other, would require more ambitious moral argument than seems likely to be successful in circumstances of deep moral disagreement and political conflict.[15]

Subsequent to *Bowers,* constitutional discourse, especially that concerning gay and lesbian rights, has moved in Sandel's direction. In *Romer v. Evans,* the Supreme Court struck down, as a denial of equal protection, an amendment to a state constitution prohibiting measures that would protect homosexuals against discrimination. The Court held that the amendment was not rationally related to any legitimate governmental purpose but instead reflected "animus" or a "bare . . . desire to harm a politically unpopular group."[16] In a vigorous dissent, Justice Scalia implicitly paid Sandel a backhanded compliment when he complained that gay and lesbian rights advocates seek "not merely a grudging social toleration, but full social acceptance, of homosexuality."[17] For Sandel, in his critique of the liberal dissents in *Bowers,* had advocated moving beyond arguments for empty toleration to arguments for acceptance and appreciation of gays and lesbians.[18]

Several years after *Romer,* in *Lawrence,* the Court held that a state law criminalizing same-sex sodomy violated a homosexual's right to privacy or autonomy. Justice Kennedy's opinion declared that it "demeans the lives" of homosexuals to respect the right of heterosexuals to autonomy without respecting an analogous right for homosexuals.[19] One of us (Fleming) applied Sandel's method to Kennedy's opinion, going through the opinion and single-mindedly differentiating the liberal strains from the republican strains: "Let us say that the liberal elements bespeak concern for choice, autonomy, toleration, and bracketing moral arguments and disagreement, while the republican elements bespeak concern for justifying freedoms on the basis of substantive moral arguments about the goods or virtues they promote, or on the basis of their significance for citizenship." That analysis showed that *Lawrence* intertwines liberal and republican concerns, emphasizing respecting autonomy together with securing the status of free and equal citizenship for all. The constitutional liberalism we advance here is tailor-made to fit and to support arguments and decisions weaving together such strands. By contrast, Sandel's civic republican theory seems to call for substantive moral arguments to the exclusion of liberal autonomy or toleration arguments.[20]

Sandel's own analysis of Justice Kennedy's opinion in *Lawrence* begins by identifying the liberal autonomy arguments sounding in choice. But, Sandel clearly was heartened by Kennedy's opinion. For it not only embodied liberal strands of choice, but also "gestured toward" republican strands of moral goods, specifically that the statute "wrongly demeaned a morally legitimate mode of life."[21] Yet, Sandel's analysis implies that Kennedy's opinion would have been still more persuasive if it had been cast more fully in terms of republican moral goods along the lines he urges.

Goodridge v. Department of Public Health, the decision of the Massachusetts Supreme Judicial Court recognizing a right to same-sex marriage under the state constitution, may be the fullest realization in a judicial opinion to date of Sandel's call for substantive moral arguments in justifying constitutional rights. Chief Justice Marshall's opinion spoke of the moral goods of marriage, most centrally "commitment," but also "the ideals of mutuality, companionship, intimacy, fidelity, and family."[22] But we hasten to add that, even in *Goodridge,* republican arguments sounding in moral goods stand side by side with liberal arguments sounding in choice, autonomy, and toleration (as Sandel acknowledges in his analysis of *Goodridge,* to be discussed later). Again, this combination—a synthesis of liberal arguments with republican arguments—is appropriate in a liberal republican constitutional democracy such as our own, and most certainly in circumstances of deep moral disagreement and political conflict.

Sandel's Aristotelian Conception of Justice in Terms of Cultivating Virtues

We now will examine the most recent articulation of Sandel's argument about the impossibility of liberal neutrality and the unavoidability of substantive moral argument about moral goods and virtues in justifying constitutional rights. In particular, we will examine one example Sandel offers: the definition of marriage and whether gay men and lesbians should be allowed to marry. We will focus on Sandel's articulation of Aristotle's method for addressing questions of political conflict: an inquiry into office, virtues, and purposes. Sandel proposes what he calls a third approach to justice, focusing on *cultivating virtues* instead of *maximizing welfare* or *respecting freedom*. Under Sandel's approach, questions of justice are not just about freedom or welfare but also about virtues and higher moral purposes. We think that Sandel's insight—that what are at stake in the same-sex marriage debate and many other conflicts are questions of worth and status—is powerful.[23] His reliance on Aristotle as an exemplar of a virtue approach to justice is also helpful. We will consider to what extent Sandel's conception is compatible with the constitutional liberal approach to the relationship among rights, responsibilities, and virtues that we propose in this book.

Sandel draws on Aristotle's conception of justice in terms of cultivating virtues, asserting:

> Debates about justice and rights are often, unavoidably, debates about the purposes of social institutions, the goods they allocate, and the virtues they honor and reward. Despite our best attempts to make law neutral on such questions, it may not be possible to say what's just without arguing about the nature of the good life.

Aristotle's approach to justice, as Sandel recounts, has two central ideas:

1. Justice is teleological. Defining rights requires us to figure out the *telos* (the purpose, end, or essential nature) of the social practice in question.
2. Justice is honorific. To reason about the telos of a practice—or to argue about it—is, at least in part, to reason or argue about what virtues it should honor and reward.

This approach, Sandel argues, differs from liberal theories of justice, because the latter "try to separate questions of fairness and rights from arguments about honor, virtue, and moral desert. They seek principles of justice that are neutral among ends, and enable people to choose and pursue their ends for themselves."[24]

Thus, Sandel sets up a dichotomy between a liberal conception of justice as respecting rights and an Aristotelian view of justice as being concerned with forming good citizens. "For Aristotle, the purpose of politics is not to set up a framework of rights that is neutral among ends. It is to form good citizens and to cultivate good character." Aristotle, in a passage Sandel quotes, criticizes a political association that merely was "a guarantor of men's rights against one another" for being a "mere covenant" or "mere alliance," instead of "being, as it should be, a rule of life such as will make the members of a polis good and just." Sandel concludes that the "highest end of political association" for Aristotle "is to cultivate the virtue of citizens." "[P]olitics is about something higher" than promoting economic exchange or maximizing economic welfare: "It's about learning how to live a good life."[25] Another implication is that the institutions of social life should be means to the end of the good life.

We reject this dichotomy: our project is to develop a constitutional liberalism that both supports rights and underwrites a formative project of inculcating civic virtues of liberal citizenship. We, like other civic liberals, are indebted to Sandel for inspiring us to think about government's formative responsibilities. However, it is not necessary to take an *either/or* approach: making arguments sounding *either* in protecting freedom of choice *or* in promoting moral goods. We should combine both types of argument.

Not only Neutral but also Naked: The Liberal Idea of Public Reason

Sandel argues that liberalism aspires not merely to state neutrality concerning competing conceptions of the good life, but indeed to a naked public square denuded of religious arguments and convictions. He criticizes Rawls's idea of public reason and conception of the Supreme Court as an exemplar of public reason.[26] Sandel quotes Rawls as providing this test for whether we are following public reason: "[H]ow would our argument strike us presented in the form of a supreme court opinion?" Rawls continues: "The justices cannot, of course, invoke their own personal morality, nor the ideals and virtues of morality generally. Those they must view as irrelevant. Equally, they cannot invoke their or other people's religious or philosophical views." Interpreting Rawls, Sandel concludes: "Like Supreme Court justices, we should set aside our moral and religious convictions, and restrict ourselves to arguments that all citizens can reasonably be expected to accept."[27]

President John F. Kennedy accepted this ideal of liberal neutrality, Sandel argues, but President Barack Obama rejects it. Sandel asserts that "[f]rom the 1960s through the 1980s, Democrats drifted toward the neutrality ideal, and largely banished moral and religious argument from their political discourse," with Martin Luther King Jr. and Robert Kennedy being exceptions.[28] By contrast, the religious right, beginning in the 1980s with the election of Ronald Reagan and the launching of the Christian Coalition, sought to "clothe the 'naked public square'" and attack the moral permissiveness of American life.[29] Liberal and Democratic response was anemic, Sandel charges; even when liberals spoke about "values," they did so awkwardly and typically meant "the values of tolerance, fairness, and freedom of choice." Here, Sandel's example is John Kerry's 2004 convention acceptance speech. Obama is the hero of this story, with Sandel quoting at length from an Obama speech about how "thousands of Americans" are "coming to realize that something is missing. . . . They want a sense of purpose, a narrative arc to their lives. . . . If we truly hope to speak to people where they're at—to communicate our hopes and values in a way that's relevant to their own—then as progressives, we cannot abandon the field of religious discourse."[30]

Sandel concludes, after excerpting this speech:

> Obama's claim that progressives should embrace a more capacious, faith-friendly form of public reason reflects a sound political instinct. It is also good political philosophy. The attempt to detach arguments about justice and rights from arguments about the good life is mistaken for two reasons: First, it is not always possible to decide questions of justice and rights without resolving substantive moral questions; and second, even where it's possible, it may not be desirable.[31]

This serves as Sandel's springboard to considering several controversial "culture war" issues: the abortion and stem cell debates and the same-sex marriage debate.[32] We have sketched Sandel's criticism of the idea of public reason, not to assess it in its own right, but to set the stage for our discussion of his analysis of same-sex marriage.

Sandel's Analysis of *Goodridge,* the Massachusetts Same-Sex Marriage Decision

Sandel argues that the question whether to recognize same-sex marriage cannot be resolved within the bounds of public reason, but requires "recourse to controversial conceptions of the purpose of marriage and the goods it honors." Thus, arguments appealing to "liberal, nonjudgmental grounds [–] whether one personally approves or disapproves of gay and lesbian relationships, individuals should be free to choose their marital partners"—will not suffice. Whether gay men and lesbians should be allowed to enter into civil marriage, Sandel argues, depends on arguments about the purpose of the social institution of marriage, which means that we must argue about "the virtues it honors and rewards." He asserts: "The debate over same-sex marriage is fundamentally a debate about whether gay and lesbian unions are worthy of the honor and recognition that, in our society, state-sanctioned marriage confers. So the underlying moral question is unavoidable."[33]

Sandel argues this is so because the state may choose among three different policies concerning marriage:

1. Recognize only marriages between a man and a woman.
2. Recognize same-sex and opposite-sex marriages.
3. Don't recognize marriage of any kind, but leave this role to private associations.[34]

Political theorist Tamara Metz refers to this third option as "the disestablishment of marriage," by analogy to the disestablishment of religion.[35] For completeness, we should round out these three with a modification of the first, which we will call Policy 4: restrict marriage to opposite-sex couples, but create a parallel institution, whether domestic partnership or civil union, for same-sex couples. Sandel notes that several states have done this, but he doesn't list it among the policy options.[36]

What about Policy 3, the disestablishment of marriage? Even though it is "purely hypothetical" and hardly anyone has embraced this proposal, Sandel claims, it "sheds light on the arguments for and against same-sex marriage." How so? It is a "libertarian solution" to the marriage debate because it "privatizes marriage,"[37] letting people marry as they please, without state sanction or interference. To the extent that the controversy over altering the definition of civil marriage entails religious disputes about marriage's purpose, this policy would allow the state to bypass such controversies by leaving the definition of marriage to religious entities. Under Policy 3, what role would the state have? Proposals vary. Liberal Michael Kinsley, for example, suggests that the state could provide domestic partnership laws to address economic and inheritance aspects of marriage.[38] Feminist Martha Fineman suggests that the economic subsidies now tied to marriage should be shifted to the caretaker/dependent relationship, stressing that adult intimate relationships could be handled by private contract.[39] Liberal feminist Metz argues for a new status, an Intimate Caregiving Union, which would include parent-child, adult-adult intimate relationships, and various other relationships.[40] This status would get at the state's most significant contemporary interest in intimate relationships and ensure that dependency and vulnerability are addressed in fair and just ways. But it, Metz argues, would avoid the problem that now exists with state establishment of marriage: because marriage is a comprehensive social institution, whose social meaning and ethical authority stem from extra-governmental sources such as religion, state regulation offends liberal principles of liberty, equality, and stability.[41]

Sandel contends that considering Policy 3 shows us that neither Policy 1 nor Policy 2 can be "defended within the bounds of liberal public reason" and "why both proponents and opponents of same-sex marriage must contend with the substantive moral and religious controversy about the purpose of marriage and the goods that define it." By contrast, with disestablishment: "Since the state would no longer confer on any family units the honorific title of marriage, citizens would be able to avoid engaging in debate about the telos of marriage, and whether gays and lesbians can fulfill it." So, too, judges could avoid "the moral and religious controversy over the purpose of marriage and the morality of homosexuality."[42]

Sandel observes that opponents of same-sex marriage argue that "the true meaning" of marriage would be dishonored by altering marriage's definition and are not "bashful about the fact that they're making a moral or religious claim."[43] However, we would point out that the arguments that opponents of same-sex marriage make in court generally eschew religious language and appeal to grounds like marriage's procreative purpose, optimal childrearing for children, and the importance of preserving tradition.[44] By contrast, proponents of a right to same-sex marriage, he says, "often try to rest their claim on neutral grounds, and to avoid passing judgment on the moral meaning of marriage." They "draw[] heavily on the ideas of nondiscrimination and freedom of choice." But such ideas alone, he argues, are not enough to justify a right to same-sex marriage.[45] He turns to *Goodridge* to explain why.

Chief Justice Marshall's opinion in *Goodridge*, Sandel observes, begins with a disclaimer—adapted from the Supreme Court in *Casey* and *Lawrence*—about the court not taking sides in the dispute among competing moral, religious, and ethical convictions about marriage and about whether same-sex couples are entitled to marry. Marshall quotes *Lawrence* (itself quoting *Casey*): "Our obligation is to define the liberty of all, not to mandate our own moral code."[46] So far, this sounds like a liberal analysis: the right to marry is a matter of autonomy and freedom of choice; to exclude same-sex couples denies them "respect for individual autonomy and equality under law."[47] In Sandel's gloss, Marshall is saying that the issue "is not the moral worth of the choice, but the right of the individual to make it."[48]

But those grounds are insufficient, Sandel contends: if the state were truly neutral, how could it draw any lines at all about who may marry, so long as the relationships were voluntary? On what grounds could it prohibit polygamy? If the state truly wanted to be neutral, he suggests, it would have to "get out of the business of conferring recognition on any marriages" (recall Policy 3 above). Instead, "[t]he real issue in the gay marriage debate is not freedom of choice but whether same-sex unions are worthy of honor and recognition by the community—whether they fulfill the purpose of the social institution of marriage." He continues: "In Aristotle's terms, the issue is the just distribution of offices and honors. It's a matter of social recognition."[49]

Sandel finds in Chief Justice Marshall's opinion a nodding toward this view of the matter. For example, in noting that the state is a third party to every marriage, Marshall brings out marriage's "honorific aspect": "Civil marriage is at once a deeply personal commitment to another human being and a highly public celebration of the ideals of mutuality, companionship, intimacy, fidelity, and family."[50] Here, Sandel argues, she "steps outside the bounds of liberal neutrality to affirm the moral worth of same-sex unions, and to offer a view about the purpose of marriage, properly conceived." What virtues or goods does marriage honor, if it is "an honorific institution"? Sandel notes that many opponents of same-sex marriage argue that the purpose of marriage is procreation, and that since same-sex couples lack the natural capacity to procreate, they lack "the relevant virtue." Marshall directly addresses and rejects this argument, locating marriage's primary purpose—its sine qua non—not in procreation but in an "exclusive loving, commitment between two partners."[51]

Sandel next stands back to ask: "[H]ow . . . is it possible to adjudicate between rival accounts of the purpose, or essence, of marriage?" Is it simply "a clash of bald assertions" or is there some way to show that one argument is more persuasive than the other? Marshall's opinion, he suggests, provides a "good illustration" of how to proceed in such cases of conflict. Her method entails "an interpretation of the purpose or essence of marriage as it currently exists." She shows that "as currently practiced and regulated by the state, [marriage] does not require the ability to procreate." From this, Sandel extrapolates: if there are "rival interpretations of a social practice, . . . how can we determine which is more plausible?"

He identifies two ways. One way is "to ask which account makes better sense of existing marriage laws, taken as a whole. Another is to ask which interpretation of marriage celebrates virtues worth honoring." Put another way, to determine "[w]hat counts as the purpose of marriage" necessitates an inquiry about "what qualities we think marriage should celebrate and affirm." This leads unavoidably to the "underlying moral and religious controversy": "What is the moral status of gay and lesbian relationships?" On this question of moral status, Sandel argues, Marshall's opinion is not neutral but concludes that the relationships formed by gay men and lesbians are as worthy of respect as opposite-sex relationships.[52] When the state denies same-sex couples the right to marry, it "confers an official stamp of approval on the destructive stereotype that same-sex relationships are inherently unstable and inferior to opposite sex relationships and are not worthy of respect." Thus, concludes Sandel:

> [W]hen we look closely at the case for same-sex marriage, we find that it cannot rest on the ideas of nondiscrimination and freedom of choice. In order to decide who should qualify for marriage, we have to think through the purpose of marriage and the virtues it honors. And this carries us onto contested moral terrain, where we can't remain neutral toward competing conceptions of the good life.[53]

Sandel's analysis is illuminating in important ways, but problematic in setting up an either/or dichotomy between nondiscrimination and freedom of choice, on the one hand, and virtues and purposes, on the other. The case for same-sex marriage does properly rest in part on "ideas of nondiscrimination and freedom of choice."[54] Sandel is right, though, to insist that it also entails inquiry into the goods and purposes of marriage and requires interpreting marriage as a contemporary social institution. That said, it is important to recognize that there is no "virtue test" for entering into civil marriage. Persons who can satisfy the minimal state qualifications may marry. Certainly, battles over access to marriage stress the symbolic importance of marriage and its aspirational meaning; arguments for extending civil marriage to same-sex couples claim that they have the same aspirations and capacity for intimate commitment and parenting. When people contend that marriage equality is a matter of basic fairness and civil rights, we should bear this in mind, lest same-sex couples be held to a standard of worth to which opposite-sex couples are not held.[55]

One can offer an alternative reading of *Goodridge* that does not require recourse to distinctively moral goods or going outside the bounds of liberalism. First, conventional constitutional law doctrine concerning Due Process (liberty) and Equal Protection, both federal and state, requires an inquiry into whether laws that are challenged are rationally related to a legitimate governmental purpose or end.[56] The analysis of purposes or ends required in these contexts is not peculiarly teleological or necessarily a moral inquiry. Nothing about liberalism precludes this conventional inquiry. To the contrary, basic principles of liberal legitimacy require it. If a law is not rationally related to a legitimate governmental purpose or end, it is not a legitimate exercise of political power in the most elemental sense. And, under conventional constitutional law doctrine, it is not constitutional. This general requirement extends far beyond the "culture war" issues like same-sex marriage implicating moral disagreement and political conflict. It applies to analyses of purposes or ends that are not moral in any ordinary sense.[57]

Second, the conclusions that laws criminalizing same-sex sodomy "demean the existence" of gays and lesbians[58] or that laws limiting marriage to opposite-sex couples "confer[] an official stamp of approval on the destructive stereotype that same-sex relationships are inherently unstable and inferior to opposite-sex relationships and are not worthy of respect"[59] are not necessarily Aristotelian or off limits to liberalism. One can interpret these holdings in Dworkinian terms: the challenged laws deny equal concern and respect.[60] Alternatively, one can put them in characteristically liberal terms as denials of dignity. That is how the Court of Appeal for Ontario put it in *Halpern v. Toronto:* "[T]he existing definition of marriage," it stated, "offends the dignity of persons in same-sex relationships."[61] That is how Dworkin argues for a right to same-sex marriage.[62] That is also how the California Supreme Court framed its decision striking down a law limiting marriage to opposite-sex couples (as we show later). Another frame for these conclusions is a Rawlsian liberal concern to secure the status of free and equal citizenship for all,[63] homosexuals and heterosexuals alike. From this standpoint, the laws at issue in *Lawrence* and *Goodridge* wrongly deny gays and lesbians this status by demeaning their existence, denying the equal moral worth of their relationships, and failing to accord them the common benefits of citizenship. All of these formulations comfortably express political liberalism's aspiration to secure the status of free and equal citizenship to all. Far from precluding such formulations, political liberalism entails them.

Finally, despite Sandel's suggestions, there is nothing in these formulations that entails that government is furthering a particular comprehensive conception of the good and thus that they are off limits to political liberalism or flout political liberalism's commitment to public reason.

Political liberalism as Rawls formulates it precludes government from imposing or promoting a particular comprehensive conception of the good,[64] for example, that of the Catholic Church. It does not preclude government from pursuing moral goods or public values that are common to a number of competing comprehensive conceptions, for example, to recall the moral goods Chief Justice Marshall invokes in *Goodridge:* commitment, mutuality, companionship, intimacy, fidelity, and family.[65] It is one thing to say, as Rawls does, that political liberalism rules out governmental imposition of a particular comprehensive conception of the good. It is quite another to say that it rules out governmental creation of institutions like marriage that pursue moral goods like those stated above. It does not. Nor does political liberalism preclude justifying constitutional rights on the basis of the moral goods promoted by protecting them.

In sum, Sandel provides a powerful and illuminating reading of the *Goodridge* same-sex marriage decision in terms of moral goods and purposes. But political and constitutional liberals can and should embrace Chief Justice Marshall's opinion. Not only does it not exceed the bounds of political liberalism or of public reason—it is, in Rawls's terms, an exemplar of public reason.

The California Marriage Cases

Like *Goodridge,* the recent California cases (both state and federal) concerning the definition of marriage provide a valuable opportunity to explore the promise of Sandel's proposed Aristotelian method for resolving the debate over same-sex marriage, which foregrounds questions of "competing notions of honor and virtue, pride and recognition."[66] At the same time, also like *Goodridge,* they suggest that his dichotomy between a liberal approach and a virtue approach is too stark. Although the success of the ballot initiative Proposition 8, amending the California Constitution to define marriage as the union between one man and one woman, in effect nullified the California Supreme Court decision in *In re Marriage Cases,* the court's opinion still warrants analysis as an instructive melding of rights and virtues arguments.

What distinguishes both the state and federal cases in California from prior litigation over same-sex marriage is that they raise and thoroughly address the question whether it is constitutional to afford same-sex couples an alternative legal status—that of domestic partnership, to which the material benefits and the respective rights and responsibilities of marriage attach—while reserving the status of marriage exclusively to same-sex couples. This helps to focus attention on what Metz helpfully calls the *meaning* side of marriage, as distinct from the *material* side.[67] It is a new stage in the struggle for marriage equality. Framing the question in this way helps people to focus on the significance of the label "marriage." Here Sandel's intuition that questions about worth are at stake is helpful: are same-sex unions viewed as equally worthy of official recognition as the unions of opposite-sex couples? Or is the creation of an alternative legal status based on a judgment that such relationships are inferior and not as worthy? So, too, these opinions afford examples of courts engaging in substantive moral argument and interpretive reasoning about the purposes of marriage. We focus primarily on the decision of the California Supreme Court from 2008, *In re Marriage Cases*,[68] and then conclude with a mention of the decision of the federal district court invalidating Proposition 8, *Perry v. Schwarzenegger,* and the federal court of appeals's affirmance of that decision.[69] It is necessary to give some background.

By referendum in a 2000 election, California voters adopted Proposition 22, which provides that "Only marriage between a man and a woman is valid or recognized in California."[70] Nonetheless, California had become one of the most hospitable states for same-sex couples. Since the enactment of a law in 1999, same-sex partners have been permitted to register with the Secretary of State as domestic partners. The preamble to California's domestic partner law states its goals: promoting equality for "caring and committed couples," "promoting family relationships and protecting family members during life crises," and reducing "discrimination on the bases of sex and sexual orientation." The legislature has steadily expanded the domestic partnership law, culminating in the dramatic expansion of the Domestic Partner Rights and Responsibilities Act of 2003 (Domestic Partner Act).[71] The upshot is that, at least since 2005, domestic partnership has functioned in California as a near-equivalent to marriage.

Marriage Cases takes up the question of whether the state must go further and provide same-sex couples with access to civil *marriage*. In a lengthy opinion, authored by Justice Ronald George, the California Supreme Court reached two basic conclusions: that the fundamental right to marry protected by the state constitution's due process clause includes the right to marry a person of the same sex and that reserving the status of marriage for heterosexuals, while limiting gays and lesbians to the second-class domestic partnership status, constitutes unconstitutional discrimination on the basis of sexual orientation in violation of the state constitution's equal protection clause.[72] On the face of it, these two holdings seem to correspond to what Sandel characterizes as the insufficient liberal arguments of freedom of choice and nondiscrimination, respectively.

Within the small number of states that have granted some kind of formal recognition to same-sex couples, there is a divide between those who grant full access to marriage and those who create an alternative legal status to provide comparable benefits. Illustrating the latter approach, Vermont's high court, in Baker v. State,[73] allowed the legislature the discretion to create an alternative legal status, civil union, to provide common benefits to same-sex couples (although the legislature subsequently in 2009 extended civil marriage to same-sex couples).[74] So did New Jersey's high court, in Lewis v. Harris.[75] Illustrating the former approach, Massachusetts's high court, in an advisory opinion subsequent to Goodridge, rebuffed the state senate when it asked whether adopting a civil union law for same-sex couples rather than allowing marriage would be sufficient. The court held that the "dissimilitude between the terms 'civil marriage' and 'civil union' is not innocuous," but assigns "same-sex, largely homosexual, couples to second-class status."[76]

The Supreme Court of California joined Massachusetts in believing that the name "marriage"—or at least the withholding of the name—means something. According to the majority opinion, the right to marry as protected by the state constitution is a "couple's right to have their family relationship accorded dignity and respect equal to that accorded other officially recognized families." Making the name of their family relationship turn on the identity of the parties undermines that equal dignity and respect. Perhaps the state could, the majority suggests, strip all unions of the name "marriage" and call them something else—that would be the disestablishment Policy 3 mentioned above. As a matter of both due process and equal protection, however, the state may not maintain one status for opposite-sex couples and another for same-sex ones.[77]

The distinctiveness of the California Supreme Court's approach is manifest when compared with that of New Jersey. In Lewis v. Harris, the state's highest court said that the naming question does not implicate constitutional questions but is instead best resolved in the "crucible of the democratic process." The majority concluded that constitutionally requiring access to "marriage"—rather than simply to the rights and responsibilities "of marriage"—would force "social acceptance" upon the citizens of New Jersey, who may not be ready for it. Any change in the longstanding definition of marriage, the majority believed, ought to come from the legislature, through "civil dialogue and reasoned discourse."[78]

This reasoning seems to treat the question of who may use the name "marriage" for their relationships as a question of policy, not constitutional rights. By contrast, the California court emphatically stated that its role is not to make decisions based on policy or what is popular, but to interpret the constitution and to protect rights under it.[79]

In addition to marriage's symbolic importance, the California Supreme Court identified other reasons why a two-tier system denies same-sex couples equal dignity and respect. To begin, the entrenched bias against gays and lesbians raises special concerns about a separate-but-equal approach. Drawing the analogy to race, the court observed that California's barring interracial marriages would have been unconstitutional even if the state had made unions using "alternative nomenclature, such as 'transracial union,'" available to interracial couples.[80] The court also pointed out the practical problem, evident from Vermont's and New Jersey's experiences with civil unions, that the public understands marriage but does not understand alternatives like civil unions or domestic partnerships. Finally, the court identified the risk that having separate tracks for opposite-sex and same-sex relationships may send a general message that government regards gay men and lesbians and their families as less worthy of respect.[81]

Thus, questions of worth do play an obvious and important role in the court's opinion. And the opinion seems to track Sandel's argument that the debate about same-sex marriage is "fundamentally" about whether same-sex couples' unions are "worthy" of the "honor and recognition" our society confers through state-sanctioned marriage.[82] Clearly, the court resolves this question in the affirmative.

But a critical step in being able to reach that judgment, says Sandel, is an Aristotelian inquiry into the purposes of the social institution of marriage and argument about "the virtues it honors" and rewards. This requires inquiry into whether same-sex unions "fulfill the purpose of the social institution of marriage," such that including gay and lesbian couples is a matter of the "just distribution of offices and honors."[83]

How does the court resolve questions about the purposes of marriage? Is it possible to detect the two strands of argument that Sandel identifies—the liberal, nonjudgmental strand and the Aristotelian, purposive strand? Does the court rely on a strategy of liberal neutrality emphasizing freedom of choice, avoiding controversial moral and religious argument? Or does it engage in substantive moral argument? As in *Goodridge*, so in *Marriage Cases*, we contend, both strands play a part in the court's resolution of the constitutional issues.

The California Supreme Court's decision offers the richest account to date of why marriage is a vital *social institution*, significant for society as well as for those who marry.[84] Metz observes that the opinion "came closer than any other to presenting a complete and compelling constitutional defense of the establishment of marriage." Marriage jurisprudence, Metz accurately says, has both an individual rights strand, which Sandel might identify with a liberal form of argument, and an institutionalist strand, which stresses society's interest in marriage and the instrumental value of marriage as a foundational social institution. She contends that the California Supreme Court moved beyond dominant "liberal discourse" about marriage by observing that protecting the right to marry requires more than merely leaving people alone, but also requires the state "to provide—define, confer, and regulate—a legal framework."[85] *Goodridge* itself made this point very clearly, speaking both of "freedom from" and "freedom to" being at stake in the right to marry.[86]

In ruling that gay and lesbian couples were entitled to marry, the California Supreme Court emphatically stressed the continuing importance of marriage both for individuals *and* for society,[87] melding an individual rights perspective with an institutionalist perspective. In doing so, it drew on many traditional arguments about why marriage matters. In this sense, the California ruling might actually be read as a conservative decision: it recognizes and seeks to preserve the important functions of marriage in an age when many couples simply cohabit and many people choose to be single. At the same time, the court's opinion is clearly also a progressive one, for it concludes that appeals to history and tradition alone are insufficient constitutional bases for excluding same-sex couples from this fundamental institution. It is also progressive in the sense that it considers and rejects a number of contemporary arguments made by the marriage movement against redefining marriage.[88]

What are the purposes of marriage? Why is it fundamental? The California Supreme Court emphasizes the unique role of marriage in providing "official recognition" to a family relationship.[89] In doing so, it employs several traditional arguments typically used by opponents of same-sex marriage. Precisely because marriage is—as conservatives have argued—unique in offering couples societal respect and dignity, the court reasoned that the state may not deny it to same-sex couples without undermining constitutional guarantees of rights to privacy, liberty, and equality.

From numerous federal and state precedents about privacy, liberty, equality, and the right to marry, the California Supreme Court distills one basic idea: the fundamental right to marry embraces the right of an individual to establish, with a loved one of his or her choice, an officially recognized *family* relationship.[90] The court makes what Sandel might call a liberal rights argument about choice but weds it to an argument about the worth of official recognition.[91]

The California Supreme Court asks: "What is society's interest in marriage?" Or what are marriage's purposes? It elaborates many reasons why both society and individuals have a stake in the institution of civil marriage. First, there is the channelling function of the family, as the "basic unit of our society."[92] Older California cases state that the family "channels biological drives that might otherwise become socially destructive," giving order to sexuality and procreation.[93] Second, civil marriage also facilitates parents' providing for "the care and education of children in a stable environment."[94] Third, society relies on marital and family relationships, which are attended by legal obligations of support, to provide crucial care for dependents and to relieve the public from, or at least share with it, the burden of support. Indeed, society favors marriage because of its necessary role in "'providing an institutional basis for defining the fundamental relational rights and responsibilities in an organized society.'"[95] These are institutionalist arguments that stress what marriage does for society.

But marriage, the court insists, is also of "fundamental significance" for those who seek to marry. Thus, one cannot look at marriage only from an *institutionalist* perspective—that is, how marriage "serve[s] the interests of society"—and ignore the *individual rights* perspective—that marriage is also a "fundamental right," an "integral component of an individual's interest in *personal autonomy*" protected by state constitutional liberty and privacy rights.[96] Marriage "cannot properly be understood as simply the right to enter into such a relationship *if (but only if)* the Legislature chooses to establish and retain it."[97] In elaborating the importance of marriage to individuals, the court makes arguments sounding more in liberal themes about a right to form and act on a conception of the good life. Marriage, for example, offers "the most socially productive and individually fulfilling relationship that one can enjoy in the course of a lifetime."[98] Indeed, constitutional precedents speak of it as part of the "pursuit of happiness."[99] The court notes that, of course, people can have and raise children outside of marriage, but "the institution of civil marriage affords official governmental sanction and sanctuary to the family unit." Civil marriage affords a public affirmation of commitment and a form of self-expression. It also enmeshes married persons in a broader network of extended family and the "broader family social structure" that is a vital part of community life.[100] Families provide a place in which personality may be developed, intimate association pursued, and values and commitments generated that reach beyond the family.

Those who argue against extending marriage to same-sex couples often appeal to some of these traditional functions of marriage. For instance, the channelling function of the family—and of family law—provided a rationale for preserving the traditional definition of marriage in *Hernandez v. Robles*[101] (in which New York's highest court upheld the state's ban on same-sex marriage) and in Justice Cordy's dissent in *Goodridge*.[102] Opponents of same-sex-marriage argued before the California Supreme Court that because of the historical link between marriage and procreation, the constitutional right to marry should be limited to opposite-sex couples. Altering the definition of marriage, they argued, would send a message that marriage no longer has to do with procreation, or with a child's needing a mother and a father.[103]

How did the California Supreme Court resolve this debate about marriage's definition and purposes? It looked to marriage law to reject the arguments centered around procreation, observing that, although channelling procreation may be a reason for marriage, the constitutional right to marry has never been confined only to couples capable of procreating. Moreover, it held that promoting "responsible procreation" among heterosexuals is not a constitutionally sufficient reason to deny same-sex couples the fundamental right to marry. As the court saw it, the state's goal of encouraging stable two-parent family relationships could be served by extending the benefits of marriage to same-sex couples (who often raise children together).[104]

Further, the court observed that providing a stable setting for procreation and childrearing is not marriage's only purpose. Marriage is also an adult relationship; state and federal precedents link it to adult happiness and to "personal enrichment."[105] The court's resistance to making marriage primarily or solely "about" children recurs in California's federal marriage case, *Perry*.[106] Moreover, the California Supreme Court pointed out that the U.S. Supreme Court has upheld the constitutional right of married couples to use contraception (thus preventing procreation).[107]

The California Supreme Court considered and rejected another argument made by the marriage movement: allowing same-sex couples to marry will "send a message" that marriage has nothing to do with procreation and childrearing, and that it is "immaterial" to the state whether a child is raised by her or his biological parents.[108] The court held that recognizing the constitutional rights of same-sex couples to marry diminishes neither the constitutional rights of opposite-sex couples nor the legal responsibilities of biological parents.[109] If anything, the court concluded, recognizing these rights "simply confirms that a stable two-parent family relationship, supported by the state's official recognition and protection, is equally as important for the numerous children in California who are being raised by same-sex couples as for those being raised by opposite-sex couples."[110] As New York's Chief Judge Judith Kaye wrote in her dissent to *Hernandez:* "There are enough marriage licenses to go around for everyone."[111] The California court reasoned here that the good of stability is relevant not just to households formed by opposite-sex couples, but also to those formed by same-sex couples. Implicitly, there is a moral judgment that these households not only will benefit from this recognition and support, but also that they are equally worthy of it.

We want to reiterate that the California Supreme Court opinion can be seen as being at once progressive and conservative. It is progressive in its unwillingness to defer completely to history and tradition when defining constitutional rights. Though the State of California had urged the court to embrace the longstanding definition of marriage as a union between a man and a woman, the court looked more critically at history and tradition. Drawing on its own precedents, and subjecting these arguments to critical scrutiny, the court stated that "history alone is not invariably an appropriate guide for determining the meaning and scope of this fundamental constitutional guarantee."[112] In rejecting wholesale deference to tradition, the court insisted that neither marriage nor constitutional concepts are static. In this sense, its reasoning resembles that of *Goodridge,* which spoke of marriage as an "evolving paradigm."[113] The court also invoked Justice Kennedy in *Lawrence:* "[T]imes can blind us to certain truths and later generations can see that laws once thought necessary and proper in fact serve only to oppress."[114]

Yet the opinion can be seen as conservative in its strong emphasis on the unique symbolic value of marriage and its invocation of the primacy of marriage. Legal scholars and activists who argue for de-centering marriage by developing domestic partnership laws and other legal statuses alternative to civil marriage[115] might criticize the majority's insistence on the inadequacy of domestic partnership as a legal alternative to marriage. The court's marshaling of traditional arguments about the importance of marriage—along with its emphasis on the risk that domestic partnership will be perceived as lesser and as inferior—may lead some progressives to lament that a real opportunity for breaking the monopoly that marriage holds on our social and legal imagination was lost. While we can argue about the society we ideally should have, for now the California Supreme Court's point is cogent: so long as marriage exists and is open only to opposite-sex couples, a marriage/domestic partnership two-track system conveys a very real and serious insult to same-sex couples, communicating that their family relationships are not worthy of equal dignity and respect.

Far from resolving the controversy over same-sex marriage, the California Supreme Court's opinion was a catalyst for the Proposition 8 campaign to amend the California Constitution by defining marriage as the union of one man and one woman.[116] These issues of worth and of the symbolic message of marriage versus domestic partnership are also central in the ongoing federal litigation concerning the constitutionality of Proposition 8, as demonstrated in *Perry*. There Chief Judge Walker of the federal district court concluded that views about the inferiority of same-sex couples and their families animated the campaign for Proposition 8 and held that it violated both the Due Process Clause and the Equal Protection Clause of the United States Constitution.[117] His lengthy opinion is heavily laden with findings of fact and citations to specific evidence on these findings to support his conclusions of law.[118] The opinion provides a rich example of the intertwining of liberal and civic republican arguments—autonomy together with worth—in justifying a right to same-sex marriage.[119]

The official proponents of Proposition 8 appealed to the Ninth Circuit. (The Supreme Court of California ruled that these proponents were "authorized to assert the state's interest in the validity of the initiative," and thus to defend its constitutionality, when the State of California refused to do so.[120]) The Ninth Circuit affirmed Judge Walker's judgment, emphasizing the "respect," "dignity," and "status" attached to marriage and concluding that Proposition 8 violated the Equal Protection Clause because it took that status and dignity away for no "legitimate purpose." The court was thus (quoting *Romer*) "left with 'the inevitable inference that the disadvantage imposed is born of animosity toward,' or, as is more likely with respect to Californians who voted for the Proposition, mere disapproval of . . . gays and lesbians as a class." Proposition 8's withdrawing a right by singling out a class in this way, the court concluded, "enacts nothing more or less than a judgment about the worth and dignity of gays and lesbians as a class."[121] We do not read the federal appellate court as making a broad statement, contra Sandel's view or our own constitutional liberalism, that moral argument has no place in what voters or legislators do. Rather, the relevant point is that the court reached its conclusion about the inevitable inference of moral disapproval after it carefully analyzed the "possible reasons" or state interests offered by proponents or their amici to justify enactment of Proposition 8 (such as encouraging responsible procreation and childrearing) and concluded that, given the state of California law before and after Proposition 8, it did not further any of them.[122] The proponents of Proposition 8 unsuccessfully sought review of this ruling by the full Ninth Circuit, and the case may eventually end up before the U.S. Supreme Court.

Choice and Worth in Justifying New York's Same-Sex Marriage Legislation

So far, we have considered Sandel's arguments about how best to justify rights, and the right to marry in particular, by examining judicial opinions. We now turn to analyze the New York legislature's vote, in June 2011, to legalize civil marriage between same-sex couples. The passage of the Marriage Equality Act vividly illustrates how arguments about rights work together with arguments about virtue or worth. Moreover, some legislators wrestled with the relationship between religious and civil marriage: how should their own religious convictions about what marriage is bear on their obligations as lawmakers to deliberate about and vote on a civil marriage bill?

Notably, the New York legislature passed the Act without any ruling by a state high court that it must do so. As noted above, in *Hernandez,* the New York Court of Appeals ruled that the state's constitution did not require opening up civil marriage to same-sex couples. The court left it open to the legislature to legalize same-sex civil marriage, and lawmakers unsuccessfully sought to do so in several prior sessions. When the legislature finally approved, and Governor Andrew Cuomo signed, the Act, the positive votes of Republican lawmakers who had opposed previous bills were critical.

Studying the statements by lawmakers in the legislative sessions as well as after the enactment of the law reveals that they justified their votes by appealing both to rights talk and to virtue talk. Some lines of argument comfortably fit what Sandel characterizes as liberal arguments sounding in the language of equal rights and basic fairness. Three examples are: marriage is a fundamental right important to human happiness—a basic civil and human right—that same-sex couples should have; as a matter of basic equality, fairness, and justice, same-sex couples should have access to the legal status of marriage and to the numerous benefits and obligations linked to that status; and a commitment to tolerance and equal respect requires treating same-sex couples equally. Lawmakers also advanced what Sandel conceives as virtue-based arguments about honor, worth, and recognition: marriage is "shorthand" for society's recognition of love, commitment, and family, and it is wrong to deny same-sex couples that recognition; and the relationships of same-sex couples have the same love and commitment as opposite-sex couples and deserve the same security and stability that the institution of marriage affords. Lawmakers also stressed the institutional benefits of marriage for society: "stable families help to build a stronger society."[123]

Opponents of the marriage law stressed that the new definition of marriage departed from religious definitions, arguing for congruence between religious and civil definitions. The most vocal opponent of the law, Democratic Senator Diaz, objected: "[W]e are trying to redefine marriage. . . . I agree with Archbishop Timothy Dolan when he said that God, not Albany, has settled the definition of marriage a long time ago."[124] Diaz referred to the "great truth[]" that "marriage is and should remain the union of husband and wife" and asserted: "Same-sex marriage is a government takeover of an institution that government did not create and should not define."[125]

By contrast, some lawmakers who voted for the bill explained how they reasoned through the conflict between religious teachings about marriage and their convictions about the "right thing" to do. It is critical, in understanding these votes, to appreciate that the final law included extensive exemptions for religious institutions, including not only the obvious exemption from performing any marriage ceremony but also from public accommodations law concerning the provision of goods and services. These exemptions (like those we discussed in Chapter 6) enabled some lawmakers to support the bill. For example, Senator Saland stressed that the bill addressed the "dual issues of religious freedoms" and marriage equality, mentioning the importance of the exemptions. He emphasized his own "rather traditional background," including his marriage of forty-six years, as well as "being raised by parents who preached to me the importance of tolerance, respect, and acceptance of others" and "always to do the right thing." His "quandary," however, as his constituents also urged him "to do the right thing," was figuring out what the right thing entailed. His "intellectual and emotional journey" ended with him defining "the right thing as treating all persons with equality, [including] within the definition of marriage."[126] In his public statement after the vote, he stressed that he appreciated that both "those for marriage equality and those who support the traditional view of marriage" have a "deep and passionate interest" in the issue. He explained that "as a traditionalist, I have long viewed marriage as a union between a man and a woman" and, as a believer in equal rights, he initially thought "civil unions for same-sex couples would be a satisfactory conclusion." However, he came to believe that equality required equal treatment as to marriage itself.[127]

Our second example is Republican Senator Grisanti. Initially, he simply opposed same-sex marriage, but he felt an obligation as a lawmaker to investigate the issue: "As a Catholic I was raised to believe that marriage is between a man and a woman. I'm not here, however, as a Senator who is just Catholic. I'm also here with a background as an attorney, through which I look at things and I apply reason." After much research and thought, he concluded: "I cannot legally come up with an argument against same-sex marriage." He made a rights-based argument that sounds in a live-and-let-live kind of tolerance, if not affirmative respect and recognition: "Who am I to say that someone does not have the same rights that I have with my wife, who I love, or have the 1300-plus rights that I share with her?" He elaborated his point about equal rights with eloquence: "I cannot deny a person, a human being, a taxpayer, a worker, or people in my district and across . . . the State of New York, and those people who make this the great state it is, the same rights that I have with my wife." Like Saland, he concluded that civil unions "do not work," but cause "chaos," and that "this state needs to provide equal rights and protections to all its residents."[128] The bill's protections for religious organizations were important to him, as a Catholic. Neither lawmaker makes an explicit argument about the equal worth of same-sex couples; however, their conclusion that basic rights or equality require opening marriage to such couples may imply that they have rejected arguments that such relationships are unworthy of legal recognition and protection.

By contrast, the role of marriage as public recognition of the equal moral worth of same-sex relationships evidently featured centrally in Governor Cuomo's private appeal to Republican lawmakers to support the bill. He reportedly told those he invited to his private residence: "'Their love is worth the same as your love.' . . . 'Their partnership is worth the same as your partnership. And they are equal in your eyes [sic] to you. That is the driving issue.'"[129] In his public statement upon passage of the bill, Cuomo spoke the language of equality and "long overdue fairness and legal security," stating: "New York has finally torn down the barrier that has prevented same-sex couples from exercising the freedom to marry and from receiving the fundamental protections that so many couples and families take for granted. . . . With the world watching, the Legislature, by a bipartisan vote, has said that all New Yorkers are equal under the law."[130] Cuomo's ability to shift from the language of moral worth and recognition to that of equality and basic fairness shows how politicians can be bilingual in justifying rights, using the rhetoric most appropriate for a particular audience.

The principal proponents of the Act similarly appealed to rights-based and virtue-based arguments. Some made the argument primarily in terms of basic human rights, fairness, and equality. For example, Assembly Speaker Sheldon Silver stated: "This is a matter of equity and justice. . . . New Yorkers should have the right to marry whom they choose."[131] Similarly, some lawmakers framed the bill as voicing the legislature's "deep-seated belief in Equality" and its rejection of "legalized discrimination."[132] Others combined rights talk and moral argument. Assemblymember Richard Gottfried, a co-sponsor of the bill, said that "both houses from both parties followed their moral compasses to point the way to extend this fundamental human right—marriage—to same-sex couples." He added that the law says that "the love, commitment, and families of same-sex couples are entitled to the same recognition the law gives to any couple."[133] During the legislative debate, Gottfried combined the appeal to marriage as a fundamental human right with an argument about moral worth: "[I]t is hard to imagine a more profoundly insulting and degrading and disrespectful statement to make about a group of New Yorkers than to say your kind are not fit to join the institution of marriage that I think we all recognize as a fundamental human right."[134] Senator Tom Duane, referring to his own long-term, intimate relationship with a same-sex partner, argued that it is *marriage* that "says that we are a family" and "recognizes that love and commitment."[135]

The relationship between civil and religious marriage featured in the speeches of some supporters of the Act. Assemblymember Deborah Glick, co-sponsor of the Act, stated: "everybody is entitled to their religious belief. But they are not, according to our Constitution, entitled to impose those religious beliefs on others." She continued: "when you take your oath of office, and declare, perhaps, by placing your hand on a Bible, that you will uphold the constitution, you don't place your hand on the Constitution of the State of New York and swear to uphold the Bible." Glick stressed the personal cost to her and her same-sex partner of being denied various benefits by the "civic institutions of this state." She shared a personal anecdote about her own grandmother's acceptance of her partner to emphasize that the "one, distilled truth about people and their relationships" was "the love of a committed relationship." She concluded: "the right to avail oneself of all the protections for that family unit should be not be denied by the State of New York, the civic institution that is the recognized and consistent shorthand that we all use to recognize and acknowledge committed, loving relationships and the families that exist within them."[136]

Glick's description of marriage as a "shorthand" for civic recognition of relationships helpfully identifies marriage's role in signaling that relationships deserve not only public but also social recognition. That it is *civic* rather than religious recognition stresses the distinction between civil and religious marriage. Thus, co-sponsor Assemblymember Daniel O'Donnell referred to his own long-term relationship and stated: "What I'm seeking is nothing from a church, or from a synagogue, or from a mosque; what I'm seeking is a piece of paper from my government . . . that conveys responsibilities and rights, which I am currently deprived from getting."[137] Finally, in responding to the argument by opponents to the bill that "we shouldn't be changing the institution of marriage," which had existed for "millennia," some proponents pointed out the continual evolution of the institution of marriage and the sharp distinctions between marriage practices that are part of "our own religious heritage" (such as polygamy) and contemporary civil marriage. Thus, Assemblyman Gottfried observed that adhering to certain biblical commandments concerning marriage—such as taking a deceased brother's wife as one's second, third, or fourth wife—"would be a criminal act in this state and . . . in every state."[138]

This sampling of arguments made in support of New York's Marriage Equality Act illustrates how rights-based and virtue-based arguments both can play a part in the processes of democratic self-government. It also suggests a recognition that civil marriage is distinct from religious marriage. By contrast, the primary statements opposing the Act insist that the definition of civil marriage must be congruent with the religious definition. After passage of the Act, Archbishop Dolan reiterated the Catholic Church's teaching that "we always treat our homosexual brothers and sisters with respect, dignity, and love," but that "we just as strongly affirm that marriage is the joining of one man and one woman in a lifelong, loving union that is open to children, ordered for the good of children and the spouses themselves." He asserted that "this definition cannot change," expressing worry that "both marriage and the family will be undermined by this tragic presumption of government in passing this legislation that attempts to redefine these cornerstones of civilization." He urged a societal return to a "true understanding of the meaning and the place of marriage, as revealed by God, grounded in nature, and respected by America's foundational principles."[139]

We will conclude by turning to the language of the Act. The Act speaks primarily in the language of rights and equality, beginning with a statement of legislative intent that declares: "Marriage is a fundamental human right." It then blends individual and institutionalist arguments, implicitly affirming the worth of same-sex relationships:

> Same-sex couples should have the same access as others to the protections, responsibilities, rights, obligations, and benefits of civil marriage. Stable family relationships help build a stronger society. For the welfare of the community and in fairness to all New Yorkers, this act formally recognizes otherwise-valid marriages without regard to whether the parties are of the same or different sex.[140]

The "Statement in Support" of the Act includes a rich mingling of arguments. After invoking *Loving*'s reference to the "freedom to marry" as "one of the vital personal rights essential to the orderly pursuit of happiness by free people," it notes that: "This bill removes the barriers in New York law that currently deprive individuals of the equal right to marry the person of their choice." Thus far, it sounds in rights talk. But the Statement goes on to characterize the issue as one of equal worth. Explaining that "[c]ivil marriage provides a comprehensive structure of state-sanctioned protections, benefits, and mutual responsibilities for couples who are permitted to marry," it states:

> [C]ouples who are denied the State's recognition, are denoted, by force of law and policy, as not equal to couples in other comparable relationships. Couples who are excluded from marriage are told by the institutions of the State, in essence, that their solemn commitment to one another has no legal weight.

The Statement explains that same-sex couples "are not simply looking to obtain additional rights, they are seeking out substantial responsibilities as well: to undertake significant and binding obligations to one another, and to lives of 'shared intimacy and mutual financial and emotional support.'" Their participation "in this crucial social institution" can "only strengthen New York's families."[141] Virtue talk here explains the melding of rights and responsibilities in civil marriage.

We turn now to the Statement's striking clarification of the relationship between civil and religious marriage: "In short, this bill grants equal access to the government-created legal institution of civil marriage, while leaving the religious institution of marriage to its own separate, and fully autonomous, sphere." How does the Act protect that sphere? Its expansive exemptions include not only the "well-established constitutional and statutory principles that no member of the clergy may be compelled to perform any marriage ceremony." It also protects the freedom of religious institutions and benevolent organizations to "choose who may use their facilities and halls for marriage ceremonies and celebrations, to whom they rent their housing accommodations, or to whom they provide religious services, consistent with their religious principles."[142] These religious exemptions evidently were critical to passage of the Act.[143]

In concluding, given Sandel's contention that appeals to substantive moral and religious argument are unavoidable on this issue, it merits mention that religious clergy and institutions were active on both sides of the debate over the Marriage Equality Act. Strong opposition by the Catholic Church contributed to the defeat of prior bills. Commentators who analyzed the factors contributing to the success, in 2011, of the Act found that one factor was the "concerted, sustained efforts by liberal Christian and Jewish clergy to advocate for [same-sex marriage] in the language of faith, to counter the language of morality voiced by foes."[144] This effort "provided a kind of political and theological cover to the moderate and conservative state senators who cast the vital swing votes" for the Act. The fact that there was religious support for the bill made it "'easier to counteract the claim of religious conservatives who say there is only one answer to this question.'"[145] Such supporters drew analogies to the critical role of religious support in passing the Civil Rights Act of 1964.[146]

Finally, it is striking that accounts of why the New York legislature finally passed the law stress that doing so had become "personal" and, thus, an imperative. "It's personal" was an idea expressed by Republican lawmakers, formerly opposed to the law, who had gay or lesbian family members. So, too, it was a personal imperative for proponents of the law, such as Governor Cuomo, who was "staggered" by the number of gay couples who sought him out to keep his campaign promise and whose girlfriend had an "openly gay brother" and frequently signaled her interest in changing the law.[147] Mayor Michael Bloomberg of New York City, who argued that "near-equality is no equality," spoke of becoming tired "of trying to explain to gay friends, relatives, and staff members why government was denying them the right to wed."[148] The personal dimension of the issue echoes the reminders in judicial opinions that same-sex couples denied the right to marry are "our friends and neighbors," seeking to share in our "common humanity."[149] This is further evidence of how issues of fairness and equal worth intertwine.

Conclusion

To recapitulate: As did the Massachusetts Supreme Judicial Court in *Goodridge,* so did the California Supreme Court in *Marriage Cases* present liberal arguments sounding in freedom of choice and nondiscrimination alongside Aristotelian or perfectionist arguments sounding in purposes, moral goods, and worth. Similarly, the New York legislature's enactment of the Marriage Equality Act shows how arguments about rights work together with arguments about virtue or worth. Sandel may be right that the latter arguments help resolve the issue. But we maintain that both types of argument can stand side by side. From the standpoint of our constitutional liberalism, this is as it should be.

Minimalism versus Perfectionism

Unlike Michael Sandel, who has put forward a perfectionist critique of liberal theories like ours for being minimalist, Cass R. Sunstein has developed a minimalist critique of liberal theories like ours for being perfectionist.[1] He calls for courts to avoid perfectionist moral arguments about the good as well as liberal autonomy arguments about the right in justifying constitutional rights. Indeed, Sunstein recommends that courts eschew arguments about abstract moral principles generally. On his view, it cheats deliberative democracy when courts, conceiving themselves to be "the forum of principle" or a forum of justice, grandly theorize about rights and moral goods and reach "maximalist" decisions that take issues of moral principle off the political agenda.[2] Instead, Sunstein argues for judicial "minimalism." He claims that law's distinctive approach to the problem of political conflict and moral pluralism should be to seek "incompletely theorized agreements" on particular outcomes, accompanied by "agreements on the narrow or low-level principles that account for them."[3] Courts should engage in reasoning by analogy from case to case, deciding cases narrowly (or "leaving things undecided") so as to leave room for political deliberation.[4]

Like Sandel, Sunstein rejects abstract liberal principles of liberty, privacy, and autonomy, but he proceeds in the opposite direction from Sandel. Sunstein finds theories like Dworkin's and ours too deep and contends that, to attain agreement in the face of moral conflict, we have to stay nearer to the surface. Sandel calls for a civic republicanism that engages in substantive moral argument, while Sunstein advocates a minimalist republicanism that avoids such argument. If Sandel argues that liberalism is too thin or minimalist in its justification for constitutional rights of privacy or autonomy, Sunstein argues that it is too thick or maximalist.

Sunstein's rejection of perfectionism and defense of minimalism rest not only on his argument concerning legitimacy—that judicial resolution of pressing moral conflicts robs the people of their right to deliberate about them—but also on an argument about the limited institutional competence of courts. He offers a number of prudential reasons concerning the likelihood that courts will get things wrong and the lack of any special qualities making judges better suited than citizens or legislatures to resolve moral conflicts. He embraces the "hollow hope" argument that courts usually cannot effectively bring about social change and that, even if they seek to vindicate constitutional rights, political and social resistance or backlash will weaken those rights and render their efforts ineffectual.[5] Thus, minimalism is superior to perfectionism given the relative institutional capacities of courts as compared with politically elected officials.

In this chapter, we focus on minimalism versus perfectionism in the justification of constitutional rights. (We encounter affinities between Sunstein's progressive critiques of liberal theories of rights and Glendon's conservative critiques considered in Chapters 2 and 3.) First, we take up perfectionism. What senses of perfectionism does Sunstein criticize? What are his critiques of perfectionism? Second, what are Sunstein's particular criticisms of liberal perfectionist justifications for the right of privacy? Are they cogent? Here we present a tale of two courts addressing the controversial issue of same-sex marriage, minimalist *Baker v. State* and perfectionist *Goodridge v. Department of Public Health*. Third, we turn to minimalism in its own right: What is minimalism? Is it just a theory of judicial review (or judicial strategy), or does it amount to a theory of the Constitution itself and a theory of the ground for constitutional rights? Is minimalism a theory for all times and circumstances or only for circumstances of moral disagreement and political conflict? Is minimalism itself a form of perfectionism? Finally, we examine the journey from Sunstein's *The Partial Constitution*[6] to his minimal Constitution: we show it to be an odyssey of the incredible shrinking constitutional theory with a perilous withering away of rights driven by exaggerated worries about moral disagreement and backlash along with the limited capacities of courts as compared with legislatures. Over and against minimalism, which is too thin to secure ordered liberty, we defend the mild perfectionist approach to justifying constitutional rights that we developed in Chapter 7: respecting autonomy and cultivating virtues and moral goods.

Perfectionism

What is perfectionism? We shall distinguish several varieties of perfectionist constitutional theory implicated by Sunstein's critique. First, there is perfectionism in political philosophy as it might be applied to constitutional theory. Sunstein states that "[t]he perfectionist approach to constitutional law should not be confused with perfectionism in political philosophy," citing John Rawls, *Political Liberalism*.[7] As discussed in Chapter 5, Rawls distinguishes between political liberalism and perfectionist liberalism (as well as perfectionist political philosophies more generally): perfectionists of all stripes believe that statecraft is soulcraft, and that the state must inculcate civic virtues or even moral excellence in the citizenry. Despite Sunstein's remark, we should acknowledge the variety of constitutional perfectionism that brings perfectionist political philosophy to bear on constitutional theory. The two best examples are the work of Sotirios A. Barber[8] and that of Michael Sandel, discussed in Chapter 7. On Barber's view, we ultimately must face up to the challenge of "supplying . . . the defect of better motives," not just by relying upon checks and balances and making "[a]mbition . . . counteract ambition"—Madison's strategy in *The Federalist* No. 51[9]—but also by inculcating civic virtues that are necessary for responsible citizenship and for the success of the constitutional order. Similarly, Sandel argues not only that government should undertake such a formative project but also that in justifying constitutional rights like privacy, we should make recourse to substantive moral goods or virtues and a conception of justice as cultivating virtues. As shown in Chapters 5 and 7, we embrace a mild perfectionist constitutional theory along these lines.

Second, we distinguish perfectionism in the sense of a theory of constitutional interpretation entailing that we should interpret the Constitution so as to make it the best it can be.[10] On this view, as Sunstein puts it, constitutional interpretation is a matter of putting the existing legal materials "in their best constructive light."[11] Furthermore, it is the quest for the interpretation that provides the best fit with and justification of the constitutional document and underlying constitutional order.[12] This sense of perfectionism—which we might call "interpretive perfectionism"—is famously associated with Dworkin, and Sunstein mentions Dworkin as a proponent of it.[13] We embrace this sense.[14] Sunstein criticizes this approach to constitutional interpretation, calling it "first-order perfectionism." But he accepts a more generic form of such perfectionism, which he calls "second-order perfectionism."[15] We will return to this idea later.

Third, what we will call "taking rights seriously" liberalism represents another sense of perfectionism. This form of perfectionism is not so much a conception of the content of constitutional rights or the ground for such rights as a conception of their stringency. These so-called perfectionists demand that we must take rights seriously in all circumstances, including war and crisis. They are liberal rights absolutists like David Cole, whom Sunstein calls the "Liberty Perfectionists" as against the "National Security Fundamentalists."[16] We might better conceive such figures not as perfectionists, but simply as rights-absolutist liberals. These liberals are strongly antipragmatic, strongly opposed to balancing rights against other considerations like national security, deeply distrustful of government, and strongly protective of individual rights, come what may. We can also imagine "taking rights seriously" conservatives (most likely libertarians).[17] As we indicate in Chapter 9, our constitutional liberalism is not such a rights-absolutism.

Finally, we might distinguish a highly generic form of constitutional "perfectionism": the idea that every constitutional theory is ultimately perfectionist in the sense that its proponents think that adoption and application of the theory will improve the constitutional order, even make the Constitution the best it can be in a general sense. Here we allude to Sunstein's statements to the effect that the battle among competing constitutional theories must be fought on perfectionist ground: theorists must show that adoption and application of their theory will improve the constitutional system as a whole.[18] He formulates and defends this view as "second-order perfectionism."[19] Our constitutional liberalism is certainly such a second-order perfectionism as well. Thus, we can see that Sunstein is criticizing perfectionism of many shapes and sizes. Some of his criticisms may apply forcefully to some versions of perfectionism but not as well or not at all to others.

What are Sunstein's criticisms of perfectionism, and are they well taken? We shall distill his many criticisms into four interrelated objections. One, perfectionism is undemocratic or, more precisely, is too intrusive on the political processes.[20] Two, perfectionism is not well suited to circumstances of moral disagreement and political conflict about basic liberties.[21] Three, perfectionism harbors hollow hopes that courts can bring about liberal social change and ignores risks of unintended consequences and backlash. And four, perfectionism does not appreciate the limited institutional capacities of courts. In the next section, we take up the first and second objections through examining Sunstein's specific criticisms of Supreme Court decisions relating to the right of privacy. On his view, these decisions problematically rest upon liberal perfectionist justifications. We assess his arguments for recasting them on minimalist grounds. In "From the Partial Constitution to the Minimal Constitution: The Incredible Shrinking Constitutional Theory," we turn to the third and fourth criticisms.

Sunstein's Call for a Minimalism that Avoids Substantive Moral Argument

Sunstein's Analysis of the Privacy Cases from *Griswold* to *Lawrence*

Unlike Sandel, who seeks to replace the liberal autonomy justification in the line of cases from *Griswold v. Connecticut*[22] to *Lawrence v. Texas*[23] with a perfectionist justification for privacy rooted in substantive moral argument about goods and virtues, Sunstein would abandon the privacy justification entirely. For him, judicial enforcement of broad privacy rights is too "adventurous" because the Due Process Clause too readily engenders expansive, antidemocratic rights of autonomy.[24]

Sunstein's justification for *Griswold* would look to neither substantive moral goods nor autonomy. Instead, Sunstein believes that the Court was too ambitious in *Griswold*. Here he seeks to build on and invigorate the idea of desuetude as a constitutional basis for courts to invalidate statutes. Rather than recognize a right to privacy, the Court should have struck down Connecticut's contraceptive ban on the ground that "citizens need not comply with laws, or applications of laws, that lack real enforcement and that find no support in anything like common democratic conviction." Sunstein contends that enforcement of the statute at issue in *Griswold* against a married couple would have lacked contemporary democratic support; the real function of the statute was to deter birth control clinics from assisting poor people. He argues that a judgment based on desuetude "would have had the large advantage of producing a narrow and incompletely theorized outcome. It might have obtained a range of agreement from people who reject any 'right of privacy' or are uncertain about its foundations and limits."[25] His minimalist approach, under which courts decide the case before them on the narrowest ground available, would seek and secure agreement on the result—invalidation of the statute—based on the low-level, narrow principle against the enforcement of obsolescent, underenforced, or selectively enforced laws. It would avoid recourse to abstract, broad, and contested rights.

Sunstein finds a ready analogy between *Griswold* and *Lawrence*. Like *Griswold*, *Lawrence* involved an old, unenforced law—a ban on sodomy. Indeed, such laws mainly served as a tool for harassment through selective enforcement on "invidious grounds."[26] In *Lawrence*, Sunstein argues, the Court should have avoided deciding whether homosexuals, like heterosexuals, have a right to privacy or autonomy. Instead, it should have struck down the law banning same-sex sodomy (but not opposite-sex sodomy) on the ground of desuetude: "Without a strong justification, the state cannot bring the criminal law to bear on consensual sexual behavior if enforcement of the relevant law can no longer claim to have significant moral support in the enforcing state or the nation as a whole."[27] By doing so, it could have avoided abstract moral reasoning about the right or the good, and even about an anticaste principle of equality, and simply struck down the old law.

Obviously, the principle of desuetude cannot justify invalidating laws in cases in which a legal prohibition does not lack real enforcement or in fact has contemporary democratic support. Restrictive abortion laws prior to *Roe v. Wade*[28] and current bans on same-sex marriage offer two illustrations. Sunstein's approach to abortion and same-sex marriage suggests just how much his commitment to deliberative democracy constrains his conception of judicial role and legal reasoning. In each case, Sunstein believes that the Equal Protection Clause, properly interpreted to incorporate an anticaste principle, forbids such laws as impermissible discrimination on the basis of sex or sexual orientation.[29] However, in both cases, he contends that it would be wrong for a court to give full vindication to that principle, because that would rob the democratic process of a chance to "participate[] in the evolving interpretation of the Constitution."[30]

Restrictive abortion laws, Sunstein argues, selectively impose on women a duty to devote their bodies to render aid to the vulnerable (fetuses). The state does not impose such a burden on men (or on parents, who are not required to donate kidneys to their children). This selective imposition stems from stereotyped "conceptions of women's proper role" and perpetuates their "second-class citizenship."[31] Thus, abortion restrictions are a form of sex discrimination. Moreover, Sunstein argues in an earlier work that just as miscegenation laws, rooted in an ideology of white supremacy, impermissibly perpetuated a racial caste system, so bans on same-sex marriage serve to perpetuate a gender caste system or gender hierarchy based on the "natural" and unequal roles of men and women.[32]

Nonetheless, Sunstein concludes that, in each instance, courts should proceed incrementally, narrowly, and cautiously. In the case of abortion, he critiques the ambitious "maximalist" decision of *Roe,* which invalidated the abortion laws of almost every state, and suggests that the Court should have proceeded slowly and incrementally, beginning with striking down laws that did not permit abortion in cases of rape and incest. Meanwhile, democratic bodies could wrestle independently with the moral questions and come to resolutions, possibly ultimately protecting a more expansive right to reproductive freedom, rooted in sex equality, than that recognized by the Court in *Roe.*[33]

Similarly, with respect to state statutes excluding gays and lesbians from marrying, it would be wrong for the Court to announce the unconstitutionality of such laws "now or as soon as it can"; such a broad ruling would be inconsistent with deliberative democracy.[34] (Nor would Sunstein invoke any fundamental constitutional right to marry, a right that he argues the Court, had it been properly minimalist, would never have recognized.[35]) Because the debate over the legal treatment of sexual orientation, including same-sex marriage, involves a fundamental moral conflict, courts should not rob the people of their right to deliberate by purporting to settle the issue and remove it from the political agenda. Instead, courts should proceed cautiously and narrowly, and allow the democratic process to come to terms with the broader and deeper issues. Nonetheless, Sunstein praised the Massachusetts Supreme Judicial Court's decision in *Goodridge,* holding that the prohibition of same-sex marriage violated the state constitution: "We should . . . celebrate *Goodridge,* not only because it ends a form of second-class citizenship for gays and lesbians but also because it exemplifies the federal system at its best."[36] That is, he argues, even if the Massachusetts Supreme Judicial Court was right to interpret the Massachusetts Constitution to support a right to same-sex marriage, the U.S. Supreme Court would be wrong, at least at the present time, to interpret the U.S. Constitution to protect such a right for the entire, morally divided nation. Later we consider *Baker v. State,* the Vermont Supreme Court decision invalidating laws limiting marriage to opposite-sex couples, as a minimalist decision and contrast it with *Goodridge* as a perfectionist decision.

A Critique of Sunstein's Analysis of the Privacy Cases

Is Sunstein's argument for judicial minimalism persuasive and sound, or does it amount to a troubling withering away of the proper role and responsibility of courts as vindicators of constitutional rights? Sunstein's minimalism represents a significant and disturbing retreat from what began, in *The Partial Constitution,* as a potentially robust interpretation of the Equal Protection Clause, assigning courts a role in protecting citizens from laws perpetuating second-class citizenship. There, he argued for an anticaste principle of equal citizenship pursuant to which society may not turn morally irrelevant characteristics—most obviously race and sex, but also sexual orientation—into systemic sources of social disadvantage.[37] To be sure, from the outset he contended that the legislative and executive branches should play the primary role in enforcing the anticaste principle because courts have limited capacities to implement any general attack on such systemic disadvantage. Nonetheless, he clearly contemplated some role for courts, leading to the reasonable conclusion that, although he rejected any broad principle of autonomy or privacy as a basis for rights, his principle of equality might secure similar protections.[38] Thus, Sunstein defended *Roe* not on privacy grounds but by analogy to *Brown v. Board of Education*[39] and through a link between race and sex discrimination: like *Brown, Roe* was a "judicial invalidation of a law contributing to second-class citizenship for a group of Americans defined in terms of a morally irrelevant characteristic."[40] And he hinted that an analogy to *Loving v. Virginia*[41] offered a foundation for judicial invalidation of bans on same-sex marriage (an analogy he subsequently called "highly controversial").[42]

In his more recent writings, however, Sunstein's position is that courts should not fully enforce such constitutional principles or give full scope to such analogies, even if they are sound; rather, courts should apply those principles narrowly and make more modest use of analogical reasoning.[43] Morally ambitious constitutional interpretation is simply not in the judge's toolbox of lawyerly methods. Sunstein's view seems to be that so long as deliberative democracy will eventually vindicate constitutional principles, courts should defer to the democratic process. In contrast with Dworkin's liberal model of courts as aggressive vindicators of constitutional rights, Sunstein's model of judicial minimalism comes perilously close to sacrificing such rights for the sake of deliberative processes. For how long should the courts stay their hand? What of the human cost to the individuals who may have legitimate claims to constitutional protection but whose rights are underenforced by the courts and who must await protection in the democratic arena? Justice delayed is not, for Sunstein, justice denied. Or justice delayed, all things considered (especially the benefits to deliberative democracy of such a delay), is justifiably denied.

Sunstein, of course, recognizes that the democratic process may have flaws and that courts have an appropriate role in protecting persons who are disadvantaged in that process. Yet his strong commitment to judicial minimalism leads to a judicial incrementalism that appears to undercut that protection in order to respect the democratic process. To return to the example of abortion, women, he argues, are a group who suffer disadvantage in the democratic process, and the courts should play a role in striking down restrictive abortion laws. But, Sunstein suggests, judicial incrementalism (for example, beginning with invalidating laws that prohibited abortion even in cases of rape and incest) would have been a better course than the "maximalist" approach of *Roe*. Furthermore, he wagers that it might have led to legislatures fashioning a broader and more accepted right of sex equality and reproductive freedom than *Roe*.[44] It is a point of considerable controversy whether, without *Roe*, state legislatures would have done so.[45] In any event, abortions sought because of rape and incest are a tiny portion of all abortions, and such a limited right would leave most pregnant women who seek to terminate their pregnancies with no legal recourse. And here, justice delayed, given the temporal nature of pregnancy, is certainly justice denied. If there are, as Sunstein contends, strong arguments for abortion rights rooted in an anticaste principle of sex equality (under the Equal Protection Clause), why must women wait for democratic vindication? This is an especially troubling prescription, given that the abortion issue has illustrated repeatedly that highly mobilized minorities opposing abortion rights can have dramatic effects on legislatures.[46] In such circumstances, courts have a vital role to play in blocking measures restricting such rights in defiance of *Roe*.[47]

To read Sunstein's critique of *Roe*, you would think three things:

- that *Roe* was a triumph of liberal perfectionist arguments and that no one has ever offered "conservative" justifications for this 7–2 Burger Court decision on grounds of consensus and common-law constitutionalism;
- that *Roe*'s justification of the right to abortion is all there is, and that the Supreme Court itself has never offered a fuller, more persuasive justification of the right; and
- that Sunstein has fully accepted controversial arguments about *Roe* most commonly associated with Mary Ann Glendon, for example, as discussed in Chapter 3, that *Roe* short-circuited the political processes that were proceeding state-by-state toward liberalization of restrictive abortion laws, thus provoking backlash against the right to abortion.[48]

We will take up the first and second points here; we will discuss the third later in connection with backlash.

Before we accept an account of *Roe* as a product of liberal perfectionism, we should recall Thomas C. Grey's classic account of *Roe* (in "Eros, Civilization and the Burger Court") as reflecting not liberal concerns for autonomy and the sexual revolution of the 1960s and 1970s, but conservative concerns for family stability and family planning.[49] Grey's account helps make sense of the fact that it was, after all, the conservative Burger Court (not the liberal Warren Court) that decided *Roe*. In fact, four of the justices in the 7–2 majority were moderate Republicans (Harry Blackmun, Warren Burger, Lewis Powell, and Potter Stewart, including three out of the four Republican justices appointed by Richard Nixon). The sole Nixon appointee to dissent was William Rehnquist. We guess these moderate, mostly midwestern Republicans (soon joined by Illinois Republican John Paul Stevens) just did not see the radical counterrevolutionary Republicans[50] (and the culture war) coming.

One could even see Blackmun's opinion in *Roe* as minimalist: an incompletely theorized agreement, and shallow rather than deep. Rather than articulating a deep justification for the right to abortion on liberal perfectionist grounds of liberty or autonomy, Blackmun simply sketched the "roots" of the right in decisions from *Meyer v. Nebraska* (1923) and *Pierce v. Society of Sisters* (1925) up through *Griswold* and *Eisenstadt v. Baird* (1972).[51] Nor did he articulate a deep justification for the right in a liberal or feminist perfectionist ground of an anticaste or antisubordination principle of sex equality (even though incipient sex equality arguments featured in pre-*Roe* federal court decisions that otherwise influenced Justice Blackmun and in "friend of the court" briefs filed in *Roe*).[52] What is more, Blackmun offered an incompletely theorized agreement acknowledging that the right could be grounded in "the Fourteenth Amendment's concept of personal liberty and restrictions upon state action" or "in the Ninth Amendment's reservation of rights to the people." He wrote an opinion with which six other Justices, perhaps for their own deeper reasons, could agree. With this incompletely theorized agreement on hand, Blackmun concluded that the right "is broad enough to encompass a woman's decision whether or not to terminate her pregnancy."[53] Granted, Sunstein may say that the "broad enough" is the problem from the standpoint of minimalism. Our point is that Blackmun's opinion is hardly the opinion that a liberal perfectionist would have written.

We should also recall that many have justified *Roe* as a consensualist decision or a common-law constitutionalist decision, not as a liberal per-fectionist decision. Some notable scholars originally justified *Roe* on grounds of consensus.[54] Given all the controversy that subsequently has surrounded the case, it is easy to forget this. Many (most recently David Strauss) have justified *Roe* as solidly grounded in common-law constitu-tionalism, saying that the critics are missing the forest for the trees and the like.[55] Despite all the controversy surrounding *Roe,* that is the way Justices O'Connor, Kennedy, and Souter evidently still see the right to abortion, after all these years, as indicated by their joint opinion in *Planned Parenthood v. Casey.*[56] Let us not forget that Justice John Marshall Harlan II is often celebrated as a great common-law constitu-tionalist—developing doctrine through reasoning by analogy from one case to the next—and that the joint opinion in *Casey* embraced his con-ception of the framework for the due process inquiry.[57] Sunstein praises O'Connor, Kennedy, and Souter for their minimalism in certain cases.[58] Souter clearly conceived of himself as the new Harlan in certain respects, most notably, in his common-law constitutionalist conception of the due process inquiry (as is evident not only in the joint opinion in *Casey* but also in his concurrence in *Washington v. Glucksberg*[59]).

In any case, the Supreme Court's justification of the right to abortion in *Roe* was not the Court's last word on the subject. It offered a fuller and more persuasive justification for the right in *Casey,* as we have discussed in Chapter 3. That justification, again, is in the form of a Harlan-style common-law constitutionalism, for it builds upon prece-dents, conceives of liberty as a "rational continuum" rather than an enu-merated list, conceives judgment as a "rational process" of "reasoned judgment" rather than mechanical application of a bright-line formula, and conceives tradition as a "living thing" rather than a hidebound his-torical practice.[60] We present *Roe* and *Casey* in this light in Chapter 9. We hasten to acknowledge that Sunstein is hardly more satisfied with *Casey* than with *Roe.* He does, though, praise the *Casey* joint opinion's intimation of an equal protection grounding for the right to abortion (as an alternative to the liberty or substantive due process grounding): "The ability of women to participate equally in the economic and social life of the Nation has been facilitated by their ability to control their reproduc-tive lives."[61] This suggests that much of Sunstein's discontent with *Roe* and *Casey* may be with liberty and substantive due process as a ground for rights as such. Indeed, he makes the general argument that liberty rights inherently are more intrusive on the political process than equality rights. Elsewhere one of us has extensively criticized that argument.[62]

Baker v. State, the Vermont Same-Sex Marriage Decision:
A Case Study in Minimalism

In *Baker v. State,* the Vermont Supreme Court held that the state law permitting only opposite-sex couples to marry violated the Common Benefits Clause of the Vermont Constitution (its counterpart to the Equal Protection Clause of the U.S. Constitution).[63] By contrast with our analysis (in Chapter 7) of *Goodridge v. Department of Public Health,* the Massachusetts same-sex marriage decision, as a triumph of both liberal autonomy arguments and perfectionist moral goods arguments, we shall present *Baker* as a case study in minimalism. The decision was minimalist in several important respects.

First, Chief Justice Amestoy bases the decision invalidating the Vermont law on the Common Benefits Clause, not the Due Process Clause; on equality, not liberty.[64] Sunstein argues that decisions based on equal protection are minimalist as compared with those based on liberty because they are less intrusive on the political process. Courts can avoid deciding, for example, whether there is a substantive fundamental right to marry that the state must afford to everyone. They can simply say: whether or not there is a fundamental right to marry, if the state provides the benefits of marriage to some couples, it must provide those benefits to all couples unless it has a good justification for not doing so. Thus, courts leave it up to legislatures whether to provide those benefits to all or to none. They do not tell legislatures that they must provide them to all on grounds of due process or liberty.

Second, Amestoy takes a minimalist approach to common benefits or equal protection at that. He writes that Vermont decisions are "broadly deferential to the legislative prerogative to define and advance governmental *ends,* while vigorously ensuring that the *means* chosen bear a just and reasonable relation to the governmental objective." Furthermore, Vermont decisions apply a "relatively uniform standard . . . rather than the rigid, multi-tiered analysis" of the U.S. Supreme Court.[65] Thus, the Vermont Supreme Court is not concerned with delineating suspect or quasi-suspect classes or the like. This has important implications for the way Amestoy writes the opinion and justifies the holding. For example, he can steer clear of deciding whether discrimination on the basis of sexual orientation is a suspect classification triggering strict scrutiny. Moreover, he feels no compulsion to argue that discrimination on the basis of sexual orientation is analogous to discrimination on the basis of race. And he can avoid deciding whether discrimination on the basis of sexual orientation is analogous to, or indeed a form of, discrimination on the basis of sex. All of these would be controversial doctrinal holdings and arguably would entail subscribing to, or presupposing acceptance of, deep, controversial normative theories or arguments.

In fact, Chief Justice Amestoy rejects the argument that laws denying marriage to same-sex couples discriminate on the basis of sex. Justice Johnson (in partial concurrence) accepts this argument.[66] What reasons does Amestoy give for rejecting this argument? He writes that the evidence does not demonstrate such a discriminatory purpose.[67] That is, when one examines the history of the adoption of the laws limiting marriage to opposite-sex couples, one finds nothing to support a purpose to discriminate against gays and lesbians. More fundamentally, we believe that Amestoy rejects these arguments because he wants to justify the decision without having to take any controversial theories on board. He wants a matter-of-fact common benefits argument, not a complex or controversial normative theory.

Amestoy also rejected arguments that denial of marriage to same-sex couples is analogous to the racial discrimination condemned in *Loving*. In that case, Virginia had defended a statute forbidding interracial marriage on the ground that it applied equally to whites and blacks: Blacks may not marry whites, and whites may not marry blacks. But the U.S. Supreme Court saw through this justification; the classification was designed to maintain white supremacy. Here Vermont defends the law on the ground that it applies equally to men and women. As Justice Johnson puts the argument, quoting from an article by Sunstein: "if a man wants to marry a man, he is barred; a woman seeking to marry a woman is barred in precisely the same way. For this reason, women and men are not treated differently."[68] Justice Johnson invoked this analogy to *Loving*, but Chief Justice Amestoy concludes that it is "misplaced."[69] Again, we believe Amestoy does so because he wants to avoid making controversial moral judgments analogizing discrimination on the basis of race to discrimination on the basis of sexual orientation or sex.

Instead of taking any of these theoretically and normatively ambitious routes, Chief Justice Amestoy writes a deliberately shallow opinion. It goes something like this. On the one hand, the couples over here (the opposite-sex couples who wish to marry) may marry and they get certain benefits if they do so. On the other hand, the couples over there (the same-sex couples who wish to marry) are not permitted to marry and therefore they do not get those benefits. And the state has offered no persuasive arguments that justify the exclusion. Therefore, the latter couples are denied common benefits. It is as simple as that.[70] No complex and controversial normative theories needed here. No complex and controversial analogies and doctrinal constructions needed either.

Third, most obviously and famously, *Baker* is minimalist in its approach to remedy for the constitutional violation. Instead of ordering the state to permit same-sex marriage, the Court leaves it to the Vermont legislature to implement the constitutional mandate by choosing a statutory scheme that will afford common benefits to same-sex couples. What arguments does the Court give for this approach? Amestoy invokes a conception of who may interpret the Constitution. Instead of conceiving courts as having ultimate or even exclusive authority to interpret the Vermont Constitution, he argues that "courts are participants [with legislatures] in the system of democratic deliberation."[71] He invokes Sunstein's theory of minimalism, and argument for courts "leaving things undecided" and open for democratic deliberation, especially in circumstances of moral disagreement and "flux" concerning rights. He quotes Sunstein for the recognition that even when courts are right about rights, they "may be counterproductive," for example, through provoking democratic or populist backlash.[72]

Chief Justice Amestoy argues that this implementation—with the legislature devising the remedy—is a "fulfillment of constitutional responsibility."[73] But Justice Johnson (in partial dissent) argues it "abdicates that responsibility."[74] Should Amestoy's approach be praised as a prudential act of judicial statesmanship? Or condemned for declaring a right without recognizing a remedy? The answer depends upon whether you are a minimalist or a champion of courts "taking rights seriously." This clash encapsulates the debate between proponents of these two approaches, epitomized by Sunstein and Dworkin, respectively.

Presumably one of the prudential reasons for Amestoy's decision to leave it to the Vermont legislature to implement a statutory scheme was his aim to include the legislature in the outcome and to avoid the populist backlash exemplified by the reaction to *Baehr v. Lewin*.[75] In that case, a plurality opinion of the Hawaii Supreme Court held that the state laws denying marriage to same-sex couples discriminated on basis of sex, only to be overturned by a state constitutional amendment returning the power to the legislature "to reserve marriage to opposite-sex couples."[76] Chapter 7 discusses a similar experience in California, where the state's highest court ordered recognition of same-sex marriage and was repudiated by Proposition 8, which defined marriage as the union of one man and one woman.

Furthermore, in bringing the legislature into the fashioning of the remedy, the risk that the Vermont Supreme Court takes is not as great as it might appear. There is every reason to believe that Amestoy, previously elected Attorney General of the state of Vermont for six consecutive terms, knew his legislature well and knew they would do right by his lights. After all, the Vermont legislature already had conferred many benefits upon same-sex couples: for example, it "has acted affirmatively to remove legal barriers so that same-sex couples may legally adopt and rear the children conceived" through assisted-reproductive technologies; "has also acted to expand the domestic relations laws to safeguard the interests of same-sex parents and their children when such couples terminate their domestic relationship"; and has removed "all prior legal barriers to the adoption of children by same-sex couples."[77] Indeed, what the legislature had already done undermined many of the state's arguments about the need to exclude same-sex couples from the benefits and protections of marriage (for example, the argument about furthering the link between procreation and childrearing). It is far less likely that a court with an unpredictable and uncooperative legislature would have taken the risk of handing over the fashioning of the remedy. What if, for example, the Vermont legislature instead had prohibited adoption by gays and lesbians? And had a mini Defense of Marriage Act? We speculate that in such circumstances a court probably would not take the minimalist, prudential route that the Vermont Supreme Court took in *Baker* and probably would not be successful if it tried to do so.

Soon after the decision, in 2000, the Vermont legislature enacted a statute recognizing same-sex civil unions but not same-sex marriage.[78] It reserved "marriage" for opposite-sex couples. Nonetheless, it afforded all of the benefits of marriage (except the expressive value of the name "marriage") to such civil unions. In 2009, as we observed in Chapter 6, the Vermont legislature enacted a statute recognizing same-sex marriage.[79] What might have prompted Vermont to move from civil unions to marriage? After living with civil unions for nine years, the good people of Vermont had seen that the skies did not fall. Nor did the skies fall in nearby Massachusetts and Connecticut, both of which had recognized same-sex marriage in the meantime. Moreover, the Vermont legislature came to see that civil unions did not afford full equality.[80] The "single, most common theme" in hearings held at the behest of Vermont legislators about the effects of the law was that "civil unions are separate, but unequal." Vermonters testified that the "two separate legal structures for conferring state benefits" sent a message that same-sex couples are inferior and "unworthy of inclusion in the marriage laws" and urged that such a system violated the Common Benefits Clause and "values deeply and widely held in Vermont."[81] And so, the Vermont legislature decided to go all the way to marriage, appealing (to use our formulation from Chapter 7) both to equality rights and to equal worth. In retrospect, we might view civil unions as a ladder to full civil rights for gays and lesbians: a ladder that ultimately can be discarded in favor of marriage.[82] Sunstein might say, yes, that is a virtue of minimalism: it does not preclude ultimate realization of full equality or full citizenship and indeed it may be a prudential route to that outcome.

Baker and *Goodridge:* A Tale of Two Courts

Let us consider a tale of two courts: The main differences between *Baker* and *Goodridge* are the very points that are vigorously debated between minimalists and perfectionists. We shall sketch five.

- **Prudence** versus unflinching commitment to **principle:** *Baker* prudentially left it to the Vermont legislature to devise the remedy (and signaled that civil unions would be sufficient). *Goodridge* and the Massachusetts Supreme Judicial Court's subsequent advisory opinion, standing on firm commitments to the principles of equality and liberty, rejected civil unions as "second-class citizenship" and ordered the legislature to permit same-sex marriage.
- Fundamentally differing conceptions of **who** may interpret the Constitution and decide how to implement it: *Baker* expresses a conception of courts along with legislatures as "participants in the system of democratic deliberation."[83] *Goodridge* takes the view that "it is the traditional and settled role of courts to decide constitutional issues."[84] These fundamentally differing conceptions shaped their different approaches to remedy.
- **Avoidance of** versus **direct engagement with** questions of the moral worth of same-sex relationships: *Baker* sought to avoid such controversial issues by focusing concretely on denial of common benefits and protections.[85] *Goodridge* focused on the denial of membership in the institution of civil marriage itself.[86] Thus, *Goodridge* confidently faced up to the very deep and controversial issues concerning moral worth and the meaning or expressive value of marriage itself that *Baker*'s prudential and minimalist approach avoided.
- **Provocation of backlash** and implications for subsequent presidential elections: In the 2000 presidential election, not a word was heard of the 1999 decision in *Baker* and Vermont's recognition of same-sex civil unions. In the 2004 presidential election, by con-

trast, the 2003 decision in *Goodridge* and Massachusetts's judicially compelled recognition of same-sex marriage was front and center: on some analyses, backlash against it swayed the outcome of the election in favor of Bush and against Kerry.[87] Bush portrayed Kerry as a liberal senator from the state of Massachusetts, which brought us same-sex marriage. No matter how many times Kerry said he was opposed to same-sex marriage and criticized the *Goodridge* decision, he could not shake this image.

- Finally, unlike *Baker, Goodridge* prompted proposals to amend the U.S. Constitution to forbid recognition of same-sex marriage. So far, those proposals have not gotten the support of two-thirds of both houses of Congress that is required under Article V to propose an amendment to the Constitution.

Which is more defensible, the minimalist route of *Baker* or the perfectionist route of *Goodridge?*[88] Before deciding that, we shall examine minimalism as a theory in its own right.

Minimalism

We begin with some questions: What is the theory of minimalism? Is it merely a theory of judicial review (or judicial strategy) that is agnostic concerning the character and commitments of the Constitution? Or is it a theory of the Constitution itself? Is minimalism a theory for all times and circumstances or only for certain times and circumstances? Despite our opening contrast between minimalism and perfectionism, is minimalism itself a form of perfectionism?

The Circumstances for Minimalism

Officially, Sunstein presents minimalism as a theory of judicial review (or judicial strategy), not as a theory of the Constitution itself. Moreover, he argues for minimalism as a theory that is appropriate in certain circumstances, for example, those of moral disagreement and political conflict about our basic liberties.[89] Yet to the extent that Sunstein's minimalism is rooted in a pragmatic or Burkean distrust of abstract theories and principles,[90] it may be a theory of judicial review for all times and circumstances. To the extent that it reflects a Learned Hand–like humility and skepticism about moral principle—witness Sunstein's pervasive refrain that "the spirit of liberty is that spirit which is not too sure that it is right"[91]—it likewise may be a theory for all circumstances. Sunstein applies this idea of the spirit of liberty not only to judges, but also to citizens. Thus, it is not merely about the justification for rights in judicial opinions, but also about how citizens themselves should conceive their basic liberties.

Similarly, to the extent that minimalism grows out of concern for the limited institutional capacities of courts,[92] it may be a theory for all circumstances. After all, it is unlikely that courts somehow could change and become more capable of making the kinds of judgments that those who are preoccupied with limited institutional capacities of courts think they are not capable of making. And, to the extent that it is rooted in a conception of common-law constitutionalism, understood in a minimalist way, it may be a theory for all circumstances. We say "understood in a minimalist way" because we might understand common-law constitutionalism to be more theoretically ambitious than minimalism. This is exemplified in the jurisprudence of Justice Harlan—for example, in his dissent in *Poe v. Ullman* justifying the right of privacy, which was embraced by the joint opinion in *Casey*—as well as in the common law approach of Strauss.[93] (We return to this matter in Chapter 9.) Finally, though Sunstein says minimalism is appropriate in circumstances of moral disagreement and political conflict, he probably would add that these are perennial circumstances in a constitutional order like our own. He might well invoke Rawls's characterization (discussed in Chapter 5) of the fact of reasonable moral pluralism as a permanent feature of a constitutional democracy such as our own, not to be regretted and not soon to pass away.[94] If Sandel argues that these circumstances entail that we inevitably must face up to questions of moral goods and moral worth through perfectionist arguments, Sunstein argues that they entail that we must avoid those questions through minimalism.

Minimalism Itself as a Form of Perfectionism

Sunstein's minimalism is best understood in terms of what motivates it: the concern that "theoretically ambitious" federal judges protecting rights of privacy or autonomy are removing too many issues (for example, abortion and same-sex intimate association) from the purview of elected legislatures and therewith popular choice.[95] Perfectionist theories of constitutional interpretation, he says, invite theoretically ambitious decisions (like *Roe* and *Lawrence*) that rob popular majorities of the opportunity to deliberate about, and through deliberation to reach consensus about, divisive moral issues. Sunstein instead proposes minimalism: "the view that judges should take narrow, theoretically unambitious steps" in deciding constitutional questions, especially concerning controversial rights.[96]

We will attempt a clearer picture of minimalism momentarily, but we note first something that is not always clear in Sunstein's argument: his position on interpretation is a two-part affair. Only one of these parts proposes anything fairly described as minimalist. The minimalist part, moreover, does not deal with constitutional interpretation; it does not advise interpreters how to find what the Constitution means. The minimalist part is rather a theory of judicial strategy. Its explicit audience is judges. Sunstein says his "focus . . . [is] on constitutional interpretation by the judiciary." While he advises judges to adopt minimalism, he leaves "citizens and their representatives" free to adopt what he calls a "first-order perfectionism"[97] and thus to interpret the Constitution so as to make it the best it can be. He attributes such perfectionism to Dworkin and would also attribute it to Sandel and us. Instead of advising judges and other interpreters how to find what the Constitution means, minimalism tells judges what to do after they have decided that question. In other words, minimalism tells judges the kind of thing they should say to the public in constitutional cases, not how to decide what the Constitution means where controversial rights are concerned.

Sunstein, however, does have a theory of how to decide what the Constitution means. That theory comprises the second part of his position. But this second part is not minimalist; it is in fact a version of perfectionism, as we shall see. Unraveling and then recombining the two parts of Sunstein's position leaves us with the following advice to judges: find what the Constitution means essentially as Dworkin does and then tell the people what is best for them to hear. Sunstein's position raises many issues about the role of judges and the nature of constitutional democracy, especially the theory of responsibility in constitutional democracy.[98] But our present interest in his position is limited. We seek to show only that his approach to constitutional interpretation is philosophic or perfectionist in nature, and his minimalism is a theory of what judges should do or say to the public after they have decided what the Constitution means.

That Sunstein's approach to constitutional interpretation is philosophic or perfectionist in nature is indicated in a preliminary way by his choice of labels. He calls Dworkin's approach "first-order perfectionism" and minimalism "second-order perfectionism," which is enough to suggest that minimalism is some diminished form of a philosophic approach or perfectionism. Looking behind these labels to what they stand for, we see that Sunstein distinguishes four strategies of judicial conduct in constitutional cases. The first strategy (associated with Thayer) is that judges should let legislation stand unless legislation "is plainly in violation of the Constitution"—i.e., a "clear mistake" in violation beyond reasonable question. The second (associated with Raoul Berger and other originalists) is that judges should ground their judgments in "the original public meaning of the [constitutional] document." The third strategy (Sunstein's approach) is minimalism, in which judges should "build modestly on their own precedents" instead of ruling "broadly or ambitiously." And the fourth strategy (associated with Dworkin) is that judges should represent the Constitution as the best it can be, "and in that sense perfect [] it." None of these strategies is "ruled out by the Constitution itself," Sunstein says, and therefore each "must be defended by reference to some account that is supplied by the interpreter."[99] These accounts, moreover, must be "perfectionist" in nature—that is, moral or philosophic.

Sunstein is clear and emphatic about this last point. We quote him in full:

> Any approach to the founding document must be perfectionist in the sense that it attempts to make the document as good as it can possibly be. Thayerism is a form of perfectionism; it claims to improve the constitutional order. Originalism, read most sympathetically, is a form of perfectionism; it suggests that constitutional democracy, properly understood, is best constructed through originalism. Minimalism is a form of perfectionism too; it rejects Thayerism and originalism on the ground that they would make the constitutional system much worse. It would appear that the debate among Thayerians, originalists, minimalists, and perfectionists must be waged on the perfectionists' own turf. And if this is so, perfectionists are right to insist that any approach to the Constitution must attempt to fit and to justify it. Perhaps the alternatives to perfectionism are all, in one or another sense, perfectionist too.[100]

This is an important passage because Sunstein recognizes that a philosophic argument is needed to defend any general approach to constitutional meaning and/or judicial strategy. Here Sunstein says something about his activity as a constitutional theorist. He has to offer a philosophic argument for minimalism, just as other theorists have to offer philosophic arguments for their positions. But this proves nothing about the activity of judges deciding concrete constitutional questions concerning controversial rights. Armed with Sunstein's philosophic argument for minimalism (whatever it may be), can judges (or any other

interpreters) use the tenets of minimalism to decide concrete constitutional questions in a manner free of controversial philosophic choices?
To see why the answer is no, we shall consider Sunstein's further observations about minimalism.

Sunstein says that "[n]o approach to constitutional interpretation
makes sense in every possible world," and that the case for each approach
"must depend, in part, on a set of judgments about institutional capacities." Thus, where "democratic processes work exceedingly fairly and
well" on their own—where there is no racial segregation, for example,
and "political speech is not banned," and "federalism and separation of
powers are safeguarded, and precisely to the right extent," all without
"judicial intervention"—then it "would make a great deal of sense" for
judges to adopt Thayer's approach to constitutional adjudication. On the
other hand, when representative institutions are behaving badly and "the
original public meaning is quite excellent" from the standpoint of honoring constitutional rights and institutions, then an originalist approach
"would seem best." Where original meanings are inadequate and courts
are more competent, morally and intellectually, than representative institutions, Dworkin's approach is best. And minimalism is best when original meaning "is not so excellent" for protecting rights and institutions,
"the democratic process is good but not great," and "judges will do
poorly if they strike out on their own, but very well if they build modestly
on their own precedents."[101]

From this it appears that before a judge can decide to go minimalist, she or he must decide the best view of constitutional rights and/
or institutions, whether the original meaning comports with the best
view of rights/institutions, how well present democratic processes are
progressing toward the best view of rights/institutions, and whether
judges are presently likely to do a better job than the democratic processes in serving the best view of rights/institutions. The complexity and
theoretical ambition of these moral and nonmoral judgments require no
elaboration. They are at least as ambitious as anything Dworkin has ever
attempted. The minimalist judge may pretend otherwise to the public.
She or he may say, for example, that a particular prosecution of homosexual intimate conduct is unconstitutional simply because prosecutions
under the relevant statute are too rare for the public to know what to
expect, and that knowing what to expect is a hallmark of the rule of law.
But what the judge says to the public is one thing, and what she or he is
thinking is another. What the judge is thinking is that public opinion on
the rights of gay men and lesbians is heading in the right direction

without judicial help, and that she or he risks mucking things up by boldly stepping ahead of public opinion and flatly declaring a constitutional right of same-sex intimate association or marriage. If there is minimalism here, it is not in how the judge understands the Constitution, it is in how she or he presents her- or himself to the public as a matter of judicial strategy.

In closing our assessment of minimalism, we want to recapitulate two main points. One, Sunstein has come out as a perfectionist: he acknowledges that his theory of minimalism, like every theory, claims to fit and justify the Constitution and to make it the best it can be. Two, Sunstein's "minimalist" judgments about cases protecting the right to privacy or autonomy are no less "theoretically ambitious" than are perfectionist analyses grounded in autonomy (or substantive moral goods or virtues). In sum, there is nothing minimalist about the theoretical and strategic judgments called for by Sunstein's minimalism.

From the Partial Constitution to the Minimal Constitution: The Incredible Shrinking Constitutional Theory

You may have seen (or heard of) the cult science fiction film, *The Incredible Shrinking Man* (or its takeoff, *The Incredible Shrinking Woman*).[102] We hope that Sunstein will not be offended if we suggest that the odyssey of his theory from *The Partial Constitution* to the minimal Constitution in his more recent works, *Radicals in Robes* and *A Constitution of Many Minds,* is that of an incredible shrinking constitutional theory. We assume he will not be since he names the fictional society for which his theory is appropriate "Smallville" to distinguish it from "Olympus," the society where he says perfectionist theories like ours are appropriate.[103]

Thinning Deliberative Democracy Down

Sunstein's theory has shrunk from a theory of perfecting deliberative democracy—or judicial reinforcement of the preconditions for its legitimacy—to a theory of largely permitting the political processes to proceed, such as they are. *The Partial Constitution* provides Sunstein's fullest exposition of a substantive vision of the Constitution as embodying a deliberative democracy. There he develops a substantive theory of the Constitution and the form of government that it embodies, as well as a theory of judicial review. His theory of judicial review would secure the preconditions for deliberative democracy, though it would leave fuller realization of some of those preconditions to legislatures and executives in the Constitution outside the courts.

Since then, Sunstein has focused on developing a theory of judicial review (or judicial strategy) over and against a theory of the Constitution: he has concentrated on the role of courts more than on the commitments of the Constitution itself. In his subsequent work, we see less and less elaboration of the substantive commitments of our Constitution and underlying constitutional scheme, conceived as a deliberative democracy. We see more and more elaboration of the problems with judicial review—the limited institutional capacities of courts, the circumstances of moral disagreement and political conflict, the brakes that social resistance, unintended consequences, and backlash put upon courts bringing about liberal social change, and the like.

From Theory of Judicial Review (or Judicial Strategy) to Theory of the Constitution Itself

Furthermore, it appears that Sunstein's constitutional aspirations and commitments have atrophied as minimalism has expanded from being a theory of judicial review (or judicial strategy) to practically being a theory of the Constitution itself. Indeed, we should ask whether *Radicals in Robes* and *A Constitution of Many Minds* express or presuppose a minimalist conception of the Constitution. What might one think if one held a minimalist view of the Constitution itself? One might think that the commitments of the Constitution are relatively thin and themselves leave most questions concerning their meaning and application undecided. And one might think that the Constitution simply says nothing about many or most things.[104] And one might think, as Holmes famously put it in his dissent in *Lochner,* that a constitution " 'is made for people of fundamentally differing views.' "[105] And one might think, as Hand famously put it, that " 'the spirit of liberty is . . . not too sure that it is right,' " whether about the obligations of justice or the commitments of the Constitution.[106] And one might be skeptical or distrustful of abstract moral principles generally, fearing that such principles are divisive and polarizing.[107] Finally, one might think that "ought implies can," that courts have limited institutional capacities to interpret a Constitution any thicker or more ambitious than the foregoing propositions entail,[108] and, therefore, that we ought to conceive of the Constitution itself as being thin enough and modest enough for their limited institutional capacities to be adequate to interpret and apply it. Here we can see a downsizing, recasting, or retrofitting of the Constitution itself to fit a conception of limited judicial capacities. Sound familiar? All of these ideas are expressed in one form or another in *Radicals in Robes* and *A Constitution of Many Minds*. To the extent they are, perhaps those works do indeed express or presuppose a minimalist view of the Constitution itself.

Exaggerated Fears about Backlash and Unintended Consequences

Exaggerated fears about backlash and unintended consequences, too, have contributed to the minimalization or evisceration of constitutional commitments. It is striking to what degree Sunstein has incorporated— into his minimalism—arguments against hollow hopes that courts can bring about liberal social change, together with worries about backlash and unintended consequences. We grant that as early as *The Partial Constitution,* Sunstein had endorsed Gerald Rosenberg's famous "hollow hope" argument.[109] Just as we should not harbor hollow hopes that courts can bring about liberal social change, so, too, we should not have exaggerated fears that courts will provoke backlash, cause unintended consequences, and make things worse when they protect controversial constitutional rights. Sunstein seems to endorse the familiar arguments about *Roe* provoking backlash, spawning the right to life movement and the like (citing Glendon, for example).[110] The causes of the emergence of the right to life movement are numerous, and many of them have nothing to do with judicial decisions—and certainly nothing to do with how broadly or narrowly, deeply or shallowly, judicial opinions are written. The revival of religious fundamentalism generally would have occurred with or without *Roe.* The right to life movement would have been born with or without *Roe,* although we do not deny the symbolic importance of *Roe* as a focal, mobilizing point for that movement.[111] More generally, the "new right," neoliberalism, and neoconservatism—countless varieties of "antiliberalism" (to use the term Stephen Holmes has used)[112]— would have emerged with or without *Roe.*

The "women's movement" and gains in women's equality and reproductive freedom also would have provoked backlash with or without *Roe.*[113] Gains in women's equality and reproductive freedom, whether furthered through legislation or judicial decision, and whether through federal courts or state legislatures, would have provoked backlash. See the forceful discussion in Susan Faludi's *Backlash: The Undeclared War against American Women.*[114] Finally, those gains would have provoked backlash regardless of whether Justice Blackmun's opinion in *Roe* had justified the right to abortion on the basis of the Due Process Clause or the Equal Protection Clause, and regardless of whether it had taken a liberal perfectionist route or a minimalist route.

Similarly, if the Supreme Court had never decided *Brown v. Board of Education,* and Congress nonetheless had passed the very civil rights laws that it in fact enacted, we very likely still would have experienced resistance to and backlash against gains in equality and civil rights for African-Americans.[115] We mention this particular example because Sunstein sometimes writes as if there is something inherent in equality that makes it less adventuresome or less intrusive on the political processes than liberty or privacy (and correspondingly less likely to provoke backlash). To take another example, the Supreme Court, after *Shapiro v. Thompson,*[116] never recognized a constitutional right to welfare,[117] and gains in the "war on poverty" mostly were pursued through the legislative processes. Nonetheless, we still have experienced backlash against welfare programs, including the "war against the poor" and "welfare reform."[118]

All of these developments—the right to life movement, resistance to gains in women's equality and reproductive freedom, resistance to gains of the civil rights movement (culminating in resistance to affirmative action programs), welfare reform, and the like—are part of a larger backlash against the 1960s and its aftermath. Liberal developments in the 1960s and 1970s provoked all manner of antiliberalism, and backlash against liberal gains, however advanced: whether through courts or legislatures, courts together with legislatures, federal or state governments (and whether through maximalist or minimalist judicial decisions). To take a hypothetical, does anyone seriously believe that if the Massachusetts Supreme Judicial Court had never decided *Goodridge,* and if instead the Massachusetts legislature on its own initiative had passed a law recognizing same-sex marriage in November 2003, the repercussions for the 2004 presidential election would have been significantly different? Granted, the attack would have been on liberal legislatures, not "activist" liberal judges, but there would have been similar repercussions. Even Michael Klarman, a prominent proponent of the view that liberal judicial decisions trigger backlash, admits in recent work that legislation recognizing same-sex marriage also does so.[119] It is telling that such legislation has prompted opponents of same-sex marriage, who previously advocated letting legislatures rather than courts decide this matter, to pursue ballot initiatives to "let the people decide" to overturn the legislation. Evidently their commitment is not to the democratic principles of the ordinarily political processes, but simply to resisting change and winning in whatever forum they can.

To offer another hypothetical, no one should believe for one second that Glendon (and people who agree with her) would have complained about the Supreme Court deciding the matter of abortion for the whole country in one bold stroke in *Roe* if the Court had reached the opposite result and interrupted the state-by-state democratic processes by holding that fetuses are full persons who are entitled to life and to equal protection along with born persons.[119] When courts make liberal decisions, they become an easy target for antiliberals' attacks, but we should not let that fool us into thinking that the primary objection is to courts attempting change rather than to liberal change as such. Law professors like Sunstein and many in his audience, because they are excessively court-centered, are especially vulnerable to falling into this way of thinking.

There is a huge measure of what Albert Hirschman famously called the "rhetoric of reaction"[120] in these tales of court decisions like *Roe* leading to unanticipated consequences and provoking backlash, even to the point of making things worse. Those who oppose liberal change make gloomy predictions and warnings about unintended consequences and backlash. Again, they warn about liberal change through whatever venue: not just courts but also legislatures and executives, not just the federal government but also state governments. On top of these warnings, they pile the argument that liberal do-gooders always make things worse, not only for the world but even (perhaps especially) for the people they seek to help and for themselves. This kind of thinking is especially rampant among law and economics scholars and those who work in their shadow. In this sense, economics indeed proves to be the "dismal science." It is important to understand that these "rhetoric of reaction" moves are not simply reactionary; people who make these moves affirmatively aim to demoralize those who push for liberal change. We fear that Sunstein has been more affected by these ideas than is warranted.

Preoccupation with the Limited Institutional Capacities of Courts

The final aspect of the downsizing of Sunstein's constitutional theory that we want to mention is his increasing preoccupation with the limited institutional capacities of courts. Sunstein offers a number of prudential reasons concerning the likelihood that courts will get things wrong and the lack of any special qualities making judges better suited than citizens or legislatures to resolve moral conflicts. Thus, he argues, judicial minimalism is appropriate given the relative institutional capacities of courts as compared with those of politically elected officials.[121] There are two opposed traditions in constitutional theory concerning the relative institutional capacities or positions of courts and legislatures. On one account, courts' independence from politics is their greatest weakness or disqualification for elaborating and protecting substantive constitutional freedoms against encroachment through the political processes. Sunstein has fully developed a version of this view. On another account, courts' independence from politics is their greatest strength or qualification for discharging such a responsibility. Dworkin has advanced a well-known version of such a view.[122] It is not possible to resolve the longstanding dispute between these traditions here. But it is worth recalling Justice Robert Jackson's formulation in the second flag salute case (invalidating a required salute), responding to Justice Felix Frankfurter in the first such case (upholding a required salute): rather than deferring to the "vicissitudes" of the political processes, courts vindicate constitutional freedoms "not by authority of [their] competence but by force of [their] commissions."[123] If the commission of the courts is to preserve the Constitution, including substantive liberties, against encroachment through the political processes, they would be abdicating their responsibility were they to side with Sunstein and against Dworkin on this dispute.

"Ought implies can," and Sunstein and other scholars who are preoccupied with the limited institutional capacities of courts say that courts simply are not competent to carry out the commission that Jackson, Dworkin, and we believe they should.[124] Such scholars might object that judges simply are not capable of being Dworkin's "Hercules" or "Platonic Guardians" (to use Hand's term).[125] We wish Dworkin had never used the alliterative formulation "Hercules"—as in "Hercules" versus "Herbert" (Lionel Adolphus Hart)—in describing judging under his theory of legal interpretation as contrasted with judging under H. L. A. Hart's legal positivism.[126] For Dworkin's formulation makes the responsibilities of judging seem too Herculean (or Olympian). And that plays into or exacerbates the worries of those who are preoccupied with the limited institutional capacities of courts.

In reality, judges throughout American history have shown themselves to be perfectly capable of making the kinds of judgments that what Dworkin calls a moral reading of the Constitution, and what Sotirios A. Barber and one of us call a philosophic approach to constitutional interpretation, require of them. (By "moral reading," we refer to a conception of the Constitution as embodying abstract moral and political principles, not codifying concrete historical rules or practices; interpreting the

Constitution on such a view requires elaborating the meaning of those principles.) In *Taking Rights Seriously,* Dworkin said his "rights thesis" is "less radical than it might first have seemed": "The thesis presents, not some novel information about what judges do, but a new way of describing what we all know they do."[127] In *Constitutional Interpretation: The Basic Questions,* Barber and one of us defend a philosophic approach to constitutional interpretation that does not require judges to be philosophers.[128] It requires only that they make philosophic choices of the sort that they have been making all along, from John Marshall through Robert Jackson through John Marshall Harlan II through John Paul Stevens through David Souter. And it presupposes that they are capable of (and justified in) making these judgments.

We venture a hypothesis about the scholars who are preoccupied with the limited institutional capacities of courts. In the first instance, they write as if they are primarily skeptical about the institutional capacities of courts to make the decisions that, for example, perfectionists say courts have a responsibility to make. They want to leave things to be decided by the legislatures, and so we presuppose that they have confidence in the institutional capacities of legislatures. Then it turns out that they are skeptical about the institutional capacities of legislatures to make the decisions that it seems they have a responsibility to make. Yet, it turns out that executives, too, have limited institutional capacities and are not capable of making the regulatory and other determinations that we might think they have a responsibility to make. The upshot is that they say we should leave decisions to markets instead of governmental regulation. (We grant that Sunstein does not go all the way with them in the embrace of markets, although he practically does so with respect to same-sex marriage, as we shall see in the conclusion.[129]) Furthermore, it is not as if these scholars are populists who have confidence in the capacities of the people themselves to make decisions either; they are greatly skeptical of the people's capacities, too. All of this skepticism about the institutional capacities of all of these institutions and the people themselves is based in part on moral skepticism and other forms of skepticism.

But it is important to see that this skepticism about capacities is driven in part by exaggerated, too-lofty conceptions of what it is that judges, legislatures, executives, and citizens have responsibilities to do in the first place. For example, those who are preoccupied with limited institutional capacities of courts think that, under a moral reading, philosophic approach, or Constitution-perfecting theory, judges must be Herculean or Platonic philosopher judges who are capable of living on Olympus.[130] In fact, again, all these approaches require is that judges be capable of doing what they have been doing all along. We do not believe that we have to live on Olympus for a moral reading, philosophic approach, or Constitution-perfecting theory to be appropriate—just down here in the United States of America. In Chapter 9, we will show that judges have been capable of engaging in a rational process of reasoned judgment in giving full meaning to our rational continuum of ordered liberty.

A Tale of Two Courts Revisited

In concluding, we return to the question we raised earlier: which is the more defensible approach to justifying constitutional rights in circumstances of moral disagreement, the minimalist route of *Baker* or the perfectionist route of *Goodridge* (defended by Sandel and analyzed in Chapter 7)? Or perhaps the middle way of our constitutional liberalism, which weaves together arguments for respecting autonomy with perfectionist arguments for cultivating virtues and moral goods?

One might have expected Sunstein to argue that the tale of two courts recounted above is a thoroughgoing vindication of his minimalism (and the route of *Baker*) over perfectionism (and the route of *Goodridge*). And one might have expected that he would find further vindication in the experience of Vermont in moving, legislatively, from same-sex civil unions to same-sex marriage. That is, one might have expected this experience to stem the "incredible shrinking" of minimalism and the exaggerated fears about backlash and the debilitating preoccupation with the limited institutional capacities of courts. To the contrary, in an evident (and questionable) strategy of conflict avoidance, Sunstein recently came out in favor of abandoning the quest for a constitutional right to same-sex marriage (or even to same-sex civil unions) and instead "privatizing marriage."[131] He would abolish state recognition of marriage altogether—whether opposite-sex or same-sex—and replace it with publicly recognized civil unions—for both opposite-sex and same-sex couples—together with privately recognized marriages. We view this move as a capitulation that shows that the "incredible shrinking" of minimalism continues unabated. And we seriously doubt that Sunstein's strategy would avoid conflict rooted in moral and religious opposition to same-sex marriage. Indeed, it might provoke even greater conflict, with moral and religious opponents contending that the quest for same-sex marriage had destroyed marriage after all!

To be sure, the struggle for full citizenship, equality, and liberty for gays and lesbians is hardly won, but we believe that the tale of two courts shows that in circumstances of moral pluralism, proponents of those goals may be successful in advancing both perfectionist and minimalist arguments. We also believe that the tale holds out hope that minimalism can be an effective route to the mild perfectionist end to which we should aspire: a constitutional right to same-sex marriage justified both on grounds of respecting autonomy and cultivating virtues and moral goods. We believe that the moral of the tale applies to other struggles for rights pitting minimalist against perfectionist strategies. Ultimately, there is no avoiding the questions of principle at the heart of these struggles if we are to interpret the Constitution so as to make it the best it can be.

CHAPTER NINE

The Myth of Strict Scrutiny
for Fundamental Rights

In this chapter, we conclude by addressing the absoluteness critique previewed in Chapters 2 and 6: that liberal theories that, in Ronald Dworkin's terms,[1] "take rights seriously" treat fundamental rights as "trumps" or absolute exemptions from governmental pursuit of goods. We assess this critique in the context of the Supreme Court's protection of basic liberties under the Due Process Clause. We show that the absoluteness critique is misplaced as against the cases and our constitutional liberalism, which protect such basic liberties stringently but not absolutely.

The Equal Protection and Due Process Clauses are said to protect "fundamental rights" that trigger "strict scrutiny." In a famous statement, Professor Gerald Gunther wrote that under the Equal Protection Clause, strict scrutiny is "strict in theory and fatal in fact"; he also stated that under that clause, rational basis scrutiny is deferential in theory and nonexistent in fact.[2] Gunther thus dramatically phrased the Supreme Court's hankerings for absoluteness and for frameworks that automatically decide cases without requiring judgment: laws are either automatically unconstitutional (on the first tier) or automatically constitutional (on the second tier). Such hankerings are subject to Mary Ann Glendon's arguments that rights talk fosters the "illusion of absoluteness" and "impoverishment" of judgment. Glendon contends that absolutist rights talk has led Americans carelessly to deploy "the rhetoric of rights" as though rights trump everything else and to develop a constitutional jurisprudence of rights isolated from "common sense," reasonable, and necessary limitations on rights in a system of "ordered liberty." She suggests that liberal theories take rights too absolutely, to the exclusion of encouraging responsibility and inculcating civic virtue.[3]

In this chapter, we explore the analogous hankerings for absoluteness and avoidance of judgment under the Due Process Clause in cases protecting rights of liberty or autonomy. These cases have been at the center of our concern throughout this book. Dissenting in *Lawrence v. Texas*, Justice Scalia stated that, under the Due Process Clause, if an asserted liberty is a "fundamental right," it triggers "strict scrutiny" that almost automatically invalidates any statute restricting that liberty. For strict scrutiny requires that the challenged statute, to be upheld, must further a "compelling governmental interest" and must be "necessary" or "narrowly tailored" to doing so. Scalia also wrote that if an asserted liberty is not a fundamental right, it is merely a "liberty interest" that triggers rational basis scrutiny that is so deferential that the Court all but automatically upholds the statute in question. For deferential rational basis scrutiny requires merely that the challenged statute, to be valid, must further a "legitimate governmental interest" and need only be "rationally related" to doing so.[4]

Lawrence deviated from this regime. The Court did not hold that homosexuals' right to autonomy was a fundamental right requiring strict scrutiny. Nor did it hold that their right was merely a liberty interest calling for highly deferential rational basis scrutiny. Instead, the Court applied an intermediate standard—what we call "rational basis scrutiny with bite"—and struck down the statute forbidding same-sex sexual conduct. Consequently, Scalia cried foul, chastising the Court for not following the rigid two-tier framework that all but automatically decides rights questions one way or the other.[5] In equal protection cases, Scalia has cried foul because strict scrutiny for affirmative action plans has not been "fatal in fact" but has required judgment.[6] In due process cases, he has cried foul because rational basis scrutiny for laws forbidding same-sex sexual conduct has not been nonexistent in fact. In both domains, and in the application of both tiers, he has called for absolute, automatic decisions that do not require judgment. Such a jurisprudence manifests both the illusion of absoluteness and the impoverishment of judgment.

We shall expose the myth of strict scrutiny for fundamental rights under the Due Process Clause. Scalia's formulation of the framework for substantive due process sounds familiar and uncontroversial. Indeed, you'll find this formulation in leading treatises and commercial outlines because these sources seek neat, rigidly maintained frameworks with clearly delineated tiers of analysis. Yet we show that the only substantive due process case ever to recognize a fundamental right implicating strict scrutiny—requiring that the statute further a compelling governmental interest and be necessary to doing so—was *Roe v. Wade*.[7] And we point out that those aspects of *Roe* were overruled in *Planned Parenthood v. Casey,* which pointedly avoided calling the right of a woman to decide whether to terminate a pregnancy a "fundamental right" and substituted an "undue burden" standard for strict scrutiny.[8] Going through due process cases protecting liberty and autonomy—from *Meyer v. Nebraska* (1923) through *Casey* (1992) and *Lawrence* (2003)—we show that due process jurisprudence is not absolutist nor does it reflect an impoverishment of judgment. None of these cases applies the framework that Scalia propounds. To the contrary, these cases reflect what *Casey* and Justice Harlan called "reasoned judgment" concerning our "rational continuum" of "ordered liberty."[9] Indeed, they have involved judgment of the very sort that Glendon calls for and that Scalia would banish. The constitutional liberalism developed in our book does not seek to protect rights absolutely or to avoid judgment in interpreting rights. Instead, it justifies such reasoned judgment, which protects important rights stringently but does not preclude government from encouraging responsibility or inculcating civic virtues.

Whence derives the myth of strict scrutiny for fundamental rights under the Due Process Clause? How did it take hold in our constitutional culture despite lacking a firm footing in the cases protecting liberty or autonomy under that clause? This myth has been propounded and perpetuated mostly by opponents of substantive due process like Scalia and Chief Justice Rehnquist. As stated previously, it has not been put forward in cases *recognizing* asserted liberties as protected under the Due Process Clause (besides *Roe,* itself repudiated in this respect in *Casey*). Instead, opponents of substantive due process have advanced the myth of strict scrutiny for fundamental rights in opinions *refusing to recognize* asserted rights. Examples include Justice White's majority opinion in *Bowers v. Hardwick,* rejecting a right of homosexuals to sexual privacy[10] (*Bowers* was overruled in *Lawrence,* hence provoking Scalia's rage in dissent); Scalia's plurality opinion in *Michael H. v. Gerald D.,* rejecting a right of unwed fathers to visit their biological children;[11] Rehnquist's majority opinion in *Washington v. Glucksberg,* rejecting a right to die including physician-assisted suicide;[12] and, most pointedly, Scalia's dissent in *Lawrence,* objecting to the Court's protection of a right of homosexuals to sexual privacy or autonomy. We will focus on the latter two.

These opponents of substantive due process perpetuate the myth in order to narrow the interpretation of the Due Process Clause, to make it harder to justify protecting rights under it. Somehow, the defenders of substantive due process have fallen for the myth and been enlisted in perpetuating it. We suppose that they have been willing participants, not because they want to make it hard to protect rights of privacy or autonomy, but instead because they want stringent protection for rights of privacy or autonomy under the Due Process Clause. After all, liberal constitutional theorists who defend substantive due process typically love talk of "taking rights seriously," and it is no surprise that they might think that the best way to take rights seriously is to declare them to be "fundamental rights" and to subject restrictions upon or regulations of them to "strict scrutiny." Indeed, typically in constitutional law, what drives jurists and scholars to impose or argue for a requirement of strict scrutiny is a desire stringently to protect the right in question, as is the case with the First Amendment and the Equal Protection Clause, two main areas of strict scrutiny. We do not, for example, trust government when it restricts freedom of speech on the basis of the content of ideas, and we are suspicious of government when it passes laws reflecting racial prejudice. In substantive due process, by contrast, what typically drives jurists like Scalia and Rehnquist to argue for the requirement of strict scrutiny is a desire narrowly to limit the recognition and protection of rights of liberty or autonomy.

Indeed, the twofold result of Scalia's and Rehnquist's myth is to make it harder to recognize rights under the Due Process Clause and then to make all cases recognizing rights but not tracking this doctrinal template of strict scrutiny—which is to say all cases protecting rights under substantive due process (besides *Roe*)—seem problematic, messy, and unrigorous. Every time the Court does not use the formulations "fundamental right," "strict scrutiny," "compelling," and "necessary," people say that something illegitimate is going on. Even liberal proponents of substantive due process are sometimes complicit in perpetuating the myth.[13]

Our larger point here is that our situation under the Due Process Clause is much like our situation under the Equal Protection Clause. In equal protection, despite official doctrine, instead of having rigidly maintained tiers that automatically decide cases and do not require judgment, we have what Justice Stevens called a "continuum of judgmental responses" (or what Justice Marshall called a "spectrum of standards") permitting judges to make the judgments they need to make.[14] Likewise in due process, despite Scalia's assertions, instead of having two rigidly policed tiers that automatically invalidate statutes or automatically uphold them, our cases reflect what *Casey* and Justice Harlan called "reasoned judgment" concerning our "rational continuum" of "ordered liberty." To paraphrase Harlan, no two-tier formula could serve as a substitute for such judgment.[15]

If the familiar framework of strict scrutiny for fundamental rights is a myth, what framework (or standards) has the Court actually applied? Put another way, what framework best fits and justifies the line of cases actually protecting substantive liberties under the Due Process Clause? We have already given away the answer: Harlan's famous conception of the Due Process inquiry advanced in his dissent in *Poe v. Ullman*. We offer interpretations of Harlan's conception that bring out how well it fits and justifies the cases over and against Scalia's and Rehnquist's conception propounding the myth of strict scrutiny for fundamental rights. And we show that the cases have not protected rights absolutely so as to preclude government from encouraging responsibility or inculcating civic virtues in the ways prescribed by our constitutional liberalism.

Reasoned Judgment Concerning the Rational Continuum of Ordered Liberty

The joint opinion of Justices O'Connor, Kennedy, and Souter in *Casey* embraced Justice Harlan's conception of the Due Process inquiry as put forward in dissent in *Poe*. It quoted the following two passages from Harlan:

> Due process has not been reduced to any formula; its content cannot be determined by reference to any code. The best that can be said is that . . . it has represented the balance which our Nation, built upon postulates of respect for the liberty of the individual, has struck between that liberty and the demands of organized society. If the supplying of content to this Constitutional concept has of necessity been a rational process, it certainly has not been one where judges have felt free to roam where unguided speculation might take them. The balance . . . is the balance struck by this country, having regard to what history teaches are the traditions from which it developed as well as the traditions from which it broke. That tradition is a living thing. A decision of this Court which radically departs from it could not long survive, while a decision which builds on what has survived is likely to be sound. No formula could serve as a substitute, in this area, for judgment and restraint.

> [T]he full scope of the liberty guaranteed by the Due Process Clause cannot be found in or limited by the precise terms of the specific guarantees elsewhere provided in the Constitution. This "liberty" is not a series of isolated points pricked out in terms of the taking of property; the freedom of speech,

press, and religion; the right to keep and bear arms; the freedom from unreasonable searches and seizures; and so on. It is a rational continuum which, broadly speaking, includes a freedom from all substantial arbitrary impositions and purposeless restraints, . . . and which also recognizes, what a reasonable and sensitive judgment must, that certain interests require particularly careful scrutiny of the state needs asserted to justify their abridgment.[16]

Interpreting these passages, the joint opinion in *Casey* added:

> The inescapable fact is that adjudication of substantive due process claims may call upon the Court in interpreting the Constitution to exercise that same capacity which by tradition courts always have exercised: reasoned judgment. Its boundaries are not susceptible of expression as a simple rule. That does not mean we are free to invalidate state policy choices with which we disagree; yet neither does it permit us to shrink from the duties of our office.[17]

To recall Chapter 8, the joint opinion is not saying that courts need the capacity to decide cases as they would on Olympus, simply the capacity to decide cases as they always have done. From this vantage point, we can see that the joint opinion is implying that originalists like Justice Scalia and minimalists like Cass Sunstein would have judges "shrink from the dut[y]" to decide cases responsibly, exercising reasoned judgment.

We shall distill five characteristics of Harlan's substantive due process jurisprudence, in contradistinction from the hankerings seen in Scalia's and Rehnquist's myth of strict scrutiny for fundamental rights under the Due Process Clause. First, Harlan conceives liberty as a "rational continuum" of "ordered liberty," not a list of fundamental rights or isolated points pricked out in the text of the Constitution. It is an abstract concept (as *Casey* put it, "ideas and aspirations"[18]), not a code of concrete, specific enumerated rights. Second, he conceives interpretation of abstract commitments like liberty as a "rational process" of "reasoned judgment," not a quest for a formula, code, or bright-line framework to avoid judgment. Third, applying these conceptions of liberty and interpretation yields a rational continuum of judgmental responses, not a rigidly maintained two-tier framework. Fourth, and relatedly, doing so requires judgment about the balance between liberty and order ("ordered liberty") and uses common-law constitutionalist reasoning by analogy from one case to the next, as opposed to making decisions by automatically invalidating or automatically upholding challenged legislation. Fifth, while Harlan agrees with Scalia that judgments about liberties must be grounded in history and tradition, Harlan unlike Scalia conceives tradition as a "living thing" or evolving contemporary consensus, not hidebound historical practices as of the time the Due Process Clause was ratified (in 1868).[19]

If the Supreme Court were to have applied Harlan's conception of the Due Process inquiry, what would our substantive due process jurisprudence look like? Instead of having two rigidly maintained tiers—strict scrutiny and deferential rational basis scrutiny—we would have a spectrum of standards or continuum of judgmental responses. That is, this jurisprudence would look basically the very way it looks today! To preview our findings, see the figure below for the spectrum of standards or continuum of judgmental responses we will see in the substantive due process cases. We have ordered them from the most stringent review to the most lenient or deferential review.

In analyzing each case, we will apply the following template: What did the case hold? Did the Court recognize a "fundamental right"? Did the Court apply "strict scrutiny"? And if not "strict scrutiny," what type of judgment did it say is required? Where appropriate, we will ask whether the Court states or assumes that the protection of rights in the case

Strict scrutiny	
Roe; Loving (Equal Protection Clause)	↓ - - - - - - - - - - - - - - - -
	Undue burden standard
	Casey
	- - - - - - - - - - - - - - - - -
	↑ "Means may not sweep unnecessarily broadly"
	Griswold
- - - - - - - - - - - - - - - - - -	- - - - - - - - - - - - - - - - -
Intermediate scrutiny	↑ "Heightened protection"
Moore; Craig (Equal Protection Clause)	*Troxel*
	- - - - - - - - - - - - - - - - -
	↑ Rational basis scrutiny with "bite"
	Lawrence; Romer (EP Clause); *Meyer; Pierce*
	- - - - - - - - - - - - - - - - -
	↑ "Accommodation" of rights and authority
	Prince
	- - - - - - - - - - - - - - - - -
	↑ "Balancing" of liberty interest against state interest
	Cruzan
Deferential rational basis scrutiny	
Bowers; Michael H.; Glucksberg	

precludes encouragement of responsibility and inculcation of civic virtue. Throughout, we shall be inquiring which framework for the Due Process inquiry—that of Scalia/Rehnquist or that of Harlan—better fits and justifies the cases. We will conclude that Harlan's framework can fit and justify all of the cases protecting rights under the Due Process Clause, and that that of Scalia and Rehnquist can fit and justify none of them.

The Substantive Due Process Cases from *Meyer* to the Present

Meyer v. Nebraska (1923)

In 1919, Nebraska enacted a statute prohibiting the teaching of any modern language other than English in any public or private grammar school (to pupils who had not successfully completed eight years of schooling). Meyer, a parochial school instructor, was convicted of violating this law by teaching German to a ten-year-old boy. The Court invalidated the statute as a deprivation of liberty in violation of the Due Process Clause.[20]

Did the Court say that the legislation violated a fundamental right? The Court proclaimed: "That the state may do much, go very far, indeed, in order to improve the quality of its citizens, physically, mentally and morally, is clear; but the individual has certain fundamental rights which must be respected." The Court clearly contemplated that the state has considerable latitude to engage in a formative project of inculcating civic virtues (and the state legislature might have thought it was doing precisely that by prohibiting the teaching of modern languages such as German). At the same time, it contemplated that the state must respect certain "fundamental rights." What are those fundamental rights? The Court gives several formulations: the teacher's "right to teach," as part of the right "to engage in any of the common occupations of life"; the parents' "right to contract" with the teacher, "to engage him so to instruct their children"; and the parents' right, and corresponding "natural duty," to control the upbringing and education of their children. More abstractly, *Meyer* intimates a fundamental theory of "the relation between individual and state" precluding the state from freely crafting its vision of ideal citizens (by contrast with the theory of Plato's ideal commonwealth in *The Republic*).[21] And it presumes that the family shares in the responsibility to carry out a formative project, thus setting the stage for conflicts of the sort we examined in Chapters 4 and 5.

Does the Court employ strict scrutiny? The Court frames the test thus: "The established doctrine is that this liberty [guaranteed by the Due Process Clause] may not be interfered with, under the guise of protecting the public interest, by legislative action which is arbitrary or without reasonable relation to some purpose [or "end"] within the competency of the state to effect." And: "[A] desirable end cannot be promoted by prohibited means." So far, the test does not look like strict scrutiny but instead like deferential rational basis scrutiny. But the Court adds: "Determination by the Legislature of what constitutes proper exercise of police power is not final or conclusive but is subject to supervision by the courts."[22] As we will see, the form that this "supervision" takes is not deferential rational basis scrutiny, but rather scrutiny with some teeth in it. The upshot is that, though the language resembles our language of deferential rational basis scrutiny, in application the inquiry looks more like rational basis scrutiny with "bite."

What is the "purpose" or end that the state legitimately may pursue? The Court states: "The desire of the Legislature to foster a homogeneous people with American ideals prepared readily to understand current discussions of civic matters is easy to appreciate." Again, as we argued in Chapter 5, the Court presumes that the government may engage in a formative project of inculcating civic virtues. What is the Court's analysis of whether the challenged statute bears a "reasonable relation" to that purpose? "Perhaps it would be highly advantageous if all had ready understanding of our ordinary speech, but this cannot be coerced by methods which conflict with the Constitution—a desirable end cannot be promoted by prohibited means." If the test actually applied is rational basis scrutiny with "bite," does the bite apply to the analysis of the end or to that of the fit between means and end? It evidently applies to both. The Court appears quite deferential to the legitimacy of the end of fostering a homogeneous people with American ideals and a common tongue. At the same time, the Court puts bite into its scrutiny of the permissibility of another asserted end, that of "protect[ing] the child's health by limiting his mental activities." The Court writes: "As the statute undertakes to interfere only with teaching which involves a modern language, leaving complete freedom as to other matters, there seems no adequate foundation for the suggestion that the purpose was to protect the child's health by limiting his mental activities." Moreover, the Court puts some bite into its scrutiny of the fit between end and means: "But the means adopted, we think, exceed the limitations upon the power of the state and conflict with rights assured to plaintiff in error."[23]

Justice Holmes's argument in dissent shows us what deferential rational basis scrutiny would look like in the context of this case. His approach is quite deferential as to end—the statute pursues "a lawful and proper [end]." It is also quite deferential as to the fit between means and end—the statute "might . . . be regarded as a reasonable or even necessary method of reaching the desired result." This is "a question upon which men reasonably might differ." Therefore, Holmes concludes, the Constitution does not "prevent[] the experiment [from] being tried."[24] It might seem that Holmes, by advocating scrutiny that is so deferential that it is practically nonexistent in fact, is anticipating a portion of Scalia's proposed framework. But unlike Scalia, who proposes such scrutiny when no fundamental rights are in play, Holmes is advocating such scrutiny across the board, even when fundamental rights are in play.

Pierce v. Society of Sisters (1925)

In 1922, Oregon enacted a law requiring parents to send their children between the ages of eight and sixteen, with limited exceptions, to public schools rather than private schools. The Society of Sisters of Holy Names, a Catholic religious order that operated several parochial schools in Oregon, and the Hill Military Academy, a private school, brought suit in federal district court. The Court struck down the law as a violation of the Due Process Clause.[25]

The Court does not speak of any "fundamental rights" as such. It frames the right in question as "the liberty of parents and guardians to direct the upbringing and education of children under their control," citing Meyer. Pierce further sketches a "fundamental theory" of the relation between the individual and the state, intimated in Meyer, which forbids the state to standardize its citizens by freely crafting its vision of ideal citizens: "The fundamental theory of liberty upon which all governments in this Union repose excludes any general power of the state to standardize its children by forcing them to accept instruction from public teachers only." The Court famously proclaims: "The child is not the mere creature of the state; those who nurture him and direct his destiny have the right, coupled with the high duty, to recognize and prepare him for additional obligations."[26]

Does the Court apply strict scrutiny? It frames the test as follows: "As often heretofore pointed out, rights guaranteed by the Constitution may not be abridged by legislation which has no reasonable relation to some purpose within the competency of the state."[27] So far, as in Meyer, the test looks less like strict scrutiny than like deferential rational basis scrutiny.

What is the "purpose" or end that the state legitimately may pursue? "No question is raised concerning the power of the state reasonably to regulate all schools, to inspect, supervise and examine them, their teachers and pupils; to require that all children of proper age attend some school, that teachers shall be of good moral character and patriotic disposition, that certain studies plainly essential to good citizenship must be taught, and that nothing be taught which is manifestly inimical to the public welfare."[28] As in *Meyer*, so here, the Court presumes that the state has considerable room to pursue a formative project of inculcating civic virtues. But both cases presume that the family shares in this responsibility; hence there will be conflicts.

What is the Court's analysis of whether the statute bears a "reasonable relation" to that purpose? It simply states the two famous propositions quoted above concerning the "fundamental theory of liberty" and that the "child is not the mere creature of the state." The Court does not methodically separate out analysis of ends from analysis of fit between means and ends (as it would do if it were applying a two-pronged formula). It simply concludes, holistically, that the statute denies protected liberty. Clearly, the Court is putting some "bite" into its analysis. It is not simply deferring to the legitimacy of the end and to the rationality of the fit between means and end. As in *Meyer*, so here, the upshot is that, though the language looks like our language of deferential rational basis scrutiny, in application the framework looks more like rational basis scrutiny with "bite."

Prince v. Massachusetts (1944)

Prince is the third in the famous trilogy of early parental liberty cases often cited as a group to support the venerable roots of substantive due process. Unlike *Meyer* and *Pierce,* however, *Prince upholds* the statute being challenged. Massachusetts's child labor laws prohibited boys under twelve and girls under eighteen from selling, exposing, or offering for sale "any newspapers, magazines, periodicals or any other articles of merchandise of any description . . . in any street or public place." The statute imposed a fine and imprisonment of up to five days on "any parent, guardian or custodian having a minor under his control who compels or permits such minor to work in violation" of the laws. One night, Mrs. Prince, the aunt and legal custodian of nine-year-old Betty Simmons, allowed Betty to distribute copies of *Watchtower* and *Consolation,* publications of the Jehovah's Witnesses, on the streets of

Brockton. Mrs. Prince was convicted of violating the law. The Court upheld the law against her claims of parental liberty and freedom of religion as well as of the child's religious liberty. The Court recognized these claims of parental authority and religious liberty as rooted in *Meyer* and *Pierce* but concluded that "Acting to guard the general interest in youth's well being, the state as *parens patriae* may restrict the parent's control by requiring school attendance, regulating or prohibiting the child's labor, and in many other ways. . . . [T]his includes, to some extent, matters of conscience and religious conviction."[29]

The Court in this case does not make any explicit reference to "fundamental rights." It states: "It is cardinal with us that the custody, care and nurture of the child reside first in the parents, whose primary function and freedom include preparation for obligations the state can neither supply nor hinder," citing *Pierce*. The Court continues: "And it is in recognition of this that these decisions have respected the private realm of family life which the state cannot enter." This line is often quoted in subsequent cases recognizing a right of privacy or autonomy. The Court also refers to the "sacred private interests" of the parent's "claim to authority in her own household and in the rearing of her children."[30] *Prince* is the only case in the trilogy to refer explicitly to the rights of the child, even characterizing *Meyer* and *Pierce* as being in part about children's rights.

Does the Court exercise strict scrutiny? As in *Meyer* and *Pierce,* so here, the Court does not put forward any framework or test that can be said to presage "strict scrutiny." Instead, it emphasizes the "clash" between parents' and children's rights, on the one hand, and state authority, on the other, and the need for making "accommodation" between them. Its outlook is one of making judgments in "accommodations" or weighing of interests rather than of strictly scrutinizing restrictions upon fundamental rights. And the Court credits the state's claim that the law is "necessary to accomplish its legitimate objectives."[31] We elaborate upon this point later.

What are the legitimate objectives that the state may pursue? According to the Court, the state may promote the healthy development of children and protect them against evils:

> The state's authority over children's activities is broader than over like actions of adults. . . . A democratic society rests, for its continuance, upon the healthy, well-rounded growth of young people into full maturity as citizens. . . . It may secure this against impeding restraints and dangers, within a broad range of selection. Among evils most appropriate for such action are the crippling effects of child employment. . . . It is too late now to doubt

that legislation appropriately designed to reach such evils is within the state's police power, whether against the parent's claim to control of the child or one that religious scruples dictate contrary action.[32]

Clearly, the state may engage in a formative project of developing citizens. In this instance, the state may restrict children's immediate exercise of their liberty, as immature citizens, in order to protect the development of their capacity for future exercises of liberty, as mature citizens.[33] What is the Court's analysis of whether the statute furthers those legitimate objectives? It credited Massachusetts's determination that "an absolute prohibition, though one limited to streets and public places and to the incidental uses proscribed, is necessary to accomplish its *legitimate* objectives." It continued: "[The state's] power to attain them is broad enough to reach these peripheral instances in which the parent's supervision may reduce but cannot eliminate entirely the ill effects of the prohibited conduct." Therefore, the Court upholds the constitutionality of the statute. "Parents may be free to become martyrs themselves. But it does not follow that they are free . . . to make martyrs of their children before they have reached the age of full and legal discretion when they can make that choice for themselves."[34] In this often-quoted formulation, the Court again stresses governmental authority to protect children's development of their full capacity for self-determination (that is, self-government), even when that entails restricting adult exercises of parental and religious liberty that may hinder such development.

The Court proclaims that decisions like *Meyer* and *Pierce* have respected the "private realm of family life which the state cannot enter." "But," it immediately insists: "the family itself is not beyond regulation in the public interest, as against a claim of religious liberty. And neither rights of religion nor rights of parenthood are beyond regulation." Here, the Court engages in a "two-step" seen in much of its constitutional family law about the regulation of marriage and parental rights and responsibilities: following quick on the heels of step one—a declaration that something is "fundamental" and "private"—is step two—a clarification that it is neither absolute nor beyond regulation. In making the "accommodation" or resolving the "clash," the Court holds that "the state has a wide range of power for limiting parental freedom and authority in things affecting the child's welfare."[35] In Chapters 5 and 6, we have addressed ways of accommodating or resolving such clashes between the government's and civil society's pursuits of their formative projects of developing citizens. *Prince* features in subsequent substantive due process liberty cases *both* for its rhetoric about the "private realm of life of family life which the state cannot enter" *and* for its assertion of the state's *parens patriae* authority to restrict parental liberty and children's rights in support of a formative project.[36]

Griswold v. Connecticut (1965)

A Connecticut statute made it a crime to use or to aid, abet, or counsel use of "any drug, medicinal article or instrument for the purpose of preventing conception." The Executive Director of Planned Parenthood League of Connecticut and a physician who was Medical Director for the League flouted the law by publicly advising married persons about the use of contraceptives. They were arrested, tried, convicted, and fined $100. The Court invalidated the law as a violation of the right of privacy.[37]

Does the Court say that the right of privacy is a "fundamental right"? Not exactly, but it does come close, saying: "The present case, then, concerns a relationship lying within the zone of privacy created by several fundamental constitutional guarantees."[38] That makes the right of privacy, like those guarantees, sound fundamental. In concurrence, Justice Goldberg uses the language of "fundamental rights," stating: "I do agree that the concept of liberty protects those personal rights that are fundamental, and is not confined to the specific terms of the Bill of Rights."[39]

The Court does not exactly lay out a framework of scrutiny, strict or otherwise. The closest it comes is to say: "Such a law cannot stand in light of the familiar principle, so often applied by this Court, that a 'governmental purpose to control or prevent activities constitutionally subject to state regulation may not be achieved by means which sweep unnecessarily broadly and thereby invade the area of protected freedoms.'"[40] Here the Court is drawing an analogy to First Amendment overbreadth analysis. Implying that prohibition of the use of contraceptives by married couples sweeps too broadly, the Court concludes, rhetorically, "Would we allow the police to search the sacred precincts of marital bedrooms for telltale signs of the use of contraceptives? The very idea is repulsive to the notions of privacy surrounding the marriage relationship."[41] However, the Court does not engage in formulaic, two-pronged analysis of whether the end is compelling and whether the means is necessary to further it. It seems fair to say that Douglas's opinion in *Griswold* applies some form of what we today would call intermediate scrutiny: not as stringent as strict scrutiny, but not as lenient as deferential rational basis scrutiny.

Griswold does not explicitly consider whether government may engage in a formative project. But as we have seen in Chapter 7, *Griswold* justifies the right of privacy on grounds of the substantive moral goods or virtues promoted by protecting it, not simply on grounds of individual choice without regard for the good of what is chosen. Douglas emphasizes protecting a sacred, traditional institution (marriage) and protects privacy in order to promote the moral goods of intimate association. In speaking of marriage as a "noble" association[42] in a case that strikes down criminal restrictions on the use of contraception, Justice Douglas says (implicitly) two things pertinent to the state's formative project concerning marriage. First, to the extent that bans on contraception serve the state's formative project of encouraging fidelity within marriage, there are limits to its ability to use coercion to do so. Second, because the goods of marital association include adult intimacy that need not aim at (and may avoid) procreation, using criminal law to channel persons into "responsible procreation" within marriage infringes upon marital privacy. *Lawrence* gleans from *Griswold* a right both to spatial and decisional privacy, or autonomy, and relies on it in recognizing a liberty of adults (heterosexual and homosexual, married and unmarried) to engage in private, consensual sexual intimacy.[43] There is a corresponding limit on the part of the state to use criminal law for a channelling function of promoting a particular understanding of sexual morality.

Loving v. Virginia (1967)

Loving holds that a miscegenation statute prohibiting and punishing interracial marriage violates both the Equal Protection Clause and the Due Process Clause. The Court begins with its Equal Protection holding. Here, the Court rejects deferential rational basis scrutiny: "We do not accept the State's contention that these statutes should be upheld if there is any possible basis for concluding that they serve a rational purpose."[44] Instead, because the case involves invidious racial discrimination, the Court writes: "At the very least, the Equal Protection Clause demands that racial classifications, especially suspect in criminal statutes, be subjected to the 'most rigid scrutiny' and, if they are ever to be upheld, they must be shown to be necessary to the accomplishment of some permissible state objective, independent of the racial discrimination which it was the object of the Fourteenth Amendment to eliminate."[45] The Court clearly demonstrates that it is well on its way toward articulating the canonical formulation of strict scrutiny under the Equal Protection Clause. The Court holds that the statute fails that test.

Next, the Court turns to its Due Process Clause holding. The Court opens by saying: "The freedom to marry has long been recognized as one of the vital personal rights essential to the orderly pursuit of happiness by free men." It continues: "Marriage is one of the 'basic civil rights of man,' fundamental to our very existence and survival."[46] Further-more, the Court holds: "To deny this fundamental freedom on so unsup-portable a basis as the racial classifications embodied in these statutes, classifications so directly subversive of the principle of equality at the heart of the Fourteenth Amendment, is surely to deprive all the State's citizens of liberty without due process of law. The Fourteenth Amend-ment requires that the freedom of choice to marry not be restricted by invidious racial discriminations."[47]

Note the thoroughgoing overlap between the Court's Due Process holding and its Equal Protection holding. To begin, when the Court characterizes the right to marry as a "basic civil right of man," and "fun-damental freedom," it does so by reference to *Skinner v. Oklahoma*, an Equal Protection case.[48] And when it holds that the statute denies due process, it emphasizes the invidious racial discrimination that subverts the principle of equality. Let us be clear: we are not reducing *Loving*'s Due Process holding to an Equal Protection holding (in the way some have, such as casebook editors who edit out the Due Process holding[49]). Nor are we implying that the Court's Due Process holding is a muddle that doesn't really tell us anything about the Due Process inquiry. To the contrary, we believe that the Due Process Clause and the Equal Pro-tection Clause overlap, and so it is no surprise (and certainly not a sign of a muddle) that the Court would hold that this statute denies both Due Process and Equal Protection for overlapping reasons. What we are suggesting is that *Loving* may not say much by way of intimating or formulating a doctrinal framework of fundamental rights and strict scrutiny under the Due Process Clause in general, or where we don't have a similar overlap with the Equal Protection Clause and invidious racial discrimination. That said, it is undeniable that *Loving* features in constitutional law and family law jurisprudence as an important root for a "fundamental right to marry."[50] Proponents and opponents of extending civil marriage to same-sex couples divide over whether its conclusion—"Under our Constitution, the freedom to marry, or not marry, a person of another race resides with the individual and cannot be infringed by the State"[51]—has force when a person's chosen partner is of the same sex.

Roe v. Wade (1973)

Texas statutes made it a crime to "procure an abortion," as therein defined, or to attempt one, except with respect to "an abortion procured or attempted by medical advice for the purpose of saving the life of the mother." Similar statutes were in existence in a majority of the states. The Court invalidated the statute on the ground that it violated the right of a woman to decide whether to terminate a pregnancy, a right rooted in personal privacy.[52] As we acknowledged, *Roe* is a substantive due process case that characterizes the right being protected as a "fundamental right." The Court, in explicating the "roots" of the right of privacy (in various precedents) in the First Amendment, the Fourth and Fifth Amendments, the penumbras of the Bill of Rights, the Ninth Amendment, or the concept of liberty guaranteed by the Fourteenth Amendment, writes: "these decisions make it clear that only personal rights that can be deemed 'fundamental' or 'implicit in the concept of ordered liberty,' are included in this guarantee of personal privacy."[53]

As we also acknowledged, *Roe* is the one substantive due process case protecting an asserted liberty that applies strict scrutiny as canonically formulated. The Court writes:

> Where certain "fundamental rights" are involved, the Court has held that regulation limiting these rights may be justified only by a "compelling state interest," *Kramer v. Union Free School District* (1969); *Shapiro v. Thompson* (1969); *Sherbert v. Verner* (1963); and that legislative enactments must be narrowly drawn to express only the legitimate state interests at stake. *Griswold v. Connecticut* (1965); *Aptheker v. Secretary of State* (1964); *Cantwell v. Connecticut* (1940); see *Eisenstadt v. Baird* (1972) (White, J., concurring in result).[54]

And, in characterizing the district court opinion's analysis, the Court uses the formulations "compelling state interest" and "necessary." It is striking that, for the idea that where "fundamental rights" are involved, it should apply strict scrutiny, the Court invokes two Equal Protection cases (*Kramer* and *Shapiro*) and a First Amendment case (*Sherbert*). It is also striking that, for the requirement that laws "must be narrowly drawn to express only the legitimate state interests at stake," the Court cites a concurrence in an Equal Protection precedent (*Eisenstadt*), two First Amendment precedents (*Aptheker* and *Cantwell*), and *Griswold* (recall that *Griswold* itself for a similar idea drew an analogy to First Amendment overbreadth doctrine but cited no Due Process precedents). That is, *Roe* bases its application of strict scrutiny on analogies to Equal Protection and First Amendment jurisprudence, without purporting to be applying established Due Process jurisprudence. The purity of strict scrutiny is compromised, though, by the Court's statement that the laws must be "narrowly drawn to express only the legitimate state interests at stake," rather than "compelling state interests." Purists would insist that "legitimate" is a code word for rational basis scrutiny, whereas "compelling" is a code word for strict scrutiny. Be that as it may, *Roe* is the closest approximation to what Scalia offers as the Court's authoritative framework, and the fullest realization of a framework requiring strict scrutiny for fundamental rights under the Due Process Clause.

But let's note that, even here, the Court does not contemplate that strict scrutiny will be "fatal in fact," automatically invalidating laws that trigger it. For one thing, Justice Blackmun rejects the argument that the right of a woman to decide whether to terminate a pregnancy is "absolute." For another, he presents the trimester framework as contemplating that some regulations justified on the grounds of protecting the health of the pregnant woman and protecting the potential life of the fetus will be upheld.[55] Finally, as we saw in Chapter 3, *Roe* contemplates that pregnant women exercise their right, not absolutely or in isolation, but in consultation with their physicians, whom it views as responsible decision makers: it presupposes that physicians have the "basic responsibility" to exercise sound professional judgment concerning this "medical decision."[56]

Moore v. City of East Cleveland (1977)

The next major substantive due process case, *Moore,* is a vindication of Justice Harlan's conception of the Due Process inquiry—a rational continuum of ordered liberty—over a fundamental rights conception triggering strict scrutiny. Justice Powell's plurality opinion wholeheartedly embraces Harlan's conception. For Powell as for Harlan, due process is a "rational continuum" of "ordered liberty," not a list of fundamental rights. And, for Powell as for Harlan, no formula—such as either absolutist strict scrutiny automatically invalidating a statute or deferential rational basis scrutiny automatically upholding it—can take the place of the rational process of reasoned judgment.

An ordinance of East Cleveland, Ohio limited occupancy of each dwelling unit to members of a single family, with "family" defined essentially as the nuclear family of parents and their children. (The ordinance, however, permitted grandparents to live with their children and their children's children, provided that all of the grandchildren were siblings rather than cousins.) Inez Moore shared her home with her son and two grandsons who were cousins rather than brothers; thus, her extended family was too extended. She was convicted of violating the ordinance. The plurality concluded that this ordinance violated the Due Process Clause.[57]

In the plurality opinion, Powell nowhere says that the Due Process inquiry seeks to mark out "fundamental rights." Instead, his formulations of the rights protected under the Due Process Clause closely track the formulations of prior cases, and he does not call them "fundamental rights." He writes: "This Court has long recognized that freedom of personal choice in matters of marriage and family life is one of the liberties protected by the Due Process Clause of the Fourteenth Amendment."[58] He continues: "A host of cases, tracing their lineage to *Meyer v. Nebraska* (1923) and *Pierce v. Society of Sisters* (1925), have consistently acknowledged a 'private realm of family life which the state cannot enter.' "[59] He also speaks of the Due Process Clause as protecting "choices concerning family living arrangements." To be sure, the city in urging the Court to uphold the regulation uses the term "fundamental rights." Powell writes:

> The city would distinguish the cases based on *Meyer* and *Pierce*. It points out that none of them "gives grandmothers any fundamental rights with respect to grandsons," and suggests that any constitutional right to live together as a family extends only to the nuclear family: essentially a couple and their dependent children.

But Powell does not adopt the city's attempt to limit liberties to "fundamental rights." Powell's response is telling: he rejects the city's proto-Scalian attempt to define the rights recognized in prior cases at a highly specific level, limiting the force of precedents to their factual circumstances involving nuclear families. To the contrary, he focuses on the reasons we protect those rights, the force and rationale of those precedents, and concludes that they justify protecting extended family living arrangements along with nuclear family living arrangements. He further invokes Harlan's dissent in *Poe* to justify this approach. Powell eschews the city's formulation of the precedents as being limited to protecting "fundamental rights" in favor of two alternative formulations: "[C]ertain rights associated with the family have been accorded shelter" and the precedents have afforded "enhanced protection to certain substantive liberties."[60] As we interpret Powell's formulations, substantive due process gives "enhanced" protection to certain substantive liberties as compared with the protection given by deferential rational basis scrutiny, but not as stringent as that given by strict scrutiny. To wit, it is a form of intermediate protection.

Finally, we acknowledge that Powell quotes Harlan using the word "fundamental." Harlan wrote: "The home derives its pre-eminence as the seat of family life. And the integrity of that life is something so fundamental that it has been found to draw to its protection the principles of more than one explicitly granted Constitutional right."[61] Here, Harlan is not saying that the Constitution enshrines "fundamental rights"

triggering strict scrutiny. Instead, he is saying that family life is fundamental in the sense that the family is a fundamental institution of our
society. This formulation is more akin to a civic republican argument
(à la Michael Sandel) about the need to protect traditional institutions
because of the substantive moral goods they foster than to an argument
for protecting individual fundamental rights against those traditional
institutions. Supporting this interpretation is Powell's argument that:
"Our decisions establish that the Constitution protects the sanctity of
the family precisely because the institution of the family is deeply rooted
in this Nation's history and tradition." The extended family, he states,
"has roots equally venerable and equally deserving of constitutional recognition" as the nuclear family. East Cleveland's ordinance, by contrast,
would "cut[] off any protection of family rights at the first convenient, if
arbitrary boundary—the boundary of the nuclear family." Powell continues in a Harlanian/Sandelian vein: "It is through the family that we
inculcate and pass down many of our most cherished values, moral and
cultural." He further states: "Decisions concerning child rearing, which
Yoder, Meyer, Pierce, and other cases have recognized as entitled to constitutional protection, long have been shared with grandparents or other
relatives who occupy the same household—indeed who may take on
major responsibility for the rearing of the children."[62] In sum, the Court
is protecting the fundamental institution of the family, not marking off
"fundamental rights" of individuals.

Just as Powell avoids the language of "fundamental rights," so he
avoids the language of strict scrutiny. Unlike Blackmun in *Roe* or Douglas
in *Griswold,* Powell in *Moore* does not cite any First Amendment or
Equal Protection cases suggesting strict scrutiny, requiring a compelling
governmental interest and necessary relationship to furthering it. Rather,
he writes: "When a city undertakes such intrusive regulation of the
family, . . . the usual judicial deference to the legislature is inappropriate."[63]
But unlike Scalia in dissent in *Lawrence,* Powell does not assume or hold
that if the Court does not apply deferential rational basis scrutiny and
automatically uphold the legislation, it must apply strict scrutiny and
automatically invalidate it. For again, Powell, like Harlan, argues that
no formula can substitute for judgment.

What judgment, if not strict scrutiny, is required? Powell writes: "Of
course, the family is not beyond regulation. See *Prince.*" He continues:
"But when the government intrudes on choices concerning family living
arrangements, this Court must examine carefully the importance of the
governmental interests advanced and the extent to which they are served
by the challenged regulation. See *Poe* (Harlan, J., dissenting)."[64] Powell's

formulation is clearly not Scalia-style strict scrutiny: he articulates no requirement of a compelling governmental interest and necessary relationship to furthering it. In fact, it sounds more like intermediate scrutiny, as developed in interpreting the Equal Protection Clause in *Craig v. Boren* (*Moore* was decided in 1977, and *Craig* in 1976). *Craig* requires an "important governmental objective[]" and that the means be "substantially related" to serving it.[65] Powell assimilates this intermediate level of review to Harlan's conception of the Due Process inquiry in his *Poe* dissent. We, like Powell, read these formulations as a whole as calling for something approximating what we now call intermediate scrutiny, not what we now call strict scrutiny.

Finally, let's examine Powell's application of this intermediate standard of review. What interests does the city claim to be advancing here? Powell writes: "The city seeks to justify [the ordinance] as a means of preventing overcrowding, minimizing traffic and parking congestion, and avoiding an undue financial burden on East Cleveland's school system." What does Powell say about "the extent to which [these governmental interests] are served by the challenged regulation"? He writes: "Although these are legitimate goals, the ordinance before us serves them marginally, at best." Notice that Powell labels the city's end as "legitimate" as distinguished from "important" or "compelling." He also writes: "Section 1341.08 has but a tenuous relation to alleviation of the conditions mentioned by the city."[66] This language, if anything, sounds like deferential scrutiny with "bite" concerning the "tenuous" or "marginal" fit between the means and the asserted "legitimate" end. In any case, it sounds more like a form of intermediate scrutiny than strict scrutiny.

In conclusion, Powell's opinion in *Moore* is quintessentially Harlanian. Due Process is a "rational continuum" of "ordered liberty," not a list of fundamental rights triggering strict scrutiny and not a formula that avoids judgment. Interpreting our commitments to liberty entails a rational process of reasoned judgment: a form of judgment lying on a continuum at an intermediate point between strict scrutiny and deferential rational basis scrutiny.

Cruzan v. Director, Missouri Department of Health (1989)

Missouri required that evidence of an incompetent person's wishes as to the withdrawal of life-sustaining treatment be proved by clear and convincing evidence. The guardians of Nancy Cruzan, a person in a "persistent vegetative state," challenged this law. The Court upheld that requirement as not violative of the Due Process Clause.[67]

Chief Justice Rehnquist for the Court notably avoids speaking of, or assuming, any "fundamental right" to die. Instead, he speaks of a "liberty interest" in refusing "unwanted medical treatment," a much weaker claim than a fundamental right. Rehnquist distinguishes between a "generalized constitutional right of privacy" and a "liberty interest."[68] By not citing to any of the line of substantive due process cases from *Meyer* and *Pierce* through *Griswold* and *Roe* about the right to make certain decisions fundamentally affecting one's destiny, he seems to suggest that the privacy/autonomy cases are not relevant. The only cases relevant on his view are cases specifically involving refusing "unwanted medical treatment."

Rehnquist does not apply strict scrutiny, instead writing: "whether respondent's constitutional rights have been violated must be determined by *balancing* his liberty interests against the relevant state interests."[69] The "balancing" he contemplates seems highly general, with no weight on the scales in favor of any "liberty interest." On our continuum of standards, balancing of this sort is clearly less stringent than the forms of intermediate scrutiny seen in *Moore* and *Griswold*. Yet it is presumably somewhat more stringent than deferential rational basis scrutiny. After all, the Court acknowledges that a "general liberty interest in refusing unwanted medical treatment" has been recognized in the cases. Accordingly, the Court may be implying that it would give that "liberty interest" more weight than, say, the "liberty interests" of opticians to pursue their livelihood in *Williamson v. Lee Optical,* the canonical case exemplifying deferential rational basis scrutiny.[70]

In any case, the Court clearly leaves plenty of room for the state to moralize against persons refusing unwanted medical treatment and to moralize in favor of what Rehnquist called its "unqualified interest in the preservation of human life."[71] *Cruzan* lends no support whatever to Scalia's formulation of the framework for the Due Process inquiry.

Planned Parenthood v. Casey (1992)

The joint opinion in *Casey* embraces Harlan's conception of the Due Process inquiry as propounded in his *Poe* dissent (much like Powell adopts it in *Moore*). *Casey* reaffirms the "essential holding" or "central holding" of *Roe* concerning the right of a woman to decide whether to terminate a pregnancy before viability. However, it rejects *Roe*'s framework of strict scrutiny for a fundamental right. The joint opinion pointedly avoids calling the right in question a "fundamental right." Surprisingly, this fact went unnoticed by many, perhaps because the joint opinion otherwise characterized the right at issue in terms familiar from the precedents, e.g., "personal autonomy," "bodily integrity," "*Griswold* liberty," and the like. And it explicitly jettisons *Roe*'s framework of strict scrutiny—requiring a compelling governmental interest and a necessary means—together with the trimester framework.[72]

What standard does the joint opinion formulate to replace strict scrutiny? It puts forward an undue burden standard. This standard does not automatically invalidate regulations of or restrictions upon abortion. Instead, as shown in Chapter 3, it inquires whether a state regulation "has the purpose or effect of placing a substantial obstacle" to or undue burden upon a woman's exercise of the right to make the "ultimate decision" whether to have an abortion.[73]

On our spectrum of standards, the undue burden standard lies between strict scrutiny and deferential rational basis scrutiny. It is, if you will, a form of intermediate (or heightened) scrutiny, though it does not follow the analytics of, say, intermediate scrutiny under the Equal Protection Clause (e.g., does not require important governmental interest or means substantially related to furthering it). And, it certainly affords more stringent protection than the "balancing" test of *Cruzan*.

How does the undue burden standard compare with rational basis scrutiny with "bite"? Its analytics are not the same, i.e., it does not put teeth into analysis of ends and fit between means and ends. But let's observe that the undue burden standard was formulated by three justices who authored the joint opinion in *Casey*—O'Connor, Kennedy, and Souter—all of whom were crucial in the majority in *Romer* and *Lawrence*, two decisions subsequently applying rational basis scrutiny with "bite" (though O'Connor would have applied such scrutiny in *Lawrence*, like *Romer*, under the Equal Protection Clause instead of the Due Process Clause). Furthermore, adoption of the undue burden standard may have been driven by concerns similar to those which drove the majority in *Lawrence* to apply rational basis scrutiny with "bite": an unwillingness to call the right in question a "fundamental right" and to apply "strict scrutiny" (if doing so implies that there can be virtually no regulation of it), together with an unwillingness to fall back on deferential rational basis scrutiny (because, at bottom, there is a big difference between, on the one hand, discriminating against, or criminalizing the sex lives of, gays and lesbians, and, on the other, regulating the business of opticians in *Williamson*[74]).

In any case, the undue burden standard is less "absolutist" than strict scrutiny, and the joint opinion in *Casey* that propounded it draped its arguments in the garb of Harlan through and through. The joint opinion emphatically did not wear the garb of fundamental rights, strict scrutiny, and all the rest of it. Indeed, Scalia grants these points in dissent in *Lawrence*.[75]

If *Casey* adopts Harlan's approach as a general conception of the Due Process inquiry, does it entail applying the undue burden standard (as distinguished from strict scrutiny) across the board to other asserted liberties? That was an open question when *Casey* was decided in 1992, but by now the answer is clearly no. To understand why, let's be clear about why the joint opinion propounded an "undue burden" standard in *Casey* instead of strict scrutiny. It did so in part because (to recall Chapter 3) it was rejecting the idea that having a right to do something (e.g., to have an abortion) insulates the right-holder from governmental moralizing seeking to persuade the right-holder not to exercise the right. It characterizes the liberty at stake as "unique," because pregnancy itself is a "unique" condition, and explains that abortion begins as an exercise of conscience but is also an act "fraught with consequences for others."[76] Thus, the government has considerable latitude to moralize against abortion by adopting regulations to facilitate "wise exercise" of the right.[77] More precisely, the government may adopt regulations aimed at encouraging women not to have an abortion, so long as it does not impose an undue burden upon or substantial obstacle to their exercising the right. Again, after all the governmental moralizing, a woman has the right to make the ultimate decision.

This account may suggest why the Court has not generally applied the undue burden standard in lieu of other available frameworks including strict scrutiny. Consider the contexts in which the Court applies strict scrutiny, like the First Amendment. Rightly or wrongly, even if many people exercise their freedom of speech irresponsibly, the Court is not about to say that the government may regulate speech and encourage people not to exercise their right to speak, so long as the government respects the ultimate decision to speak or does not impose undue burdens upon or substantial obstacles to the right to speak.[78] To take another example, in the area of freedom of religion, the Court does not find governmental persuasion in favor of religious belief acceptable.[79] The clearest candidate for application of an undue burden standard might have been the right to die, including the right to physician-assisted suicide. It was conceivable that, for such a right, just as for the right to abortion—with which it is often joined—the Court would have said: there is a right, but not a "fundamental right" that would preclude governmental regulation. It is a right to make the "ultimate decision," not a right to be insulated from governmental moralizing seeking to persuade one not to exercise the right. On this view, the right to die (including physician-assisted suicide) would be a right where the government may encourage right-holders to make the decision conscientiously and responsibly—deliberating about what respect for the sanctity of life requires—so long as it respects the right of the individual to make the ultimate decision, rather than coercing what the government thinks is the right decision.

Washington v. Glucksberg (1997)

But this is not the approach the Court took with respect to the right to die (including physician-assisted suicide) in *Washington v. Glucksberg*. That case concerned the constitutionality of a Washington law prohibiting physician-assisted suicide.[80] Instead, the Court rejected the asserted right and took the occasion generally to narrow the Due Process inquiry. For one thing, Rehnquist's opinion of the Court specifically rejected Harlan's conception of the Due Process inquiry, which had been embraced by the joint opinion in *Casey*. For another, Rehnquist took steps toward propounding the myth of strict scrutiny for fundamental rights under the Due Process Clause. The Court articulated what it called "our established method" for the Due Process inquiry. Whenever the Court says something like "our established method is" or "it is well settled that," it is likely about to put forward a new method and to utter something controversial. This is certainly borne out here.

Rehnquist asserts that under "[o]ur established method of substantive-due-process analysis," only if the Court recognizes a "fundamental right" will it "requir[e] more than a reasonable relation to a legitimate state interest" to justify a statute. To Justice Souter's contrary argument in concurrence that *Casey* had adopted Justice Harlan's conception of the Due Process inquiry, Rehnquist retorted:

> Justice Souter, relying on Justice Harlan's dissenting opinion in *Poe v. Ullman*, would largely abandon this restrained methodology, and instead ask "whether [Washington's] statute sets up one of those 'arbitrary impositions' or 'purposeless restraints' at odds with the Due Process Clause of the Fourteenth Amendment," (quoting *Poe* (Harlan, J., dissenting)). In our view, however, the development of this Court's substantive-due-process jurisprudence . . . has been a process whereby the outlines of the "liberty" specially protected by the Fourteenth Amendment—never fully clarified, to be sure, and perhaps not capable of being fully clarified—have at least been carefully refined by concrete examples involving fundamental rights found to be deeply rooted in our legal tradition. This approach tends to rein in the subjective elements that are necessarily present in due-process judicial review. In addition, by establishing a threshold requirement—that

a challenged state action implicate a fundamental right—before requiring more than a reasonable relation to a legitimate state interest to justify the action, it avoids the need for complex balancing of competing interests in every case.

In a footnote, Rehnquist adds:

> In Justice Souter's opinion, Justice Harlan's *Poe* dissent supplies the "modern justification" for substantive-due-process review. But although Justice Harlan's opinion has often been cited in due-process cases, we have never abandoned our fundamental-rights-based analytical method. . . . True, the Court relied on Justice Harlan's dissent in *Casey,* but . . . we did not in so doing jettison our established approach. Indeed, to read such a radical move into the Court's opinion in *Casey* would seem to fly in the face of that opinion's emphasis on stare decisis.[81]

It was particularly rich of Rehnquist to jujitsu Souter with *Casey*'s emphasis on stare decisis, especially since in dissent he had called *Casey*'s application of it a "judicial Potemkin Village." Now Rehnquist asserts that *Casey*'s reliance on Harlan's *Poe* dissent was a one-off moment because *Casey,* and this Court, has so valued stare decisis. In *Glucksberg,* Rehnquist is doing the very thing he accused the joint opinion in *Casey* of doing: constructing a Potemkin Village—here, the myth of strict scrutiny for fundamental rights under the Due Process Clause—and using stare decisis to pass off his new creation as always having been there.[82]

We will focus on Rehnquist's claim that only if the Court recognizes a "fundamental right" will it "requir[e] more than a reasonable relation to a legitimate state interest to justify the action." The Court claims that, to be protected under the Due Process Clause, an asserted liberty must be a "fundamental right." And it claims that it applies a rigidly dichotomous two-tier framework: either "more than a reasonable relation" (if a fundamental right is in play) or deferential rational basis scrutiny (if no fundamental right is in play). Note that Rehnquist, unlike Scalia in dissent in *Lawrence,* does not go all the way to saying that "fundamental rights" trigger "strict scrutiny." He says only that they "requir[e] more than a reasonable relation to a legitimate state interest to justify the action." And so, once the Court in *Glucksberg* holds that there is no fundamental right to die, it falls back on deferential rational basis scrutiny. The Court is highly deferential concerning the legitimacy of the ends and of the fit between means and ends, and it readily upholds the law prohibiting physician-assisted suicide.

Who provides the better account of the "established method of substantive-due-process analysis," Rehnquist or Souter (who embraces Harlan's conception in *Poe*)? Are *Meyer, Pierce, Prince, Griswold,*

Loving, Roe, Moore, Cruzan, and *Casey* more consistent with Rehnquist's account or Souter's? Which method better fits and justifies the cases protecting liberties under the Due Process Clause? Souter clearly can account for all of these cases—as the joint opinion in *Casey* did through the framework of "reasoned judgment." He also could readily account for the subsequent cases of *Troxel* and *Lawrence,* to be discussed next. One of us has argued elsewhere that Rehnquist can account for none of them.[83] The latter is no surprise when we realize two things: that Rehnquist is offering this "established method" as a method of damage control—he can't overrule the substantive due process cases but he can try to drain them of any generative vitality for future cases—and that he is laying the groundwork for the myth of strict scrutiny for fundamental rights under the Due Process Clause (subsequently to be fully propounded by Scalia in dissent in *Lawrence*). The only cases where the Court has taken pains to insist that, to receive protection, the right must be "fundamental," have been cases like *Bowers, Michael H.,* and *Glucksberg,* where the Court was taking pains to justify rejecting the asserted right. And in all of those cases, the opinions were met with criticisms in dissents that their way of formulating the right was not true to the challengers' claims or to our history and tradition.[84]

Troxel v. Granville (2000)

Troxel drew attention for the fact that, at a time when the Court was narrowing its interpretation of the Due Process Clause in cases like *Glucksberg,* it affirmed the vitality of the "big three" early substantive due process cases. Justice O'Connor's plurality opinion in *Troxel* cited *Meyer, Pierce,* and *Prince* in support of its statement that "[t]he liberty interest at issue in this case—the interest of parents in the care, custody, and control of their children—is perhaps the oldest of the fundamental liberty interests recognized by this court." After citing subsequent cases, O'Connor further states: "[i]t cannot now be doubted that the Due Process Clause . . . protects the fundamental right of parents to make decisions concerning the care, custody, and control of their children."[85]

Under a Washington statute, grandparents were permitted to petition a court for visitation of grandchildren, and the court was permitted to order visitation rights if they served the best interest of the children, over and against a mother's judgments concerning the care, custody, and control of her children. The Court held that the statute violated the Due Process Clause.

The plurality opinion of Justice O'Connor writes: "The Fourteenth

Amendment . . . includes a substantive component that 'provides heightened protection against government interference with certain fundamental rights and liberty interests.'"[86] As quoted above, the opinion
speaks of the "fundamental right of parents to make decisions concerning the care, custody, and control of their children," but it also
speaks of "fundamental liberty interests" and "liberty interests." The
latter formulations may suggest less stringent protection than that
accorded "fundamental rights" or may signal that a form of review
weaker than "strict scrutiny" is to be applied.

The plurality opinion nowhere speaks of "strict scrutiny," and indeed
it does not put forth a framework of scrutiny. Thus, family law scholars
have commented that *Troxel* simultaneously reiterated the rhetoric of
"fundamental" parental liberty, while declining to apply strict scrutiny.[87] The closest it comes is to say that "certain fundamental rights and
liberty interests" trigger "heightened protection." That is why Justice
Thomas objects, in concurrence, to the failure to apply strict scrutiny.
He writes: "I agree with the plurality that this Court's recognition of a
fundamental right of parents to direct the upbringing of their children
resolves this case." He continues: "The opinions of the plurality, Justice
Kennedy, and Justice Souter recognize such a right, but curiously none of
them articulates the appropriate standard of review. I would apply strict
scrutiny to infringements of fundamental rights."[88]

If not "strict scrutiny," what standard of "heightened protection" does
the plurality apply? Without specifying a framework for according
"heightened protection," the plurality concludes that the statute is
"breathtakingly broad" by allowing "any third party seeking visitation
to subject any decision by a parent concerning visitation of the parent's
children to state-court review." The constitutional flaw the plurality
identifies is the failure, in the statute and in its application by the state
court, to "give [any] special weight at all" to the "presumption that fit
parents act in the best interests of their children." As the plurality puts it:
"Accordingly, so long as a parent adequately cares for his or her children
(i.e., is fit), there is normally no reason for the State to inject itself into the
private realm of the family to further question the fit parents' ability to
make the best decision" regarding their children. (Note the allusion to
Prince's language about the "private realm" of the family.) It concludes:
"The Due Process Clause does not permit a State to infringe on the fundamental right of parents to make child rearing decisions simply because
a state judge believes a 'better' decision could be made."[89]

Justice Stevens's dissent brings out that in cases like *Troxel*, the Court
has engaged in "balancing" of interests rather than "strict scrutiny" pro-

tecting well-nigh absolute fundamental rights. And he expresses concern to protect children against arbitrary decisions by parents. Stevens observes: "Our cases leave no doubt that parents have a fundamental liberty interest in caring for and guiding their children, and a corresponding privacy interest—absent exceptional circumstances—in doing so without the undue interference of strangers to them and to their child." But, he continues: "A parent's rights with respect to her child have thus never been regarded as absolute . . . [but] must be balanced against the State's long-recognized interests as *parens patriae,* . . . and, critically, the child's own complementary interest in preserving relationships that serve her welfare and protection." Expressing concern to protect children from arbitrary parental decisions, Stevens argues: "While . . . the Federal Constitution certainly protects the parent-child relationship from arbitrary impairment by the State . . . we have never held that the parent's liberty interest in this relationship is so inflexible as to establish a rigid constitutional shield, protecting every arbitrary parental decision from any challenge against a threshold finding of harm."[90]

Clearly, *Troxel* does not support Scalia's (and Thomas's) claim that cases involving "fundamental rights" apply "strict scrutiny" under the Due Process Clause. All things considered, the "heightened protection" given in *Troxel* is a form of intermediate scrutiny.

Lawrence v. Texas (2003)

Enter *Lawrence,* which invalidated a Texas law criminalizing certain same-sex intimate sexual conduct under the Due Process Clause.[91] What does it do to the framework for the Due Process inquiry? For one thing, it overrules *Bowers* and rejects its narrow specification of the asserted right as a "fundamental right to engage in homosexual sodomy."[92] Echoing Blackmun's dissent in *Bowers,* Kennedy says that *Bowers* and *Lawrence* are no more about the right to commit homosexual sodomy than *Griswold* is about the right to have sexual intercourse using contraceptives. Instead, both cases are about liberty "in its spatial and more transcendent dimensions" (or autonomy).[93] For another, *Lawrence* emphatically rejects *Bowers*'s (and by implication *Michael H.*'s and *Glucksberg*'s) conception of the Due Process inquiry.

The Court does not ask whether the asserted liberty is a "fundamental right." In this respect, *Lawrence* is unlike *Bowers* and *Glucksberg,* to be sure, but right in line with the decisions protecting liberties under the Due Process Clause. Nor does the Court apply strict scrutiny, just as it did not in any of the other Due Process cases protecting an asserted liberty (besides *Roe,* itself repudiated in this respect in *Casey*). Yet, it did not for that reason fall back on deferential rational basis scrutiny, again unlike *Bowers* and *Glucksberg* but very like the Due Process cases protecting asserted liberties. Instead, *Lawrence* applied rational basis scrutiny with "bite" (as we discuss later).

Did the Court in *Lawrence* embrace Harlan's conception of the Due Process inquiry (as the joint opinion had in *Casey*)? This option certainly would seem to have been on the table. All three authors of the joint opinion in *Casey*—Kennedy, O'Connor, and Souter—were in the majority of six in *Lawrence*. But the Court, officially, did not do so. The majority did not make Harlan's concurrence in *Poe* the centerpiece of the opinion. But its approach is true to Harlan's approach in several senses. The *Lawrence* opinion embodies a common-law constitutionalism: the Court proceeds by analogy from rights already protected for straights to protecting analogous rights for gays and lesbians. Indeed, the Court concluded that it would be anomalous to protect liberty/autonomy for straights but not the analogous liberty/autonomy for gays and lesbians.

Insofar as the Court conceives the Due Process inquiry as an inquiry into what liberties traditionally have been protected, it makes two Harlanian moves. First, it frames the right asserted quite abstractly: liberty in its spatial and more transcendent dimensions, not, as *Bowers* framed it, a "fundamental right to engage in homosexual sodomy." Second, the Court conceives tradition as a "living thing" or evolving contemporary consensus, not, as *Bowers* assumed, hidebound historical practices (what was on the statute books or in the common law as of 1868). Thus, Kennedy's opinion focuses on the "emerging awareness" of the past 50 years,[94] or how we have "broken from" (to recall Harlan's formulation) tradition conceived as hidebound historical practices regarding gays and lesbians. Indeed, Kennedy's opinion retraces *Bowers*'s steps, saying that the pattern of 26 out of 50 states repealing their antisodomy laws between 1961 and 1986 should have signaled, even in 1986 (when *Bowers* was decided), that we were witnessing tradition as a living thing, reflecting an evolving contemporary consensus against criminalization of sexual intimacy and in favor of respecting sexual autonomy.[95] Finally, *Lawrence* is Harlanian in its ease with carefully scrutinizing a statute without laboring under any compulsion to articulate a rigid formula or framework that will substitute for making reasoned judgments.

The reader may ask, if *Lawrence* is so Harlanian, why didn't the Court officially embrace Harlan's conception of the Due Process inquiry, as the joint opinion did in *Casey*? Here we can only speculate, but there is a speculation available that is so obvious that it may in fact be sound.

In *Poe,* Harlan propounded his conception and applied it to sexual privacy. While he argued for an abstract "right to be let alone" as part of the rational continuum of ordered liberty, he confined that right basically to a right of marital privacy for opposite-sex couples within the home. He specifically exempted, as beyond what he was willing to credit as part of the rational continuum of ordered liberty, any right of homosexuals to sexual privacy.[96] To be sure, one can embrace Harlan's conception of the Due Process inquiry without accepting Harlan's own application of it. There is no contradiction in general and certainly not in particular if tradition is indeed a "living thing" that could have evolved between 1961 (*Poe*) and 2003 (*Lawrence*). Among the notables who have taken this route are Charles Fried, famously the law clerk for Harlan at the time Harlan wrote the dissent in *Poe.* Fried, for example, embraced Harlan's method but argued that *Bowers* was wrongly decided.[97] Laurence Tribe and Michael Dorf also took this approach, embracing Harlan's method and using it to argue that *Bowers* was wrongly decided.[98] The Court could have gone that route. For whatever reasons, it officially did not. But again, its conception of the Due Process inquiry and its application of it are Harlanian in spirit if not officially in name.

Scalia's Dissent in *Lawrence*

We are now in a position to assess Scalia's dissent in *Lawrence,* with which this chapter opened. Again, Scalia says that the Court's established framework for the Due Process Clause has two rigidly policed, dichotomous tiers: either fundamental right, triggering strict scrutiny, or mere liberty interest, triggering deferential rational basis scrutiny.[99] As stated, Scalia claims that only "fundamental rights" get greater protection than that afforded under deferential rational basis scrutiny. What is more, White in *Bowers* had offered the two famous phrases from *Palko* and *Moore*—"implicit in the concept of ordered liberty" and "deeply rooted in this Nation's history and tradition"—as *alternative* formulations for deciding whether an asserted liberty was protected—as if you just had to satisfy one or the other.[100] By contrast, Scalia in dissent in *Lawrence* offers them as independent requirements—and claims that you have to satisfy *both.* He claims that an asserted liberty has to be both implicit in the concept of ordered liberty and deeply rooted in this nation's history and tradition.[101]

Whereas *Bowers,* much like *Glucksberg,* spoke of "heightened" scrutiny but did not specify a framework of what that heightened scrutiny would consist of, Scalia speaks of "strict" scrutiny and says that the established framework is to require a compelling governmental interest and a necessary relationship between the statute and that interest.[102] *Bowers, Glucksberg,* and Scalia's dissent in *Lawrence* contemplate a rigid two-tier framework: if the Court is not prepared to declare an asserted liberty a "fundamental right" triggering heightened or strict scrutiny, it falls back on deferential rational basis scrutiny. For them, there is nothing in between—notwithstanding all of the cases that have gone before and which we have shown to lie in between. We have shown this framework to be false through and through, a myth of Scalia's and Rehnquist's making.

Scalia also refers to the Court's method in *Lawrence*—which we call rational basis scrutiny with "bite"—as "unheard of."[103] To say that an approach is "unheard of" is one of Scalia's favorite put-downs. In *Casey,* he referred to the joint opinion's conception of "reasoned judgment" as unheard of, even though it was a well-known and much celebrated approach famously propounded by Justice Harlan. The joint opinion there claimed to be following the Court's "established method" and we have shown that it can account for the cases protecting liberties under the Due Process Clause. That was not enough to stop Scalia from haughtily asserting that this was a "new" method never heard of before that day.[104]

Let's address Scalia's claim that Kennedy's approach to scrutinizing the Texas law in *Lawrence* was "unheard of." It is demonstrably false in two important respects. For one thing, Kennedy's method closely resembles Harlan's well-known framework (as shown above). For another, Kennedy's method closely resembles Kennedy's own approach, under the Equal Protection Clause, to measures reflecting animus against gays and lesbians in *Romer.*[105] And let's not forget that Scalia there objected to this very approach as unheard of.[106] In *Romer,* instead of applying strict scrutiny, intermediate scrutiny, or deferential rational basis scrutiny, the Court applied rational basis scrutiny with "bite"–putting some teeth into its scrutiny of both the legitimacy of the end and the fit between means and end. *Lawrence* is not the first case in which the Court has adapted an analysis in the Equal Protection Clause context to the Due Process Clause context. And that analysis was already familiar in the Equal Protection Clause context from cases like *City of Cleburne v. Cleburne Living Center* and *U.S. Department of Agriculture v. Moreno,* which had looked askance at laws reflecting "animosity" toward, or a "bare desire to harm," a "politically unpopular group" without applying "strict scrutiny" to them.[107]

We have analogous situations regarding gays and lesbians in relation to the Equal Protection Clause and the Due Process Clause. In *Romer,* the Court was not about to say that discrimination on the basis of sexual orientation should be recognized as a suspect classification triggering strict scrutiny under the Equal Protection Clause. Nor, on the other hand, was it about to say that discrimination on the basis of sexual orientation should be subjected to merely deferential rational basis scrutiny (just like regulations discriminating against opticians in *Williamson*). Similarly, in *Lawrence,* the Court was not about to say that the right of gays and lesbians to sexual autonomy is a fundamental right triggering strict scrutiny. (In fact, the joint opinion in *Casey* wouldn't even any longer say that the right to abortion is a "fundamental right.") Nor, on the other hand, was it about to say that laws criminalizing homosexual sexual intimacy should be subjected to merely deferential rational basis scrutiny (just like regulations of opticians in *Williamson*). And so, in *Romer* under the Equal Protection Clause as well as in *Lawrence* under the Due Process Clause, the Court has eschewed rigorously policing frameworks of three tiers or two tiers and instead applied rational basis scrutiny with "bite"; not as stringent as strict scrutiny and not as lenient as deferential rational basis scrutiny. In *Romer,* the Court put some bite into its scrutiny of the asserted legitimate governmental interest: whereas *Bowers* presumed that the preservation of traditional sexual morality was a legitimate governmental interest,[108] *Romer* saw "animosity" toward a "politically unpopular group" and held this not to be a legitimate governmental interest.[109] In *Romer,* the Court also put some teeth into its analysis of the fit between the means and the end.[110] *Lawrence* applies a similar analysis with "bite."[111] And so, contrary to Scalia, the level of scrutiny in *Lawrence* had been heard of in *Romer.*

Vermont and Massachusetts Same-Sex Marriage Decisions

We should look briefly at *Baker v. State* and *Goodridge v. Department of Public Health,* the Vermont and Massachusetts same-sex marriage decisions, in light of our analysis here. In *Baker,* in interpreting the Vermont Constitution's Common Benefits Clause (its counterpart to the U.S. Constitution's Equal Protection Clause), the Vermont Supreme

Court expressly disavows the U.S. Supreme Court's equal protection jurisprudence, with its aspirations to rigidly police a three-tier framework.[112] Instead, the court basically says—to paraphrase Stevens's famous statement that "[t]here is only one Equal Protection Clause"[113]— there is only one Common Benefits Clause. The opinion embodies a view like those of Stevens and Marshall concerning the U.S. Constitution's Equal Protection Clause: it reflects a continuum of judgmental responses or spectrum of standards, not a rigidly tiered framework.[114] The Vermont Supreme Court applies something like rational basis scrutiny with "bite" across the board, putting teeth into analysis of ends and especially of fit between means and ends, but not the teeth of strict scrutiny: "That approach may be described as broadly deferential to the legislative prerogative to define and advance governmental *ends,* while vigorously ensuring that the *means* chosen bear a just and reasonable relation to the governmental objective." Applying that standard, the court invalidates the law limiting marriage to opposite-sex couples on the ground that it denies common benefits to same-sex couples.[115]

Goodridge, analogous to *Baker,* does not share the U.S. Supreme Court's hankering for a rigid three-tier analysis under the Equal Protection Clause as well as for a rigid two-tier analysis under the Due Process Clause. At first blush, it appears very different from the substantive due process jurisprudence of the U.S. Supreme Court (if you believe the myth of strict scrutiny for fundamental rights under the Due Process Clause). Instead, the Massachusetts Supreme Judicial Court says its inquiry is to put teeth into its analysis of ends and of fit between means and ends, though not the teeth of strict scrutiny: "Not every asserted rational relationship is a 'conceivable' one, and rationality review is not 'toothless.' Statutes have failed rational basis review even in circumstances where no fundamental right or 'suspect' classification is implicated."[116] That sounds a lot like rational basis scrutiny with "bite," *Lawrence* and *Romer* style. And so, if the analysis of this chapter is sound, maybe the Massachusetts court's approach to due process (and to equal protection) is not so different from that of the U.S. Supreme Court after all. Perhaps it confirms the wisdom of Harlan's approach. Perhaps it is taking, clear-headedly, the approach that the U.S. Supreme Court has groped toward and unofficially followed, notwithstanding the myth of strict scrutiny for fundamental rights under the Due Process Clause. In sum, these leading state supreme court decisions have gone the same way as Stevens/Marshall in equal protection and Harlan in due process. They will hear nothing of the myth of strict scrutiny for fundamental rights put out by Scalia and Rehnquist.

Debunking the Myth of Strict Scrutiny for Fundamental Rights

We now realize why students are baffled concerning what the doctrinal framework for substantive due process is. And why they are especially baffled to be told that, to be protected under the Due Process Clause, a liberty must be held to be a fundamental right, which triggers strict scrutiny and all the rest of it. Students reading the cases from *Meyer* and *Pierce* on down the line for the first time simply don't see that—and that is no wonder since it is not in the cases. It is a myth of Scalia's and Rehnquist's making.

To recapitulate: Scalia and Rehnquist have propounded the myth of strict scrutiny for fundamental rights under the Due Process Clause to make it harder to protect liberties. For Scalia and Rehnquist (not to mention White in *Bowers*), the ideal state of affairs would be to abolish substantive due process altogether, to overrule all of the precedents protecting substantive liberties under the Due Process Clause and, going forward, to protect no such substantive liberties. But they do not have the votes to accomplish their ideal state of affairs. For Scalia and Rehnquist (along with White), the second-best state of affairs is to formulate a framework that will narrow the precedents, drain them of generative vitality, and make it difficult if not impossible to protect "new" liberties under the Due Process Clause and make it easy to uphold laws restricting liberty.

It might seem that the fact that the cases have not followed this framework would be a strike against the framework. That is, when one offers a framework to account for an area of doctrine, ordinarily one seeks to show that it fits and justifies the cases. If the framework doesn't fit and justify the cases, that suggests that the framework is inadequate. But Scalia and Rehnquist treat the fact that the cases have not followed this framework as a strike against the cases! They propound the myth of strict scrutiny for fundamental rights under the Due Process Clause, even though none of the cases protecting liberties under the Due Process Clause have conformed to that framework (besides *Roe*, itself repudiated in this respect in *Casey*). Then they criticize those cases for failing to follow the framework. They criticize the cases, accordingly, as illegitimate and as a mess suggesting the inherent unruliness, incoherence, and illegitimacy of the whole undertaking. Again, instead of acknowledging, from the fact that the cases don't fit the framework, that the framework is inadequate, Scalia can criticize the cases for not following the framework. Thus, Scalia and Rehnquist try to have it both ways: propound a new framework to shut down the protection of liberty under the Due Process Clause and then criticize the precedents for failing rigorously to have followed that framework! Tellingly, opinions by White, Scalia, and Rehnquist (in *Bowers*, *Michael H.*, *Glucksberg*, and dissent in *Bowers*) proclaim that this is the established framework and cite one another (cases denying protection of liberties) in support of this claim, but they do not—and cannot—cite cases actually protecting rights as supporting this framework.

Conclusion

Notwithstanding the myth of strict scrutiny for fundamental rights under the Due Process Clause and the absoluteness critique, the cases protecting basic liberties under the Due Process Clause reflect what *Casey* and Justice Harlan called "reasoned judgment" concerning our "rational continuum" of "ordered liberty."[117] The cases themselves dispel any illusion of absoluteness concerning rights of privacy or autonomy and avoid the impoverishment of judgment that Scalia seeks and Glendon decries. Our constitutional liberalism justifies such reasoned judgment, protecting important rights stringently but not precluding government from encouraging responsibility or inculcating civic virtues. It enables us to pursue ordered liberty through taking rights, responsibilities, and virtues seriously.

Epilogue: Pursuing Ordered Liberty

In considering communitarian, civic republican, and progressive arguments that our constitutional system takes individual rights too seriously, to the neglect of responsibilities, virtues, and the common good, we have responded to the charges of irresponsibility, neutrality, wrongness, and absoluteness. We have countered claims that liberalism promotes "liberty as license" through developing a constitutional liberalism that aspires to pursue "ordered liberty"—"to secure conditions favorable to the pursuit of happiness"[1]—by taking rights, responsibilities, and virtues seriously. Our constitutional liberalism, a synthesis of liberalism, civic republicanism, and feminism, does so through a formative project of government and civil society encouraging responsibility and cultivating citizens' capacities for democratic and personal self-government. It also provides a framework for resolving clashes of rights so as to promote ordered liberty and equal citizenship for all, not the absolutism of one liberty to the exclusion of other constitutional commitments. Furthermore, it justifies constitutional rights not solely to protect choices, without regard for the good of what is chosen, but also to promote moral goods essential to ordered liberty. And it protects basic liberties stringently but not absolutely, through reasoned judgment concerning what is essential to a scheme of ordered liberty. Finally, instead of conceiving the Constitution merely as protecting people from government, our constitutional liberalism views it as imposing affirmative obligations upon government to pursue positive benefits like the ends proclaimed in the Preamble, for which We the People ordained and established the Constitution. Those positive benefits include securing the blessings of ordered liberty to ourselves and our posterity.

Notes

1. Rights, Responsibilities, and Virtues

1. Anthony Giddens, *The Third Way: The Renewal of Social Democracy* (Cambridge, UK: Polity Press, 1998), 65. See also "Progressive Policy Institute: The Third Way" ("Third Way politics seeks . . . a new social compact based on individual rights and responsibilities"), http://www.dlc.org/ppi/ppi_ka.cfm?knlgAreaID=128 (accessed 2/8/12).
2. Barack Obama, "Inaugural Address," http://www.whitehouse.gov/the-press-office/president-barack-obamas-inaugural-address (accessed 4/9/10).
3. Ronald Dworkin, *Taking Rights Seriously* (Cambridge, MA: Harvard University Press, 1977), vii, xi, 184.
4. Michael J. Sandel, *Democracy's Discontent: America in Search of a Public Philosophy* (Cambridge, MA: Belknap Press of Harvard University Press, 1996), 6, 129–133.
5. 763 N.W.2d 862, 883 (Iowa 2009).
6. Olmstead v. United States, 277 U.S. 438, 478 (1928) (Brandeis, J., dissenting).
7. See, e.g., William A. Galston, *Liberal Purposes: Goods, Virtues, and Diversity in the Liberal State* (Cambridge: Cambridge University Press, 1991); William A. Galston, *Liberal Pluralism: The Implications of Value Pluralism for Political Theory and Practice* (Cambridge: Cambridge University Press, 2002); Stephen Macedo, *Liberal Virtues: Citizenship, Virtue, and Community in Liberal Constitutionalism* (Oxford: Clarendon Press, 1990); Stephen Macedo, *Diversity and Distrust: Civic Education in a Multicultural Democracy* (Cambridge, MA: Harvard University Press, 2000). See also Corey Brettschneider, *Democratic Rights: The Substance of Self-Government* (Princeton, NJ: Princeton University Press, 2007); Corey Brettschneider, *When the State Speaks, What Should it Say? How*

Democracies Can Protect Expression and Promote Equality (Princeton, NJ: Princeton University Press, 2012).

8. See John Rawls, *Political Liberalism* (New York: Columbia University Press, 1993).

9. Ronald Dworkin, *Life's Dominion: An Argument About Abortion, Euthanasia, and Individual Freedom* (New York: Knopf, 1993); Ronald Dworkin, *Is Democracy Possible Here? Principles for a New Political Debate* (Princeton, NJ: Princeton University Press, 2006); Ronald Dworkin, *Justice for Hedgehogs* (Cambridge, MA: Belknap Press of Harvard University Press, 2011).

10. Rawls, *Political Liberalism*, xxvii, 196, 199.

11. James E. Fleming, *Securing Constitutional Democracy: The Case of Autonomy* (Chicago, IL: University of Chicago Press, 2006).

12. Linda C. McClain, *The Place of Families: Fostering Capacity, Equality, and Responsibility* (Cambridge, MA: Harvard University Press, 2006).

13. Steven Wall, *Liberalism, Perfectionism and Restraint* (Cambridge: Cambridge University Press, 1998), 8. See also Colin Farrelly and Lawrence B. Solum, eds., *Virtue Jurisprudence* (New York: Palgrave Macmillan, 2008).

14. An influential statement of this critique is Mary Ann Glendon, *Rights Talk: The Impoverishment of Political Discourse* (New York: Free Press, 1991).

15. Amitai Etzioni, *The Spirit of Community: Rights, Responsibilities, and the Communitarian Agenda* (New York: Crown, 1993), 161.

16. Planned Parenthood v. Casey, 505 U.S. 833 (1992); Gonzales v. Carhart, 550 U.S. 124 (2007).

17. Robin West, "Foreword: Taking Freedom Seriously," 104 *Harvard Law Review* 43, 81, 82-83 (1990) (criticizing Dworkin, *Taking Rights Seriously*).

18. Robin West, "From Choice to Reproductive Justice: De-Constitutionalizing Abortion Rights," 118 *Yale Law Journal* 1394 (2009).

19. See, e.g., E. J. Dionne Jr., ed., *Community Works: The Revival of Civil Society in America* (Washington, DC: Brookings Institution Press, 1998); *A Nation of Spectators: How Civic Disengagement Weakens America and What We Can Do About It* (College Park, MD: National Commission on Civic Renewal, 1998); *A Call to Civil Society: Why Democracy Needs Moral Truths* (New York: Institute for American Values, 1998).

20. Mary Ann Glendon, "Introduction: Forgotten Questions," in Mary Ann Glendon and David Blankenhorn, eds., *Seedbeds of Virtue: Sources of Competence, Character, and Citizenship in American Society* (Lanham, MD: Madison Books, 1995), 1, 4, 12.

21. *A Call to Civil Society*, 7.

22. See Nancy L. Rosenblum, *Membership and Morals: The Personal Uses of Pluralism in America* (Princeton, NJ: Princeton University Press, 1998), 10–15, 36–41.

23. John Rawls, *A Theory of Justice* (Cambridge, MA: Belknap Press of Harvard University Press, 1971), 440–442.

24. On this "liberal expectancy," see Rosenblum, *Membership and Morals.*

25. DeShaney v. Winnebago County Department of Social Services, 489 U.S. 189 (1989), expresses the recent Supreme Court's conception of the Constitution as a charter of negative liberties. The most powerful argument for instead conceiving the Constitution as a charter of positive benefits is Sotirios A. Barber, *Welfare and the Constitution* (Princeton, NJ: Princeton University Press, 2003). See also Sotirios A. Barber and James E. Fleming, *Constitutional Interpretation: The Basic Questions* (New York: Oxford University Press, 2007), 35–55.

26. *The Federalist* No. 51 (Madison), ed. Clinton Rossiter (New York: New American Library, 1961), 322.

27. Fleming, *Securing Constitutional Democracy,* 3–4.

28. Rawls, *Political Liberalism,* 19.

29. 347 U.S. 483, 493 (1954).

30. See Nomi Maya Stolzenberg, " 'He Drew a Circle that Shut Me Out': Assimilation, Indoctrination, and the Paradox of a Liberal Education," 106 *Harvard Law Review* 581 (1993).

31. Susan Moller Okin and Rob Reich, "Families and Schools as Compensating Agents in Moral Development for a Multicultural Society," 28 *Journal of Moral Education* 283, 296 (1999).

32. We borrow the term "weedbeds of vice" from Eileen McDonagh, who suggested it in conversation.

33. See Abner S. Greene, *Against Obligation: The Multiple Sources of Authority in a Liberal Democracy* (Cambridge, MA: Harvard University Press, 2012).

34. 468 U.S. 609 (1984).

35. 530 U.S. 640 (2000).

36. 461 U.S. 574 (1983).

37. 130 S. Ct. 2971 (2010).

38. Sandel, *Democracy's Discontent,* 95–108.

39. Michael J. Sandel, *Public Philosophy: Essays on Morality in Politics* (Cambridge, MA: Harvard University Press, 2005), 142 (analyzing Lawrence v. Texas, 539 U.S. 558 (2003)).

40. Michael J. Sandel, *Justice: What's the Right Thing To Do?* (New York: Farrar, Straus & Giroux, 2009), 253–254 (analyzing Goodridge v. Department of Public Health, 798 N.E.2d 941 (Mass. 2003)).

41. 183 P.3d 384 (Cal. 2008). Proposition 8, discussed in Chapter 7, partially overruled *Marriage Cases.* Strauss v. Horton, 207 P.3d 48, 61 (Cal. 2009).

42. Cass R. Sunstein, *Radicals in Robes: Why Extreme Right-Wing Courts Are Wrong for America* (New York: Basic Books, 2005), 31–41.

43. Cass R. Sunstein, *Legal Reasoning and Political Conflict* (New York: Oxford University Press, 1996); Cass R. Sunstein, *One Case at a Time: Judicial Minimalism on the Supreme Court* (Cambridge, MA: Harvard University Press, 1999); Cass R. Sunstein, *A Constitution of Many Minds: Why the Founding Document Doesn't Mean What It Meant Before* (Princeton, NJ: Princeton University Press, 2009).

44. Cass R. Sunstein, "What Did *Lawrence* Hold? Of Autonomy, Desuetude, Sexuality, and Marriage," 2003 *Supreme Court Review* 27, 30.

45. Baker v. State, 744 A.2d 864 (Vt. 1999); *Goodridge*, 798 N.E.2d 941 (Mass. 2003).

46. Cass R. Sunstein, *The Partial Constitution* (Cambridge, MA: Harvard University Press, 1993).

47. Gerald Gunther, "Foreword: In Search of Evolving Doctrine on a Changing Court: A Model for a Newer Equal Protection," 86 *Harvard Law Review* 1, 8 (1972).

48. Glendon, *Rights Talk*, 18, 40–41.

49. *Lawrence*, 593 (Scalia, J., dissenting).

50. Ibid., 593–594.

51. See Grutter v. Bollinger, 539 U.S. 306, 349 (2003) (Scalia, J., dissenting).

52. 410 U.S. 113, 153–155 (1973).

53. *Casey*, 876–878.

54. 262 U.S. 390 (1923).

55. Poe v. Ullman, 367 U.S. 497, 543, 549 (1961) (Harlan, J., dissenting); *Casey*, 847–849.

2. Rights and Irresponsibility

1. "Who Owes What to Whom?," *Harper's*, Feb. 1991, 43, 44. For a contemporaneous examination of the relationship between the Bill of Rights and citizen responsibilities, see "Symposium, Individual Responsibility and the Law," 77 *Cornell Law Review* 955 (1992).

2. "The Responsive Communitarian Platform: Rights and Responsibilities" holds that "a communitarian perspective [balancing rights and responsibilities] must be brought to bear on the great moral, legal, and social issues of our time" and suggests an array of responsibilities to achieve that balance. See "The Responsive Communitarian Platform: Rights and Responsibilities," 2 *Responsive Community* (Winter 1991–1992), 5. Amitai Etzioni distinguishes "responsive" from "collectivistic" communitarians: the former, he argues, do not "trample" autonomy. Amitai Etzioni, *The New Golden Rule: Community and Morality in a Democratic Society* (New York: Basic Books, 1996), 5.

3. "Responsive Communitarian Platform," 7, 14. See also Mary Ann Glendon, *Rights Talk: The Impoverishment of Political Discourse* (New York: Free Press, 1991), 109–120.

4. "The Democratic Platform: A 'New Covenant' with Americans," *New York Times*, July 15, 1992, A10; "Remarks at a White House Interfaith Breakfast," 29 *Weekly Compilation of Presidential Documents* 1657 (Aug. 30, 1993) (Government Accounting Office); "The Inauguration: 'We Force the Spring': Transcript of Address by President Clinton," *New York Times*, Jan. 21, 1993, A15.

5. Ed Gillespie and Bob Schellhas, eds., *Contract with America* (New York: Times Books, 1994), 13–14.

6. "Progressive Policy Institute: The Third Way," http://www.dlc.org/ppi /ppi_ka.cfm?knlgAreaID=128 (accessed 2/8/12).

7. Barack Obama, *The Audacity of Hope* (New York: Random House, 2006), 55; Amitai Etzioni, "Conservatism is Dead: Long Live Liberalism? (Part III)," *The Huffington Post*, July 16, 2008, http://www.huffingtonpost .com/amitai-etzioni/conservatism-is-dead-long_b_113096.html (accessed 2/6/12); David Brooks, "McCain and Obama," *New York Times*, Jan. 8, 2008, A23.

8. Barack Obama, "Inaugural Address," http://www.whitehouse.gov/the-press -office/president-barack-obamas-inaugural-address (accessed 4/9/10).

9. Lloyd Weinreb observes: "Rights, it is sometimes suggested, are anticommunitarian. That view of rights misses their true import. Rights may, of course, be abused. But without rights, there is no freedom and no responsibility." Lloyd L. Weinreb, *Oedipus at Fenway Park: What Rights Are and Why There Are Any* (Cambridge, MA: Harvard University Press, 1994), 12.

10. See Glendon, *Rights Talk*, 15, 104–105. Glendon's examples in which law may encourage or appear to condone irresponsibility include: the "no duty to rescue" rule in tort law; the constitutional embrace of that rule in DeShaney v. Winnebago County Department of Social Services, 489 U.S. 189 (1989), which speaks of the Constitution as a charter of negative liberties and appears to sanction parental irresponsibility; and the law and policies surrounding child support. Ibid., 97–98, 105, 135. In the first two instances, Glendon criticizes judicial opinions for failing to explain the moral infrastructure of American society, notwithstanding the absence of legal obligations. Ibid., 15, 95–98, 102–105, 174–175.

11. Ibid., 14. Our explication includes Glendon's subsequent work.

12. Statement by Dr. Mary Ann Glendon, "Freedom and Moral Truth, The United Nations: A Family of Nations: A Seminar on the Address of his Holiness John Paul II to the United Nations Organization," May 8, 1996, http://www.holyseemission.org/glendon.html (accessed 4/9/10).

13. Glendon, *Rights Talk*, 55 (quoting Olmstead v. United States, 277 U.S. 438, 478 (1928) (Brandeis, J., dissenting)).

14. Mary Ann Glendon, "Looking for 'Persons' in the Law," Dec. 2006, http:// www.firstthings.com/article/2007/01/looking-for-8220persons8221in -the-law-16 (accessed 4/22/10). Glendon's work on rights often draws on Catholic Social Thought; she has represented the Vatican in UN human rights events and is President of the Roman Catholic Church's Pontifical Academy of Social Sciences.

15. Ibid.

16. Glendon, *Rights Talk*, 13 (quoting United Nations UDHR, Article 29 (1949)).

17. Ibid., 9 (citing a survey by People for the American Way). See ibid., 18–46.

18. See ibid., 10–11, 13, 32–37, 115–117. For Glendon's appeal to "ordered liberty," see ibid., 10 (citing Palko v. Connecticut, 302 U.S. 319, 325 (1937)); ibid., 127–128. For her analysis of Tocqueville, see ibid., 117–120 (citing 1 Alexis De Tocqueville, *Democracy in America*, ed. J. P. Mayer

and trans. George Lawrence (New York: Anchor, 1969), 63, 70, 93–94; Alexis De Tocqueville, *The Old Regime and the French Revolution,* trans. Stuart Gilbert (New York: Anchor, 1955), xiii)). For particular historical texts, see *The Federalist* No. 55 (Madison), ed. Clinton Rossiter (New York: New American Library, 1961), 341; George Washington, "Farewell Address," reprinted in William B. Allen, ed., *George Washington: A Collection* (Indianapolis, IN: Liberty Press, 1988), 521. See also Steven Calabresi and Gary Lawson, "Foreword: The Constitution of Responsibility," 77 *Cornell Law Review* 955 (1992) (arguing that the Founders presupposed citizen responsibility as a vital support of government and took for granted the vitality of civil society, morality, and religion).

19. See Glendon, *Rights Talk,* 4–7, 87, 115–117, 136–138.
20. Glendon, "Looking for 'Persons' in the Law."
21. Glendon, *Rights Talk,* xii, 8, 174–175.
22. Ibid., 15, 177.
23. Ibid., 148–158.
24. See ibid., 60–66, 95–96, 104–105, 151–158.
25. See ibid., passim.
26. Amitai Etzioni, *The Spirit of Community: Rights, Responsibilities, and the Communitarian Agenda* (New York: Crown, 1993), 3.
27. Ibid., 10 (stating that this "symbolic" finding triggered the dialogue that launched the responsive communitarian movement); "Responsive Communitarian Platform," 12.
28. Steirer v. Bethlehem Area School District, 987 F.2d 989, 999 (3d Cir. 1993) ("[g]overnments may require individuals to perform certain well-established 'civic duties,' such as military service and jury duty, and impose legal sanctions for the failure to perform"), *cert. denied,* 510 U.S. 824 (1993); "Responsive Communitarian Platform," 12 (arguing that "serving on juries" is a "fully obligatory" duty to the polity); see also N.Y. Jud. Law §527 (McKinney 2009) (imposing a civil penalty for failing to respond to jury summons or to attend jury service).
29. Compare Karl Zinsmeister, "Parental Responsibility and the Future of the American Family," 77 *Cornell Law Review* 1005, 1011 (1992).
30. "Responsive Communitarian Platform," 7–10.
31. Etzioni, *The Spirit of Community,* 89–97.
32. See ibid., 23–30 (reviewing the "state of the union's morality" and including as evidence of "moral erosion" rates of divorce, social attitudes toward sex and marriage, high rates of "chronic malingering at work," the use of physical force against others, insider trading in financial markets, political scandals, and the marketing of unsafe products).
33. The responsive communitarians attack interpretations of the Second and Fourth Amendments that are invoked to oppose crime prevention measures and some of them support civil disarmament. Amitai Etzioni and Steven Hellend, "The Case for Domestic Disarmament" (1992), http://www.gwu.edu/~ccps/pop_disarm.html (Communitarian Position Paper).
34. See Stephen Holmes, *The Anatomy of Antiliberalism* (Cambridge, MA:

Harvard University Press, 1993), 4; Ronald Dworkin, *Life's Dominion: An Argument about Abortion, Euthanasia, and Individual Freedom* (New York: Knopf, 1993), 14; Steven J. Heyman, "The First Duty of Government: Protection, Liberty and the Fourteenth Amendment," 41 *Duke Law Journal* 507 (1991). An infamous decision of the Rehnquist Court, *DeShaney*, 196, 202, rejected this view, concluding that the Due Process Clauses "confer no affirmative right to governmental aid," that the state of Wisconsin "had no constitutional duty to protect [a child] against his father's violence," and that failure to do so did not violate the Due Process Clause.

35. See Etzioni, *The Spirit of Community*, 30 (stating that "illegal and immoral behaviors have broken through [the] important line of voluntary self-restraint").

36. Unless otherwise indicated, we have drawn on the work of Etzioni and Galston for the composite account in this Section. See Etzioni, *The Spirit of Community*, 12–13, 23–24; William A. Galston, *Liberal Purposes: Goods, Virtues, and Diversity in the Liberal State* (Cambridge: Cambridge University Press, 1991), 267–270.

37. Galston, *Liberal Purposes*, 268–270.

38. See, e.g., Glendon, *Rights Talk*, 6, 15–16.

39. But see Etzioni, *The Spirit of Community*, 11–12, 23–25 (arguing that it was not the challenge to authority that was the problem, but the absence of new social forms and consensus).

40. Ibid., 23–24; Galston, *Liberal Purposes*, 268–270.

41. Etzioni, *The Spirit of Community*, 248.

42. Etzioni, *The New Golden Rule*, 65.

43. In a famous speech about Martin Luther King Jr., President Clinton contrasted the gains of the civil rights movement with such contemporary problems as violence committed by African-Americans against African-Americans, teen pregnancy, and family breakdown, stressing that Dr. King fought for rights for blacks, but not for the freedom of them to kill each other. Douglas Jehl, "Clinton Delivers Emotional Appeal on Stopping Crime," *New York Times*, Nov. 14, 1993, A1.

44. An example communitarians offer is women's entry into the workforce, which, together with less restrictive divorce laws, they argue, have had a dramatic impact on patterns of childcare in the home, resulting in insufficient attention to the nurture and education of children. See Glendon, *Rights Talk*, 127–128.

45. Cass R. Sunstein, "Rightalk," *New Republic*, Sept. 2, 1991, 33, 34 (reviewing Glendon, *Rights Talk*).

46. Michael Schudson, *The Good Citizen: A History of American Civic Life* (New York: Free Press, 1998), 291, 302.

47. Daniel P. Moynihan, "Defining Deviancy Down," 62 *American Scholar* 17 (1993). On "demoralization," see Etzioni, *The New Golden Rule*, 95–96 (quoting Gertrude Himmelfarb on the need to "remoralize" civil society).

48. See, e.g., Galston, *Liberal Purposes,* 269 (arguing that key U.S. Supreme Court decisions on issues such as "school prayer, pornography, criminal justice, and abortion" spurred the assault on traditional morality, "widened individual freedom," and called for neutrality in areas "previously seen as the legitimate arena for collective moral judgment").

49. Glendon, *Rights Talk,* 105–108 (criticizing U.S. divorce law as "having embraced principles of free terminability of marriage and spousal self-sufficiency after divorce," while failing "to assure *either* public or private responsibility for the casualties").

50. Francis Fukuyama, *Trust: The Social Virtues and the Creation of Prosperity* (New York: Free Press, 1995), 314.

51. See Etzioni, *The Spirit of Community,* 6 (arguing that "[o]nce, rights were very solemn moral/legal claims, ensconced in the Constitution and treated with much reverence," but that today, people attempt to elevate every personal desire and special interest to the status of a legal right). See ibid., 5–7.

52. See, e.g., Charles J. Sykes, *A Nation of Victims* (New York: St. Martins Press, 1992); John Taylor, "Don't Blame Me! The New Culture of Victimization," *New York Magazine,* June 3, 1991, 27, 29 (diagnosing the "inextricably linked concepts" of "victimization," whereby the principle of individual responsibility for one's actions is almost a relic, and the growth of a "rights industry" (quoting Etzioni)).

53. See Taylor, "Don't Blame Me!," 32.

54. "Responsive Communitarian Platform," 14.

55. See Wesley N. Hohfeld, "Some Fundamental Legal Conceptions as Applied in Judicial Reasoning," 23 *Yale Law Journal* 16, 28–44 (1913).

56. Richard H. Fallon, Jr., "Individual Rights and the Powers of Government," 27 *Georgia Law Review* 343, 344 n.4 (1993).

57. J. M. Balkin, "The Hohfeldian Approach to Law and Semiotics," 44 *University of Miami Law Review* 1119, 1129 (1990).

58. See Joseph W. Singer, "The Legal Rights Debate in Analytical Jurisprudence from Bentham to Hohfeld," 1982 *Wisconsin Law Review* 975, 1056–1067. Mill's "harm principle" is: "[T]he sole end for which mankind are warranted, individually or collectively, in interfering with the liberty of action of any of their number, is self-protection. . . . [T]he only purpose for which power can be rightfully exercised over any member of a civilised community, against his will, is to prevent harm to others."
    John Stuart Mill, *On Liberty,* ed. David Spitz (New York: Norton, 1975) (1859), 10–11 (footnotes omitted).

59. See "Responsive Communitarian Platform," 13–14 (stating that "[s]uggestions that [the First Amendment] should be curbed to bar verbal expressions of racism, sexism, and other slurs seem to us to endanger the essence of the First Amendment, which is most needed when what some people say is disconcerting to some others"). Communitarians favor nonlegal remedies to educate and promote tolerance. See Etzioni, *The Spirit of Community,* 192–206.

60. See Etzioni, *The Spirit of Community*, 11, 163–191.

61. "Responsive Communitarian Platform," 8, 17. See Galston, *Liberal Purposes*, 286–287 (supporting "braking" mechanisms for parents contemplating divorce).

62. See Jean Elshtain et al., "A Communitarian Position Paper on the Family," http://www.gwu.edu/~ccps/pop_fam.html (detailing proposals that call for attention to "cultural values" of "excessive careerism or acquisitiveness" that detract from childcare and advocating a "children first" principle for divorce law to "slow the rush to divorce"). See also Galston, *Liberal Purposes*, 281.

63. See Mill, *On Liberty*, 10–11, 70–74, 87.

64. See Etzioni, *The Spirit of Community*, 7–8 (rejecting libertarian challenges to seatbelt and motorcycle helmet laws and noting that "[r]eckless individuals . . . do not absorb many of the consequences of their acts").

65. See Mill, *On Liberty*, 5–6, 14–15, 62–63.

66. See, e.g., Etzioni, *The Spirit of Community*, 7–8; Glendon, *Rights Talk*, 8, 40; James Q. Wilson, *The Moral Sense* (New York: Free Press, 1993), 250.

67. See, e.g., Glendon, *Rights Talk*, x–xi (criticizing the proliferation of rights talk as promoting "unrealistic expectations" and ignoring "both social costs and the rights of others").

68. Ronald Dworkin, *Taking Rights Seriously* (Cambridge, MA: Harvard University Press, 1977), vii, xi, 184.

69. Ibid., 194, 269.

70. See Glendon, *Rights Talk*, 18, 40 (quoting Dworkin, *Taking Rights Seriously*, 269).

71. Dworkin, *Taking Rights Seriously*, 190–191. Nonetheless, if one acknowledges the final circumstance as a justification, one would be "treating the right in question as not among the most important or fundamental." Ibid.

72. Some laws that do not directly restrict fundamental rights, but incidentally burden them, may be constitutional. Michael C. Dorf, "Incidental Burdens on Fundamental Rights," 109 *Harvard Law Review* 1175 (1996).

73. Ronald Dworkin, *Is Democracy Possible Here? Principles for a New Political Debate* (Princeton, NJ: Princeton University Press, 2006), 10, 17–18. See also Dworkin, *Life's Dominion*, 148–154, 166–168, 237–241.

74. Dworkin, *Life's Dominion*, 113–118.

75. Dworkin, *Taking Rights Seriously*, 198–199, 204, 205.

76. Ronald Dworkin, *Justice for Hedgehogs* (Cambridge, MA: Belknap Press of Harvard University Press, 2011).

77. Etzioni, *The Spirit of Community*, 7 (citing Sunstein, "Rightalk," 34).

78. James B. White, "Looking at Our Language: Glendon on Rights," 90 *Michigan Law Review* 1267, 1273 (1992).

79. See T. Alexander Aleinikoff, "Constitutional Law in the Age of Balancing," 96 *Yale Law Journal* 943, 963–972 (1987); Fallon, "Individual Rights," 346–347, 360–364, 372 (arguing that individual rights and governmental powers must be defined by reference to conflicting interests that must be

balanced but suggesting that his approach is not inconsistent with Dworkin's).

80. Glendon, *Rights Talk*, 177.

81. Ibid., 138.

82. Ibid., 38–39 (discussing example of German property law); ibid. (quoting the Canadian Charter of Rights and Freedoms, Canada Act 1982, R.S.C. app. II, no. 44 (1985)).

83. Thomas D. Barton, "Reclaiming Law Talk," 81 *California Law Review* 803, 807, 812 (1993).

84. See Roger Pilon, "Freedom, Responsibility, and the Constitution: On Recovering Our Founding Principles," 68 *Notre Dame Law Review* 507, 510 & n.8 (1993) (citing the Responsive Communitarian Platform as implying such an understanding of rights).

85. Holmes, *The Anatomy of Antiliberalism*, 4.

86. See "Responsive Communitarian Platform," 13 ("The First Amendment is as dear to communitarians as it is to libertarians and many other Americans.").

87. Whitney v. California, 274 U.S. 357, 371 (1927), *overruled by* Brandenburg v. Ohio, 395 U.S. 444 (1969).

88. See, e.g., Mari J. Matsuda et al., *Words That Wound: Critical Race Theory, Assaultive Speech, and the First Amendment* (Boulder, CO: Westview Press, 1993); see also Cass R. Sunstein, *Democracy and the Problem of Free Speech* (New York: Free Press, 1993), 180–193, 197–208; Steven J. Heyman, *Free Speech and Human Dignity* (New Haven, CT: Yale University Press, 2008).

89. See Catharine A. MacKinnon, *Only Words* (Cambridge, MA: Harvard University Press, 1993).

90. See, e.g., Regina v. Butler, 1 S.C.R. 452 (Can.1992) (upholding restrictions on pornography in view of the harm to society, including the effect on attitudes toward women).

91. Compare Note, "A Communitarian Defense of Group Libel Laws," 101 *Harvard Law Review* 682 (1988).

92. United States v. Stevens, 130 S. Ct. 1577, 1585 (2010).

93. We allude to the title of Matsuda, *Words That Wound*.

94. Snyder v. Phelps, 131 S. Ct. 1207, 1213, 1216–1217 (2011).

95. Ibid., 1223 (Alito, J., dissenting) (citation omitted).

96. Ibid., 1216–1218, 1219, 1220 (citations omitted).

97. Devin Dwyer, "From Retirement, Justice John Paul Stevens Dissents in Funeral Protest Case," May 5, 2011, http://abcnews.go.com/blogs /politics/2011/05/justice-john-paul-stevens-dissents-in-funeral-protests -case/ (accessed 11/14/11).

98. *Snyder*, 1222 (Alito, J., dissenting).

99. Ibid., 1222, 1228, 1229.

100. See Stanley Fish, "Sticks and Stones," http://opinionator.blogs.nytimes. com/2011/03/07/sticks-and-stones/ (accessed 11/14/11) (quoting Chief Justice Roberts in *United States v. Stevens*).

101. "Responsive Communitarian Platform," 14.

102. Galston, *Liberal Purposes*, 281.

103. Etzioni, *The Spirit of Community*, 38.

104. Dworkin, *Taking Rights Seriously*, 188. Some philosophers have argued that there is a moral right to do wrong, but Galston denies this. See Jeremy Waldron, "A Right to Do Wrong," 92 *Ethics* 21 (1981); William A. Galston, "On the Alleged Right to Do Wrong: A Response to Waldron," 93 *Ethics* 320 (1983); Jeremy Waldron, "Galston on Rights," 93 *Ethics* 325 (1983).

105. Glendon, "Looking for 'Persons' in the Law."

106. See, e.g., Joel Feinberg, *Rights, Justice, and the Bounds of Liberty: Essays in Social Philosophy* (Princeton, NJ: Princeton University Press, 1980), 156.

107. Etzioni, *Spirit of Community*, 36.

108. Amitai Etzioni, "Individualism—within History," *The Hedgehog Review* (Spring 2002), 49–50.

109. "Responsive Communitarian Platform," 17.

110. Etzioni, *The Spirit of Community*, 30, 40.

111. See ibid., 34–39; Robin West, "Foreword: Taking Freedom Seriously," 104 *Harvard Law Review* 43, 71–72 (1990).

112. Galston, *Liberal Purposes*, 213, 222; Glendon, *Rights Talk*, 127; compare Stephen Macedo, *Liberal Virtues: Citizenship, Virtue, and Community in Liberal Constitutionalism* (Oxford: Clarendon Press, 1990), 233–240.

113. See Macedo, *Liberal Virtues*, 234.

114. See Mill, *On Liberty*, 70–72.

115. Ronald Dworkin, *Sovereign Virtue: The Theory and Practice of Equality* (Cambridge, MA: Harvard University Press, 2000), 237–284, 283. Liberalism, however, is not "neutral toward ethical ideals that directly challenge its own." Ibid., 283.

116. See Dworkin, *Justice for Hedgehogs*, 368–371, 375–378.

117. See, e.g., Galston, *Liberal Purposes*.

118. Ibid., 178, 182.

119. See, e.g., *MacNeil/Lehrer NewsHour: Conversation* (PBS television broadcast, May 25, 1993), LEXIS, NEWS Library, SCRIPT File ("our rights, which are kind of knives . . . cut us off from our identity and membership in the American Nation") (statement of Benjamin Barber, political scientist at Rutgers University); Jesse Birnbaum, "Crybabies: Eternal Victims, Hypersensitivity and Special Pleading Are Making a Travesty of the Virtues that used to be Known as Individual Responsibility and Common Sense," *Time*, Aug. 12, 1991, 16 ("I have [an] image of human beings as porcupines, with rights as their quills.") (quoting Roger Conner, executive director of the American Alliance for Rights and Responsibilities); compare Roberto M. Unger, *The Critical Legal Studies Movement* (Cambridge, MA: Harvard University Press, 1986), 36 ("The right is a loaded gun that the right holder may shoot at will in his corner of town. . . . [T]he give-and-take of communal life . . . [is] incompatible with this view of right[s].").

120. In this chapter, we discuss examples involving constitutional rights. Our monitoring of newspapers reveals frequent use of the terms "irresponsible" and "irresponsibility" to criticize decisions, conduct, or speech. Such references involve individuals, corporations, institutions, and governments and include journalistic, fiscal, governmental, corporate, environmental, parental, sexual, and personal irresponsibility. Charges of the failure of responsibility both as accountability and as autonomy are common.

121. For example, the Responsibility Project, sponsored by Liberty Mutual Insurance Company, placed a series of ads inviting readers to consider the responsible thing to do. See http://responsibility-project.libertymutual .com/#fbid=pPVCzh3c9iR (accessed 11/27/11). Kent Greenfield objects to some appeals to "personal responsibility" because they allow "some people to avoid responsibility." For example, "Cheeseburger Bills," which stress personal responsibility for food consumption choices, limit liability of food manufacturers in lawsuits claiming that they contribute to persons' obesity. He counters that responsibility for obesity is "shared": "[f]ast-food executives bear the responsibility for the choices they make" to develop and push certain foods, just as Congress should bear responsibility for agricultural subsidies that make fast-food cheaper than healthy food. Kent Greenfield, *The Myth of Choice: Personal Responsibility in a World of Limits* (New Haven, CT: Yale University Press, 2011), 157–160.

122. Thus, we support the idea that government and private actors may properly "nudge" people to act in ways that will improve their well-being without violating their liberty. Richard H. Thaler and Cass R. Sunstein, *Nudge: Improving Decisions about Health, Wealth, and Happiness* (New Haven, CT: Yale University Press, 2008). Thaler and Sunstein propose a "libertarian paternalism" that tries to "nudge" people toward better choices through structuring the "architecture" of choice (e.g., putting fruit first in the cafeteria line). They argue that this is "liberty-preserving" and eschews coercion. Ibid., 1–11. This type of persuasion is compatible with the formative project we advance. Greenfield counters that sometimes "nudges" are not enough; governmental regulation and even bans may be necessary. Greenfield, *The Myth of Choice,* 196–200.

123. Scott Swenson, "*Snyder v. Phelps:* In the Court of Public Opinion, Snyder Wins," *Huffington Post,* March 3, 2011, http://www.huffingtonpost.com /scott-swenson/snyder-v-phelps-in-the-co_b_831069.html (accessed 11/14/11).

124. Commenting on the absence of self-regulation by the gun industry, one observer remarked, "The premise seems to be that if they've got the right to do something, then that's the right thing to do." Erik Larson, "The Story of a Gun," *Atlantic,* Jan. 1993, 48.

125. The notion that social responsibility should factor into the exercise of rights is prominent in debates over responsible and irresponsible entertainment, entertainers, and corporate producers of such entertainment.

126. Todd S. Purdum, "Terror in Oklahoma: The President; Shifting Debate to the Political Climate, Clinton Condemns 'Promoters of Paranoia,'" *New York Times,* Apr. 25, 1995, A19.

127. Helene Cooper and Jeff Zeleny, "Obama Calls Americans to a New Era of Civility," *New York Times,* Jan. 13, 2011, A1.

128. Patrik Jonsson, "Can a New 'National Civility Institute' Calm Political Rancor?," Feb. 21, 2011, http://www.csmonitor.com /USA/Politics/2011 /0221/Can-a-new-national-civility-institute-calm-political-rancor(accessed 11/14/11) (quoting Fred DuVal, Arizona Board of Regents, on aims of the Institute).

129. A recent example is the Health Initiative undertaken in 2007 by the Council of Fashion Designers of America (CFDA) "to raise awareness of eating disorders in the fashion industry and to change the aesthetic on the New York runways and in magazines from extreme thinness to a more realistic ideal." CFDA, "Healthier Standards—An Op-Ed by CFDA President Diane von Furstenberg and Director of the Harris Center Dr. David Herzog," http://www.cfda/com /healthier-standards-%E2%80%93-an-op -ed-by-cfda-president-diane-von-furstenberg-and-director-of-the -harris-center-dr-david-herzog/ (accessed 11/14/11). CFDA stated: "Designers share a responsibility to protect women, and very young girls in particular, within the business, sending the message that beauty is health." CFDA, "Health Initiative," www.cfda.com/health-initiative (accessed 11/15/11).

130. See Dworkin, *Taking Rights Seriously,* 189 n.1.

131. For example, journalist Matt Richter and the *New York Times* staff won a 2010 Pulitzer Prize for their "Driven to Distraction" series. The series had "enormous impact," spurring federal and employer bans. *"The New York Times* Wins Three 2010 Pulitzer Prizes," *New York Times,* April 13, 2010, A7.

132. See Jennifer Friesen, *State Constitutional Law: Litigating Individual Rights, Claims, and Defenses,* vol. 1 (LexisNexis, 4th ed. 2006), Appendix 5: State Free Speech and Press Provisions. The language quoted in text is from New York's constitution. Ibid., 5–109. Identical or similar language appears in 41 other state constitutions. Ibid., 5–103 to 5–114.

133. See, for example, Hill v. Colorado, 530 U.S. 703 (2000) (upholding against First Amendment challenge a Colorado statute prohibiting any person from knowingly approaching within eight feet of another person near a health care facility—for the purposes of handing out literature or engaging in "oral protest, education, or counseling" of that person—without that person's consent).

134. Shaila Dewan, "Anti-Abortion Billboards on Race Split Atlanta," *New York Times,* Feb. 6, 2010, A9. President Clinton said abortion should be "safe and legal but rare." Robin Toner, "Settling in: Easing Abortion Policy; Clinton Orders Reversal of Abortion Restrictions Left by Reagan and Bush," *New York Times,* Jan. 23, 1993. President Obama has appealed to find common ground on reducing the need for abortion. "Remarks by the President in Commencement Address at the University of Notre Dame," May 17, 2009, http://www.whitehouse.gov/the-press-office/remarks -president-notre-dame-commencement (accessed 8/1/11).

135. See, e.g., Gabriel Winant, "O'Reilly's Campaign against Murdered Doctor," May 31, 2009, http://www.salon.com/2009/05/31/tiller_2/ (accessed 11/21/11) (characterizing Bill O'Reilly's repeated verbal attacks on Kansas doctor George Tiller as "sensationally irresponsible"); Robert Mackey, "Doctor Was Target of O'Reilly's Rhetoric," *The Lede,* http://thelede.blogs.nytimes.com/2009/06/01/doctor-was-target-of-oreillys-rhetoric/ (accessed 11/21/11) (debating question of responsibility of "heated rhetoric" for violent attacks, including killing of Dr. Tiller).

136. Etzioni, *The Spirit of Community,* 201 (quoting Antonin Scalia, "Law, Liberty and Civic Responsibility," in Bradford P. Wilson, ed., *Rights, Citizenship and Responsibilities: The Proceedings of Freedoms Foundation's Symposium on Citizen Responsibilities* (Washington, DC: Freedoms Foundation, 1984), 3). It seems odd for Justice Scalia to make this assertion, given his own positivist insistence on the gap between moral rights and constitutional rights.

137. Planned Parenthood v. Casey, 505 U.S. 833, 995 (1992) (Scalia, J., concurring in part and dissenting in part).

138. One important implication of recognizing that rights do not equate with rightness is the moral responsibility of citizens to oppose unjust laws and engage in civil disobedience. See John Rawls, *A Theory of Justice* (Cambridge, MA: Belknap Press of Harvard University Press, 1971), 388–391; Dworkin, *Taking Rights Seriously,* 184–222.

139. See Kristin Luker, "The Hard Road to *Roe,*" *New York Times,* Feb. 20, 1994, § 7, 7 (reviewing David J. Garrow, *Liberty and Sexuality: The Right to Privacy and the Making of* Roe v. Wade (New York: Scribner, 1994)) (stating that "[b]etween roughly 1967 and 1972, there was a huge shift in American attitudes about sexuality" as to the moral permissibility of both premarital sex and abortion).

140. See Bowers v. Hardwick, 478 U.S. 186, 212 (1986) (Blackmun, J., dissenting) ("'[W]e have ample evidence for believing that people will not abandon morality . . . merely because some private sexual practice which they abominate is not punished by the law.'") (quoting H. L. A. Hart, "Immorality and Treason," in Louis J. Blom-Cooper, ed., *The Law as Literature* (London: Bodley Head, 1961), 220, 225); ibid., 211 ("'[W]e apply the limitations of the Constitution with no fear that freedom to be intellectually and spiritually diverse or even contrary will disintegrate the social organization.'") (quoting West Virginia Board of Education v. Barnette, 319 U.S. 624, 641–642 (1943)).

141. See Rawls, *A Theory of Justice,* 504–515; see also John Rawls, *Political Liberalism* (New York: Columbia University Press, 1993), 324–340.

142. Wilson, *The Moral Sense,* 250.

143. See, e.g., Dworkin, *Sovereign Virtue,* 281–284.

144. Pilon, "Freedom, Responsibility, and the Constitution," 510–511.

145. Holmes, *The Anatomy of Antiliberalism,* 4.

146. See Mill, *On Liberty,* 71–72, 78–79.

147. *Casey,* 850.

148. Rawls, *Political Liberalism,* 36.

149. William A. Galston, "The Theory and Practice of Free Association in a Pluralist Liberal Democracy," in Elizabeth J. Reid, ed., *In the States, across the Nation, and Beyond* (Urban Institute, 2003), 39, 43–45. Etzioni argues that "responsive" communitarians, by contrast to social conservatives, insist on a relatively more modest set of shared values and recognize more room for disagreement. Etzioni, *The New Golden Rule,* 16–17.

150. See Dworkin, *Life's Dominion,* 167–168.

151. Ibid., 206.

152. Macedo, *Liberal Virtues,* 231 ("[T]o be free is to be capable of making choices, of making mistaken or even bad choices.").

153. See Etzioni, *The Spirit of Community,* 201 (quoting Scalia, "Law, Liberty and Civic Responsibility," 4).

154. Such commitments are manifest in the liberal political theory of John Rawls, as well as in Macedo's and Galston's civic liberalisms. See Galston, *Liberal Purposes,* 173–175, 227–231; Macedo, *Liberal Virtues,* 207–212, 214–216; Rawls, *Political Liberalism,* 19, 334–338.

3. Taking Responsibilities as well as Rights Seriously

1. Ronald Dworkin, *Taking Rights Seriously* (Cambridge, MA: Harvard University Press, 1977).

2. Robin West, "Foreword: Taking Freedom Seriously," 104 *Harvard Law Review* 43, 81, 82–83, 85 (1990).

3. Robin West, "From Choice to Reproductive Justice: De-Constitutionalizing Abortion Rights," 118 *Yale Law Journal* 1394 (2009).

4. Planned Parenthood v. Casey, 505 U.S. 833 (1992).

5. Ibid., 856.

6. "Report of the South Dakota Task Force to Study Abortion" (December 2005), 47–48, http://www.dakotavoice.com/Docs/South%20Dakota%20Abortion%20Task%20Force%20Report.pdf (accessed 1/28/12).

7. 550 U.S. 124 (2007).

8. *Casey,* 852.

9. Roe v. Wade, 410 U.S. 113, 164–166 (1973).

10. *Casey,* 877–878.

11. Ibid., 851.

12. John Locke, *A Letter Concerning Toleration,* ed. Patrick Romanell (Indianapolis, IN: Liberal Arts Press, 1955) (1689).

13. *Casey,* 847, 850, 852–853, 869.

14. Thornburgh v. American College of Obstetricians & Gynecologists, 476 U.S. 747, 760–762 (1986); City of Akron v. Akron Center for Reproductive Health, 462 U.S. 416, 423–424, 444–445 (1983).

15. *Casey,* 877–878.

16. Ibid., 872, 877–878, 887.

17. Ibid., 882–883 (overruling in part *Thornburgh* and *Akron*).

18. Ibid., 852.

19. Ibid., 877, 887.

20. *Carhart,* 141 (quoting Congressional finding).

21. Mary Ann Glendon, *Abortion and Divorce in Western Law: American Failures, European Challenges* (Cambridge, MA: Harvard University Press, 1987); Mary Ann Glendon, *Rights Talk: The Impoverishment of Political Discourse* (New York: Free Press, 1991).

22. For example, Mary Ann Glendon, "Looking for 'Persons' in the Law," December 2006, http://www.firstthings.com/article/2007/01/looking-for -8220persons8221in-the-law-16 (accessed 4/9/10).

23. Glendon, *Abortion and Divorce,* 1–9, 16, 18–20, 40–57, 52–58, 62, 155–157 (providing and quoting the text of the French Abortion Law of 1975).

24. Ibid., 17, 20.

25. Ibid., 59–62.

26. Ibid., 47–50 (speculating about what "compromise legislation" would look like). Constitutional law scholar Laurence Tribe counters that "the history of abortion law reform in the United States seriously undermines this claim." Laurence H. Tribe, *Abortion: The Clash of Absolutes* (New York: Norton, 1990), 49–51. Ronald Dworkin challenges Glendon's contrast between "individual rights" and "social solidarity" and points out differences between Europe and the United States that make her expectation "seem unrealistic." Ronald Dworkin, *Life's Dominion: An Argument about Abortion, Euthanasia, and Individual Freedom* (New York: Knopf, 1993), 60–67.

27. Glendon, *Abortion and Divorce,* 49.

28. Prepared Statement of Mary Ann Glendon, Origins and Scope of *Roe v. Wade:* Hearing before the Subcommittee on the Constitution of the Committee on the Judiciary, House of Representatives, 104th Congress, Second Session, April 22, 1996, Serial No. 80, 54.

29. On this "laggard" status and probable reasons for it, see Eileen McDonagh, *The Motherless State: Women's Political Leadership and American Democracy* (Chicago, IL: University of Chicago Press, 2009).

30. *Casey,* 866, 874, 875.

31. Glendon, "Looking for 'Persons' in the Law."

32. Advertisement: "A New American Compact: Caring about Women, Caring for the Unborn," *New York Times,* July 14, 1992, A23.

33. Ibid.

34. "The America We Seek: A Statement of Pro-Life Principle and Concern," May 1996, http://www.firstthings.com/article/2007/10/005-the -america-we-seek-a-statement-of-pro-life-principle-and-concern-16 (accessed 4/22/10).

35. "We Hold these Truths: A Statement of Christian Conscience and Citizenship, July 4, 1997," http://www.peopleforlife.org/truths.html (accessed 4/22/10).

36. "The America We Seek."

37. Glendon, *Rights Talk,* 48, 60–61.

38. Ibid., 61–65. In 1992, the German Parliament passed legislation intended to reconcile the restrictive laws of the former West Germany with the more permissive laws of the former East Germany. When the Bundesverfassungsgericht (Federal Constitutional Court) considered the compromise legislation, the Pregnant Women's and Family Assistance Act, the court "upheld central features of the proposed counseling scheme, but insisted on the revision of other features to make them more unambiguously pro-life." Mary Anne Case, "Perfectionism and Fundamentalism in the Application of the German Abortion Laws," in Susan H. Williams, ed., *Constituting Equality: Gender Equality and Comparative Constitutional Law* (New York: Cambridge University Press, 2009), 93, 97 (discussing Schwangerschaftsabbruch II Judgment, 88 BverfGE 203 (F.R.G.)). For example, the court stated that the counseling should not merely be informational, but "the counselors must try to encourage the woman to continue her pregnancy and show her opportunities for a life with the child." Case, "Perfectionism and Fundamentalism," 97–98 (quoting from official translation of opinion). The court insisted that abortion "would remain a wrongful act," but if a woman underwent the counseling, she would "receive a certificate in effect permitting her to obtain a first trimester abortion without risk of criminal sanctions." Ibid., 98.
39. Glendon, *Rights Talk*, 65.
40. *Casey*, 893.
41. Glendon, "Looking for 'Persons' in the Law."
42. Mary Ann Glendon and Eric W. Greene, "Selective Humanism: The Legacy of Justice William Brennan," 24 *The Human Life Review* 65 (1998).
43. Glendon, "Looking for 'Persons' in the Law"; see *Casey*, 887 ("wise exercise").
44. "The America We Seek" (stating that a "national effort" to enact laws like Pennsylvania's in all 50 states would be "a modest but important step toward the America we seek"). Restrictions on late-term abortions and on specific methods are other examples.
45. Ibid.
46. *Casey*, 852 (citation omitted).
47. Glendon, *Abortion and Divorce*, 27, 28 (quoting Judgment of Feb. 25, 1975, BverfG, 39 Entscheidungen des Bundesverfassungsgerichts [BVerfGE] 1 (F.R.G.), translated in the Abortion Decision of February 25, 1975, of the Federal Constitutional Court, Federal Republic of Germany 63 (Edmund C. Jann trans., 1975)).
48. West, "Taking Freedom Seriously," 52–54.
49. Glendon, *Rights Talk*, 47–66, 81–82.
50. Ibid., 39–40. See Chapter 2 for discussion of Glendon's critique of Dworkin's conception of rights.
51. Ronald Dworkin, "The Great Abortion Case," *New York Review of Books*, June 29, 1989, 49, 51.
52. Dworkin, *Life's Dominion*, 166, 160–168.

53. Ibid., 150, 153.

54. Ibid., 81–84, 167.

55. Ibid., 148–154.

56. Ibid., 153, 173–174.

57. Ibid., 150–159.

58. Ibid., 151.

59. Ronald Dworkin, *Is Democracy Possible Here? Principles for a New Political Debate* (Princeton, NJ: Princeton University Press, 2006), 10, 17.

60. Dworkin, *Life's Dominion*, 4, 15, 167–168.

61. Dworkin's characterization of the majority, liberal position suggests an impressive degree of fit between public approval of reasons for abortion and women's actual reasons. Other contemporaneous assessments suggest less of a fit. Linda C. McClain, "The Poverty of Privacy?," 3 *Columbia Journal of Gender and Law* 119, 164–172 (1992) (citing other assessments).

62. Dworkin, *Life's Dominion*, 60. Dworkin's liberal position might not capture, for example, feminist arguments that start from the premise not of the presumptive "wrongness" of abortion but of a moral and legal right to abortion based on the requirements of women's well-being and reproductive health. See, e.g., Rosalind P. Petchesky, *Abortion and Woman's Choice: The State, Sexuality, and Reproductive Freedom* (Boston: Northeastern University Press, rev. ed. 1990), 368–401.

63. Dworkin, *Life's Dominion*, 32–34, 97–100 (arguing that, in addition to cases of rape or incest, liberals think that abortion is justified in instances of serious "frustration" of the life of the eventual child or of the woman and other family members, e.g., a "very grave physical deformity" of the child, "economically barren" family circumstances, risk to the pregnant woman's life, or a permanent and grave impact on the woman's or her family's life or the life of the child if born).

64. Glendon, "Looking for 'Persons' in the Law."

65. Ronald Dworkin, *Justice for Hedgehogs* (Cambridge, MA: Belknap Press of Harvard University Press, 2011), 368–378.

66. Ronald Dworkin, *Sovereign Virtue: The Theory and Practice of Equality* (Cambridge, MA: Harvard University Press, 2000), 237–284.

67. Martha Nussbaum, "Aristotelian Social Democracy," in R. Bruce Douglass et al., eds., *Liberalism and the Good* (New York: Routledge, 1990), 203, 228–230 (arguing for the importance of a governmental role in moving citizens "across the threshold into capability to choose well").

68. Ronald Dworkin, *Freedom's Law: The Moral Reading of the American Constitution* (Cambridge, MA: Harvard University Press, 1996), 121–122. See also Dworkin, *Life's Dominion*, 153.

69. PEW Research Center, "Issue Ranks Lower on the Agenda; Support for Abortion Slips" (Oct. 1, 2009), http://www.people-press.org/files/legacy-pdf/549.pdf, 3, 21 (reporting "continued polarization over abortion"; that a plurality (32 percent) cite religious beliefs as "main influence on abortion

opinion"; and that "[m]ore than half of those who say abortion should be illegal (53 percent) cite religious beliefs as the primary influence on their views, compared with only 11 percent among supporters of legal abortion.") (accessed 11/29/11).

70. See Lee v. Weisman, 505 U.S. 577 (1992).

71. Carol Sanger similarly asks, in the context of mandatory ultrasound rules: "when or to what extent may the state persuade a person not to exercise a constitutional right?" She argues that mandatory ultrasound crosses the boundary between persuasion (in the service of informed consent) and coercion. See Carol Sanger, "Seeing and Believing: Mandatory Ultrasound and the Path to a Protected Choice," 56 *UCLA Law Review* 351, 360–361, 399–400 & n.189 (2008).

72. Dworkin's argument in the context of abortion may open the door to governmental moralizing and across-the-board encouragement of responsibility with respect to rights; responsibility may prove to be an idea that is not easily cabined. Compare Archibald Cox, *The Warren Court: Constitutional Decision as an Instrument of Reform* (Cambridge, MA: Harvard University Press, 1968), 6 ("Once loosed, the idea of Equality is not easily cabined."). Notably, while he has undertaken responsibility talk with respect to abortion and euthanasia, he has not done so with respect to freedom of speech. Dworkin, *Freedom's Law,* 195–243.

73. "Report of the South Dakota Task Force to Study Abortion," 47–48.

74. Sanger, "Seeing and Believing," 362, 396–397.

75. For example, Mill contended that no one's opinions deserve the name of knowledge "except so far as he has either had forced upon him by others, or gone through of himself, the same mental process which would have been required of him in carrying on an active controversy with opponents." John Stuart Mill, *On Liberty,* ed. David Spitz (New York: Norton, 1975) (1859), 44.

76. *See* Carey Goldberg and Janet Elder, "Public Still Backs Abortion, but Wants Limits, Poll Says," *New York Times,* Jan. 16, 1998, A1 (reporting shift in public opinion from general acceptance of abortion to a "permit but discourage model"). Poll data both from 1992 (when *Casey* was decided) and more recent years indicates a very large majority support "[a] law requiring doctors to inform patients about alternatives to abortion before performing the procedure." In 2003, 88 percent favored such a law; 86 percent favored one in 1992. Gallup, "Abortion," Nov. 18, 2011, http://www.gallup.com/1576/abortion.aspx (accessed 11/18/11). A similar percentage supported a 24-hour waiting period in a July 2011 poll. In that poll, public opinion was closely divided on "[a] law requiring women seeking an abortion to be shown an ultrasound image of her fetus at least 24 hours before the procedure," with 50 percent favoring and 46 percent opposing. Ibid.

77. For example, one feminist theorist has suggested requiring health care providers to offer voluntary counseling sessions concerning relevant ethical issues for all pregnant women and their partners, whether they plan to

continue or terminate their pregnancies. Ruth Colker, "Feminism, Theology, and Abortion: Toward Love, Compassion, and Wisdom," 77 *California Law Review* 1011, 1067 (1989).

78. Amy Gutmann and Dennis Thompson, *Democracy and Disagreement* (Cambridge, MA: Belknap Press of Harvard University Press, 1996), 34–39 (critiquing Rawls's attempt to resolve abortion conflict by appeal to political values and arguing that abortion is a paradigm of deliberative disagreement, on which consensus may remain elusive); John Rawls, *Political Liberalism* (New York: Columbia University Press, expanded ed. 1996), lv–lvi & n.31 (acknowledging that, despite his argument that a reasonable balance of political values might yield a right to abortion, the disputed abortion question may lead to a "stand-off"); Robert P. George, "Public Reason and Political Conflict: Abortion and Homosexuality," 106 *Yale Law Journal* 2475, 2485–2495 (1997) (disputing Rawls's appeal to political values and arguing for need to appeal to comprehensive doctrines). On conscientious disagreement over the morality of abortion in various circumstances, see Dworkin, *Life's Dominion,* 30–67.

79. *Carhart,* 159. For more detailed analysis of *Carhart,* see Joanna Grossman and Linda McClain, "New Justices, New Rules: The Supreme Court Upholds the Federal Partial-Birth Abortion Ban Act of 2003," *FindLaw's Writ: Legal Commentary,* May 1, 2007, http://writ.news.findlaw.com /commentary/20070501_mcclain.html; Joanna Grossman and Linda McClain, "*Gonzales v. Carhart*: How the Supreme Court's Validation of the Federal Partial-Birth Abortion Ban Act Affects Women's Constitutional Liberty and Equality," *FindLaw's Writ: Legal Commentary,* May 7, 2007, http://writ.news.findlaw.com/commentary/20070507_mcclain.html.

80. *Carhart,* 183–184 (Ginsburg, J., dissenting).

81. Ibid., 159–160.

82. Brief of Sandra Cano, the Former "Mary Doe" of Doe v. Bolton, and 180 Women Injured by Abortion as Amici Curiae In Support of Petitioner, Gonzales v. Carhart, 5, 21; see Doe v. Bolton, 410 U.S. 179 (1973).

83. Brief of Sandra Cano, 21.

84. *Carhart,* 171–172, 183–184, 185 (Ginsburg, J.., dissenting) (citing works by feminist legal scholars Reva Siegel and Sylvia Law).

85. House Bill No. 1217, §1(5) (2011) (amending S.D. Codified Laws §34-23A).

86. Planned Parenthood Minnesota, North Dakota, South Dakota, and Ball v. Rounds, 650 F. Supp. 2d 972, 977 (D. S. D. 2009) (quoting S.D. Codified Laws §34-23A-10), aff'd in part, rev'd in relevant part, and remanded, 653 F.3d 662, 668-670 (8th Cir. 2011).

87. Ibid., 978.

88. Reva B. Siegel, "The Right's Reasons: Constitutional Conflict and the Spread of Woman-Protective Antiabortion Argument," 57 *Duke Law Journal* 1641 (2008).

89. See La. Rev. Stat. Ann. § 40:1299.35.6(A)(5)(c) (2011) (quoting *Casey*). See also Alabama's Woman's Right to Know Act, which includes legislative findings that "[t]he medical, emotional, and psychological consequences of

an abortion are serious and can be lasting or life threatening." Ala. Code §26-23A-2 (1975).

90. House Bill No. 1217, §§6, 7(4), 3(3)(a).

91. Planned Parenthood Minnesota, North Dakota, South Dakota, and Ball v. Daugaard, 799 F. Supp. 2d 1048, 1060 (D. S. D. 2011).

92. See *Casey*, 919–920 (Stevens, J., concurring in part and dissenting in part).

93. Rebecca J. Cook et al., "Unethical Female Stereotyping in Reproductive Health," 109 *International Journal of Gynecology and Obstetrics* 255, 256 (2010); Chris Guthrie, "*Carhart*, Constitutional Rights, and the Psychology of Regret," 81 *Southern California Law Review* 877, 902 (2008) (arguing that empirical evidence does not support Justice Kennedy's analysis of regret and that "the prospect of regret" does not justify "limiting a woman's right to choose or any other right ostensibly protected by the Constitution").

94. See Karen Ball, "Defending Nebraska's Child-Abandonment Law," *Time*, Nov. 18, 2008, http://www.time.com/time/printout/0,8816,1859951,00. html (accessed 11/11/10) (reporting that Nebraska's law, unlike other state laws, used the word "child" instead of "infant," "result[ing] in an epidemic of abandoned children—with some parents driving from Florida, Arizona, and Georgia to drop off their problem kids"). Nebraska promptly amended the law to cover only infants up to 30 days old. Child welfare experts opined that this parental action "highlighted . . . a widespread shortage of public and private aid, especially mental health services, for overstressed families and teenagers." Eric Eckholm, "Nebraska Limits Safe Haven Law to Infants," *New York Times*, Nov. 22, 2008, A10.

95. Planned Parenthood of the Heartland v. Heineman, 724 F. Supp. 2d 1025, 1045 & n.12 (D. Neb. 2010).

96. Cook et al., "Unethical Female Stereotyping in Reproductive Health," 256.

97. Brief of the Institute for Reproductive Health Access and Fifty-Two Clinics and Organizations as Amici Curiae in Support of Respondents in Gonzales v. Planned Parenthood Federation of America et al., No. 05-1382 & No. 05-380, 1, 29.

98. An often-cited study is Aida Torres and Jacqueline Darroch Forrest, "Why Do Women Have Abortions?," 20 *Family Planning Perspectives* 169 (1988). More recent studies include Akinrinola Bankole, Susheela Singh, and Taylor Hass, "Reasons Why Women Have Induced Abortions: Evidence from 27 Countries," 24 *International Family Planning Perspectives* 117 (1998); Lawrence B. Finer et al., "Reasons U.S. Women Have Abortions: Quantitative and Qualitative Perspectives," 37 *Perspectives on Sexual and Reproductive Health* 110 (2005).

99. Finer et al., "Reasons U.S. Women Have Abortions," 117 (examining women's reasons in 1987 and 2004).

100. Ibid., 116–118.

101. Ibid., 119.

102. West, "From Choice to Reproductive Justice," 1409, 1409–1411.

103. Ibid., 1403.

104. 448 U.S. 297 (1980).

105. 489 U.S. 189 (1989).

106. See *Harris,* 329 (Brennan, J., dissenting, joined by Justices Marshall and Blackmun); ibid., 337 (Marshall, J., dissenting); ibid., 348 (Blackmun, J., dissenting); *DeShaney,* 203 (Brennan, J., dissenting, joined by Justices Marshall and Blackmun); ibid., 212 (Blackmun, J., dissenting).

107. See, e.g., *Casey,* 944 (Rehnquist, C. J., concurring in part and dissenting in part); ibid., 979 (Scalia, J., concurring in part and dissenting in part); *DeShaney,* 191 (Rehnquist, C. J., and Scalia, J., joining majority); Michael H. v. Gerald D., 491 U.S. 110, 113 (1989) (Scalia, J., plurality opinion, in which Rehnquist, C.J., joined); *Roe,* 171 (Rehnquist, J., dissenting).

108. Our conception of the Constitution as a charter of positive benefits, not merely a charter of negative liberties, is indebted to Sotirios A. Barber, *Welfare and the Constitution* (Princeton, NJ: Princeton University Press, 2003). See also Sotirios A. Barber and James E. Fleming, *Constitutional Interpretation: The Basic Questions* (New York: Oxford University Press, 2007), 35–55.

109. Linda Greenhouse and Reva B. Siegel, *Before* Roe v. Wade: *Voices That Shaped the Abortion Debate before the Supreme Court's Ruling* (New York: Kaplan Publishing, 2010); Reva B. Siegel, "*Roe*'s Roots: The Women's Rights Claims that Engendered *Roe,*" 90 *Boston University Law Review* 1875 (2010).

110. West, "From Choice to Reproductive Justice," 1422–1443 (citing Reva Siegel, "Constitutional Culture, Social Movement Conflict and Constitutional Change: The Case of the De Facto ERA," 94 *California Law Review* 1323, 1395–1397 (2006)).

111. Ibid., 1415, 1425, 1427.

112. *Griswold,* 381 U.S. 479 (1965); *Eisenstadt,* 405 U.S. 438 (1972).

113. West, "From Choice to Reproductive Justice," 1428–1430.

114. For example, on June 30, 2011, a federal district court issued a preliminary injunction against several sections of South Dakota's most recent restrictive abortion law, House Bill 1217, which required women to visit a pregnancy help center and a physician to screen her for being at risk of coercion, on the ground that it violated women's First Amendment and Fourteenth Amendment rights. *Daugaard.* See "The Courts Step in: Judges' Recent Rulings Show How Extreme Antiabortion Measures Have Become," *New York Times,* July 14, 2011, A22.

115. "Statement of President Obama on the 36th Anniversary of Roe v. Wade," Jan. 22, 2009, http://www.whitehouse.gov/the_press_office/Statementof PresidentObamaonthe36thAnniversaryofRoevWade(accessed 11/26/11).

116. For example, Naomi Cahn and June Carbone propose, since abortion is the "family values issue least amenable to compromise," to "change the subject" in the battles over family planning from abortion to contraception by deemphasizing "rights talk" about abortion and rallying around the greater centrality of contraception to women's reproductive autonomy. See Naomi Cahn and June Carbone, *Red Families v. Blue Families: Legal Polarization*

and the Creation of Culture (New York: Oxford University Press, 2010), 205, 208. We believe that the intense controversy over contraception at both the state and federal levels, for example, the opposition to the Affordable Care Act's requirements concerning insurance coverage for contraception, suggests that changing the subject may not be so easy or effective.

117. For example, Rawls suggests that a balance of such important political values as due respect for life, the equality of women, and orderly social reproduction would yield at least a limited right to abortion. Rawls, *Political Liberalism*, 243 n.32. But see ibid., lv–lvi & n.31 (acknowledging that the disputed abortion question may lead to a "stand-off").

118. For some helpful entry points into an extensive literature, see Asian Communities for Reproductive Justice, *A New Vision* (2005), http://reproductivejustice.org/assets/docs/ACRJ-A-New-Vision.pdf (accessed 11/21/11); Religious Coalition for Reproductive Choice, "Reproductive Justice," http://www.rcrc.org/calltojustice (accessed 11/21/11); Angela Hooten, "A Broader Vision of the Reproductive Rights Movement: Fusing Mainstream and Latina Feminism," 13 *Journal of Gender, Social Policy & the Law* 1 (2005); Anita Allen, "On Infertility and Racial Justice," Feb. 7, 2010, *Reproductive Rights Blog*, http://lawprofessors/typepad.com/reproductive_rights (accessed 3/29/11); Mary Lyndon Shanley, "Infertility, Social Justice, and Equal Citizenship," in Linda C. McClain and Joanna L. Grossman, eds., *Gender Equality: Dimensions of Women's Equal Citizenship* (New York: Cambridge University Press, 2009), 327–344. For older, but still valuable, sources, see Petchesky, *Abortion and Women's Choice*, 388–401; Laurie Nsiah-Jefferson, *Reproductive Laws, Women of Color, and Low-Income Women*, in Sherrill Cohen & Nadine Taub, eds., *Reproductive Laws for the 1990s* (Clifton, NJ: Humana Press, 1988), 15–38.

119. Robin West, "The Nature of the Right to an Abortion," 45 *Hastings Law Journal* 961, 964 (1994) (arguing that *Casey*'s attempt to recognize women's reproductive responsibility lacks a model of mutual responsibility, whereby government accepts responsibility to secure women's equal citizenship (invoking Rawls's model of justice)).

4. Civil Society's Role in Cultivating the "Seedbeds of Virtue"

1. We appreciate that "civil society–revivalist" is a broad category that may be both over- and underinclusive. Nonetheless, it is possible to find common themes among the various scholars, public commentators, and political figures who have called for reviving or renewing civil society. We do not mean the term "civil society–revivalist" to be derogatory. The term "revival" occurs in such works as E. J. Dionne Jr., ed., *Community Works: The Revival of Civil Society in America* (Washington, DC: Brookings Institution Press, 1998). Another common term is "renewal." See Robert K. Fullinwider, ed., *Civil Society, Democracy, and Civic Renewal* (Lanham, MD: Rowman & Littlefield, 1999).

2. Mary Ann Glendon and David Blankenhorn, eds., *Seedbeds of Virtue: Sources of Competence, Character, and Citizenship in American Society* (Lanham, MD: Madison Books, 1995).

3. See Nancy L. Rosenblum and Robert C. Post, eds., *Civil Society and Government* (Princeton, NJ: Princeton University Press, 2002).

4. On this "liberal expectancy," see Nancy L. Rosenblum, *Membership and Morals: The Personal Uses of Pluralism in America* (Princeton, NJ: Princeton University Press, 1998).

5. See James E. Fleming, *Securing Constitutional Democracy: The Case of Autonomy* (Chicago, IL: University of Chicago Press, 2006), 18–20; Linda C. McClain, *The Place of Families: Fostering Capacity, Equality, and Responsibility* (Cambridge, MA: Harvard University Press, 2006), 40–42, 106–131.

6. Krishan Kumar, "Civil Society: An Inquiry into the Usefulness of an Historical Term," 44 *British Journal of Sociology* 375, 376 (1993).

7. Don Eberly, "The Coming Social Renaissance . . . ," *The Civil Society Project,* Vol. 99, No. 2., p. 1, http://www.civilsocietyproject.org/_files /SocialRenaissance.pdf (accessed 11/23/11).

8. Todd S. Purdum, "Clinton Calls for Volunteers in Communities and Schools," *New York Times,* May 11, 1996, §1, 8.

9. John M. Broder, "For Hillary Clinton at 50, Yet Another Beginning," *New York Times,* Oct. 26, 1997, § 1, 20; Hillary Rodham Clinton, *It Takes a Village* (New York: Simon & Schuster, 10th anniversary ed. 2006).

10. Hillary Rodham Clinton, "Civil Society: The Space That Matters Most," *New Perspectives Quarterly,* Spring 1998, 12.

11. Robert D. Putnam, *Bowling Alone: The Collapse and Revival of American Community* (New York: Simon & Schuster, 2000). Putnam has also published a well-received scholarly book on the importance of social capital: *Making Democracy Work: Civic Traditions in Modern Italy* (Princeton, NJ: Princeton University Press, 1993).

12. *Better Together: Saguaro Seminar on Civic Engagement in America,* December 2000, 6, http://www.bettertogether.org/pdfs/FullReportText .pdf (accessed 11/23/11). Putnam is Director of the Saguaro Seminar.

13. Mary Ann Glendon, "Introduction: Forgotten Questions," in Glendon and Blankenhorn, eds., *Seedbeds of Virtue,* 1, 2.

14. Exec. Order No. 13,199, 66 Fed. Reg. 8499 (Jan. 29, 2001); The White House, *Rallying the Armies of Compassion* (2001), http://archives.hud. gov/reports/rally.pdf (accessed 11/22/11). For President Obama's initiative, see Press Release, "Obama Announces White House Office of Faith-based and Neighborhood Partnerships" (Feb. 5, 2009), http://www.whitehouse .gov/the-press-office/obama-annouces-white-house-office-faith-based-and -neighborhood-partnerships (accessed 11/22/11); and President's Advisory Council on Faith-Based and Neighborhood Partnerships, *A New Era of Partnerships: Report of Recommendations to the President* (March 2010), http://www.whitehouse.gov/sites/default/files/microsites/ofbnp-council -final-report.pdf (accessed 11/22/11).

15. President Obama, "Remarks by the President at Parallel Civil Society Summit," Metropol Hotel, Moscow, Russia, July 7, 2009, http://www .whitehouse.gov/the_press_office/remarks-by-the-president-at-parallel -civil-society-summit (accessed 7/13/11).

16. Eberly, "The Coming Social Renaissance . . . ," 1; Don Eberly, "Compassion: America's Most Consequential Export," *The Civil Society Project,* May 15, 2007, http://www.civilsocietyproject.org/articles/index.php?fuse Action=article&agID=31&artID=144 (accessed 11/23/11).

17. Omar G. Encarnación, "Review Article: Civil Society Reconsidered," 38 *Comparative Politics* 357, 359–361 (2006); see also Philippe C. Schmitter, "Twenty-Five Years, Fifteen Findings," 21 *Journal of Democracy* 17, 24 (2010) (Finding 9: "Civil society has figured prominently and favorably in the literature on democratic transition and consolidation, but it may be a mixed blessing.").

18. See Don Eberly, "Civic Renewal vs. Moral Renewal," *Policy Review: Journal of American Citizenship,* Sept.–Oct. 1998, 44.

19. *A Nation of Spectators: How Civic Disengagement Weakens America and What We Can Do about It* (College Park, MD: National Commission on Civic Renewal, 1998).

20. *A Call to Civil Society: Why Democracy Needs Moral Truths* (New York: Institute for American Values, 1998). The Institute for American Values recently released an essay elaborating on its mission "to study and strengthen civil society." See *Propositions 5* (2011), http://www.centerfor publicconversation.org/propositions/2011–10.pdf. That essay states: "Within the focus on civil society, the Institute's three current priorities are marriage, thrift, and public conversation." As to marriage, the essay repeats *A Call to Civil Society*'s articulation of the family as "the seedbed institution of civil society," and of marriage as "the basis of the family." Ibid., 5.

21. See *A Nation of Spectators,* 5–12; *A Call to Civil Society,* 3, 6, 7–13, 13–16. Illustrating the overlap between these two strands, Mary Ann Glendon, William Galston, and Jean Bethke Elshtain were part of each group.

22. See, e.g., Amitai Etzioni, *The Spirit of Community: Rights, Responsibilities, and the Communitarian Agenda* (New York: Crown, 1993); William A. Galston, *Liberal Purposes: Goods, Virtues, and Diversity in the Liberal State* (New York: Cambridge University Press, 1991); Mary Ann Glendon, *Rights Talk: The Impoverishment of Political Discourse* (New York: Free Press, 1991); "The Responsive Communitarian Platform: Rights and Responsibilities," 2 *Responsive Community* (Winter 1991–1992), 4.

23. Glendon, "Introduction: Forgotten Questions," 2, 12.

24. *The Federalist* No. 55 (Madison), ed. Clinton Rossiter (New York: New American Library, 1961), 346. For invocations of *Federalist* No. 55, see, e.g., *A Nation of Spectators,* 4; *A Call to Civil Society,* 7; Glendon, *Rights Talk,* 116.

25. Glendon, *Rights Talk,* 116–120.

26. For a sophisticated account acknowledging proposals, even in the country's earliest years, for a national educational system, see Ken I. Kersch, *Constructing Civil Liberties: Discontinuities in the Development of American Constitutional Law* (Cambridge: Cambridge University Press, 2004), 237–244.

27. Alexis de Tocqueville, *Democracy in America,* ed. J. P. Mayer and trans. George Lawrence (New York: Anchor, 1969) (1848 ed.), 513–517: "Americans of all ages, all stations in life, and all types of disposition are forever forming associations. There are not only commercial and industrial associations in which all take part, but others of a thousand different types— religious, moral, serious, futile, very general and very limited, immensely large and very minute." Ibid., 513.

28. *A Nation of Spectators,* 9. Putnam observes: "When Tocqueville visited the United States in the 1830s, it was the Americans' propensity for civic association that most impressed him as the key to their unprecedented ability to make democracy work." Putnam, *Bowling Alone,* 65.

29. Glendon, *Rights Talk,* 117–118; *A Call to Civil Society,* 8.

30. Glendon, "Introduction: Forgotten Questions," 2.

31. See generally Glendon and Blankenhorn, eds., *Seedbeds of Virtue;* Glendon, *Rights Talk,* 65–75, 173–174; *A Call to Civil Society,* 16.

32. Glendon, *Rights Talk,* 75.

33. William M. Sullivan, "Reinstitutionalizing Virtue in Civil Society," in Glendon and Blankenhorn, eds., *Seedbeds of Virtue,* 185, 188–189.

34. Glendon, "Introduction: Forgotten Questions," 12.

35. Galston, *Liberal Purposes,* 222.

36. See *A Call to Civil Society,* 7–13; *A Nation of Spectators,* 8, 12–19; Glendon, "Introduction: Forgotten Questions," 1–9.

37. *A Nation of Spectators,* 8; see also *A Call to Civil Society,* 7 ("[S]elf-government begins with governing the self.").

38. See, e.g., *A Call to Civil Society,* 7; *A Nation of Spectators,* 8–13; David Blankenhorn, "Conclusion: The Possibility of Civil Society," in Glendon and Blankenhorn, eds., *Seedbeds of Virtue,* 271, 275.

39. Meyer v. Nebraska, 262 U.S. 390 (1923); Pierce v. Society of the Sisters, 268 U.S. 510 (1925); Prince v. Massachusetts, 321 U.S. 158 (1944).

40. McClain, *The Place of Families.*

41. Glendon, *Rights Talk,* xii, 8, 174–175.

42. Ibid., 174.

43. Putnam, *Bowling Alone,* 22–23.

44. Francis Fukuyama, *Trust: The Social Virtues and the Creation of Prosperity* (New York: Free Press, 1996), 28–29.

45. Council of Economic Advisers, *Teens and Their Parents in the 21st Century: An Examination of Trends in Teen Behavior and the Role of Parental Involvement* (2000), 18–23, http://clinton3.nara.gov/WH/EOP/CEA /html/Teens_Paper_Final.pdf (accessed 11/29/11); National Center on Addiction and Substance Abuse at Columbia University, *The Importance*

of Family Dinners VII (September 2011), http://www.casacolumbia.org/upload/2011/2011922familydinnersVII.pdf (accessed 2/28/12).

46. See Christopher Beem, "Civil Is Not Good Enough," 6 *Responsive Community* (Summer 1996), 47, 50 ("What of the family, the 'seedbed of civic virtue'? Surely many families positively exemplify the most deleterious tendencies of our materialistic, individualistic culture.").

47. *A Call to Civil Society,* 10; *A Nation of Spectators,* 14.

48. *The Civic Mission of Schools* (New York: Carnegie Corporation of New York and Center for Information and Research on Civic Learning and Engagement, 2003), 13.

49. See *A Call to Civil Society,* 6–7, 14; *A Nation of Spectators,* 8–11, 40–42.

50. Thus, after reviewing the empirical evidence on the role of voluntary associations, Miriam Galston concluded: "it no longer seems useful for civic renewal advocates to continue to portray associational life as critical for cultivating moral values and public spiritedness in individuals or promoting attitudes and practices conducive to reflective self-governance. In general, voluntary associations can at most serve as a vehicles for strengthening, harnessing, and directing their members' existing moral and public-spirited attitudes." Miriam Galston, "Civic Renewal and the Regulation of Nonprofits," 13 *Cornell Journal of Law & Public Policy* 289, 401 (2004).

51. Yael Tamir, "Revisiting the Civic Sphere," in Amy Gutmann, ed., *Freedom of Association* (Princeton, NJ: Princeton University Press, 1998), 214, 219–220.

52. For a cautionary, comical tale of virtue and vice in bowling leagues, see the Coen brothers' 1998 film *The Big Lebowski.*

53. See Amitai Etzioni, "On Social and Moral Revival," 9 *Journal of Political Philosophy* 356, 361–363 (2001) (citing to Nina Eliasoph, *Avoiding Politics: How Americans Produce Apathy in Everyday Life* (Cambridge: Cambridge University Press, 1998), a study of several voluntary associations finding that members "engaged in very little dialogue concerning the public good or matters related to the social or moral order").

54. John Rawls, *Political Liberalism* (New York: Columbia University Press, 1993), 194–195.

55. *A Nation of Spectators,* 14, 46.

56. Ibid., 40–41.

57. Rosenblum, *Membership and Morals.*

58. *Federalist* No. 51 (Madison), 322.

59. Rosenblum, *Membership and Morals,* 10–15, 36–41.

60. Ibid., 41. In an influential essay, Peter Berger and Richard John Neuhaus wrote, some decades ago, that "mediating structures"—families, religious institutions, voluntary associations, and neighborhoods—"are essential for a vital democratic society." Peter L. Berger and Richard John Neuhaus, *To Empower People: The Role of Mediating Structures in Public Policy* (Washington, DC: American Enterprise Institute, 1977), 6.

61. Rosenblum, *Membership and Morals,* 42.

62. Ibid., 45–50, 350.

63. Ibid., 62–63.

64. John Rawls, *A Theory of Justice* (Cambridge, MA: Belknap Press of Harvard University Press, 1971), 440–442.

65. Rosenblum, *Membership and Morals*, 62–63.

66. Ibid., 48.

67. Nancy L. Rosenblum, *On the Side of the Angels: An Appreciation of Parties and Partisanship* (Princeton, NJ: Princeton University Press, 2008).

68. Jane Mansbridge, "Using Power/Fighting Power: The Polity," in Seyla Benhabib, ed., *Democracy and Difference: Contesting the Boundaries of the Political* (Princeton, NJ: Princeton University Press, 1996), 46, 47, 55, 58.

69. Mark Tushnet has suggested that "[a] paradox lies at the heart of this interest in revitalizing the institutions of civil society as a check on government: Those institutions are themselves constituted by government, not in the sense that they are called into being by government, but in the sense that their boundaries are defined by the government." Mark Tushnet, "The Constitution of Civil Society," 75 *Chicago-Kent Law Review* 379, 380 (2000). See also Abner S. Greene, *Against Obligation: The Multiple Sources of Authority in a Liberal Democracy* (Cambridge, MA: Harvard University Press, 2012) (arguing that our constitutional order authorizes and protects multiple repositories of power).

70. Jack M. Balkin, *Living Originalism* (Cambridge, MA: Harvard University Press, 2011), 74–75.

71. *A Nation of Spectators*, 41, 43 n.12 (citing Jean L. Cohen, "American Civil Society Talk," in Fullinwider, ed., *Civil Society, Democracy, and Civic Renewal*, 55, 69).

72. Seyla Benhabib, "Toward a Deliberative Model of Democratic Legitimacy," in Benhabib, ed., *Democracy and Difference*, 67, 73–74, 84.

73. See John Rawls, "The Idea of Public Reason Revisited," 64 *University of Chicago Law Review* 765, 775 n.28 (1997).

74. *A Call to Civil Society*, 16 (citing John Rawls, "Kantian Constructivism [sic] Moral Theory," 77 *Journal of Philosophy* 515, 543 (1980)).

75. See Fleming, *Securing Constitutional Democracy*, 37, 43–46; Linda C. McClain, "'Atomistic Man' Revisited: Liberalism, Connection, and Feminist Jurisprudence," 65 *Southern California Law Review* 1171, 1204–1206 (1992).

76. Jennifer Nedelsky, *Law's Relations: A Relational Theory of Self, Autonomy, and Law* (New York: Oxford University Press, 2011), 4; see also Catriona Mackenzie and Natalie Stoljar, eds., *Relational Autonomy* (New York: Oxford University Press, 2000).

77. Rawls, *Political Liberalism*, 14, 18, 84.

78. *A Nation of Spectators* criticizes an understanding of individual liberty that stresses self-expression, self-realization, and personal choice but does not specifically link that understanding to a conception of the person attributed to Rawls. *A Nation of Spectators*, 6–7.

79. Rawls, *Political Liberalism*, 36–37, 144.

80. *A Call to Civil Society,* 16, 18, 21.

81. Rawls, *Political Liberalism,* 133–172.

82. *A Call to Civil Society,* 16.

83. Rawls, *Political Liberalism,* 9, 81, 302, 332.

84. See McClain, *The Place of Families,* 40–42, 106–131; Fleming, *Securing Constitutional Democracy,* 18–20.

85. *A Call to Civil Society,* 12, 27.

86. Amy Gutmann and Dennis Thompson, *Democracy and Disagreement* (Cambridge, MA: Belknap Press of Harvard University Press, 1996), 26.

87. See Michael J. Sandel, *Democracy's Discontent: America in Search of a Public Philosophy* (Cambridge, MA: The Belknap Press of Harvard University Press, 1996), 320.

88. William A. Galston, *Liberal Pluralism: The Implications of Value Pluralism for Political Theory and Practice* (New York: Cambridge University Press, 2002), 4–7, 30. Galston says that liberal pluralism not only allows for "the possibility of a shared understanding of justice" but also "allows for considerable variation reflecting cultural distinctiveness, political decision making, and the particular circumstances in which a community may find itself." Ibid., 128. He adds: "Pluralism is not a confession of philosophical incompleteness or incapacity; it is an assertion of philosophical truth." Ibid., 131.

89. *A Call to Civil Society,* 7; Glendon, "Introduction: Forgotten Questions," 1–3; *A Nation of Spectators,* 13.

90. *A Call to Civil Society,* 18.

91. Ibid.; *A Nation of Spectators,* 13.

92. Glendon, *Rights Talk,* 110–138; Glendon, "Introduction: Forgotten Questions," 9.

93. *A Nation of Spectators,* 13.

94. Rawls, "The Idea of Public Reason Revisited," 788.

95. See Glendon, *Rights Talk,* 174; William A. Galston, "Won't You Be My Neighbor?," *American Prospect* (May–June 1996), 16, 17; see also Kathryn Kish Sklar, "A Historical Model of Women's Voluntarism and the State, 1890–1920," in Fullinwider, ed., *Civil Society, Democracy, and Civic Renewal,* 185 (discussing how traditions of voluntarism and of limited government led women's voluntary organizations in the Progressive Era to address many social problems).

96. Tocqueville, *Democracy in America,* 590, 592, 601.

97. Ibid., 600–603.

98. Ibid., 12, 600.

99. Jocelyn M. Boryczka, "The Separate Spheres Paradox: Habitual Inattention and Democratic Citizenship," in Jill Locke and Eileen Hunt Botting, eds., *Feminist Interpretations of Alexis de Tocqueville* (University Park: Pennsylvania State University Press, 2009), 285.

100. Jean Bethke Elshtain, "Women, Equality, and the Family," 11 *Journal of Democracy* 157, 162–163 (2000).

101. *Better Together,* 15–16.

102. Ibid., 23, 77–78, 97.

103. Ibid., 7.

104. *A Call to Civil Society*, 24.

105. President Obama, Remarks at White House Forum on Workplace Flexibility, March 31, 2010, http://www.whitehouse/gov/the-press-office/remarks-president-workplace-flexibility-forum (accessed 5/12/10).

106. Ibid.

107. In announcing the creation of the White House Council on Women and Girls, President Obama emphasized that work/family balance, health care, preventing violence against women, and economic security were "not just women's issues," but also "family" and "economic" issues. "President Obama Announces White House Council on Women and Girls," March 11, 2009, http://www.whitehouse/gov/the_press_office/President-Obama-Announces-White-House-Council-on-Women-and-Girls (accessed 11/23/11).

108. See Mona Harrington, *Care and Equality: Inventing a New Family Politics* (New York: Knopf, 1999); Martha Albertson Fineman, *The Autonomy Myth: A Theory of Dependency* (New York: New Press, 2004); McClain, *The Place of Families*, 85–114; Eva Kittay and Ellen K. Fedder, eds., *The Subject of Care: Feminist Perspectives on Dependency* (Lanham, MD: Rowman and Littlefield, 2003).

109. Jane Mansbridge, "Feminism and Democratic Community, in John W. Chapman and Ian Shapiro, eds., *Democratic Community* (New York: New York University Press, 1993), 362.

110. Susan Moller Okin, *Justice, Gender, and the Family* (New York: Basic Books, 1989). See John Stuart Mill, *The Subjection of Women*, in John Stuart Mill and Harriet Taylor Mill, *Essays on Sex Equality*, ed. Alice S. Rossi (Chicago, IL: University of Chicago Press, 1970), 174–175. For an illuminating evaluation of the complexity of John Stuart Mill's writings on gender, particularly on marriage and divorce, the division of labor in the family, and family violence, see Nancy J. Hirshmann, *Gender, Class, and Freedom in Modern Political Theory* (Princeton, NJ: Princeton University Press, 2008), 238–249.

111. See Robin West, *Caring for Justice* (New York: New York University Press, 1997). Carol Gilligan identified an "ethic of care" as characteristic of women's moral reasoning but also noted the risk of the equation of care with female self-sacrifice. See Carol Gilligan, *In a Different Voice* (Cambridge, MA: Harvard University Press, 1982).

112. This is a familiar line of feminist argument. See, e.g., Catharine A. MacKinnon, *Toward a Feminist Theory of the State* (Cambridge, MA: Harvard University Press, 1989); Robin West, *Progressive Constitutionalism: Reconstructing the Fourteenth Amendment* (Durham, NC: Duke University Press, 1994); Mary E. Becker, "The Politics of Women's Wrongs and the Bill of 'Rights': A Bicentennial Perspective," 59 *University of Chicago Law Review* 453 (1992); Tracy E. Higgins, "Democracy and Feminism," 110 *Harvard Law Review* 1657 (1997).

113. For elaboration, see McClain, *The Place of Families.*

114. Rawls, "The Idea of Public Reason Revisited," 791.

115. See *A Call to Civil Society,* 19–20; *A Nation of Spectators,* 13. For example, in 2000, the Institute for American Values, publisher of *A Call to Civil Society,* released the statement, "The Marriage Movement: A Statement of Principles," http://www.americanvalues.org/pdfs/marriage movement.pdf (accessed 11/22/11). Signatories include prominent civil society–revivalists, for example, David Blankenhorn, Don Eberly, Jean Bethke Elshtain, William Galston, and Mary Ann Glendon.

116. *A Nation of Spectators,* 7.

117. Margaret F. Brinig, *Family, Law, and Community: Supporting the Covenant* (Chicago, IL: University of Chicago Press, 2010), 60, 69.

118. McClain, *Place of Families,* 134–147 (discussing studies).

119. Kathryn Edin and Maria Kefalas, *Promises I Can Keep: Why Poor Women Put Motherhood before Marriage* (Berkeley: University of California Press, 2005). On women seeking a "partnership of equals," see "Testimony of Kathryn Edin" before House Ways and Means Committee Hearing on Welfare and Marriage, May 22, 2001.

120. See Pepper Schwartz, *Love between Equals: How Peer Marriage Really Works* (New York: Free Press, 1994); McClain, *The Place of Families,* 141–154 (arguing for egalitarian marriage and noting Galston's support). Similarly, Etzioni advocates peer marriage as part of a communitarian reconstruction of the family. Etzioni, *The New Golden Rule,* 179–180.

121. Nan D. Hunter, "Marriage, Law, and Gender: A Feminist Inquiry," 1 *Law & Sexuality* 9 (1991); Chai R. Feldblum, "Gay is Good: The Moral Case for Marriage Equality and More," 17 *Yale Journal of Law and Feminism* 139, 171–184 (2005).

122. Both reports assume this in that their discussions of "the family" and of its importance for moral and civic renewal clearly presuppose the "intact" heterosexual, two-parent, married family. See, e.g., *A Call to Civil Society,* 7, 18; *A Nation of Spectators,* 13. Both are silent on same-sex marriage. For an argument that the original Constitution did not presuppose a particular ideal of family form and that several family forms coexisted at the founding, including the slaveholding family, see Mark E. Brandon, *Family, Change, and the American Constitutional Order* (Lawrence, KS: University Press of Kansas, forthcoming 2013).

123. See Don Eberly, "Families, Fathers, and the Making of Democratic Citizens," *The Civil Society Project,* Vol. 99, No. 1, http://www.civilsociety project.org/_files/FathersDemocraticCitizens.pdf?PHPSESSID=b0ebd48 af6a6cbd680839266093cdecb (accessed 11/22/11).

124. David Blankenhorn, *The Future of Marriage* (New York: Encounter Books, 2007), 205; Eberly, "Families, Fathers, and the Making of Democratic Citizens," 6 (arguing that "fathers are the first to be written out of the family script" if family definitions become more elastic).

125. *Better Together,* 75–76.

126. Rawls, "The Idea of Public Reason Revisited," 788 n.60.

127. Mary Ann Glendon, *Abortion and Divorce in Western Law: American Failures, European Challenges* (Cambridge, MA: Harvard University Press, 1987).

128. Galston, *Liberal Purposes,* 273; see also William A. Galston, "Civil Society, Civic Virtue, and Liberal Democracy," 75 *Chicago-Kent Law Review* 603, 608–611 (2000); Galston, "Won't You Be My Neighbor?," 11–14.

129. Galston, *Liberal Purposes,* 268–270.

130. James Q. Wilson, "Liberalism, Modernism, and the Good Life," in Glendon and Blankenhorn, eds., *Seedbeds of Virtue,* 17, 20, 25, 26, 29.

131. We are dubious about some of these supposed losses, e.g., "the social marginalization of religious believers," the reports of which we believe have been greatly exaggerated, and "a certain confusion over sexual roles," if by this Wilson means to refer to liberals and feminists challenging traditional assumptions about sexual roles and to gay men and lesbians coming out of the closet to challenge such assumptions.

132. Galston's work generally does not manifest such ambivalence about diversity or pluralism. In his book *Liberal Purposes,* whose subtitle is *Goods, Virtues, and Diversity in the Liberal State,* he provides a rich substantive account of liberal democratic virtues that are appropriate for a culturally and morally diverse society.

133. Rogers M. Smith, "Beyond Tocqueville, Myrdal, and Hartz: The Multiple Traditions in America," 87 *American Political Science Review* 549, 549, 550 (1993).

134. Rogers M. Smith, *Civic Ideals: Conflicting Visions of Citizenship in U.S. History* (New Haven, CT: Yale University Press, 1997), 2, 3.

135. Adam B. Seligman, *The Idea of Civil Society* (New York: Free Press, 1992), 186, 187.

136. See Peter J. Spiro, "The Citizenship Dilemma," 51 *Stanford Law Review* 597 (1999) (reviewing Smith, *Civic Ideals*).

137. Robert D. Putnam, "E Pluribus Unum: Diversity and Community in the Twenty-first Century—The 2006 Johan Skytte Prize Lecture," 30 *Scandinavian Political Studies* 137, 137, 164–165 (2007).

138. William A. Galston, "Political Economy and the Politics of Virtue: U.S. Public Philosophy at Century's End," *Good Society,* Winter 1998, 1, 9.

139. Ibid. (mentioning Sanford Levinson, *Constitutional Faith* (Princeton, NJ: Princeton University Press, 1988)). A recent work developing the ideas of a "constitutional faith" and "constitutional redemption" that is congenial to Galston's aspiration is Jack M. Balkin, *Constitutional Redemption: Political Faith in an Unjust World* (Cambridge, MA: Harvard University Press, 2011).

140. Galston, *Liberal Pluralism,* 126–127.

141. Rawls, *Political Liberalism,* 37, 144.

142. Ibid.; Rawls, "The Idea of Public Reason Revisited," 771.

143. See Glendon, *Rights Talk,* 141 (criticizing interpretations of separation of church and state limiting the ability of religious organizations to play a role

in meeting social needs and praising Bowen v. Kendrick, 487 U.S. 589 (1988), for upholding the involvement of religious organizations in addressing teen pregnancy as signaling that "more creative uses of the structures of civil society may now be permissible in the American welfare state").

144. *A Call to Civil Society,* 10.

145. Don Eberly, "Compassionate Conservatism: Voluntary Associations and the Remoralization of America," *Essays on Civil Society,* Vol. 2000, No. 1 (on file with the authors).

146. *A Nation of Spectators,* 16–17; *A Call to Civil Society,* 21. Several revivalists (e.g., Glendon, Galston, Blankenhorn, and Elshtain) are also affiliated with the Responsive Communitarian movement, whose platform urges that government "should step in only to the extent that other social subsystems fail." "The Responsive Communitarian Platform," 11, 12.

147. The George W. Bush administration attempted to address this problem by barring direct funding of pervasively religious services but allowing individuals to purchase such services by government vouchers.

148. For an analysis of the "faith-based" initiative launched by President George W. Bush that uses this distinction, see Linda C. McClain, "Unleashing or Harnessing 'Armies of Compassion': Reflections on the Faith-Based Initiative," 39 *Loyola University Chicago Law Journal* 361 (2008).

149. Stephen V. Monsma, *Putting Faith in Partnerships: Welfare-to-Work in Four Cities* (Ann Arbor: University of Michigan Press, 2004), 153–166. On the fear of "vendorism," see Stanley Carlson-Thies, "Faith-Based Institutions Cooperating with Public Welfare: The Promise of the Charitable Choice Provision," in Derek H. Davis and Barry Hankins, eds., *Welfare Reform and Faith-Based Organizations* (Waco, TX: Baylor University J.M. Dawson Institute of Church-State Studies, 1999), 29, 36.

150. See John J. DiIulio, Jr., "The Lord's Work: The Church and Civil Society," in Dionne, ed., *Community Works,* 50–58 (describing efforts of African-American inner-city ministers to prevent juvenile violence in Boston). DiIulio was the first director of President Bush's Office of Faith-Based and Community Initiatives.

151. Tocqueville, *Democracy in America,* 521–522.

152. Kumar, "Civil Society," 391; see also Keith E. Whittington, "Revisiting Tocqueville's America: Society, Politics, and Association in the Nineteenth Century," 42 *American Behavioral Science* 21 (1998).

153. Tocqueville, *Democracy in America,* 671–679.

154. Robert W. Hefner, "Civil Society: Cultural Possibility of a Modern Ideal," *Society,* Mar.–Apr. 1998, 16; see also Michael Walzer, "The Idea of Civil Society," *Dissent* (Spring 1991), 293, 301.

155. Walzer, "The Idea of Civil Society," 302.

156. See Berger and Neuhaus, *To Empower People,* 6.

157. Rawls, *A Theory of Justice,* 386–388.

158. John Rawls, *The Law of Peoples* (Cambridge, MA: Harvard University Press, 1999), 15.

159. Rawls, *Political Liberalism,* 14, 44.

160. Ibid., 41, 43.

161. Rawls, "The Idea of Public Reason Revisited," 789–790.

162. Rawls, *Political Liberalism,* 10, 11 (emphasis added), 14.

163. See Rosenblum, *Membership and Morals,* 50–58.

164. Rawls, *Political Liberalism,* 41.

165. Ibid., 261.

166. Rawls, "The Idea of Public Reason Revisited," 791.

167. Ibid., 788–790. Okin asked: why not? See Susan Moller Okin, "Justice and Gender: An Unfinished Debate," 72 *Fordham Law Review* 1537 (2004).

168. Rawls, "The Idea of Public Reason Revisited," 789.

169. Rawls, *A Theory of Justice,* 386–388.

170. Rawls, *Political Liberalism,* 82 (citation omitted).

171. Rawls, "The Idea of Public Reason Revisited," 791 (citation omitted).

172. Ibid., 774–775 & nn.28 & 30.

173. Mansbridge, "Using Power/Fighting Power," 58.

174. See Balkin, *Living Originalism,* 74–99.

5. Government's Role in Promoting Civic Virtues

1. Romer v. Evans, 517 U.S. 620, 636–637 (1996) (Scalia, J., dissenting).

2. Steven Wall, *Liberalism, Perfectionism and Restraint* (Cambridge: Cambridge University Press, 1998), 8. See also Colin Farrelly and Lawrence B. Solum, eds., *Virtue Jurisprudence* (New York: Palgrave Macmillan, 2008).

3. For this distinction, see Linda C. McClain, "Toleration, Autonomy, and Governmental Promotion of Good Lives: Beyond 'Empty' Toleration to Toleration as Respect," 59 *Ohio State Law Journal* 19 (1998).

4. Kent Greenfield, "Happy Illegal Holiday!," *New York Times,* Sept. 17, 2011, A19.

5. 319 U.S. 624 (1943).

6. Sanford Levinson, *Our Undemocratic Constitution: Where the Constitution Goes Wrong (and How We the People Can Correct It)* (New York: Oxford University Press, 2006).

7. Kate Zernike, "On Day Devoted to Constitution, a Fight over It," *New York Times,* Sept. 17, 2011, A1.

8. See, e.g., Rust v. Sullivan, 500 U.S. 173 (1991).

9. DeShaney v. Winnebago County Department of Social Services, 489 U.S. 189 (1989), expresses the recent Supreme Court's conception of the Constitution as a charter of negative liberties. The most powerful argument for instead conceiving the Constitution as a charter of positive benefits is Sotirios A. Barber, *Welfare and the Constitution* (Princeton, NJ: Princeton University Press, 2003). See also Sotirios A. Barber and James E. Fleming, *Constitutional Interpretation: The Basic Questions* (New York: Oxford University Press, 2007), 35–55.

10. *The Federalist* No. 51 (Madison), ed. Clinton Rossiter (New York: New American Library, 1961), 322.

11. Michael J. Sandel, *Democracy's Discontent: America in Search of a Public*

Philosophy (Cambridge, MA: Belknap Press of Harvard University Press, 1996), 6, 129–133.

12. John Rawls, *Political Liberalism* (New York: Columbia University Press, 1993), 19. See James E. Fleming, *Securing Constitutional Democracy: The Case of Autonomy* (Chicago, IL: University of Chicago Press, 2006). See also Corey Brettschneider, *Democratic Rights: The Substance of Self-Government* (Princeton, NJ: Princeton University Press, 2007).

13. Rawls, *Political Liberalism*, xx, 10–15, 99, 154, 206.

14. Sandel, *Democracy's Discontent*, 3–7.

15. Joseph Raz, *The Morality of Freedom* (Oxford: Clarendon Press, 1986), 124–133. See also William A. Galston, *Liberal Purposes: Goods, Virtues, and Diversity in the Liberal State* (Cambridge: Cambridge University Press, 1991), 140–162.

16. Susan Moller Okin, "*Political Liberalism,* Justice, and Gender," 105 *Ethics* 23, 28 (1994).

17. See Will Kymlicka, "Liberal Egalitarianism and Civic Republicanism: Friends or Enemies?," in Anita L. Allen and Milton C. Regan, Jr., eds., *Debating Democracy's Discontent: Essays on American Politics, Law, and Public Philosophy* (New York: Oxford University Press, 1998), 131.

18. Rawls, *Political Liberalism*, 194–195, 205.

19. Ibid., 151, 187, 193.

20. Okin, "*Political Liberalism*," 25, 39–43 (quoting and discussing Rawls, *Political Liberalism*, xxix).

21. John Rawls, "The Idea of Public Reason Revisited," 64 *University of Chicago Law Review* 765, 790–791 (1997).

22. See Vivian E. Hamilton, "Immature Citizens and the State," 2010 *Brigham Young University Law Review* 1055.

23. Center for Civic Education, *National Standards for Civics and Government* (1994), Introduction, http://www.civiced.org/index.php?page=stds_toc_intro (accessed 8/4/11); see, e.g., Idaho Const. art IX, § 1; Minn. Const. art. XIII, § 1; Ark. Const. art. XIV, § 1.

24. William A. Galston, *Liberal Pluralism: The Implications of Value Pluralism for Political Theory and Practice* (Cambridge: Cambridge University Press, 2002), 126–127.

25. For an insightful account of this tension, see Maxine Eichner, *The Supportive State: Families, Government, and America's Political Ideals* (New York: Oxford University Press, 2010), 133–141 (arguing that, even acknowledging "weighty" parental interests, given the need to sustain a "vigorous liberal democracy," the state's interest in developing civic virtues must "trump"). For an argument that teaching tolerance is intolerant because it threatens fundamentalists' way of life, see Nomi Maya Stolzenberg, "'He Drew a Circle that Shut Me Out': Assimilation, Indoctrination, and the Paradox of a Liberal Education," 106 *Harvard Law Review* 581 (1993).

26. Stephen Macedo, *Diversity and Distrust: Civic Education in a Multicultural Democracy* (Cambridge, MA: Harvard University Press, 2000), 233.

27. William A. Galston, "Civil Society, Civic Virtue, and Liberal Democracy," 75 *Chicago-Kent Law Review* 603, 604–605 (2000).

28. Susan Moller Okin and Rob Reich, "Families and Schools as Compensating Agents in Moral Development for a Multicultural Society," 28 *Journal of Moral Education* 283, 286 (1999).

29. Nancy L. Rosenblum, "Democratic Families: 'The Logic of Congruence' and Political Identity," 32 *Hofstra Law Review* 145, 156 (2003).

30. Troxel v. Granville, 530 U.S. 57, 65–66 (2000) (quoting Pierce v. Society of Sisters, 268 U.S. 510, 535 (1925)).

31. *The Role of Civic Education: A Report of the Task Force on Civic Education* (Center for Civic Education, prepared for Second Annual White House Conference on Character Building for a Democratic, Civil Society, May 19–20, 1995), 1.

32. Macedo, *Diversity and Distrust,* 45–87.

33. 347 U.S. 483, 493 (1954). Anne Dailey builds on references in *Brown* and *Barnette* to the relationship between children's "hearts and minds" and good citizenship to argue that early caregiving relationships in the family are critical for cultivating democratic citizenship. Anne C. Dailey, "Developing Citizens," 91 *Iowa Law Review* 431 (2006).

34. Bethel School District v. Fraser, 478 U.S. 675, 681 (1986) (alteration in original) (quoting Ambach v. Norwick, 441 U.S. 68, 76–77 (1979)).

35. *Brown,* 493.

36. Steve Farkas and Ann M. Duffett, *High Schools, Civics, and Citizenship: What Social Studies Teachers Think and Do* (American Enterprise Institute, September 2010), 2, http://www.aei.org/files/2010/09/30/High -Schools-Civics-Citizenship-Full-Report.pdf (accessed 8/20/11).

37. Seattle School District No. 1 of King County v. State, 585 P.2d 71, 94–95 (Wash. 1978) (quoted in Kimberly A. Yuracko, "Education Off the Grid: Constitutional Constraints on Home Schooling," 96 *California Law Review* 123, 155 n.159 (2008)).

38. Macedo, *Diversity and Distrust,* 237, 243. See Abner S. Greene, *Against Obligation: The Multiple Sources of Authority in a Liberal Democracy* (Cambridge, MA: Harvard University Press, 2012) (arguing that our constitutional order authorizes and protects multiple repositories of power).

39. For a similar view, although emphasizing children's liberty interests, see Hamilton, "Immature Citizens."

40. See *11 Principles of Effective Character Education* (Character Education Partnership, 2010), http://www.character.org/wp-content/uploads /2011/12/ElevenPrinciples_new2010.pdf, 20 (schools should invite parents to "reinforce," in the home, the "core values" taught at school) (accessed 11/29/11).

41. *The Civic Mission of Schools* (Carnegie Corporation of New York and Center for Information and Research on Civic Learning and Engagement, 2003), 14; "The Responsive Communitarian Platform: Rights and Responsibilities," 2 *Responsive Community* (Winter 1991–1992), 7–10.

42. *National Standards for Civics and Government,* "Introduction," 1.

43. On this core, see *High Schools, Civics, and Citizenship,* 13.
44. *The Civic Mission of Schools,* 4, 11.
45. Ibid., 5, 15. See also *High Schools, Civics, and Citizenship,* 2, 23–24. Testing indicates that "young people's political and civic knowledge is inadequate." *The Civic Mission of Schools,* 19 (results of NAEP Civics Assessment).
46. *The Civic Mission of Schools,* 5, 12.
47. *National Standards for Civics and Government,* "Introduction," 1.
48. *The Civic Mission of Schools,* 13-14 (emphasis in original). In family disengagement, the report mentions lower rates of discussion between young people and parents of "politics, government, or current events." Meira Levinson criticizes this "civic empowerment gap" and its consequences and calls for, among other things, an "empowering" form of civic education to help African-American, Hispanic, nonnative born, and poor students become active, engaged, efficacious citizens. Meira Levinson, *No Citizen Left Behind* (Cambridge, MA: Harvard University Press, 2012), 23–59.
49. *National Standards for Civics and Government,* "Introduction," 1.
50. *The Civic Mission of Schools,* 10.
51. Ibid., 23.
52. *High Schools, Civics, and Citizenship,* 5, 35.
53. *National Standards for Civics and Government,* "Organizing Questions and Content Summary," 2–3.
54. *The Civic Mission of Schools,* 30. Such civic education would prepare students well to participate in the intergenerational project of redeeming the Constitution's promises. Jack M. Balkin, *Living Originalism* (Cambridge, MA: Harvard University Press, 2011).
55. See *A New Civic Mission of Schools, Carnegie Review* (New York: Carnegie Corporation, Spring 2011), 11.
56. *National Standards for Civics and Government,* "Introduction," 1 (emphasis added).
57. *A New Civic Mission of Schools,* 13 (quoting Peter Levine, Director, Center for Information and Research on Civic Learning and Engagement, Tufts University).
58. Sen. Lamar Alexander, "Getting Back to Basics: Teaching Our Children What It Means to Be American," 3 *Carnegie Reports,* Spring 2005, 52.
59. *The Civic Mission of Schools,* 13; see *A New Civic Mission of Schools,* 18 (citing American Bar Association's Division for Public Education, *Paths to 21st Century Competencies through Civic Education Classrooms,* http://www.abanet.org/publiced).
60. *High Schools, Civics, and Citizenship,* 24.
61. *National Standards for Civics and Government,* "Preface," 1 (quoting National Education Goals included in Goals 2000: Educate America Act of 1994).
62. Here we refer to slogans of President Bill Clinton and the Democratic Leadership Council. On independence and not being needlessly dependent, see Galston, *Liberal Purposes,* 221–222. We do not intend to embrace uncritically the idea of "independence." See Martha Albertson Fineman,

The Autonomy Myth: A Theory of Dependency (New York: New Press, 2004).

63. *High Schools, Civics, and Citizenship,* 24.

64. Rawls, *Political Liberalism,* 36–37; Galston, *Liberal Pluralism,* 126.

65. *High Schools, Civics, and Citizenship,* 13.

66. *The Civic Mission of Schools,* 10, 24.

67. See, e.g., Amy Gutmann, *Democratic Education* (Princeton, NJ: Princeton University Press, 1987), 50–52; Macedo, *Diversity and Distrust,* 233–240; Suzanna Sherry, "Responsible Republicanism: Educating for Citizenship," 62 *University of Chicago Law Review* 131, 157, 172 (1995); Meira Levinson, *The Demands of Liberal Education* (New York: Oxford University Press, 1999), 103–104.

68. See, e.g., Galston, *Liberal Purposes,* 254.

69. 827 F.2d 1058 (6th Cir. 1987).

70. Ibid., 1060 (quoting Tenn. Code Ann. § 49–6–1007 (1986 Supp.)).

71. Ibid., 1068–1069.

72. Ibid., 1071 (Kennedy, J., concurring).

73. See, e.g., Macedo, *Diversity and Distrust,* 240.

74. Wisconsin v. Yoder, 406 U.S. 205, 235 (1972) (finding such education adequate); ibid., 245–246 (Douglas, J., dissenting).

75. Macedo, *Diversity and Distrust,* 202, 207, 232 (emphasis omitted).

76. See Stolzenberg, "'He Drew a Circle,'" 611–633.

77. Galston, *Liberal Purposes,* 251–254; Galston, *Liberal Pluralism,* 101–109, 115–121.

78. Some accounts that do discuss the issue include Gutmann, *Democratic Education,* 12–13, 113–115; Rosemary C. Salomone, *Visions of Schooling: Conscience, Community, and Common Education* (New Haven, CT: Yale University Press, 2000), 234–236. Here, we are confining discussion to the role of common public schools.

79. See Harold G. Grasmick et al., "The Effects of Religious Fundamentalism and Religiosity on Preference for Traditional Family Norms," 60 *Sociological Inquiry* 352, 353 (1990).

80. *Mozert,* 1062.

81. Amy Gutmann and Dennis Thompson, *Democracy and Disagreement* (Cambridge, MA: Belknap Press of Harvard University Press, 1996), 63–67 (defending reading exercise at issue in *Mozert* picturing a boy cooking while a girl reads to him).

82. See Holloway Sparks, "Dissident Citizenship, Democratic Theory, Political Courage, and Activist Women," 12 *Hypatia* 74, 75 (Fall 1997).

83. *The Role of Civic Education.*

84. *Bethel School District,* 681 (quoting *Ambach,* 76–77).

85. Toni Marie Massaro, *Constitutional Literacy: A Core Curriculum for a Multicultural Nation* (Durham, NC: Duke University Press, 1993), 140–152.

86. Galston, *Liberal Pluralism,* 126–127.

87. Harper v. Poway Unified School District, 445 F.3d 1166, 1196 (9th Cir. 2006).

88. Galston, *Liberal Pluralism,* 126.

89. Erik Eckholm, "In Suburb, Battle Goes Public on Bullying of Gay Students," *New York Times,* Sept. 13, 2011, A1.

90. Ibid.

91. Ibid.; Erick Eckholm, "Eight Suicides in Two Years at Anoka-Hennepin School District," *New York Times,* Sept. 13, 2011, A4.

92. The suicides of 15-year old Irish immigrant Phoebe Prince, and before her, 11-year old Carl Walker-Hoover, after relentless bullying, were catalysts for Massachusetts's new antibullying law and for new school policies. See An Act Relative to Bullying in Schools, Chapter 92 of the Acts of 2010 (Mass. Session Laws, May 3, 2010); Alyssa Giacobbe, "Who Failed Phoebe Prince?," *Boston Magazine,* June 2010, 112. The suicide of Rutgers University freshman Tyler Clementi, after his roommate secretly filmed and then broadcast over the Internet an intimate encounter between Clementi and another man, spurred New Jersey to pass the nation's toughest anti-bullying law. Anti-bullying Bill of Rights Act, Assembly, No. 3466 (New Jersey, Nov. 2010), http://www.njleg.state.nj.us (accessed 11/27/11); Matt Friedman, "N.J. Governor Approves Toughest Anti-bullying Law in the Country," Jan. 7, 2011, http://www.nj.com.news (accessed 11/27/11). At the time of Clementi's death, Rutgers was launching "Project Civility," to get students to think about how they treat others. Lisa W. Foderaro, "Private Moment Made Public, Then a Fatal Jump," *New York Times,* Sept. 29, 2010, www.nytimes.com (accessed 11/27/11).

93. See Anti-bullying Bill of Rights Act.

94. *The Civic Mission of Schools,* 28.

95. Charles M. Blow, "The Bleakness of the Bullied," *New York Times,* Oct. 15, 2011, A19 (citing 2005 Harris interactive survey, "From Teasing to Torment: School Climate in America").

96. 514 F.3d 87 (1st Cir. 2008).

97. Ibid., 92, 93 (the superintendent clarified this policy after the parents' clash with the school principal over the applicability of the notice requirement).

98. Ibid., 91–92.

99. Ibid., 94.

100. Ibid., 94–95.

101. See Perry v. Schwarzenegger, 704 F. Supp. 2d 921, 930, 975, 979, 988–990 (N.D. Calif. 2010), *aff'd,* Perry v. Brown, 671 F. 3d 1052 (9th Cir. 2012).

102. *Parker,* 100 (quoting Stolzenberg, " 'He Drew a Circle,' " 637).

103. Ibid., 100.

104. Ibid., 102.

105. Ibid., 102, 105–106.

106. 293 F. Supp. 2d 780 (E.D. Mich. 2003).

107. Ibid., 789, 791–792.

108. Ibid., 782–783.

109. Ibid., 794.
110. Ibid., 802.
111. Ibid., 804 (quoting McCollum v. Board of Education, 333 U.S. 203, 216–217 (1948) (Frankfurter, J., concurring)), 806.
112. Ibid., 811 (citing *Brown*), 813.
113. 445 F.3d 1166 (9th Cir. 2006), *vacated as moot*, 549 U.S. 1262 (2007).
114. Ibid., 1171.
115. Ibid., 1171, 1172.
116. Ibid., 1185–1186 (citing *Fraser*).
117. Ibid., 1177 (citing Tinker v. Des Moines, 393 U.S. 503, 509, 514 (1969)).
118. Ibid., 1177–1182 (quoting ibid., 1196 n.7 (Kozinski, J., dissenting)).
119. Ibid., 1186 (citing Employment Division v. Smith, 494 U.S. 872, 879 (1990)).
120. Ibid., 1189–1190 (citing *Fraser*).
121. Ibid., 1196, 1196 n.7 (Kozinski, J., dissenting).
122. Ibid., 1182.
123. Bob Jones University v. United States, 461 U.S. 574, 593 (1983); Roberts v. United States Jaycees, 468 U.S. 609, 624 (1984).
124. National Center for Education Statistics, "Issue Brief: 1.5 Million Home-schooled Students in the United States in 2007," December 2008, 1.
125. Home School Legal Defense Association (HSLDA), "Our Mission," http://www.hslda.org/about/mission.asp (accessed 10/27/11).
126. Combs v. Homer Center School District, 468 F. Supp. 2d 738, 763 (W.D. Pa. 2006), *aff'd in part, vacated in part,* 540 F.3d 231 (3rd Cir. 2008).
127. Milton Gaither, "Homeschooling in the USA: Past, Present, and Future," 7(3) *Theory and Research in Education* 331, 342 (2009). Gaither explains: "By the 1970s disillusionment with government schooling had become quite fashionable." On the left was John Holt, "a leading school critic" who by the mid 1970s "was urging parents to liberate their children from them." Ibid., 336. "In the 1960s and 1970s most conservatives were still trying to keep public school values consistent with their own," but were shocked and devastated by the Supreme Court's decisions "outlawing organized school prayer and school-sponsored Bible reading." One reaction was to turn to Protestant day schools, but by the early 1980s, "the Christian homeschooling movement was born." Ibid., 338. By the mid-1980s, the uneasy alliance between left/secular and right/conservative Christian broke apart, and HSLDA emerged as the leader of conservative Protestant homeschoolers. Ibid., 341.
128. Michael Farris, "The Third Wave of Homeschool Persecution" (speech delivered at Christian Home Educators of Ohio conference on Oct. 7, 2010), http://www.hslda.org/courtreport/V26N6/V26N601.asp?PrinterFriendly =True (accessed 10/27/11). In this speech, Farris attributes the "new ortho-doxy" to legal scholars concerned about homeschooling parents insulating their children from constitutional norms of tolerance. He discusses Yuracko, "Education Off the Grid"; Catharine Ross, "Fundamentalist Challenges to Core Democratic Values: Exit and Homeschooling," 18 *William and Mary*

Bill of Rights Journal 991 (2010); and Martha Albertson Fineman, "Taking Children's Interests Seriously," in Martha Albertson Fineman, ed., *What Is Right For Children?: The Competing Paradigms of Religion and Human Rights* (Burlington, VT: Ashgate Publishing Co., 2009), 233.

129. Farris, "The Third Wave of Homeschool Persecution." Farris appeals to the Universal Declaration of Human Rights, Art. 26 ("Parents have a prior right to choose the kind of education that shall be given to their children") to support his claim.

130. Hamilton, "Immature Citizens," 174, 175.

131. Yuracko, "Education Off the Grid," 156–158.

132. Rob Reich, "The Civic Perils of Homeschooling," 59 *Educational Leadership* 56 (April 2002); see also Ross, "Fundamentalist Challenges to Core Democratic Values."

133. Ross, "Fundamentalist Challenges to Core Democratic Values," 1013.

134. Yuracko, "Education Off the Grid."

135. For a chilling report on several such instances, see Erik Eckholm, "Preaching Virtues of Spanking, Even as Deaths Fuel Debate," *New York Times,* Nov. 7, 2011, A1.

136. For helpful discussions of this idea, see Galston, *Liberal Pluralism,* 93–96; Hamilton, "Immature Citizens"; Ira C. Lupu, "The Separation of Powers and the Protection of Children," 61 *University of Chicago Law Review* 1317 (1994).

137. Fineman, "Taking Children's Interests Seriously," 229.

138. Meyer v. Nebraska, 262 U.S. 390, 401 (1923) ("that the state may do much, go very far, indeed, in order to improve the quality of its citizens, physically, mentally, and morally, is clear"); *Prince,* 170 ("Parents may be free to become martyrs themselves. But it does not follow they are free, in identical circumstances, to make martyrs of their children. . . .").

139. *Pierce,* 534.

140. See National Center for Education Statistics, *Homeschooling in the United States: 2003.* This report indicates that "31 percent of homeschooled children had parents who cited concern about the environment of other schools, such as safety, drugs, or negative peer pressure, as the most important reason . . . and 30 percent . . . said the most important reason was to provide religious or moral instruction. . . . [A]nother 16 percent . . . said dissatisfaction with the academic instruction available at other schools was their most important reason for homeschooling." Ibid., iv. An NCES "Issue Brief" confirms these reasons, also finding that "from 2003 to 2007, the percentage of students whose parents reported homeschooling to provide religious or moral instruction increased from 72 percent to 83 percent." NCES, "Issue Brief: 1.5 Million Homeschooled Students in the United States in 2007," 2. Concern about the school environment was the most important reason for 21 percent and dissatisfaction with academic instruction for 17 percent.

141. Ross, "Fundamentalist Challenges to Core Democratic Values," 1002, 1005.

142. Morse v. Frederick, 551 U.S. 393, 424 (2007) (Alito, J., concurring).

143. Yuracko, "Education Off the Grid," 129.

144. Hamilton v. Hamilton, 2007 WL 711830 (N.J. Super. Ch. 2007).

145. Jonathan L. v. Superior Court, 81 Cal. Rptr. 3d 571, 593, 594 (Cal. App. 2 Dist. 2008).

146. Eckholm, "Preaching Virtues of Spanking."

147. Janice Aurini and Scott Davies, "Choice without Markets: Homeschooling in the Context of Private Education," 26 *British Journal of Sociology of Education* 461, 469–471 (2005) (exploring the "expressive" logic of homeschooling: that children are "too precious to be entrusted to the care of others"). The authors note affinities to the literature on "intensive parenting." Ibid., 470.

148. For an argument about the return to the home as the proper site of education, see Alan C. Carlson, "Reinventing the Schoolroom: Education as Homecoming," http://frc.org/get.cfm?i=PL03G01 (accessed 11/20/11). On the role of women both as activists in the homeschooling movement and as homeschoolers, see Milton Gaither, "Why Homeschooling Happened?," *educational HORIZONS*, Summer 2008, 226, 232–235. The intensive mothering point also applies to families who homeschool not primarily for religious reasons. Highly educated women find, in effect, a "workplace" in the home by investing in their child's education.

149. Bruce S. Cooper and John Sureau, "The Politics of Homeschooling: New Developments, New Challenges," 21 *Educational Policy* 110 (2007).

150. NCES, *Homeschooling in the United States: 2003*, 19 (reporting that "students in two-parent households where one parent was in the labor force were about 5 times more likely to be homeschooled than were students in two-parent households where both parents were in the labor force").

151. Yuracko, "Education Off the Grid," 128–130 (detailing how, as a result of HSDLA's efforts, "state laws regulating homeschooling have become increasingly lenient"; only twenty-five states require standardized testing and evaluation of homeschooled students, and ten do not even require parents to "notify the state of their intent to homeschool").

152. See Combs v. Homer-Central School District, 540 F.3d 231 (3rd Cir. 2008) (describing requirements of Pennsylvania's education law).

153. California school districts "are attempting to reach out to homeschooling families," through such programs as the Community Home Education Program. See Cooper and Sureau, "The Politics of Homeschooling," 127. School districts generally have prevailed against homeschooling parents who have asserted a "right" to opt their children in selectively to public school activities. One rationale is that public schools were not receiving state financial support for those students. Ibid., 120–122.

154. For this proposal, see Ross, "Fundamentalist Challenges to Core Democratic Values."

155. Patricia M. Lines, "Homeschooling Comes of Age," *The Public Interest*, Summer 2000, 74, 84 (2000).

156. Andy Sullivan, "Homeschoolers Emerge as Republican Foot Soldiers," http://www.reuters.com/article/2011/10/03/us-usa-campaign-home schoolers-idUSTRE7925IL20111003 (accessed 10/27/11).

157. HSLDA explains that "to help our member families equip the next generation for active, effective citizenship, HSLDA founded Generation Joshua in 2004," which "provides young people with education on Christian citizenship, and opportunities for young people to receive hands-on training in how our nation's political system works." "About HSLDA: Frequently Asked Questions," http://www.hsdla.org/about (accessed 10/27/11).

158. Ibid.

6. Conflicts between Liberty and Equality

1. Meyer v. Nebraska, 262 U.S. 390, 399–400 (1923).

2. See Abner S. Greene, *Against Obligation: The Multiple Sources of Authority in a Liberal Democracy* (Cambridge, MA: Harvard University Press, 2012).

3. For a kindred work, see Corey Brettschneider, *When the State Speaks, What Should It Say? How Democracies Can Protect Expression and Promote Equality* (Princeton, NJ: Princeton University Press, 2012). Brettschneider stresses the distinction between expressive and coercive state action, emphasizing how the state may use its expressive capacities of democratic persuasion to promote the values of free and equal citizenship. See also Abner S. Greene, "Government of the Good," 53 *Vanderbilt Law Review* 1 (2000).

4. 468 U.S. 609 (1984).

5. 530 U.S. 640 (2000).

6. 461 U.S. 574 (1983).

7. 130 S. Ct. 2971 (2010).

8. T. M. Scanlon perceptively and rigorously argues that we should acknowledge clashes of such higher order interests or values, but not clashes of institutionally specified rights. See T. M. Scanlon, "Adjusting Rights and Balancing Values," 72 *Fordham Law Review* 1477, 1478–1479 (2004) (replying to James E. Fleming, "Securing Deliberative Democracy," 72 *Fordham Law Review* 1435 (2004)). In this section, we draw upon James E. Fleming, *Securing Constitutional Democracy: The Case of Autonomy* (Chicago, IL: University of Chicago Press, 2006), chapter 8.

9. See John Rawls, *Political Liberalism* (New York: Columbia University Press, 1993), 223, 295.

10. John Rawls, *A Theory of Justice* (Cambridge, MA: Belknap Press of Harvard University Press, 1971), 541–548; Rawls, *Political Liberalism*, 294–299.

11. Ronald Dworkin, *Taking Rights Seriously* (Cambridge, MA: Harvard University Press, 1977).

12. 341 U.S. 494, 517–561 (1951) (Frankfurter, J., concurring).
13. 310 U.S. 586 (1940).
14. 319 U.S. 624, 646–671 (1943) (Frankfurter, J., dissenting).
15. Walter F. Murphy, James E. Fleming, Sotirios A. Barber, and Stephen Macedo, *American Constitutional Interpretation* (New York: Foundation Press, 4th ed. 2008), 1325–1326 (reprinting letter from Felix Frankfurter to Harlan Fiske Stone concerning *Minersville*).
16. *Dennis,* 579–581 (Black, J., dissenting).
17. *Barnette,* 630–631.
18. Ibid., 642.
19. See, e.g., Dworkin, *Taking Rights Seriously;* Alexander Meiklejohn, "The First Amendment Is an Absolute," 1961 *Supreme Court Review* 245. Leading political philosophers who take a similar stance include Rawls and Scanlon. See Rawls, *Political Liberalism,* 344, 352–356; Thomas M. Scanlon, "A Theory of Freedom of Expression," 1 *Philosophy and Public Affairs* 204 (1972).
20. Rawls, *Political Liberalism,* 295–296.
21. Ibid., 294 & n.10, 295, 299.
22. Ibid., 358–359.
23. Ibid., 296.
24. We should make clear that our aim is to apply a Rawlsian view, not to explicate Rawls's own views.
25. 424 U.S. 1, 49 (1976).
26. *Roberts,* 625–627. The many thoughtful analyses of the problems implicated by *Roberts* include Amy Gutmann, *Identity in Democracy* (Princeton, NJ: Princeton University Press, 2003), 99–103; Nancy L. Rosenblum, *Membership and Morals: The Personal Uses of Pluralism in America* (Princeton, NJ: Princeton University Press, 1998), 158–176; George Kateb, "The Value of Association," in Amy Gutmann, ed., *Freedom of Association* (Princeton, NJ: Princeton University Press, 1998), 35; Nancy L. Rosenblum, "Compelled Association: Public Standing, Self-Respect, and the Dynamic of Exclusion," in Gutmann, ed., *Freedom of Association,* 75.
27. *Buckley,* 49.
28. American Booksellers Association v. Hudnut, 771 F.2d 323, 328 (7th Cir. 1985), *aff'd mem.,* 475 U.S. 1001 (1986).
29. *Boy Scouts,* 653.
30. *Roberts,* 625, 626.
31. Ibid., 626–627.
32. See Rosenblum, *Membership and Morals,* 158–176; William A. Galston, "Civil Society, Civic Virtue, and Liberal Democracy," 75 *Chicago-Kent Law Review* 603, 604–605 (2000).
33. *Roberts,* 626.
34. See Rosenblum, *Membership and Morals,* 163–164; Rosenblum, "Compelled Association," 80, 85.
35. *Boy Scouts,* 644, 657. For fuller discussion of *Boy Scouts,* the issues it raises, and its implications for freedom of association, see, e.g., Andrew

Koppelman with Tobias Barrington Wolff, *A Right to Discriminate? How the Case of* Boy Scouts of America v. James Dale *Warped the Law of Free Association* (New Haven, CT: Yale University Press, 2009); Laura A. Rosenbury, "Between Home and School," 155 *University of Pennsylvania Law Review* 833 (2007); Richard A. Epstein, "The Constitutional Perils of Moderation: The Case of the Boy Scouts," 74 *Southern California Law Review* 119 (2000); Darren Lenard Hutchinson, "'Closet Case': *Boy Scouts of America v. Dale* and the Reinforcement of Gay, Lesbian, Bisexual, and Transgender Invisibility," 76 *Tulane Law Review* 81 (2001); Madhavi Sunder, "Cultural Dissent," 54 *Stanford Law Review* 495 (2001).

36. N.J. Stat. Ann. §§ 10:5–4, 10:5–5 (West 2002); see also *Boy Scouts,* 645, 661–662.

37. *Boy Scouts,* 657.

38. Ibid., 647, 659. The New Jersey Court stated: "It is unquestionably a compelling interest of this State to eliminate the destructive consequences of discrimination from our society." It continued: "Like other similar statutes, the [Law Against Discrimination] serves a compelling state interest and 'abridges no more speech or associational freedom than is necessary to accomplish that purpose.'" Dale v. Boy Scouts of America, 734 A.2d 1196, 1227, 1228 (N.J. 1999) (citing *Roberts,* 629).

39. 517 U.S. 620 (1996).

40. 539 U.S. 558 (2003).

41. See *Romer,* 626–631; *Lawrence,* 574–575.

42. *Lawrence,* 578.

43. See Fleming, *Securing Constitutional Democracy,* 154–160.

44. Koppelman and Wolff, *A Right To Discriminate?,* 108–111. Deborah Hellman argues that discrimination is "wrongful" when it draws distinctions in a way that "demeans," that is, expresses "that the other is less worthy of concern and respect . . . in a manner that has power." Deborah Hellman, *When Is Discrimination Wrong?* (Cambridge, MA: Harvard University Press, 2008), 157.

45. *Dale,* 1242 (Handler, J., concurring).

46. *Boy Scouts,* 653.

47. *Roberts,* 627.

48. *Boy Scouts,* 696 (Stevens, J., dissenting).

49. 388 U.S. 1 (1967).

50. *Boy Scouts,* 699–700 (Stevens, J., dissenting).

51. See the much criticized analysis of whites' claim of freedom not to associate with blacks in Herbert Wechsler, "Toward Neutral Principles of Constitutional Law," 73 *Harvard Law Review* 1, 34 (1959).

52. Rehnquist probably would have rejected any analogy between discrimination on the basis of race and discrimination on the basis of sexual orientation. Scalia, in dissent in *Romer,* took umbrage at such analogies. See *Romer,* 636 (Scalia, J., dissenting).

53. Rawls, *Political Liberalism,* 37.

54. 461 U.S. 574 (1983).

55. Ibid., 591 (quoting Perin v. Carey, 65 U.S. 465, 501 (1861)).

56. Ibid., 593 (emphasis added) (citations omitted).

57. Ibid., 580–581.

58. *Loving*, 3.

59. *Bob Jones University*, 603 (quoting United States v. Lee, 455 U.S. 252, 257–258 (1982)).

60. Ibid., 605.

61. Ibid., 603–604.

62. Ibid., 586, 591–592 (emphasis added).

63. See Linda C. McClain, "Unleashing or Harnessing 'Armies of Compassion'?: Reflections on the Faith-Based Initiative," 39 *Loyola University Chicago Law Journal* 361 (2008) (discussing the George W. Bush administration). President Obama also supports faith-based partnerships. "Obama Announces White House Office of Faith-Based and Neighborhood Partnerships," Feb. 5, 2009, http://www.whitehouse.gov/the_press_office/ObamaAnnounces WhiteHouseOfficeofFaith-basedandNeighborhoodPartnerships/ (accessed 2/28/12).

64. *Bob Jones University*, 609–610 (Powell, J., concurring) (quoting Jackson v. Statler Found., 496 F.2d 623, 639 (2d Cir. 1974) (Friendly, J., dissenting from denial of reconsideration en banc)).

65. Ibid., 609 n.3.

66. Mississippi University for Women v. Hogan, 458 U.S. 718, 733 (1982).

67. *Bob Jones University*, 610 n.4 (Powell, J., concurring) (quoting *Hogan*, 745 (Powell, J., dissenting)).

68. Ibid. (quoting Wolman v. Walter, 433 U.S. 229, 262 (1977) (Powell, J., concurring in part, concurring in the judgment in part, and dissenting in part)).

69. See, e.g., Robert K. Vischer, *Conscience and the Common Good: Reclaiming the Space between Person and State* (Cambridge: Cambridge University Press, 2010).

70. *Bob Jones University*, 610. However, Powell emphasizes that "the balancing of these substantial interests is for *Congress* to perform" and resists any suggestion that the IRS is "invested with authority to decide which public policies are sufficiently 'fundamental' to require denial of tax exemptions." Ibid., 611.

71. See Michael W. McConnell, "The New Establishmentarianism," 75 *Chicago-Kent Law Review* 453 (2000).

72. *Roberts*, 625.

73. Ibid. (citing Heart of Atlanta Motel v. United States, 379 U.S. 241, 250 (1964) (quoting S. Rep. No. 872, at 16–17)). On the import of *Heart of Atlanta Motel* for challenges to contemporary antidiscrimination law, see Linda C. McClain, "Involuntary Servitude, Public Accommodations Laws, and the Legacy of *Heart of Atlanta Motel, Inc. v. United States*," 71 *Maryland Law Review* 79 (2011).

74. *Roberts*, 624.

75. Jonathan Turley, "An Unholy Union: Same-Sex Marriage and the Use of Governmental Programs to Penalize Religious Groups and Unpopular Practices," in Douglas Laycock et al., eds., *Same-Sex Marriage and Religious Liberty: Emerging Conflicts* (Lanham, MD: Rowman & Littlefield, 2008), 68.

76. Douglas W. Kmiec, "Same-Sex Marriage and the Coming Antidiscrimination Campaigns against Religion," in Laycock et al., *Same-Sex Marriage and Religious Liberty,* 109–110.

77. *Boy Scouts,* 659.

78. Letter of Eric Holder, Office of the Attorney General, to Hon. John A. Boehner, Feb. 23, 2011, 4; S 598, The Respect for Marriage Act: Assessing the Impact of DOMA on American Families, Hearing before the Committee on the Judiciary, U.S. Senate, 112th Congress, July 20, 2011; Jackie Calmes and Peter Baker, "Obama Endorses Same-Sex Marriage, Taking Stand on Charged Social Issue," *New York Times,* May 10, 2012, A1.

79. Hearing on the Respect for Marriage Act (statement of Sen. Patrick J. Leahy), 1–2.

80. Ibid., 2 ("second-class families"); 4–6 (testimony by Rep. John Lewis, Ga.) (linking issue to civil rights struggle against racial discrimination and to "issues of dignity").

81. *Romer* forbids "singling out" a certain class of citizens for disfavored legal status or making "a class of persons a stranger to [state] law." *Romer,* 620. *Lawrence* interprets *Romer* as prohibiting laws "born of animosity toward the class of persons affected." *Lawrence,* 574–575. Relying on *Romer,* a federal court of appeals recently held that DOMA was unconstitutional. Massachusetts v. U.S. DHHS, No. 10-2204 (1st Cir. May 31, 2012).

82. 130 S. Ct. 2971 (2010).

83. Ibid., 2978.

84. Ibid., 2979 (quoting Hastings College of Law Policy on Nondiscrimination).

85. Ibid.

86. Ibid., 2980.

87. *Boy Scouts,* 672 (Stevens, J., dissenting) (characterizing Boy Scouts' alleged policy against homosexuality as a "secret" policy).

88. *Christian Legal Society,* 2979–2981.

89. Ibid., 2981.

90. Ibid.

91. Ibid., 2985 (quoting *Roberts,* 623).

92. Ibid. (citing *Boy Scouts,* 659).

93. Ibid., 2986.

94. Grove City College v. Bell, 465 U.S. 555 (1984).

95. *Christian Legal Society,* 2986.

96. Ibid. (quoting Norwood v. Harrison, 413 U.S. 455, 463 (1973)).

97. *Christian Legal Society,* 2988 (quoting Rosenberger v. Rector & Visitors of the University of Virginia, 515 U.S. 819, 829 (1995)).

98. Ibid., 2990 (citation omitted).

99. Ibid. (citation omitted).

100. Toni M. Massaro, "*Christian Legal Society v. Martinez:* Six Frames," 38 *Hastings Constitutional Law Quarterly* 569, 617–618 (2011).

101. *Christian Legal Society,* 2994.

102. Ibid., 2997 (Stevens, J., concurring).

103. Ibid., 2997–2998.

104. Ibid., 2998 (emphasis added).

105. 334 U.S. 1 (1948) (holding that state courts may not enforce racially restrictive land use covenants).

106. 466 U.S. 429 (1984) (holding that state court erred in denying mother custody because of her interracial marriage and the likely prejudice against her child; stating that "[t]he Constitution cannot control such prejudices but neither can it tolerate them. Private biases may be outside the reach of the law, but the law cannot, directly or indirectly, give them effect.").

107. *Romer,* 623, 632 (stating that "the first Justice Harlan admonished this Court that the Constitution 'neither knows nor tolerates classes among citizens,'" Plessy v. Ferguson (1896) (dissenting opinion), and concluding that Amendment 2 lacked a rational relationship to legitimate state interests and seemed "inexplicable by anything but animus toward the class that it affects").

108. *Christian Legal Society,* 3000 (Alito, J., dissenting) (quoting United States v. Schwimmer, 279 U.S. 644, 654–655 (1929) (Holmes, J., dissenting)).

109. Ibid., 3010 (quoting *Boy Scouts,* 648).

110. Ibid., 3015–3016 (citing Brief for Gays & Lesbians for Individual Liberty as Amici Curiae Supporting Petitioner at 35, *Christian Legal Society,* 130 S. Ct. 2971 (2010) (No. 08–1371)).

111. See generally Laycock et al., *Same-Sex Marriage and Religious Liberty.* In *Boy Scouts,* the majority observed that as public accommodations laws have expanded to cover more places, "the potential for conflict between state public accommodations laws and the First Amendment rights of organizations has increased." *Boy Scouts,* 657.

112. See Laycock et al., *Same-Sex Marriage and Religious Liberty.*

113. Manhattan Declaration: A Call of Christian Conscience, http://www .manhattandeclaration.org/pdfs/ManhattanDeclaration.pdf (accessed 11/21/09).

114. Press Release, *National Religious Leaders Release Historic Declaration on Christian Conscience,* http://demossnews.com/ManhattanDeclaration /news/national_religious_leaders_release_historic_declaration_on_christian _consci (accessed 11/21/09).

115. The Manhattan Declaration cites to Genesis 2:23–24 and Ephesians 5:32–33.

116. Goodridge v. Department of Public Health, 798 N.E.2d 941, 968 (Mass. 2003) ("prejudice"); Baker v. State, 744 A.2d 864, 885 (Vt. 1999)

("animus"); Perry v. Schwarzenegger, 704 F.Supp. 2d 921, 1002 (N.D. Cal. 2010) ("animus"), *aff'd*, Perry v. Brown, 671 F. 3d 1052 (9th Cir. 2012).

117. One such threat that we note here but do not address in text is efforts to "weaken or eliminate conscience clauses," such that "pro-life institutions" and "pro-life" health care professionals must refer for abortions or even perform or participate in them. Manhattan Declaration.

118. For a thoughtful analysis, see Martha Minow, "Should Religious Groups Be Exempt from Civil Rights Laws?," 48 *Boston College Law Review* 781, 831–843 (2007).

119. Manhattan Declaration.

120. Harriet Bernstein and Luisa Paster, DCR Docket No. PN34XB-03008, Finding of Probable Cause, Dec. 29, 2008, at 4. After a finding that this practice violated New Jersey's public accommodations law, the Ocean Grove Camp Meeting Association of the United Methodist Church, which owned the pavilion, adopted a new policy that it would not rent out the pavilion for any weddings, avoiding further liability under that law. Janice Moore and Emily Sonnessa v. Ocean Grove Camp Meeting Association, DCR Docket No. PN34XB-0312, Finding of No Probable Cause, Dec. 29, 2008.

121. Manhattan Declaration. The United States Conference of Catholic Bishops (USCCB) has warned of similar "challenges" to religious liberty, including redefining marriage, and invoked Tocqueville and the buffering role of churches and other "intermediate institutions" that "stand between the power of the government and the conscience of individuals" and "contribut[e] immensely to the common good." Archbishop William E. Lori, "Address on Religious Liberty" (November 2011), http://www.usccb .org/about/leadership/usccb-general-assembly/archbishop-lori-religious -liberty-november-2011-address.cfm (accessed 11/29/11). Lori is the head of a new USCCB Ad Hoc Committee for Religious Liberty.

122. Ken I. Kersch observes the curious "Declarationist Triptych," in contemporary conservative movement politics, of Thomas Jefferson, Abraham Lincoln, and Martin Luther King Jr. as constitutional "Great Men" or redeemers. Ken I. Kersch, "Beyond Originalism: Conservative Declarationism and Constitutional Redemption," 71 *Maryland Law Review* 229 (2011).

123. Robin Fretwell Wilson, "Matters of Conscience: Lessons for Same-Sex Marriage from the Healthcare Context," in Laycock et al., *Same-Sex Marriage and Religious Liberty,* 101.

124. For some contemporaneous news accounts, see, e.g., Richard Philbrick, "Church Told: Mixed Nuptial Bans Must Go—Let Wisdom Rule, Committee Urges," *Chicago Tribune,* May 22, 1965, C7 (Presbyterian church); Richard Philbrick, "Synod Votes to Fight Ban on Interracial Weddings," *Chicago Tribune,* July 6, 1965, B4 (United Church of Christ); "Ban on Interracial Couples Assailed by Catholic Group," *New York Times,* Nov. 24, 1963, 16.

125. "Truman's Sympathy with Dixie, also against Mixed Marriage," *Boston Globe,* Sept. 12, 1963, 10.

126. Minow, "Should Religious Groups Be Exempt From Civil Rights Laws?," 791.

127. Chai R. Feldblum, "Moral Conflict and Conflicting Liberties," in Laycock et al., *Same-Sex Marriage and Religious Liberty,* 152–153.

128. *Roberts,* 636 (O'Connor, J., concurring).

129. Civil Rights Act of 1964, 42 U.S.C. §§ 2000a to 2000a-6. The Senate Report invoked the English common law reasoning that "one who employed his private property for purposes of commercial gain by offering goods or services to the public must stick to his bargain." S. Rep. No. 872, quoted in *Heart of Atlanta Motel,* 285 (Douglas, J., concurring).

130. For the characterization of the U.S. Constitution as embodying a "large commercial republic," and for its tendency to moderate extreme religious claims, see Sotirios A. Barber and James E. Fleming, *Constitutional Interpretation: The Basic Questions* (New York: Oxford University Press, 2007), 41–45.

131. P.A. 96–1513, 2010 Ill. Legis. Serv.

132. Chap. 61, 2009 N.H. Laws 64 (codified at N.H. Rev. Stat. Ann. Sec. 457:37 & 457:46).

133. 2011 Session Laws of New York, Ch. 95 (A. 8534) (McKinney's) (effective July 24, 2011); AO8354 Memo ("Statement in Support"), p. 3, www.assembly.state.ny.us/leg (accessed 8/30/11); Danny Hakim, "Exemptions Were Key to Vote on Gay Marriage," *New York Times,* June 26, 2011, 18.

134. Marriage Equality Act, § 10-B.

135. Thomas Kaplan, "Rights Collide as Town Clerk Sidesteps Role in Gay Marriages," *New York Times,* Sept. 27, 2011, A1 (quoting Governor Cuomo).

136. See Clerk Informational Memorandum, New York State Department of Health, July 13, 2011 ("No application for a marriage license shall be denied on the ground that the parties are of the same or a different sex."); Kaplan, "Rights Collide"; "Ledyard Clerk Controversy Headed for Courts?," Nov. 13, 2011, http://auburnpub.com/news/local/article_6922ee6c-0da6-11e1-b3ed-001cc4c03286.html (accessed 11/28/11) (reporting that the couple, Katie Carmichael and Dierdre DiBaggio, were considering legal action and that the Courage Fund would support the newly reelected clerk, Rose Marie Belforti, in such a challenge); Lori, "Address on Religious Liberty," 5 (listing as threat to religious liberty "a county clerk in New York State who faces legal action because she refuses to take part in same-sex marriages"). For a general argument for exemptions or accommodations in such cases, see Robin Fretwell Wilson, "Insubstantial Burdens: The Case for Government Employee Exemptions to Same-Sex Marriage Laws," 5 *Northwestern Journal of Law and Social Policy* 318 (2010).

137. See, e.g., "Statement of the Bishops of New York State on Same-Sex Marriage," June 24, 2011, http://www.archny.org/news/events/news-press-releases /?i=20810 (accessed 10/17/11).

138. 744 A.2d 864 (Vt. 1999).

139. An Act Relating to Civil Unions, 2000 Vt. ALS 91.

140. P.A. 3, 2009 Vt. Acts & Resolves 33 (as codified at Vt. Stat. Ann. tit. 15 & 18 scattered sections).

141. For example, Rep. Grad of Moretown explained her vote: "Through testimony on this bill I learned that civil unions do[] not [provide "equal access, benefits, and privileges under the law"] but create[] a separate status for same-sex couples and their children who are often discriminated against, stigmatized and marginalized." Vermont House of Representatives, House Journal, 2009–2010 sess., April 3, 2009, 529–530, http://www.leg.state .vt.us/docs/2010/Permanent/House/248434.pdf (accessed 11/29/11). Rep. Ram of Burlington explained, evoking the Jim Crow era: "To say that Civil Unions offered the same rights as marriage is nothing less than saying once upon a time there [were] two drinking fountains that both dispense the same water." Ibid., 531.

142. Minow, "Should Religious Groups Be Exempt from Civil Rights Laws?," 824.

143. Robert D. Putnam and David E. Campbell, *American Grace: How Religion Divides and Unites Us* (New York: Simon and Schuster Paperbacks, 2012), 401–406; Mark Arsenault, "Same-Sex Marriage No Longer Such a Divisive Political Issue," *Boston Globe,* March 27, 2011, 9.

144. Susannah Meadows, "Passing the Torch at Bob Jones U.," *Newsweek,* Jan. 29, 2005. See also Jennifer Berry Hawes, "This Is His Father's World: The New President of Bob Jones University Is the Founder's Great-Grandson. He Brings a Fresh Tone to the Greenville School's Fundamentalist Christian Mandate," *The Post and Courier* (Charleston, SC), July 20, 2005.

145. "Christian University 'Profoundly Sorry' for Racist Policies," *USA Today,* Nov. 24, 2008, http://www.usatoday.com/news/education/2008-11-24 -bob-jones-university-race_N.htm (accessed 4/10/11).

146. *Goodridge,* 973.

7. Autonomy versus Moral Goods

1. Michael J. Sandel, *Democracy's Discontent: America in Search of a Public Philosophy* (Cambridge, MA: Belknap Press of Harvard University Press, 1996). For a range of critical and sympathetic essays on Sandel's work, see Anita L. Allen and Milton C. Regan, Jr., eds., *Debating Democracy's Discontent: Essays on American Politics, Law, and Public Philosophy* (New York: Oxford University Press, 1998).

2. 539 U.S. 558 (2003).

3. Cass R. Sunstein, *Legal Reasoning and Political Conflict* (New York: Oxford University Press, 1996); Cass R. Sunstein, *One Case at a Time: Judicial Minimalism on the Supreme Court* (Cambridge, MA: Harvard University Press, 1999); Cass R. Sunstein, *A Constitution of Many Minds: Why the Founding Document Doesn't Mean What It Meant Before* (Princeton, NJ: Princeton University Press, 2009).

4. Cass R. Sunstein, "What Did *Lawrence* Hold? Of Autonomy, Desuetude, Sexuality, and Marriage," 2003 *Supreme Court Review* 27, 30.

5. See Ronald Dworkin, *Justice for Hedgehogs* (Cambridge, MA: Belknap Press of Harvard University Press, 2011); John Rawls, *A Theory of Justice* (Cambridge, MA: Belknap Press of Harvard University Press, 1971); John Rawls, *Political Liberalism* (New York: Columbia University Press, 1993).

6. Michael J. Sandel, *Justice: What's the Right Thing To Do?* (New York: Farrar, Straus & Giroux, 2009), 6–10, 19–21, 140–166.

7. We also believe that there are notable and unexpected affinities between Sandel's and Dworkin's conceptions. See Linda C. McClain and James E. Fleming, "Respecting Freedom and Cultivating Virtues in Justifying Constitutional Rights," 91 *Boston University Law Review* 1311, 1311–1314 (2011).

8. See William A. Galston, *Liberal Purposes: Goods, Virtues, and Diversity in the Liberal State* (Cambridge: Cambridge University Press, 1991), 3; William A. Galston, *Liberal Pluralism: The Implications of Value Pluralism for Political Theory and Practice* (Cambridge: Cambridge University Press, 2002), 3; Stephen Macedo, *Liberal Virtues: Citizenship, Virtue, and Community in Liberal Constitutionalism* (Oxford: Oxford University Press, 1990), 3–8; Stephen Macedo, *Diversity and Distrust: Civic Education in a Multicultural Democracy* (Cambridge, MA: Harvard University Press, 2000), 8–10. See also Corey Brettschneider, *When the State Speaks, What Should it Say? How Democracies Can Protect Expression and Promote Equality* (Princeton, NJ: Princeton University Press, 2012).

9. James E. Fleming, *Securing Constitutional Democracy: The Case of Autonomy* (Chicago, IL: University of Chicago Press, 2006), 141–160; James E. Fleming and Linda C. McClain, "In Search of a Substantive Republic," 76 *Texas Law Review* 509, 518–522 (1997) (reviewing, in part, Sandel, *Democracy's Discontent*).

10. Sandel, "Moral Argument and Liberal Toleration: Abortion and Homosexuality," 77 *California Law Review* 521, 521–522 (1989).

11. 478 U.S. 186, 190–196 (1986).

12. Sandel, "Moral Argument," 529–531, 533–538.

13. Sandel, *Democracy's Discontent*, 107.

14. *Lawrence*, 564–579; Michael J. Sandel, *Public Philosophy: Essays on Morality in Politics* (Cambridge, MA: Harvard University Press, 2005), 142.

15. Fleming, *Securing Constitutional Democracy*, 154–160; Fleming and McClain, "In Search of a Substantive Republic," 530–538.

16. 517 U.S. 620, 632, 634 (quoting U.S. Department of Agriculture v. Moreno, 413 U.S. 528, 534 (1973)), 635–636 (1996).

17. Ibid., 646 (Scalia, J., dissenting).

18. Sandel, "Moral Argument," 533–538. For an elaboration of the contrast between "empty toleration" and "toleration as respect," see Linda C. McClain, "Toleration, Autonomy, and Governmental Promotion of Good

Lives: Beyond 'Empty' Toleration to Toleration as Respect," 59 *Ohio State Law Journal* 19 (1998).

19. *Lawrence,* 575, 578–579.

20. Fleming, *Securing Constitutional Democracy,* 154–160; ibid., 154–155; Fleming and McClain, "In Search of a Substantive Republic," 530–538.

21. Sandel, *Public Philosophy,* 142.

22. 798 N.E.2d 941, 954 (Mass. 2003).

23. "Challenged by the insights of Michael Sandel," Chai Feldblum advocates "judgmental moral arguments" in support of marriage equality for same-sex couples. Chai R. Feldblum, "Gay Is Good: The Moral Case for Marriage Equality and More," 17 *Yale Journal of Law & Feminism* 139, 157, 159 (2005).

24. Sandel, *Justice,* 186, 187, 207.

25. Ibid., 193 (quoting Aristotle, *The Politics,* ed. and trans. Ernest Barker (Oxford: Oxford University Press, 1946), Book III, ch. ix [1282b]).

26. Ibid., 248, 249–251. Rawls uses the formulation "exemplar of public reason." Rawls, *Political Liberalism,* 236.

27. Sandel, *Justice,* 249 (quoting Rawls, *Political Liberalism,* 236, 254).

28. Ibid.

29. Ibid., 249–250 (quoting Richard John Neuhaus, *The Naked Public Square* (Grand Rapids, MI: William B. Eerdmans, 1984)).

30. Ibid., 250 (quoting Barack Obama, U.S. Senator, "One Nation . . . Under God?," Keynote Address at Sojourners/Call to Renewal-sponsored Pentecost Conference (June 28, 2006), in *Sojourners,* November 2006, 10–11).

31. Ibid., 251.

32. See ibid., 251–260.

33. Ibid., 253–254. By contrast, Elizabeth Brake argues that it *is* possible for political liberalism, applying "neutrality and public reason," to justify a "minimally restricted law of marriage"—which would allow same-sex marriage—on the ground that "the social bases of caring relationships are primary goods." Elizabeth Brake, "Minimal Marriage: What Political Liberalism Implies for Marriage Law," 120 *Ethics* 302, 303, 326 (2010). We do not agree with her that political liberalism requires the disestablishment of monogamous marriage and recognition of group marriage. See Elizabeth Brake, *Minimizing Marriage: Marriage, Morality, and the Law* (New York: Oxford University Press, 2012).

34. Sandel, *Justice,* 254.

35. Tamara Metz, *Untying the Knot: Marriage, the State, and the Case for Their Divorce* (Princeton, NJ: Princeton University Press, 2010), 113–114, 119–120.

36. Sandel, *Justice,* 254.

37. Id. at 254–255 (internal quotation omitted).

38. Michael Kinsley, "Abolish Marriage: Let's Really Get the Government Out of Our Bedrooms," *Washington Post,* July 3, 2003, A23. See also

Richard H. Thaler and Cass R. Sunstein, *Nudge: Improving Decisions about Health, Wealth, and Happiness* (New Haven, CT: Yale University Press, 2008), 215–226 (arguing for "privatizing marriage").

39. Martha Albertson Fineman, *The Autonomy Myth: A Theory of Dependency* (New York: New Press, 2004), 121–123.

40. Metz, *Untying the Knot,* 119–127. See also Maxine Eichner, *The Supportive State: Families, Government, and American's Political Ideals* (New York: Oxford University Press, 2010), 110–112.

41. Metz, *Untying the Knot,* 114–119, 125–127.

42. Sandel, *Justice,* 256.

43. Ibid.

44. See, e.g., Perry v. Schwarzenegger, 704 F. Supp. 2d 921, 930–932 (N.D. Cal. 2010) (observing that, by contrast to arguments that proponents of Proposition 8 made in the official campaign to pass it, which "conveyed to voters that same-sex relationships are inferior to opposite-sex relationships and dangerous to children," in the litigation over Proposition 8, proponents stressed that it promoted marriage's "central purpose" of promoting naturally procreative relationships and promoted " 'statistically optimal' childrearing households; that is, households in which children are raised by a man and a woman married to each other") , *aff'd,* Perry v. Brown, 671 F. 3d 1052 (9th Cir. 2012). Prominent conservative opponents may also eschew religious arguments out of court. See Sherif Girgis, Robert P. George, and Ryan T. Anderson, "What Is Marriage?," 34 *Harvard Journal of Law & Public Policy* 245, 247 (2010) (contending that their argument for "legally enshrining" the "conjugal view of marriage" requires "no appeal to religious authority").

45. Sandel, *Justice,* 256.

46. Ibid., 256, 257 (quoting *Goodridge,* 948 (quoting *Lawrence,* 571 (quoting Planned Parenthood v. Casey, 505 U.S. 833, 850 (1992)).

47. *Goodridge,* 949.

48. Sandel, *Justice,* 257.

49. Ibid., 257–258.

50. Ibid., 258 (quoting *Goodridge,* 954).

51. Ibid., 258–259. Similarly, in recognizing same-sex marriage, the Iowa Supreme Court rejected the argument that same-sex couples could not achieve the goods of marriage because they could not procreate naturally. It held that such couples were similarly situated to opposite-sex couples with regard to government's purposes in regulating marriage because they were "in committed and loving relationships, many raising families," and "official recognition of their status provides an institutional basis for defining their fundamental relational rights and responsibilities." Varnum v. Brien, 763 N.W.2d 862, 883 (Iowa 2009).

52. Sandel, *Justice,* 258–259, 259–260.

53. Ibid. (quoting *Goodridge,* 962).

54. Ibid.

55. One could argue that bans on underage, incestuous, and bigamous mar-

riages express a view of marital vice, that is, what forms of marriage are bad. And we do not deny that family law and social norms reflect ideals about how spouses should treat each other once they marry. Our point is that there is no required showing of virtue on the part of the parties seeking to marry.

56. See, e.g., Erwin Chemerinsky, *Constitutional Law: Principles and Policies* (New York: Wolters Kluwer, 4th ed. 2011), 551–552 (federal doctrine); *Goodridge*, 960 (state doctrine).

57. See, e.g., Williamson v. Lee Optical, 348 U.S. 483 (1955).

58. *Lawrence*, 578.

59. *Goodridge*, 962.

60. See Ronald Dworkin, *Is Democracy Possible Here? Principles for a New Political Debate* (Princeton, NJ: Princeton University Press, 2006), 72–73 (interpreting *Lawrence*); ibid., 86–89 (arguing for a right to same-sex marriage).

61. [2003] 172 O.A.C. 276, para. 107, para. 148.

62. Dworkin, *Is Democracy Possible Here?*, 86–89.

63. See Rawls, *Political Liberalism*, 335.

64. Ibid., 37.

65. *Goodridge*, 954.

66. Sandel, *Justice*, 261.

67. Metz, *Untying the Knot*, 35–37, 41–44.

68. 183 P.3d 384 (Cal. 2008). Our analysis of *In re Marriage Cases* draws upon Joanna Grossman and Linda McClain, "The California Supreme Court Rules in Favor of Marriage for Same-Sex Couples, Part I: Why Domestic Partnerships are Not Enough," *FindLaw's Writ: Legal Commentary,* May 27, 2008, http://writ.news.findlaw.com/grossman/20080527.html; Joanna Grossman and Linda McClain, "The California Supreme Court Rules in Favor of Marriage for Same-Sex Couples, Part II: How Conservative Reasons Led to a Progressive Result," *FindLaw's Writ: Legal Commentary,* May 28, 2008, http://writ.news.findlaw.com/grossman/20080528.html.

69. 704 F. Supp. 2d 921 (N.D. Cal. 2010), *aff'd,* Perry v. Brown, 671 F. 3d 1052 (9th Cir. 2012).

70. Proposition 22 (2000) (codified as Cal. Fam. Code § 308.5 (2000), held unconstitutional by *Marriage Cases*, 453.

71. *Marriage Cases*, 413, 414–416.

72. Ibid., 446, 452.

73. 744 A.2d 864 (Vt. 1999).

74. 2009 Vt. Acts & Resolves 33 (codified in Vt. Stat. Ann. tit. 15 & 18).

75. 908 A.2d 196 (N.J. 2006).

76. In re Opinions of the Justices to the Senate, 440 Mass. 1201, 1207 (2004).

77. *Marriage Cases*, 398, 400. See also ibid., 428, 429, 434–435.

78. *Lewis*, 221, 222, 223.

79. *Marriage Cases*, 398–399, 448.

80. Ibid., 435.

81. Ibid., 445–446.
82. Sandel, *Justice,* 254.
83. Ibid., 257–258, 260.
84. *Marriage Cases,* 419–427.
85. Metz, *Untying the Knot,* 38, 38–40.
86. *Goodridge,* 959.
87. *Marriage Cases,* 422–426.
88. Ibid., 428–430, 430–433.
89. Ibid., 428.
90. See ibid., 398–399, 400, 418, 421, 423–427.
91. Ibid., 427.
92. Ibid., 422, 423. On the "channelling" function of family law, see Carl E. Schneider, "The Channelling Function in Family Law," 20 *Hofstra Law Review* 495 (1992); Linda C. McClain, "Love, Marriage, and the Baby Carriage: Revisiting the Channelling Function of Family Law," 28 *Cardozo Law Review* 2133 (2007).
93. *Marriage Cases,* 422 (quoting De Burgh v. De Burgh, 250 P.2d 598, 601 (Cal. 1952)).
94. Ibid. (quoting *De Burgh,* 601).
95. Ibid. (quoting Elden v. Sheldon, 758 P.2d 582 (Cal. 1988)).
96. Ibid., 423, 425, 426.
97. Ibid.
98. Ibid., 422 (quoting *Elden,* 586 (internal quotations omitted)).
99. Ibid. (quoting Perez v. Sharp, 198 P.2d 17, 18 (Cal. 1948) (internal quotations omitted)).
100. Ibid., 425.
101. 855 N.E.2d 1, 21 (N.Y. 2006).
102. *Goodridge,* 995–996 (Cordy, J., dissenting) ("Paramount among its many important functions, the institution of marriage has systematically provided for the regulation of heterosexual behavior, brought order to the resulting procreation, and ensured a stable family structure in which children will be reared, educated, and socialized.").
103. *Marriage Cases,* 430, 432.
104. Ibid., 431, 432, 433.
105. Ibid., 432.
106. *Perry,* 947–950.
107. *Marriage Cases,* 432 (discussing Griswold v. Connecticut, 381 U.S. 479 (1965)).
108. Ibid.
109. Ibid., 433 ("By recognizing this circumstance we do not alter or diminish either the legal responsibilities that biological parents owe to their children or the substantial incentives that the state provides to a child's biological parents to enter into and raise their children in a stable, long-term committed relationship.").
110. Ibid.

111. Ibid., 451 (quoting *Hernandez*, 30 (Kaye, C.J., dissenting)).
112. Ibid., 399.
113. *Goodridge*, 967.
114. *Marriage Cases*, 451 (quoting *Lawrence*, 579).
115. See, e.g., Nancy D. Polikoff, *Beyond (Straight and Gay) Marriage: Valuing All Families Under the Law* (Boston, MA: Beacon Press, 2008), 3; Nancy D. Polikoff, "Ending Marriage as We Know It," 32 *Hofstra Law Review* 201, 202 (2003).
116. See Cal. Const. art. I, § 7.5 ("Only marriage between a man and a woman is valid or recognized in California.").
117. *Perry*, 930–932. See ibid., 991.
118. See ibid., 953–991, 993.
119. On questions of worth, see, e.g., ibid., 973 (Finding 58) ("Proposition 8 places the force of law behind stigmas against gays and lesbians, including: gays and lesbians do not have intimate relationships similar to heterosexual couples; gays and lesbians are not as good as heterosexuals; and gay and lesbian relationships do not deserve the full recognition of society."); ibid., 974 (Finding 60) ("Proposition 8 reserves the most socially valued form of relationship (marriage) for opposite-sex couples."); and ibid., 999–1000 ("The evidence supports two points which together show Proposition 8 does not advance any of the [state's] identified interests: (1) same-sex parents and opposite-sex parents of are equal quality . . . and (2) Proposition 8 does not make it more likely that opposite-sex couples will marry and raise offspring biologically related to both parents."). On themes of marriage as an important choice, see, e.g., ibid., 961 (Finding 34) ("Marriage is the state recognition and approval of a couple's choice to live with each other, to remain committed to one another and to form a household based on their own feelings about one another and to join in an economic partnership and support one another and any dependents."); and ibid., 993 ("The right to marry has been historically and remains the right to choose a spouse and, with mutual consent, join together and form a household.").
120. See Perry v. Brown, 265 P. 3d 1002, 1015 (Cal. 2011) (in response to Order Certifying a Question to the Supreme Court of California, 628 F.3d 1191, 1192 (9th Cir. 2011)).
121. Perry v. Brown, 671 F. 3d 1052, 1092–1094 (9th Cir. 2012).
122. For example, without deciding the merits of the argument that families with two biological parents provide the optimal setting for childrearing or whether this would be a legitimate governmental interest, the court pointed out that Proposition 8 in no way altered California law governing parentage, under which same-sex partners (as domestic partners and under other laws) had identical rights to spouses or opposite-sex couples with regard to forming families and raising children. Ibid., 1086–1089.
123. Assemblymember Richard N. Gottfried, "Gottfried Hails Passage of Marriage Bill," June 24, 2011, http://assembly.state.ny.us/mem/Richard-N -Gottfried/story/43607/ (accessed 10/5/11).

124. Remarks by Senator Diaz, New York Senate Transcript, June 24, 2011, http://open.nysenate.gov/legislation/transcript/regular-session-06-24 -2011 (accessed 9/25/11).

125. Ruben Diaz and Michael Long, "If the NY Senate Passes Gay Marriage, It's Republicans Who Will Take the Heat," June 22, 2011, http://www .nysenate.gov/press-release/if-ny-senate-passes-gay-marriage-its -republicans-who-will-take-heat-ruben-diaz (accessed 2/25/12).

126. Remarks by Senator Saland, New York Senate Transcript, June 24, 2011, http://open.nysenate.gov/legislation/transcript/regular-session-06-24 -2011 (accessed 2/25/12).

127. "Senator Saland's Statement on Marriage Equality," June 25, 2011, http:// www.nysenate.gov/print/105811 (accessed 10/5/11).

128. Senator Grisanti, New York Senate Transcript, June 24, 2011, http://open .nysenate.gov/legislation/transcript/regular-session-06-24-2011 (accessed 2/25/12).

129. Michael Barbaro, "Behind Gay Marriage, an Unlikely Mix of Forces," *New York Times,* June 26, 2011, § 1, 1, 19.

130. "Governor Cuomo Announces Passage of Marriage Equality Act," June 24, 2011, http://www.governor.ny.gov/press/062411passageofmarriage equality (accessed 11/30/11).

131. "Assembly Passes Historic Marriage Equality Act: Measure Would Allow Same-Sex Partners to Legally Marry in New York State," June 15, 2011, http://assembly.state.ny.us/Press/20110615a/ (accessed 10/5/11).

132. Daniel J. O'Donnell, "Assembly Member O'Donnell Leads Marriage Equality Act to Passage for Fourth Time," June 15, 2011, http://assembly .state.ny.us/mem/?ad=069&sh=story&story=43099 (accessed 11/30/11).

133. Gottfried, "Gottfried Hails Passage of Marriage Bill."

134. Richard Gottfried, Remarks on Marriage Equality Legislation, June 15, 2011 (our transcription from video clip), http://assembly.state.ny.us/mem /Richard-N-Gottfried (accessed 10/5/11).

135. Remarks by Sen. Duane, New York Senate Transcript, June 24, 2011, 41, http://open.nysenate.gov/legislation/transcript/regular-session-06-24 -2011 (accessed 9/25/11).

136. Deborah Glick, Remarks on Marriage Equality Vote, June 15, 2011 (our transcription from video clip), http://assembly.state.ny.us/mem/?ad=066 (accessed 10/5/11).

137. Daniel J. O'Donnell, Remarks on Marriage Equality Act, June 15, 2011 (our transcription from video clip), http://assembly.state.ny.us/mem/?ad =069 (accessed 10/5/11).

138. Richard Gottfried, Remarks on Marriage Equality Legislation, June 15, 2011 (our transcription from video clip), http://assembly.state.ny.us/mem /Richard-N-Gottfried (accessed 10/5/11).

139. Statement of the Bishops of New York State on Same-Sex Marriage, June 24, 2011, http://www.archny.org/news-events/news-press-releases/index .cfm?i=20810 (accessed 10/17/11).

140. New York Marriage Equality Act, A8354, 2011–2012 Sess. (N.Y. 2011). This Bill is codified as Marriage Equality Act, NY Domestic Relations §10-a (2011). We cite to the Bill itself because it includes a statement of purpose and statement of support, which we quote in text.

141. A8354, "Statement in Support."

142. Ibid; see also "Purpose."

143. Danny Hakim, "Exemptions Were Key to Vote on Gay Marriage," *New York Times,* June 26, 2011, 18.

144. Samuel G. Freedman, "How Clergy Helped a Same-Sex Marriage Law Pass," *New York Times,* July 16, 2011, A14 (describing personal journey and organizing efforts of Ms. Taylor Sweringen).

145. Ibid. (quoting Julian E. Zelizer, history professor at Princeton).

146. Ibid.

147. Barbaro, "Behind Gay Marriage, An Unlikely Mix of Forces," 9.

148. Michael Barbaro, "Mayor States Case, Emphatically and Personally, for Gay Marriage," *New York Times,* May 27, 2011, A21.

149. See *Goodridge,* 949 (describing the plaintiffs in a way as to make clear that gay men and lesbians are our friends and neighbors, not alien others who bear no resemblance to heterosexuals); 955 ("common humanity"); 973 (Greaney, J., concurring) ("plaintiffs are members of our community, our neighbors, our coworkers, our friends"). See also *Baker,* 889 ("common humanity").

8. Minimalism versus Perfectionism

1. Cass R. Sunstein, *Radicals in Robes: Why Extreme Right-Wing Courts Are Wrong for America* (New York: Basic Books, 2005), 31–41.

2. Cass R. Sunstein, *Legal Reasoning and Political Conflict* (New York: Oxford University Press, 1996), 48–50, 59–61 (criticizing Ronald Dworkin, "The Forum of Principle," 56 *New York University Law Review* 469 (1981), *reprinted in* Ronald Dworkin, *A Matter of Principle* (Cambridge, MA: Harvard University Press, 1985), 33). There are affinities between Sunstein's view and Robin West's progressive call, discussed in Chapter 3, for "de-constitutionalizing" abortion rights by turning from courts to legislatures for their protection. See Robin West, "From Choice to Reproductive Justice: De-Constitutionalizing Abortion Rights," 118 *Yale Law Journal* 1394 (2009).

3. Sunstein, *Legal Reasoning and Political Conflict,* 4, 37.

4. Cass R. Sunstein, *One Case at a Time: Judicial Minimalism on the Supreme Court* (Cambridge, MA: Harvard University Press, 1999).

5. Sunstein, *Legal Reasoning and Political Conflict,* 177 (pointing out that judges confront only small-scale pieces of systemic controversies, are drawn from relatively narrow segments of society, and generally lack any philosophical training or other unique bases for moral evaluation); 176 (endorsing the argument made in Gerald N. Rosenberg, *The Hollow Hope: Can Courts Bring about Social Change?* (Chicago, IL: University of Chicago Press, 1991)).

6. Cass R. Sunstein, *The Partial Constitution* (Cambridge, MA: Harvard University Press, 1993).

7. Sunstein, *Radicals in Robes,* 254 n.9 (citing John Rawls, *Political Liberalism* (New York: Columbia University Press, 1993)).

8. See Sotirios A. Barber, *Welfare and the Constitution* (Princeton, NJ: Princeton University Press, 2003), 53–64, 118–142.

9. *The Federalist* No. 51 (Madison), ed. Clinton Rossiter (New York: New American Library, 1961), 322.

10. Sunstein, *Radicals in Robes,* 32; see James E. Fleming, *Securing Constitutional Democracy: The Case of Autonomy* (Chicago, IL: University of Chicago Press, 2006), 16, 211, 225.

11. Sunstein, *Radicals in Robes,* 32 (quoting Ronald Dworkin, *Law's Empire* (Cambridge, MA: Harvard University Press, 1986), 229).

12. Fleming, *Securing Constitutional Democracy,* 5, 24, 63, 84; see Dworkin, *Law's Empire,* 239; Cass R. Sunstein, "Second-Order Perfectionism," 75 *Fordham Law Review* 2867, 2869–2870, 2872–2874 (2007).

13. Sunstein, *Radicals in Robes,* 32.

14. Fleming, *Securing Constitutional Democracy,* 5, 24, 63, 84.

15. Sunstein, "Second-Order Perfectionism," 2870.

16. Sunstein, *Radicals in Robes,* 151–152, 260 n.2 (citing David Cole as a "Liberty Perfectionist").

17. The Cato Institute offers illustrations. See, e.g., Brief of the Cato Institute as Amicus Curiae in Support of Petitioner, Hamdan v. Rumsfeld, 548 U.S. 557 (2006) (No. 05–184); Cato Inst., "Cato Handbook for Congress: Policy Recommendations for the 108th Congress," chs. 12, 13, 19 (2003), http://www.cato.org/pubs/handbook/handbook108.html (accessed 11/30/11).

18. Sunstein, *Radicals in Robes,* 41.

19. Sunstein, "Second-Order Perfectionism," 2870.

20. Sunstein, *Radicals in Robes,* 35, 39, 51, 247, 251.

21. Sunstein, *Legal Reasoning and Political Conflict,* 3–7, 46–48; Sunstein, *One Case at a Time,* 5, 50–51; Sunstein, *Radicals in Robes,* 35, 100–101, 129.

22. 381 U.S. 479 (1965).

23. 539 U.S. 558 (2003).

24. See, e.g., Cass R. Sunstein, "Liberal Constitutionalism and Liberal Justice," 72 *Texas Law Review* 305, 312 (1993) (suggesting that reliance on equal protection principles could provide a narrower and more secure basis for judicial decisions).

25. Sunstein, *Legal Reasoning and Political Conflict,* 155, 156.

26. Ibid.

27. Sunstein, "What Did *Lawrence* Hold? Of Autonomy, Desuetude, Sexuality, and Marriage," 2003 *Supreme Court Review* 27, 30.

28. 410 U.S. 113 (1973).

29. See Sunstein, *Legal Reasoning and Political Conflict,* 180–181; Sunstein, *The Partial Constitution,* 270–275, 402 n.17.

30. Sunstein, *Legal Reasoning and Political Conflict*, 181.

31. See ibid., 180.

32. Sunstein, *The Partial Constitution*, 402 n.17.

33. See Sunstein, *Legal Reasoning and Political Conflict*, 180–181.

34. Ibid., 181.

35. See Sunstein, *One Case at a Time*, 156 (contending that the opinion in Loving v. Virginia, 388 U.S. 1 (1967), which ruled that a ban on miscegenation was unconstitutional, was maximalist because it rested in part on a right to marry grounded in substantive due process, not simply on equal protection).

36. Cass R. Sunstein, "Massachusetts Gets It Right: Federal Appeal," *New Republic*, Dec. 22, 2003, 21, 22 (discussing *Goodridge*, 798 N.E. 2d 941 (Mass. 2003)). In the same issue of the magazine, Jeffrey Rosen wrote the piece sounding in judicial minimalism that some might have expected Sunstein to write. See Jeffrey Rosen, "Massachusetts Gets It Wrong on Gay Marriage: Immodest Proposal," *New Republic*, Dec. 22, 2003, 19.

37. See Sunstein, *The Partial Constitution*, 258–259.

38. See Fleming, *Securing Constitutional Democracy*, chapter 3.

39. 347 U.S. 483 (1954).

40. Sunstein, *The Partial Constitution*, 260.

41. 388 U.S. 1 (1967).

42. Sunstein, *Legal Reasoning and Political Conflict*, 95; Sunstein, *The Partial Constitution*, 402 n.17.

43. Sunstein, *Legal Reasoning and Political Conflict*, 180–181; Sunstein, *One Case at a Time*, 159–161.

44. See Sunstein, *Legal Reasoning and Political Conflict*, 180–181.

45. Compare Mary Ann Glendon, *Abortion and Divorce in Western Law: American Failures, European Challenges* (Cambridge, MA: Harvard University Press, 1987), 47–50 (arguing that a "decision leaving abortion regulation basically up to state legislatures would have encouraged constructive activity by partisans of both sides") with Laurence H. Tribe, *Abortion: The Clash of Absolutes* (New York: Norton, 1990), 49–51 (stating that "the history of abortion law reform in the United States seriously undermines [Glendon's] claim").

46. See Tribe, *Abortion*, 143–147.

47. See "The Courts Step in: Judges' Recent Rulings Show How Extreme Antiabortion Measures Have Become," *New York Times*, July 14, 2011, A22.

48. Sunstein, *Radicals in Robes*, 104–105, 248–249, 268 n.4 (citing Glendon, *Abortion and Divorce in Western Law*).

49. Thomas C. Grey, "Eros, Civilization and the Burger Court," 43 *Law & Contemporary Problems* 83 (1980).

50. Elsewhere, one of us has distinguished between "preservative conservatives" and "counter-revolutionary conservatives." See Fleming, *Securing Constitutional Democracy*, 117.

51. *Roe*, 152–153 (citing, among others, Meyer v. Nebraska, 262 U.S. 390 (1923); Pierce v. Society of Sisters, 268 U.S. 510 (1925); Griswold v.

Connecticut, 381 U.S. 479 (1965); and Eisenstadt v. Baird, 405 U.S. 438 (1972)).

52. Blackmun subsequently came to accept the gender equality ground for the right to abortion as well as the liberty or privacy ground. See Planned Parenthood v. Casey, 505 U.S. 833, 926–929 (1992) (Blackmun, J., concurring in part and dissenting in part). On the recognition of the sex equality dimension of the abortion issue in feminist argument and abortion litigation prior to *Roe,* and its effacement in *Roe* in favor of a more medical rights model, see Reva B. Siegel, "*Roe*'s Roots: The Women's Rights Claims That Engendered *Roe,*" 90 *Boston University Law Review* 1875 (2010) (discussing influence on Blackmun of Judge Lumbard's opinion in Abele v. Markle, 342 F. Supp. 800 (D. Conn. 1972)); on the "disconnect" between the "new feminist discourse of women's rights" presented in amicus briefs in *Roe* and the Court's opinion, see Linda Greenhouse, "How the Supreme Court Talks about Abortion: The Implications of a Shifting Discourse," 42 *Suffolk Law Review* 41, 45–46 (2008). To be sure, the Court's Equal Protection jurisprudence was in its inception at the time of *Roe.* Judge Lumbard, nonetheless, reasoned that "women's roles" and legal status, as well as "societal attitudes," had changed since the enactment of Connecticut's 1860 abortion law, and that once-reasonable regulations might no longer be so. Siegel, "*Roe*'s Roots," 1897–1898.

53. *Roe,* 153.

54. See, e.g., Michael J. Perry, "Abortion, the Public Morals, and the Police Power: The Ethical Function of Substantive Due Process," 23 *UCLA Law Review* 689 (1976); Harry H. Wellington, "Common Law Rules and Constitutional Double Standards: Some Notes on Adjudication," 83 *Yale Law Journal* 221 (1973).

55. David A. Strauss, *The Living Constitution* (New York: Oxford University Press, 2010), 92–97; Philip B. Heymann and Douglas E. Barzelay, "The Forest and the Trees: *Roe v. Wade* and Its Critics," 53 *Boston University Law Review* 765 (1973).

56. *Casey,* 846–853, 857–859.

57. Ibid., 848–850 (quoting Poe v. Ullman, 367 U.S. 497, 542, 543 (1961) (Harlan, J., dissenting)).

58. Sunstein, *Radicals in Robes,* 29–30, 44, 146, 245 (praising O'Connor); ibid., 31, 245 (praising Kennedy); ibid., 188–190 (praising Souter).

59. 521 U.S. 702, 756 n.4, 763–773 (1997) (Souter, J., concurring).

60. *Casey,* 848–850 (quoting *Poe,* 542, 543 (Harlan, J., dissenting)).

61. Ibid., 856. See Sunstein, *The Partial Constitution,* 284 (discussing this aspect of *Casey*).

62. Fleming, *Securing Constitutional Democracy,* 50–59.

63. Baker v. State, 744 A.2d 864 (Vt. 1999).

64. Ibid., 869–870.

65. Ibid., 871, 878.

66. Ibid., 905–906 (Johnson, J., concurring in part and dissenting in part).

67. Ibid., 880 n.13.
68. Ibid., 906 (Johnson, J., concurring in part and dissenting in part) (quoting Cass R. Sunstein, "Homosexuality and the Constitution," 70 *Indiana Law Journal* 1, 19 (1994)).
69. Ibid., 880 n.13.
70. To be sure, the court had to consider the state's arguments justifying the differential treatment: the government's interest in "furthering the link between procreation and child rearing," the supposed advantages of opposite-sex partners over same-sex partners with respect to childrearing, and "maintaining uniformity with other jurisdictions." But the court rejects all of those arguments as unpersuasive, confidently concluding that "none of the interests asserted by the State provides a reasonable and just basis for the continued exclusion of same-sex couples from the benefits incident to a civil marriage license under Vermont law." *Baker*, 884–886.
71. Ibid., 888 (quoting Cass R. Sunstein, "Leaving Things Undecided," 110 *Harvard Law Review* 4, 101 (1996)). For the centrality of the question who may interpret the Constitution in struggles over its meaning and application, see Walter F. Murphy, James E. Fleming, Sotirios A. Barber, and Stephen Macedo, *American Constitutional Interpretation* (New York: Foundation Press, 4th ed. 2008).
72. *Baker*, 888.
73. Ibid.
74. Ibid., 904 (Johnson, J., concurring in part and dissenting in part).
75. Ibid., 888 (discussing the Hawaii Supreme Court decision in Baehr v. Lewin, 852 P.2d 44 (Hawaii 1993)).
76. Hawaii Const., art. I, §23.
77. *Baker*, 882, 884–885.
78. An Act Relating to Civil Unions, 2000 Vt. Acts & Resolves 91.
79. 2009 Vt. Acts & Resolves 33 (codified in Vt. Stat. Ann. tit. 15 & 18).
80. As we noted in Chapter 6, for example, Rep. Grad of Moretown explained her vote: "Through testimony on this bill I learned that civil unions do[] not [provide "equal access, benefits, and privileges under the law"] but create[] a separate status for same-sex couples and their children who are often discriminated against, stigmatized and marginalized." Vermont House of Representatives, House Journal, 2009–2010 sess., April 3, 2009, 529–530, http://www.leg.state.vt.us/docs/2010/Permanent/House/248434 .pdf (accessed 11/29/11). Rep. Ram of Burlington explained, evoking the Jim Crow era: "To say that Civil Unions offered the same rights as marriage is nothing less than saying once upon a time there [were] two drinking fountains that both dispense the same water." Ibid., 531.
81. Report of the Vermont Commission on Family Recognition and Protection (Office of Legislative Council, April 21, 2008), 6, http:/www.leg.state.vt.us /WorkGroups/FamilyCommission/VCFRP_Report.pdf (accessed 2/28/11).
82. See, e.g., William N. Eskridge, Jr. and Darren R. Spedale, *Gay Marriage: For Better or for Worse? What We've Learned from the Evidence* (New

York: Oxford University Press, 2006); William N. Eskridge, Jr., *Equality Practice: Civil Unions and the Future of Gay Rights* (New York: Routledge, 2002).

83. *Baker,* 888.
84. *Goodridge,* 966.
85. *Baker,* 886.
86. *Goodridge,* 949.
87. See, e.g., Michael Klarman, *From the Closet to the Altar: Courts, Backlash, and the Struggle for Same-Sex Marriage* (New York: Oxford University Press, 2012). According to Klarman, there may have been some local backlash in Vermont in reaction to *Baker,* but there was considerable national backlash affecting the 2004 presidential election in response to *Goodridge.*
88. The *Baker* route (same-sex civil unions) has been followed by the New Jersey Supreme Court (and, subsequently, legislature), the Hawaii legislature, the Connecticut legislature (initially), the New Hampshire legislature (initially), and the Delaware and Rhode Island legislatures. The Illinois legislature passed a law recognizing civil unions for both same-sex and opposite-sex couples. The *Goodridge* route (same-sex marriage) has been followed by the Connecticut Supreme Court (invalidating the Connecticut civil union law), the Iowa Supreme Court, the Vermont legislature (ultimately), the New Hampshire legislature (ultimately), the District of Columbia Council, the New York legislature, and the California Supreme Court (but rejected by ballot initiative (Proposition 8) in November 2008, itself declared unconstitutional by a federal district court in 2010 and by a federal court of appeals in 2011). As this book goes to press, Maryland and Washington have enacted legislation to allow same-sex marriage, subject to voter approval in November 2012. In addition, several states now have broad protection for domestic partnerships: Oregon, Nevada, and California. For a map detailing these protections by state, see the Freedom to Marry website: http://www.freedomtomarry.org/states/ (accessed 2/28/12).
89. Sunstein, *Radicals in Robes,* 27–30, 247.
90. See ibid., 12; Cass R. Sunstein, "Burkean Minimalism," 105 *Michigan Law Review* 353 (2006).
91. Sunstein, *Radicals in Robes,* 35, 129 (quoting Learned Hand, *The Spirit of Liberty,* ed. Irving Dilliard (New York: Knopf, 1953), 190).
92. Ibid., 35, 127; Sunstein, "Second-Order Perfectionism," 2867–2870.
93. *Casey,* 848–850 (discussing *Poe,* 542, 543 (Harlan, J., dissenting)). For an analysis of more and less theoretically ambitious conceptions of common-law constitutionalism, see Benjamin C. Zipursky, "Neither Minimalism nor Perfectionism: Reflections on Sunstein's and Fleming's Efforts to Find the Sweet Spot in Constitutional Theory," 75 *Fordham Law Review* 2997 (2007). For analysis of Strauss's common law constitutionalism as a theoretically ambitious moral reading of the Constitution, see James E. Fleming, "Living Originalism and Living Constitutionalism as Moral Readings of the American Constitution," 92 *Boston University Law Review* 1171 (2012).

94. Rawls, *Political Liberalism*, 36–37, 136, 144.
95. See Sunstein, "Second-Order Perfectionism," 2876. In this section, "Minimalism Itself as a Form of Perfectionism," we draw upon Sotirios A. Barber and James E. Fleming, *Constitutional Interpretation: The Basic Questions,* (New York: Oxford University Press, 2007), 140–144.
96. Sunstein, "Second-Order Perfectionism," 2868.
97. Ibid., 2870.
98. See Barber and Fleming, *Constitutional Interpretation,* 52–55.
99. Sunstein, "Second-Order Perfectionism," 2867–2869.
100. Ibid.; see also Sunstein, *Radicals in Robes,* 41.
101. Sunstein, "Second-Order Perfectionism," 2867, 2868.
102. *The Incredible Shrinking Man* (Universal Studios 1957); *The Incredible Shrinking Woman* (Universal Pictures 1981).
103. Sunstein, "Second-Order Perfectionism," 2868.
104. See Sunstein, *Radicals in Robes,* 86.
105. Ibid., 47 (quoting Lochner v. New York, 198 U.S. 45, 76 (1905) (Holmes, J., dissenting)).
106. Ibid., 35 (quoting Hand, *The Spirit of Liberty,* 190).
107. See ibid., 12.
108. See ibid., 127; Sunstein, "Second-Order Perfectionism," 2867–2870, 2878–2880.
109. Sunstein, *The Partial Constitution,* 375 n.42 (stating that he drew "heavily [on Rosenberg, *The Hollow Hope*] for the discussion of *Brown* and *Roe*").
110. Sunstein, *Radicals in Robes,* 104–105, 248–249, 268 n.4 (citing Glendon, *Abortion and Divorce in Western Law*).
111. Linda Greenhouse and Reva Siegel detail that conflict concerning abortion was already in evidence between 1970 and 1972, as public support for decriminalizing abortion grew, and that "right-to-life" organizations were already encouraging single-issue voting to combat liberalization of abortion laws. See Linda Greenhouse and Reva B. Siegel, *Before* Roe v. Wade: *Voices That Shaped the Abortion Debate before the Supreme Court's Ruling* (New York: Kaplan Publishing, 2010), 218–220, 256–259.
112. Stephen Holmes, *The Anatomy of Antiliberalism* (Cambridge, MA: Harvard University Press, 1993).
113. See Greenhouse and Siegel, *Before* Roe v. Wade, 218–220, 256–259 (detailing, for example, how opposition to abortion was part of a broader conservative attack on the Equal Rights Amendment and on "secular humanism" and a defense of "family values").
114. Susan Faludi, *Backlash: The Undeclared War against American Women* (New York: Crown, 1991).
115. 347 U.S. 483 (1954). Rebecca Zietlow, we should note, contrasts the "massive resistance" that followed *Brown* with the "rapid pace of . . . acceptance" of the education and public accommodations parts of the Civil Rights Act of 1964. She attributes this in part to the fact that the political branch, Congress, enacted a law that was "the result of an overwhelming

national consensus in favor of civil rights." Rebecca E. Zietlow, "To Secure These Rights: Congress, Courts and the 1964 Civil Rights Act," 57 *Rutgers Law Review* 945, 996–999 (2005).

116. 394 U.S. 618 (1969).

117. The most important case in which the Court declined to recognize a right to welfare is Dandridge v. Williams, 397 U.S. 471 (1970).

118. See, e.g., Herbert J. Gans, *The War against the Poor: The Underclass and Antipoverty Policy* (New York: Basic Books, 1995). Thus, in the 1990s Congressional debates that led to the enactment of the Personal Responsibility and Work Opportunity Reconciliation Act (PRWORA), Republicans, in particular, targeted the "unintended consequences" of the legislative programs of the New Deal and "Great Society" eras (including Aid for Families with Dependent Children (AFDC)). See Ed Gillespie and Bob Schellhas, eds., *Contract with America* (New York: Times Books, 1994), 65–68. PRWORA replaced AFDC with the Temporary Assistance for Needy Families block grant. PRWORA, Title I (Temporary Assistance for Needy Families), Pub. L. No. 104–193, 110 Stat. 2105 (1996) (codified as amended in scattered sections of 42 U.S.C.).

119. See Glendon, *Abortion and Divorce in Western Law.*

120. Albert O. Hirschman, *The Rhetoric of Reaction: Perversity, Futility, Jeopardy* (Cambridge, MA: Belknap Press of Harvard University Press, 1991).

121. Sunstein, *Legal Reasoning and Political Conflict,* 177; Sunstein, *Radicals in Robes,* 127.

122. See, e.g., Dworkin, *A Matter of Principle,* 33–71; Ronald Dworkin, *Taking Rights Seriously* (Cambridge, MA: Harvard University Press, 1977).

123. West Virginia Board of Education v. Barnette, 319 U.S. 624, 638, 640 (1943), *overruling* Minersville School District v. Gobitis, 310 U.S. 586 (1940).

124. See Sunstein, "Second-Order Perfectionism," 2867–2870, 2878–2880.

125. Dworkin, *Taking Rights Seriously,* 105; Learned Hand, *The Bill of Rights* (Cambridge, MA: Harvard University Press, 1958), 73 ("For myself it would be most irksome to be ruled by a bevy of Platonic Guardians, even if I knew how to choose them, which I assuredly do not.").

126. Dworkin, *Taking Rights Seriously,* 105–130.

127. Ibid., 90.

128. Barber and Fleming, *Constitutional Interpretation,* 155–170.

129. See, e.g., Cass R. Sunstein, *Free Markets and Social Justice* (New York: Oxford University Press, 1997).

130. Sunstein, "Second-Order Perfectionism," 2869.

131. Richard H. Thaler and Cass R. Sunstein, *Nudge: Improving Decisions about Health, Wealth, and Happiness* (New Haven, CT: Yale University Press, 2008), 215–226.

9. The Myth of Strict Scrutiny for Fundamental Rights

1. See Ronald Dworkin, *Taking Rights Seriously* (Cambridge, MA: Harvard University Press, 1977).
2. Gerald Gunther, "Foreword: In Search of Evolving Doctrine on a Changing Court: A Model for a Newer Equal Protection," 86 *Harvard Law Review* 1, 8 (1972).
3. Mary Ann Glendon, *Rights Talk: The Impoverishment of Political Discourse* (New York: Free Press, 1991), 14, 40 ("absoluteness"), passim ("impoverishment" of judgment).
4. 539 U.S. 558, 593–594 (2003) (Scalia, J., dissenting).
5. Ibid., 593–594.
6. See Grutter v. Bollinger, 539 U.S. 306, 349 (2003) (Scalia, J., dissenting).
7. 410 U.S. 113 (1973).
8. 505 U.S. 833, 847, 876 (1992).
9. Ibid., 848–849; Poe v. Ullman, 367 U.S. 497, 543, 549 (1961) (Harlan, J., dissenting).
10. 478 U.S. 186 (1986).
11. 491 U.S. 110 (1989).
12. 521 U.S. 702 (1997).
13. Michael C. Dorf with Trevor Morrison, *Constitutional Law* (New York: Oxford University Press, 2011), 209. Ultimately, after speaking of the Court's "doctrinal meanderings," they put the matter rightly: "Nonetheless, taking a bird's eye, rather than a worm's eye, view of the topic, we can see that the Court will apply some form of heightened scrutiny to laws that infringe the freedom of competent adults to make important decisions about family formation, child-rearing, and bodily autonomy."
14. City of Cleburne v. Cleburne Living Center, 473 U.S. 432, 451 (1985) (Stevens, J., concurring); San Antonio Independent School District v. Rodriguez, 411 U.S. 1, 98 (1973) (Marshall, J., dissenting).
15. *Poe,* 542.
16. Ibid., 542, 543.
17. *Casey,* 849.
18. Ibid., 901.
19. Contrast *Poe,* 542 (Harlan's view of tradition as a "living thing") with Michael H. v. Gerald D., 491 U.S. 110 (1989) (Scalia's view of tradition as concrete historical practices embodied in the common law and statute books as of 1868, the year the Fourteenth Amendment was ratified).
20. 262 U.S. 390 (1923).
21. Ibid., 399–402.
22. Ibid., 399–401.
23. Ibid., 401, 402, 403.
24. Ibid., 412.
25. 268 U.S. 510 (1925).
26. Ibid., 534–535.
27. Ibid., 535.

28. Ibid., 534
29. 321 U.S. 158, 160–163, 166 (1944).
30. Ibid., 165, 166.
31. Ibid., 165, 170.
32. Ibid., 168.
33. For this distinction, see Vivian E. Hamilton, "Immature Citizens and the State," 2010 *Brigham Young University Law Review* 1055.
34. *Prince,* 170 (emphasis added).
35. Ibid., 166, 167.
36. Indeed, one might have expected this case to support the Court ruling *against* the Amish parents in *Wisconsin v. Yoder,* 406 U.S. 205 (1972).
37. 381 U.S. 479 (1965).
38. Ibid., 485.
39. Ibid., 485–486 (Goldberg, J., concurring).
40. Ibid., 485 (quoting NAACP v. Alabama, 357 U.S. 449 (1958)).
41. Ibid., 485–486.
42. Ibid., 486.
43. *Lawrence,* 562, 564–566.
44. 388 U.S. 1, 8 (1967).
45. Ibid., 11 (quoting Korematsu v. United States, 324 U.S. 214, 216 (1944)).
46. Ibid., 12 (citing Skinner v. Oklahoma, 316 U.S. 535, 541 (1942)).
47. Ibid.
48. Ibid.
49. See, e.g., Geoffrey R. Stone, Louis Michael Seidman, Cass R. Sunstein, Mark V. Tushnet, and Pamela S. Karlan, *Constitutional Law* (New York: Wolters Kluwer, 6th ed. 2009), 518–519.
50. See Joanna L. Grossman and John DeWitt Gregory, "The Legacy of *Loving,*" 51 *Howard Law Journal* 15, 19 (2007).
51. *Loving,* 12.
52. *Roe,* 152–153.
53. Ibid., 152 (quoting Palko v. Connecticut, 302 U.S. 319, 325 (1937)).
54. Ibid., 155–156.
55. Ibid., 153–154, 162–163.
56. Ibid., 165–166. See Linda Greenhouse and Reva B. Siegel, *Before* Roe v. Wade: *Voices That Shaped the Abortion Debate before the Supreme Court's Ruling* (New York: Kaplan Publishing, 2010).
57. 431 U.S. 494 (1977) (Powell, J., plurality opinion).
58. Ibid., 499 (quoting Cleveland Bd. of Education v. LaFleur, 414 U.S. 632, 639–640 (1974)).
59. Ibid. (citing, e.g., *Prince; Roe; Yoder; Griswold; Poe* (Harlan, J., dissenting); compare *Loving; Skinner*).
60. Ibid., 494, 500, 501, 502.
61. Ibid., 503 n.12 (quoting *Poe,* 551–552 (Harlan, J., dissenting)).
62. Ibid., 502, 503, 504, 505.
63. Ibid., 499.
64. Ibid.

65. Craig v. Boren, 429 U.S. 190 (1976).

66. *Moore,* 499–500.

67. 497 U.S. 261 (1990).

68. Ibid., 262, 279 n.7.

69. Ibid., 279 (emphasis added).

70. 348 U.S. 483 (1955) (applying highly deferential rational basis scrutiny to economic regulations under both the Equal Protection Clause and the Due Process Clause).

71. *Cruzan,* 282.

72. *Casey,* 872, 876.

73. Ibid., 877.

74. *Williamson* is the canonical case for highly deferential rational basis scrutiny under both the Due Process and Equal Protection Clauses.

75. *Lawrence,* 588.

76. *Casey,* 852, 877–878.

77. Ibid., 887.

78. Contrast recent cases, like Snyder v. Phelps, 131 S. Ct. 1207, 1213, 1216–1217, 1219 (2011), where the Supreme Court stated that "in public debate [we] must tolerate insulting, and even outrageous, speech in order to provide adequate 'breathing space' to the freedoms protected by the First Amendment," with earlier cases, like Whitney v. California, 274 U.S. 357, 371 (1927), where the Court stated that freedom of speech does not confer a right to speak "without responsibility," for that would be an "unbridled license" or "abuse" of freedom. *Whitney* was overruled by Brandenburg v. Ohio, 395 U.S. 444 (1969).

79. See, e.g., Lee v. Weisman, 505 U.S. 577 (1992).

80. 521 U.S. 702 (1997).

81. Ibid., 720–722 & n.17.

82. *Casey,* 966 (Rehnquist, C.J., concurring in part and dissenting in part). For these observations, we are indebted to our research assistant Eric Lee.

83. Fleming, *Securing Constitutional Democracy,* 120–123.

84. See Blackmun's and Stevens's dissents in *Bowers,* 199, 217; Brennan's dissent in *Michael H.,* 139; and Stevens's and Breyer's concurrences in *Glucksberg,* 743, 790.

85. 530 U.S. 57, 65, 66 (2000).

86. Ibid., 65 (citing *Glucksberg,* 720).

87. David Meyer, "Constitutional Pragmatism for a Changing American Family," 32 *Rutgers Law Journal* 711, 711 (2001).

88. *Troxel,* 80.

89. Ibid., 58, 59, 67, 68, 69, 72–73.

90. Ibid., 86, 87, 88, 89.

91. *Lawrence,* 578.

92. *Bowers,* 191.

93. *Lawrence,* 564, 562. See *Bowers,* 204 (Blackmun, J., dissenting).

94. *Lawrence,* 571–572.

95. Ibid., 572.

96. *Poe,* 550, 553.
97. Charles Fried, *Order and Law: Arguing the Reagan Revolution—A First-hand Account* (New York: Simon & Schuster, 1991), 82–83.
98. Laurence H. Tribe and Michael C. Dorf, *On Reading the Constitution* (Cambridge, MA: Harvard University Press, 1991), 116–117.
99. *Lawrence,* 586 (Scalia, J., dissenting).
100. *Bowers,* 191–192.
101. *Lawrence,* 596.
102. Ibid., 593.
103. Ibid., 586.
104. *Casey,* 1000 (Scalia, J., concurring in part and dissenting in part).
105. Romer v. Evans, 517 U.S. 620, 634–635 (1996).
106. Ibid., 639 (Scalia, J., dissenting).
107. *Romer,* 634–635 (citing U.S. Department of Agriculture .v. Moreno, 413 U.S. 528, 534 (1973)); City of Cleburne v. Cleburne Living Center, 473 U.S. 432, 446-447 (1985) (also citing *Moreno*).
108. *Bowers,* 196.
109. *Romer,* 634.
110. Ibid., 635.
111. See *Lawrence,* 578.
112. 744 A.2d 864, 877–878 (Vt. 1999).
113. *Craig,* 211 (Stevens, J., concurring).
114. See James E. Fleming, "'There Is Only One Equal Protection Clause': An Appreciation of Justice Stevens's Equal Protection Jurisprudence," 74 *Fordham Law Review* 2301 (2006) (analyzing Stevens's and Marshall's equal protection jurisprudences).
115. *Baker,* 867, 871, 873.
116. 798 N.E.2d 941, 959–960 & n.20 (Mass. 2003).
117. *Poe,* 543 (Harlan, J., dissenting) ("rational continuum"); *Casey,* at 849 ("reasoned judgment").

Epilogue: Pursuing Ordered Liberty

1. Olmstead v. United States, 277 U.S. 438, 478 (1928) (Brandeis, J., dissenting).

Acknowledgments

In this book, we develop a constitutional liberalism for pursuing ordered liberty through taking not only rights but also responsibilities and virtues seriously. We are grateful to many responsible and virtuous colleagues for advice and support concerning this project. Both of us owe a special debt to the late John Rawls for his formative work on political liberalism and his modeling of constructive engagement with liberalism's critics. We benefitted from his inspiration and encouragement of early formulations of our constitutional liberalism. With Rawls as a model, we could never doubt that securing basic liberties does not rule out, but entails, encouraging responsibility and cultivating civic virtues. Special thanks also go to Jim's longtime co-author Sotirios Barber for numerous conversations about particular pieces as well as the whole project, including co-authorship of a book, *Constitutional Interpretation: The Basic Questions* (Oxford University Press, 2007), whose vision of the American Constitution is reflected in this work. We trust that Sot will be heartened by the mild form of perfectionism that we develop here, even if it may be too thin for his blood.

Over the years, we have engaged in fruitful discussions and exchanges with many friends and colleagues about criticisms and defenses of liberalism. In particular, we would like to thank Anita Allen-Castellito, David Blankenhorn, Corey Brettschneider, Mike Dorf, Maxine Eichner, Chris Eisgruber, Jean Bethke Elshtain, Amitai Etzioni, Dick Fallon, Martha Albertson Fineman, Samuel Freeman, William Galston, Abner Greene, Joanna Grossman, Will Harris, Steve Heyman, Charles Kelbley, Ken Kersch, Sandy Levinson, Sharon Lloyd, Steve Macedo, Eileen

McDonagh, Tamara Metz, Frank Michelman, Martha Minow, the late Walter Murphy, Joshua Rabinowitz, Nancy Rosenblum, Larry Sager, Mary Lyndon (Molly) Shanley, Larry Solum, Dennis Thompson, Bill Treanor, Robin West, and Ben Zipursky.

Boston University School of Law provided generous support for conferences and symposia organized by Jim which have borne fruit in this book: "*Justice for Hedgehogs:* A Conference on Ronald Dworkin's Book" (2009); "*Justice: What's the Right Thing To Do?:* A Symposium on Michael Sandel's Book" (2010); and the "Symposium on Jack Balkin's *Living Originalism* and David Strauss's *The Living Constitution*" (2011). We are grateful to those scholars for the chance to engage with their work in ways that have informed our own, to Dean Maureen O'Rourke for generous financial support, and to our BU colleagues in constitutional theory and jurisprudence for participating in those events and contributing papers to the published symposium issues in *Boston University Law Review.*

We would be remiss if we did not also thank Jim's previous institution, Fordham University School of Law, for likewise abundantly supporting conferences and symposia organized by Jim which yielded works that are reflected in this book: "The Constitution and the Good Society" (2000); "Rawls and the Law" (2003); and "Minimalism versus Perfectionism in Constitutional Theory" (2006). For this support we are indebted to two generous deans, John Feerick and Bill Treanor. And we are grateful to colleagues in constitutional theory and jurisprudence at Fordham who took part in those events and published papers in the symposium issues in *Fordham Law Review.*

We want to thank Ronald Dworkin for writing a sympathetic response to what became a portion of Chapter 3; Tim Scanlon for writing a thoughtful comment on what became the first part of Chapter 6; Michael Sandel for illuminating colloquy in response to what became Chapter 7; and Cass Sunstein for publishing an exchange that is reflected in what became Chapter 8.

We have had the opportunity to present earlier versions of chapters of this book to various audiences and appreciate the valuable comments we received. We thank our colleagues at BU for their helpful feedback in several faculty workshops. We also benefitted from presenting a draft chapter to the Boston Area Public Law Study Group (thanks to Ken Kersch and Shep Melnick) and delivering another as the 2011 Constitution Day Lecture at Northeastern University (thanks to Eileen McDonagh and Michael Toomey). Jim presented early drafts of chapters in the 2010 Princeton University Constitutional Law Schmooze, sponsored by the

Princeton University Program in Law and Public Affairs (thanks to Kim Scheppele), in a symposium at Cornell Law School (thanks to Eduardo Penalver and Mike Dorf), and in a faculty workshop at Wayne State University Law School (thanks to Steve Winter). Linda benefitted from presenting chapters in progress in a conference on "Twenty Years after *Employment Division v. Smith*" held at Cardozo School of Law (thanks to Marci Hamilton), in the Distinguished Speaker Series at American University's Washington College of Law (thanks to Lewis Grossman and Robert Tsai), at a meeting of the Feminist Research Network Collaborative held at George Washington University Law School (thanks to Naomi Cahn and Maxine Eichner), and at a Feminism and Legal Theory Workshop held at Emory University School of Law (thanks to Martha Fineman). Both of us, over the years, have benefitted from presenting early versions of the constitutional liberalism that we develop here in the Georgetown University Law Center Discussion Group on Constitutional Law, convened by Mark Tushnet, and later the University of Maryland Constitutional Law Schmooze, convened by Mark Graber.

We thank Elizabeth Knoll, our editor at Harvard University Press, for her encouragement and support of this project. We are also indebted to Corey Brettschneider, Sandy Levinson, and an anonymous reviewer for numerous insightful comments on the entire manuscript. Any failures and limitations in the book are, of course, our own.

We are grateful to Boston University School of Law for summer research grants and for sabbatical leaves during the spring 2010 semester. Again, we appreciate the generous support of Dean Maureen O'Rourke. The David Saul Smith Award for Excellence in Legal Scholarship generously facilitated our completing this book. Jim acknowledges the financial support provided by The Honorable Frank R. Kenison Distinguished Scholar in Law fund and Linda acknowledges similar support from the Paul M. Siskind Research Scholar fund.

We thank our research assistants, current or former BU Law students Christine Dieter, Courtney Sartor Gesualdi, Avalon Johnson, Eric Lee, Natalie Logan, Christy Renworth, Jameson Rice, Emily Strauss, and Hallie Van Duren for their conscientious work on research, cite checking, and editing. We are especially grateful to Christine, Courtney, Christy, and Emily for reading the manuscript in its final stages and making innumerable helpful suggestions. Stephanie Weigmann, Head of Legal Information Services, Pappas Library, at BU Law, provided invaluable help with research. Reference librarian Jennifer Ekblaw also helped during the final stages of preparation of the manuscript. We also want to acknowledge Danielle Amber Papa for highly competent secretarial assistance.

This book builds on the frameworks set forth in our prior books: James E. Fleming, *Securing Constitutional Democracy: The Case of Autonomy* (University of Chicago Press, 2006), and Linda C. McClain, *The Place of Families: Fostering Capacity, Equality, and Responsibility* (Harvard University Press, 2006). We include several revised passages from those books. This book draws from, partially incorporates, but extensively revises material from the following co-authored and individual law review articles: McClain and Fleming, "Respecting Freedom and Cultivating Virtues in Justifying Constitutional Rights," 91 *Boston University Law Review* 1311 (2011); McClain and Fleming, "Some Questions for Civil Society–Revivalists," 75 *Chicago-Kent Law Review* 301 (2000); Fleming, "The Incredible Shrinking Constitutional Theory: From the Partial Constitution to the Minimal Constitution," 75 *Fordham Law Review* 2885 (2007); Fleming, "Securing Deliberative Democracy," 72 *Fordham Law Review* 1435 (2004); McClain, "Religious and·Political Virtues and Values in Congruence or Conflict: On *Smith, Bob Jones University,* and *Christian Legal Society,*" 32 *Cardozo Law Review* 1959 (2011); and McClain, "Rights and Irresponsibility," 43 *Duke Law Journal* 989 (1994). We also have adapted brief portions from the following works: Fleming and McClain, "In Search of a Substantive Republic," 76 *Texas Law Review* 509 (1997); Fleming, "Taking Responsibilities as well as Rights Seriously," 90 *Boston University Law Review* 839 (2010); McClain, "Negotiating Gender and (Free and Equal) Citizenship: The Place of Associations," 72 *Fordham Law Review* 1569 (2004); McClain, "The Domain of Civic Virtue in a Good Society: Families, Schools, and Sex Equality," 69 *Fordham Law Review* 1617 (2001); and McClain, "Toleration, Autonomy, and Governmental Promotion of Good Lives: Beyond 'Empty' Toleration to Toleration as Respect," 59 *Ohio State Law Journal* 19 (1998).

Although we express some skepticism, in this book, about the role of family "table talk" in fostering civic virtues, we are grateful to our daughters, Sarah McClain Fleming and Katherine Amelia McClain Fleming, for enduring as well as participating in many discussions about the book's concerns for rights, responsibilities, and virtues. Parenting provides rich lessons in both humility and hope concerning the formative project of encouraging responsibility and inculcating civic virtues. We are encouraged by the civic education that Sarah and Katherine are receiving in their local public school and the opportunities it affords them for training in engaged, responsible citizenship.

Index

formative project of inculcating, 2,
8–12, 82, 112, 115, 183, 209
governmental promotion of, 112–145
inequality within families and, 96–100
needed to sustain constitutional
democracy, 10, 82, 85–86, 209
reciprocity as a, 84, 88, 91, 116
relationship to personal virtue, 88, 89
respect for diversity as a, 128, 140
role of families in fostering, 84, 85
role of wives and mothers in fostering,
85, 96–100
sex equality as a, 126–127
shared authority between parents and
schools in inculcating, 10–11,
119–121
tolerance as a, 10, 86, 114, 118, 122,
124, 126, 128–139, 140, 142
See also Civic education; Civil society
Civil Rights Act of 1964, 162, 173, 205
See also Antidiscrimination laws
Civil rights movement:
backlash against, 231
counterpublics in, 92
and decline of civil society, 101–103
legacy of, 25, 27–29
marriage equality and, 163
Civil society:
as buffer against government, 8–9, 82,
106, 146, 160, 170, 172
and civic renewal, 84–85
civic role of families, 82–85, 87–88,
95–101
"civil society-revivalists" on, 8, 81–106
congruence with democratic norms, 8,
11–12, 82–83, 90–93, 99, 107–109,
119, 128, 146–147, 153–154,
158–161, 163, 168
erosion of, 8, 81, 83–86, 101–102
as fostering democratic self-
government, 87, 92–93, 104–106
as fostering personal self-government,
87, 109–111
as fostering self-respect, 91, 109–111
illiberal groups in, 90, 91
imbalance between rights and
responsibilities in, 85
inequality and, 86, 101–103
and moral renewal, 84–85
public sphere and, 92–93
roles and regulation of, 9, 105–111
as "seedbeds of virtue," 8–9, 18, 24,
81–90, 95–99, 146

sex inequality in family and, 95–99
as source of social capital, 81, 84, 86,
88, 91, 97–98, 100
as supplementing government,
104–106, 159
Civil unions:
as alternative to same-sex marriage,
175, 185, 221
argument for replacing marriage with,
235
Baker and, 14, 175, 218–223
enacted by several state legislatures,
338n88
Illinois civil union law, 173–174
as ladder to same-sex marriage, 175,
222
as "second-class" citizenship or denial
of equal dignity and respect, 175,
192, 193, 221, 222
Vermont civil union law, 175, 221
See also *Baker v. State*; *Lewis v. Harris*
Clinton, Hillary (First Lady), 84
Clinton, William Jefferson (President), 19,
43, 83, 281n43, 287n134
Cohen, Jean L., 302n71
Cole, David, 210
Colson, Chuck, 170
Communitarianism:
analysis of abortion law, 56–62
on "moral state of the union,"
26–27
new communitarian critiques of rights,
18–49
See also Irresponsibility critique of
rights; Responsive Communitarian
Platform
Comprehensive conceptions of the
good, 94, 108, 115, 148, 150,
189–190
Conflict:
among basic liberties, 11–12, 147, 148,
149–150, 151–157
between democratic and associational
values, 11–12, 82–83, 146–147,
163
between freedom of association and
equal citizenship, 2, 11–12, 147, 151,
169
between liberty and equality, 146–176
between religious and political values,
157–169
between religious liberty and same-sex
marriage, 170–176